Data Mining and Machine Learning in the Era of Big Knowledge and Large Models

Data Mining and Machine Learning in the Era of Big Knowledge and Large Models

Guest Editors

Jing Zhang

Chenyang Bu

MDPI

Basel • Beijing • Wuhan • Barcelona • Belgrade • Novi Sad • Cluj • Manchester

Guest Editors

Jing Zhang
School of Cyber Science and Engineering
Southeast University
Nanjing
China

Chenyang Bu
Key Laboratory of Knowledge Engineering with Big Data (The Ministry of Education of China)
Hefei University of Technology
Hefei
China

Editorial Office
MDPI AG
Grosspeteranlage 5
4052 Basel, Switzerland

This is a reprint of the Special Issue, published open access by the journal *Mathematics* (ISSN 2227-7390), freely accessible at: https://www.mdpi.com/si/mathematics/0UM1MFXF7R.

For citation purposes, cite each article independently as indicated on the article page online and as indicated below:

Lastname, A.A.; Lastname, B.B. Article Title. *Journal Name* **Year**, *Volume Number*, Page Range.

ISBN 978-3-7258-6644-1 (Hbk)
ISBN 978-3-7258-6645-8 (PDF)
https://doi.org/10.3390/books978-3-7258-6645-8

Contents

About the Editors . . . . **vii**

Preface . . . . **ix**

Jing Zhang and Wan Zhang
Where Are Data Mining and Machine Learning Headed in the Era of Big Knowledge and Large Models?
Reprinted from: *Mathematics* **2026**, *14*, 233, https://doi.org/10.3390/math14020233 . . . . **1**

Yanxia Lyu, Yuhang Liu, Qianqian Zhao, Ziwen Hao and Xin Song
SFSIN: A Lightweight Model for Remote Sensing Image Super-Resolution with Strip-like Feature Superpixel Interaction Network
Reprinted from: *Mathematics* **2025**, *13*, 1720, https://doi.org/10.3390/math13111720 . . . . **7**

Dong-Her Shih, Feng-I Chung, Ting-Wei Wu, Shuo-Yu Huang and Ming-Hung Shih
Advanced Trans-EEGNet Deep Learning Model for Hypoxic-Ischemic Encephalopathy Severity Grading
Reprinted from: *Mathematics* **2024**, *12*, 3915, https://doi.org/10.3390/math12243915 . . . . **26**

Dong-Her Shih, Feng-I. Chung, Ting-Wei Wu, Bo-Hao Wang and Ming-Hung Shih
Advanced Trans-BiGRU-QA Fusion Model for Atmospheric Mercury Prediction
Reprinted from: *Mathematics* **2024**, *12*, 3547, https://doi.org/10.3390/math12223547 . . . . **53**

Raz Lapid, Almog Dubin and Moshe Sipper
Fortify the Guardian, Not the Treasure: Resilient Adversarial Detectors
Reprinted from: *Mathematics* **2024**, *12*, 3451, https://doi.org/10.3390/math12223451 . . . . **87**

Lama Al-Zahrani and Maha Al-Yahya
Pre-Trained Language Model Ensemble for Arabic Fake News Detection
Reprinted from: *Mathematics* **2024**, *12*, 2941, https://doi.org/10.3390/math12182941 . . . . **108**

Guoquan Yuan, Xinjian Zhao, Liu Li, Song Zhang and Shanming Wei
Few-Shot Learning Sensitive Recognition Method Based on Prototypical Network
Reprinted from: *Mathematics* **2024**, *12*, 2791, https://doi.org/10.3390/math12172791 . . . . **125**

Zhenrong Deng, Zheng Huang, Shiwei Wei and Jinglin Zhang
KCB-FLAT: Enhancing Chinese Named Entity Recognition with Syntactic Information and Boundary Smoothing Techniques
Reprinted from: *Mathematics* **2024**, *12*, 2714, https://doi.org/10.3390/math12172714 . . . . **139**

Liting Wei, Yun Li, Weiwei Wang and Yi Zhu
Enhancing Knowledge-Concept Recommendations with Heterogeneous Graph-Contrastive Learning
Reprinted from: *Mathematics* **2024**, *12*, 2324, https://doi.org/10.3390/math12152324 . . . . **157**

Fangling Leng, Fan Li, Yubin Bao, Tiancheng Zhang and Ge Yu
DABC: A Named Entity Recognition Method Incorporating Attention Mechanisms
Reprinted from: *Mathematics* **2024**, *12*, 1992, https://doi.org/10.3390/math12131992 . . . . **173**

Qun Zhao, Shicheng Cui, Yuelong Zhu, Rui Li and Xudong Zhou
A Novel Online Hydrological Data Quality Control Approach Based on Adaptive Differential Evolution
Reprinted from: *Mathematics* **2024**, *12*, 1821, https://doi.org/10.3390/math12121821 . . . . **188**

Xinjian Zhao, Weiwei Miao, Guoquan Yuan, Yu Jiang, Song Zhang and Qianmu Li
Abnormal Traffic Detection System Based on Feature Fusion and Sparse Transformer
Reprinted from: *Mathematics* **2024**, *12*, 1643, https://doi.org/10.3390/math12111643 . . . . **206**

Wan Zhang and Jing Zhang
Hallucination Mitigation for Retrieval-Augmented Large Language Models: A Review
Reprinted from: *Mathematics* **2025**, *13*, 856, https://doi.org/10.3390/math13050856 . . . . **220**

About the Editors

Jing Zhang

Jing Zhang is a Full Professor of Computer Science and Artificial Intelligence in the School of Cyber Science and Engineering at Southeast University, China. He received his Ph.D. degree in Computer Science from Hefei University of Technology, China, in 2015. He worked as a Visiting Scholar (Professor) at several universities and institutes such as the University of Pittsburg (2019-2020), University of Technology, Sydney (2017), and Zhejiang Lab (2023). His research interests include data mining, machine learning, and trustworthy artificial intelligence. He has published more than 120 articles in prestigious journals, such as *TPAMI*, *JMLR*, *TKDE*, *TNNLS*, *TCYB*, and *TMM*, and top-tier conferences, such as ICML, SIGKDD, AAAI, SIGIR, ICDM, CIKM, WSDM, etc. He has been granted three funds from the National Natural Science Foundation of China and more than ten funds from the provincial government and enterprises. He is a Senior Member of IEEE and serves as a Senior PC member for a number of AI-related top-tier conferences and a reviewer for more than 40 international journals.

Chenyang Bu

Chenyang Bu is an associate professor at the Key Laboratory of Knowledge Engineering with Big Data (Ministry of Education of China), Hefei University of Technology, Hefei, China. He received his Ph.D. degree from the University of Science and Technology of China. His current research interests include knowledge-driven optimization and the bidirectional enhancement of knowledge graphs and large language models. He has published multiple papers in leading international conferences and journals, including KDD, WWW, IJCAI, AAAI, and *IEEE/ACM Transactions*. He serves as an SPC member for IJCAI, a youth editorial board member of the journal *Artificial Intelligence in Health*, and served as the Web Chair of the IEEE International Conference on Knowledge Graph (IEEE ICKG, 2021–2023). He is a recipient of the 2024 Youth Talent Support Program of the Anhui Association for Science and Technology.

Preface

In recent years, the fields of data mining and machine learning have undergone a transformative shift with the advent of big data and the development of increasingly complex models. The integration of advanced algorithms with vast amounts of data has enabled unprecedented insights and predictions across various domains, including cybersecurity, healthcare, finance, marketing, and more. On the one hand, ongoing emergence of new applications generates massive amounts of heterogeneous data, calling for more complex and comprehensive data mining techniques to better explore and exploit data. On the other hand, many novel machine learning models, such as Transformer, graph neural networks, etc., provide more powerful tools for analyzing and modeling data. However, this field still faces the problem that machine learning models cannot adapt to massive amounts of highly dynamic, heterogeneous, constantly evolving, and imperfectly labeled data. This severely hinders the transformation of big data into big knowledge and large models.

To address the challenges in the development of data mining and machine learning in the current age, we started this Special Issue in January 2024 to encourage researchers all over the world to submit their high-quality original work related to all aspects of this field. After over two years of hard work from all authors, reviewers, and editors, of the 21 articles submitted, 13 were finally accepted for publication after the peer-review process, an acceptance rate of 61.9 percent. The published articles cover a range of topics from the basic models and algorithms to the new applications. Although submission to this Special Issue is now closed, the need for further in-depth research and development remains. We believe this Special Issue, "Data Mining and Machine Learning in the Era of Big Knowledge and Large Models," has addressed some significant existing knowledge gaps. The collective impact of these contributions is profound, aligning with the core purpose: to enhance the breadth and quality of knowledge acquisition and to promote intelligent systems to better serve humanity. It will inspire more researchers to devote themselves to this thread and make more contributions in the future.

In the end, we would like to take this opportunity to express our most profound appreciation to the MDPI Book Reprint, the editorial team of the *Mathematics* journal, especially Suri Wang, Section Managing Editor of this Special Issue, the talented authors, and hardworking and professional reviewers.

Jing Zhang and Chenyang Bu
Guest Editors

mathematics MDPI

Editorial

Where Are Data Mining and Machine Learning Headed in the Era of Big Knowledge and Large Models?

Jing Zhang [1,2,*,†] and Wan Zhang [1]

[1] School of Cyber Science and Engineering, Southeast University, Nanjing 211189, China; zhangwan@seu.edu.cn
[2] Engineering Research Center of Blockchain Application, Supervision and Management, Southeast University, Ministry of Education, Nanjing 211189, China
* Correspondence: jingz@seu.edu.cn
† Current address: Jiulonghu Campus, Southeast University, No. 2 SEU Road, Nanjing 211189, China.

1. Introduction

The advent of big knowledge, whose basis is massive volumes of heterogeneous data, and the success of large pre-trained models have revolutionized artificial intelligence. Data mining and machine learning, once focused on pattern detection from curated datasets, now grapple with complex, noisy, heterogeneous, and dynamic data sources. Looking back at the progress in data mining and machine learning in recent years, we have identified several noteworthy trends related to this Special Issue as follows:

First, Transformer [1], a deep learning framework that strongly relies on attention mechanisms to model the relationships between elements in an input sequence, has had a revolutionary impact on the field of machine learning. The core components of the Transformer include multi-head self-attention and a feed-forward network, and it incorporates sequence order information through positional encoding. This design allows the model to simultaneously focus on all positions in the input sequence, thus efficiently processing data from multiple modalities such as natural language, speech, and images. It has become the cornerstone of modern NLP. Pre-trained language models, such as BERT [2] and GPT [3], are based on the Transformer architecture, achieving breakthrough performance in tasks such as text classification, machine translation, and question answering. It has driven the development of cross-modal learning. The Vision Transformer segments images into patches and, analogous to a word input Transformer, achieves performance comparable to or even better than CNNs on the ImageNet classification task [4]. Also, it has facilitated the development of large-scale models and driven the evolution from specialized models to general-purpose foundational models.

Second, self-supervised learning (SSL) has become one of the mainstream paradigms of modern machine learning. The core idea of SSL is to train models by automatically constructing supervisory signals from unlabeled data, thereby avoiding reliance on large amounts of manually labeled data. SSL has made significant progress in recent years. Contrastive learning [5] effectively improves representation quality by bringing the representations of different augmented views of the same data sample closer together while simultaneously pushing the representations of different samples further apart. Masked autoencoders, such as MAE [6], achieve efficient visual representation learning by reconstructing occluded image patches. Multimodal self-supervised learning, such as CLIP [7], performs exceptionally well on zero-shot classification tasks through image-text contrastive learning. SSL has driven the learning paradigm shift from "small data *plus* strong supervision" to "big data *plus* weak supervision".

 https://doi.org/10.3390/math14020233

Third, as data mining and machine learning algorithms are widely deployed in the real world, their security and trustworthiness are increasingly challenging. The primary challenges include adversarial attacks, model extraction, data poisoning, privacy leakage, and insufficient interpretability of model decisions. This direction has attracted increasing attention from the research community and has made rapid progress in recent years. For example, adversarial training focuses on improving training efficiency, expanding the scope of defense, and balancing the "robustness–accuracy trade-off" between natural precision and robustness [8]. As model sizes increase, hallucination becomes a typical problem in large models, referring to outputs that seem reasonable but are actually incorrect, unfounded, or irrelevant to the input context [9]. The academic community has conducted in-depth research on the detection, mitigation, and evaluation of large-scale illusions, resulting in representative achievements such as the fine-grained fact evaluation framework FactScore [10], retrieval augmentation generation [11], and Chain-of-Thought [12].

Finally, the combination of big knowledge and large models is profoundly transforming the application of artificial intelligence in several key fields. By integrating language understanding capabilities derived from massive amounts of parameters with factual support from external knowledge, these systems significantly improve accuracy, interpretability, and credibility in specialized domains. This paradigm has achieved breakthroughs in fields such as healthcare, scientific research, legal services, education, and intelligent decision-making. The synergy between big knowledge and large models is driving AI from "general dialogue" to "professional intelligence," with its core trend being the enhancement of system reliability and usability through retrieval augmentation, knowledge alignment, and multimodal fusion.

The research articles published in this special issue demonstrate the technological development trends in the era of big knowledge and large models from the four aspects mentioned above. While they do not cover all the characteristics of this era, they are sufficient to provide some insights for the research community.

2. An Overview of Published Articles

The list of published contributions is as follows:

The study "Abnormal Traffic Detection System Based on Feature Fusion and Sparse Transformer" by Xinjian Zhao, Weiwei Miao, Guoquan Yuan, Yu Jiang, Song Zhang, and Qianmu Li was published in May 2024, which proposed a feature fusion and sparse transformer-based anomalous traffic detection system. The system utilizes a feature fusion network to encode the traffic data sequences and extract features, fusing them into coding vectors through shallow and deep convolutional networks. Then, it uses a sparse transformer to capture the complex relationships between network flows. Finally, a multilayer perceptron is used to classify the traffic and achieve anomaly traffic detection. The study shows that the feature fusion network improves feature extraction from small sample data, the deep encoder enhances the understanding of complex traffic patterns, and the sparse transformer reduces the computational and storage overhead and improves the scalability of the model.

The study "A Novel Online Hydrological Data Quality Control Approach Based on Adaptive Differential Evolution" by Qun Zhao, Shicheng Cui, Yuelong Zhu, Rui Li, and Xudong Zhou was published in June 2024, which proposed an online hydrological data quality control method based on an adaptive differential evolution algorithm according to the characteristics of hydrological data. The method takes into account the characteristics of continuity, periodicity, and seasonality, forming a Periodic Temporal Long Short-Term Memory predictive control model. Considering the real-time nature of the data, an adaptive differential evolution algorithm is used to optimize the above model, creating an Online Composite Predictive Control Model that provides confidence intervals and recommended values for control and replacement. The proposed method can effectively manage data quality, providing a solid data foundation for hydrological data analysis.

The study "DABC: A Named Entity Recognition Method Incorporating Attention Mechanisms" by Fangling Leng, Fan Li, Yubin Bao, Tiancheng Zhang, and Ge Yu was published in June 2024 and proposed an entity recognition method based on the DeBERTa-Attention-BiLSTM-CRF model. The proposed method first extracts features using a DeBERTa model. Then, the attention mechanism is introduced to further enhance the extracted features. Finally, it uses a BiLSTM to further capture the long-distance dependencies in the text and obtain the predicted sequences through the CRF layer, and then identify the entities in the text. This work advances the development of complex Chinese named entity recognition.

The study "Enhancing Knowledge-Concept Recommendations with Heterogeneous Graph-Contrastive Learning" by Liting Wei, Yun Li, Weiwei Wang, and Yi Zhu was published in July 2024 and proposed a novel multi-task strategy for knowledge-concept recommendations, namely Knowledge-Concept Recommendations with Heterogeneous Graph-Contrastive Learning. It considers learners and their structural neighbors as positive contrastive pairs to construct self-supervision signals on the predefined meta-path from heterogeneous information networks as auxiliary tasks, which can capture the higher-order neighbors of learners by presenting different perspectives. Then, the information noise-contrastive estimation loss is regarded as the main training objective to increase the differentiation of learners from different professional backgrounds. This study demonstrates the crucial role of contrastive learning on knowledge graphs in recommendation systems.

The study "KCB-FLAT: Enhancing Chinese Named Entity Recognition with Syntactic Information and Boundary Smoothing Techniques" by Zhenrong Deng, Zheng Huang, Shiwei Wei, and Jinglin Zhang was published in August 2024, which proposed an innovative model KCB-FLAT to enhance Chinese named entity recognition performance by integrating enriched semantic information with the word-boundary smoothing. It extracts various types of syntactic data and utilizes a key-value memory network to generate syntactic feature embeddings for Chinese characters. Subsequently, it employs an encoder named Cross-Transformer to thoroughly combine syntactic and lexical information to address the entity boundary segmentation errors caused by lexical information. Finally, it introduces boundary smoothing, combined with a regularity-conscious function, to capture the internal regularity of entities, reducing the overconfidence of models.

The study "Few-Shot Learning Sensitive Recognition Method Based on Prototypical Network" by Guoquan Yuan, Xinjian Zhao, Liu Li, Song Zhang, and Shanming Wei was published in September 2024, which proposed a prototype network-based named entity recognition method, namely the FSPN-NER model, to solve the problem of difficult recognition of sensitive data in data-sparse text. The model utilizes the positional coding model to pre-train the data and perform feature extraction, then computes the prototype vectors to achieve entity matching, and finally introduces a boundary detection module to enhance named entity recognition. This work shows the effectiveness of prototype networks utilizing a few labeled data and category prototypes to enhance the generalization of models.

The study "Pre-Trained Language Model Ensemble for Arabic Fake News Detection" by Lama Al-Zahrani and Maha Al-Yahya was published in September 2024, which investigated an ensemble of transformer-based models, such as AraBERT, MARBERT, AraELECTRA, AraGPT2, and ARBERT, using them in the tasks of Arabic fake news detection. Arabic possesses complex linguistic patterns and contexts, leading to performance degradation in standalone Transformer-based fake news detection systems. This study evaluated various ensemble methods, including weighted average ensemble, hard voting, and soft voting, to determine the most effective techniques for improving the learning model and increasing prediction accuracy.

https://doi.org/10.3390/math14020233

The study "Fortify the Guardian, Not the Treasure: Resilient Adversarial Detectors" by JRaz Lapid, Almog Dubin, and Moshe Sipper was published in November 2024, which introduced a robust adversarial detection method via adversarial retraining (RADAR). RADAR aims to fortify adversarial detectors against such adaptive attacks while preserving the classifier's accuracy. It employs adversarial training by incorporating adversarial examples, i.e., crafted to deceive both the classifier and the detector, into the training process. This dual optimization enables the detector to learn and adapt to sophisticated attack scenarios. Improving the ability of machine learning models to cope with adversarial attacks is an important direction for the development of trustworthy artificial intelligence. This article provides a unique example.

The study "Advanced Trans-BiGRU-QA Fusion Model for Atmospheric Mercury Prediction" by Dong-Her Shih, Feng-I. Chung, Ting-Wei Wu, Bo-Hao Wang, and Ming-Hung Shih was published in November 2024, which proposed a novel advanced Trans-BiGRU-QA hybrid model to predict the atmospheric mercury concentration accurately. This study demonstrates the role of feature engineering methods and sliding window-based time series processing methods in environmental pollution prediction.

The study "Advanced Trans-EEGNet Deep Learning Model for Hypoxic-Ischemic Encephalopathy Severity Grading" by Dong-Her Shih, Feng-I Chung, Ting-Wei Wu, Shuo-Yu Huang, and Ming-Hung Shih was published in December 2024, which proposed a deep learning method for rapid classification and assessment of hypoxic–ischemic encephalopathy severity in newborns. The method addresses data imbalance and noise interference through data preprocessing techniques. The combination of an EEGNet and a Transformer with an attention mechanism improves the computation time and feature extraction. This article demonstrates the important applications of the Transformer architecture and data preprocessing methods in the classification and assessment of key diseases.

The study "Hallucination Mitigation for Retrieval-Augmented Large Language Models: A Review" by Wan Zhang and Jing Zhang, published in March 2025, was a review article in this issue. It particularly focuses on hallucination in retrieval-augmented large language models. First, the causes of hallucinations from different sub-tasks in the retrieval and generation phases are carefully examined. Then, a comprehensive framework is proposed to address the hallucinations in retrieval-augmented LLMs after reviewing current hallucination mitigation techniques. In addition, it reviews hallucination-reduction methods based on detection and correction, and discusses the promising future research directions. This article has significant reference value for the study of hallucination mitigation.

The study "SFSIN: A Lightweight Model for Remote Sensing Image Super-Resolution with Strip-like Feature Superpixel Interaction Network" by Yanxia Lyu, Yuhang Liu, Qianqian Zhao, Ziwen Hao, and Xin Song was published in May 2025, which proposed a novel lightweight super-resolution model for remote sensing images, namely a strip-like feature superpixel interaction network (SFSIN). It utilizes the Transformer to capture global context information through long-range dependencies and the CNNs to perform shape-adaptive convolutions. By stacking strip-like feature superpixel interaction modules, it aggregates strip-like features to enable deep feature extraction from local and global perspectives. It also uses the convolutional block attention module with upsampling convolution to integrate deep features from spatial and channel dimensions to improve reconstruction performance. The proposed method effectively reduces the number of parameters and computational complexity of super-resolution techniques, making it easier to use in resource-constrained edge environments.

The published articles are listed below:

1. Zhao X.; Miao W.; Yuan G.; Jiang Y.; Zhang S.; Li Q. Abnormal Traffic Detection System Based on Feature Fusion and Sparse Transformer. *Mathematics* **2024**, 12(11), 1643. https://doi.org/10.3390/math12111643.

https://doi.org/10.3390/math14020233

2. Zhao Q.; Cui S.; Zhu Y.; Li R.; Zhou X. A Novel Online Hydrological Data Quality Control Approach Based on Adaptive Differential Evolution. *Mathematics* **2024**, 12(12), 1821. https://doi.org/10.3390/math12121821.
3. Leng F.; Li F.; Bao Y.; Zhang T.; Ye G. DABC: A Named Entity Recognition Method Incorporating Attention Mechanisms. *Mathematics* **2024**, 12(13), 1992. https://doi.org/10.3390/math12131992.
4. Wei L.; Li Y.; Wang W.; Zhu Y. Enhancing Knowledge-Concept Recommendations with Heterogeneous Graph-Contrastive Learning. *Mathematics* **2024**, 12(15), 2324. https://doi.org/10.3390/math12152324.
5. Deng Z.; Huang Z.; Wei S.; Zhang J. KCB-FLAT: Enhancing Chinese Named Entity Recognition with Syntactic Information and Boundary Smoothing Techniques. *Mathematics* **2024**, 12(17), 2714. https://doi.org/10.3390/math12172714.
6. Yuan G.; Zhao X.; Li L.; Zhang S.; Wei S. Few-Shot Learning Sensitive Recognition Method Based on Prototypical Network. *Mathematics* **2024**, 12(17), 2791. https://doi.org/10.3390/math12172791.
7. Al-Zahrani L.; Al-Yahya M. Pre-Trained Language Model Ensemble for Arabic Fake News Detection. *Mathematics* **2025**, 12(18), 2941. https://doi.org/10.3390/math12182941.
8. Lapid R.; Dubin A.; Sipper M. Fortify the Guardian, Not the Treasure: Resilient Adversarial Detectors. *Mathematics* **2024**, 12(22), 3451. https://doi.org/10.3390/math12223451.
9. Shih D.-H.; Chung F.-I.; Wu T.-W.; Wang B.-H.; Shih M.-H. Advanced Trans-BiGRU-QA Fusion Model for Atmospheric Mercury Prediction. *Mathematics* **2024**, 12(22), 3547. https://doi.org/10.3390/math12223547.
10. Shih D.-H.; Chung F.-I.; Wu T.-W.; Huang S.-Y.; Shih M.-H. Advanced Trans-EEGNet Deep Learning Model for Hypoxic-Ischemic Encephalopathy Severity Grading. *Mathematics* **2024**, 12(24), 3915. https://doi.org/10.3390/math12243915.
11. Zhang W.; Zhang J. Hallucination Mitigation for Retrieval-Augmented Large Language Models: A Review. *Mathematics* **2025**, 13(5), 856. https://doi.org/10.3390/math13050856.
12. Lyu Y.; Liu Y.; Zhao Q.; Hao Z.; Song X. SFSIN: A Lightweight Model for Remote Sensing Image Super-Resolution with Strip-like Feature Superpixel Interaction Network. *Mathematics* **2025**, 13(11), 1720. https://doi.org/10.3390/math13111720.

3. Conclusions

The objectives of this Special Issue on "Data Mining and Machine Learning in the Era of Big Knowledge and Large Models" were successfully achieved through the incorporation of groundbreaking research in these fields. Each contribution significantly advanced the understanding and capabilities of big knowledge and large model technologies, focusing on Transformer-based named entity recognition, knowledge recommendation, time series analysis, model integration, data quality improvement, hallucinations, and innovative application development. The collective impact of these studies is profound, aligning with the core purpose: to enhance the breadth and quality of knowledge acquisition and to promote intelligent systems to better serve humanity. This Special Issue stands as a testament to the potential of relevant technologies in shaping a more informed, efficient, and smart world.

Acknowledgments: I would like to extend my appreciation to the authors for their diligent research, the reviewers for providing insightful comments and constructive suggestions, and the editors and proofreading team for their meticulous attention to detail, ensuring high-quality publishing in terms of both research content and printing standards.

https://doi.org/10.3390/math14020233

Conflicts of Interest: The authors declare no conflicts of interest.

References

1. Vaswani, A.; Shazeer, N.; Parmar, N.; Uszkoreit, J.; Jones, L.; Gomez, A.N.; Kaiser, Ł; Polosukhin, I. Attention is all you need. *Adv. Neural Inf. Process. Syst.* **2017**, *30*, 6000–6010.
2. Devlin, J.; Chang, M.W.; Lee, K.; Toutanova, K. BERT: Pre-training of deep bidirectional transformers for language understanding. In Proceedings of the 2019 Conference of the North American Chapter of the Association for Computational Linguistics: Human Language Technologies, Minneapolis, MN, USA, 2–7 June 2019; Volume 1, pp. 4171–4186.
3. Yenduri, G.; Ramalingam, M.; Selvi, G.C.; Supriya, Y.; Srivastava, G.; Maddikunta, P.K.R.; Raj, G.D.; Jhaveri, R.H.; Prabadevi, B.; Wang, W.; et al. GPT (generative pre-trained transformer)—A comprehensive review on enabling technologies, potential applications, emerging challenges, and future directions. *IEEE Access* **2024**, *12*, 54608–54649. [CrossRef]
4. Dosovitskiy, A.; Beyer, L.; Kolesnikov, A.; Weissenborn, D.; Zhai, X.; Unterthiner, T.; Dehghani, M.; Minderer, M.; Heigold, G.; Gelly, S.; et al. An image is worth 16 $\times$ 16 words: Transformers for image recognition at scale. In Proceedings of the 2021 International Conference on Learning Representations, Vienna, Austria, 3–7 May 2021.
5. Hu, H.; Wang, X.; Zhang, Y.; Chen, Q.; Guan, Q. A comprehensive survey on contrastive learning. *Neurocomputing* **2024**, *610*, 128645. [CrossRef]
6. He, K.; Chen, X.; Xie, S.; Li, Y.; Dollár, P.; Girshick, R. Masked autoencoders are scalable vision learners. In Proceedings of the IEEE/CVF Conference on Computer Vision and Pattern Recognition, New Orleans, LA, USA, 18–24 June 2022; pp. 16000–16009.
7. Radford, A.; Kim, J.W.; Hallacy, C.; Ramesh, A.; Goh, G.; Agarwal, S.; Sastry, G.; Askell, A.; Mishkin, P.; Clark, J.; et al. Learning transferable visual models from natural language supervision. In Proceedings of the International Conference on Machine Learning, Virtual, 18–24 July 2021; pp. 8748–8763.
8. Qian, Z.; Huang, K.; Wang, Q.F.; Zhang, X.Y. A survey of robust adversarial training in pattern recognition: Fundamental, theory, and methodologies. *Pattern Recognit.* **2022**, *131*, 108889. [CrossRef]
9. Huang, L.; Yu, W.; Ma, W.; Zhong, W.; Feng, Z.; Wang, H.; Chen, Q.; Peng, W.; Feng, X.; Qin, B.; et al. A survey on hallucination in large language models: Principles, taxonomy, challenges, and open questions. *ACM Trans. Inf. Syst.* **2025**, *43*, 1–55. [CrossRef]
10. Min, S.; Krishna, K.; Lyu, X.; Lewis, M.; Yih, W.T.; Koh, P.W.; Iyyer, M.; Zettlemoyer, L.; Hajishirzi, H. Factscore: Fine-grained atomic evaluation of factual precision in long form text generation. In Proceedings of the 2023 Conference on Empirical Methods in Natural Language Processing, Singapore, 6–10 December 2023; pp. 12076–12100.
11. Izacard, G.; Lewis, P.; Lomeli, M.; Hosseini, L.; Petroni, F.; Schick, T.; Dwivedi-Yu, J.; Joulin, A.; Riedel, S.; Grave, E. Atlas: Few-shot learning with retrieval augmented language models. *J. Mach. Learn. Res.* **2023**, *24*, 11912–11954.
12. Kojima, T.; Gu, S.S.; Reid, M.; Matsuo, Y.; Iwasawa, Y. Large language models are zero-shot reasoners. *Adv. Neural Inf. Process. Syst.* **2022**, *35*, 22199–22213.

https://doi.org/10.3390/math14020233

mathematics

MDPI

Article

SFSIN: A Lightweight Model for Remote Sensing Image Super-Resolution with Strip-like Feature Superpixel Interaction Network

Yanxia Lyu [1,2,*], Yuhang Liu [1], Qianqian Zhao [1], Ziwen Hao [1] and Xin Song [1,2]

[1] School of Computer and Communication Engineering, Northeastern University at Qinhuangdao, Qinhuangdao 066000, China; 202212004@stu.neuq.edu.cn (Y.L.); 202212007@stu.neuq.edu.cn (Q.Z.); 2272197@stu.neu.edu.cn (Z.H.); sxin78916@neuq.edu.cn (X.S.)

[2] Hebei Key Laboratory of Marine Perception Network and Data Processing, Northeastern University at Qinhuangdao, Qinhuangdao 066004, China

* Correspondence: lyx@neuq.edu.cn

Abstract: Remote sensing image (RSI) super-resolution plays a critical role in improving image details and reducing costs associated with physical imaging devices. However, existing super-resolution methods are not applicable to resource-constrained edge devices because they are hampered by a large number of parameters and significant computational complexity. To address these challenges, we propose a novel lightweight super-resolution model for remote sensing images, a strip-like feature superpixel interaction network (SFSIN), which combines the flexibility of convolutional neural networks (CNNs) with the long-range learning capabilities of a Transformer. Specifically, the Transformer captures global context information through long-range dependencies, while the CNN performs shape-adaptive convolutions. By stacking strip-like feature superpixel interaction (SFSI) modules, we aggregate strip-like features to enable deep feature extraction from local and global perspectives. In addition to traditional methods that rely solely on direct upsampling for reconstruction, our model uses the convolutional block attention module with upsampling convolution (CBAMUpConv), which integrates deep features from spatial and channel dimensions to improve reconstruction performance. Extensive experiments on the AID dataset show that SFSIN outperforms ten state-of-the-art lightweight models. SFSIN achieves a PSNR of 33.10 dB and an SSIM of 0.8715 on the $\times 2$ scale, outperforming competitive models in both quantity and quality, while also excelling at higher scales.

Keywords: remote sensing image; super-resolution; lightweight; Transformer; strip-like feature

MSC: 68-XX; 68Txx; 68T10

1. Introduction

In the era of big knowledge and large models, the scale and complexity of data are increasing exponentially, which brings unprecedented opportunities and challenges for machine learning algorithms. Remote sensing images (RSIs) are acquired from airborne or satellite sensors and analyze surface objects using electromagnetic wave reflection functions, commonly used in computer vision tasks such as image classification, object detection, and change detection. As an important data source for obtaining geospatial information, RSIs play a central role in various areas such as environmental monitoring [1], urban planning [2], agricultural supervision [3], and disaster management [4]. RSIs provide important information that enables accurate analysis and decision-making in these areas.

However, the quality of RSIs is inevitably affected by atmospheric turbulence, lighting conditions, noise, motion blur, and intrinsic properties of the sensors during the acquisition process. These imaging conditions and hardware performance limitations result in suboptimal resolution and image quality [5,6]. Upgrading physical imaging equipment not only incurs additional costs, but also extends the deployment cycle of remote sensing systems. Conversely, improving the resolution of RSIs can significantly improve the efficiency of data use and provide more accurate and reliable information for scientific research and practical applications. Therefore, this paper aimed at developing super-resolution (SR) methods to improve RSI quality.

Transformer models [7–9] are gaining attention due to their remarkable ability to capture long-range dependencies, which is particularly advantageous when processing complex image features. In contrast, CNNs [10–14] perform shape-adaptive convolutions along tubular features, allowing them to effectively adapt to objects of different shapes. Both approaches offer unique strengths and offer diverse solutions for super-resolution tasks.

In the flourishing of large-scale knowledge and models, the richness of data provides sufficient information for model training, but also puts forward higher requirements for model complexity and efficiency. Although the introduction of advanced technologies such as residual connections and attention mechanisms have significantly improved the performance of CNN-based SR models, challenges related to large model sizes, high computational requirements, and memory usage remain critical research areas. These issues limit the practical use of SR models, especially in resource-constrained environments such as real-time remote sensing applications. To mitigate these limitations, ongoing research focuses on developing more efficient architectures, such as lightweight networks [15] and pruning techniques [16].

While these efficiency advances have primarily targeted natural images with regular textures (e.g., DIV2K, Set5, Set14, or Urban100 datasets), RSIs capture highly diverse and irregular structures such as roads, rivers, and other complex ground features, which pose a number of other challenges. These subtleties introduce additional complexity when applying traditional SR methods optimized for more regular and consistent textures. Therefore, traditional SR methods have difficulty in accurately reconstructing RSIs, particularly in preserving the finer details inherent in these image types.

Furthermore, existing SR models designed for natural images often overlook the inherent features of RSIs. This is because RSIs often contain features that vary significantly in size, shape, and texture, requiring the development of special algorithms tailored to these unique features. Traditional convolution methods [17,18] fundamentally struggle to effectively capture stripy and irregular features in RSIs. Although Transformer-based methods can model long-range dependencies, dividing images into fixed-size patches leads to increased computational complexity, memory consumption, and boundary artifacts that degrade the overall quality of the reconstruction.

As shown in Figure 1, RSIs frequently contain elongated structures such as roads, rivers, and urban boundaries. These strip-like features exhibit irregular geometries and varying scales, posing significant challenges to traditional convolution-based methods. For instance, fixed receptive fields in standard convolutions may fail to capture fragmented road networks or curved river boundaries (e.g., the winding road in Figure 1), leading to blurred or discontinuous reconstructions.

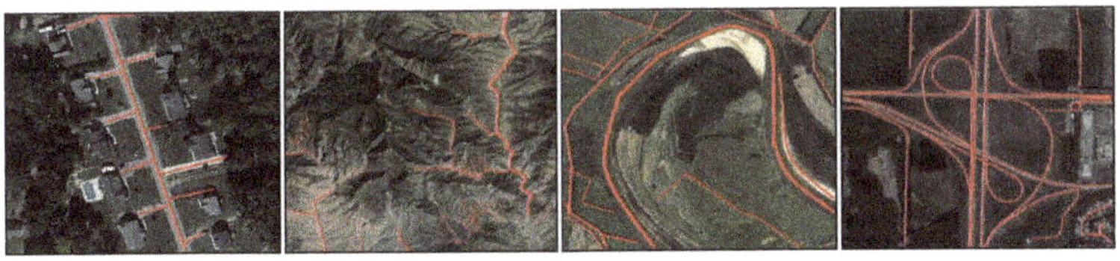

Figure 1. Example of RSIs with strip-like features.

To overcome these challenges, we propose a hybrid CNN–Transformer network that includes the strip-like feature superpixel interaction (SFSI) module. This hybrid design combines the Transformer's ability to capture long-range dependencies with CNNs that perform shape-adaptive convolutions along strip-like features. SFSI combines dynamic snake convolutions [19], which are very effective in capturing strip-like structures, with superpixel clustering [20] to reduce computational complexity while preserving critical structural information.

Additionally, existing SR models [8,10–12,21] typically rely on standard convolutions and PixelShuffle for the final reconstruction phase, which may not fully utilize the available spatial and channel information. To address this limitation, we introduce the convolutional block attention module with upsampling convolution (CBAMUpConv), which leverages the convolutional block attention module (CBAM) [22] to improve spatial and channel attention during feature extraction. By applying this attention mechanism to local, global, and strip-like features, our method significantly improves the model's ability to capture and exploit essential structural details, resulting in superior reconstruction performance, especially in preserving strip-like and complex features that are critical for RSIs.

Our contributions are summarized as follows:

1. We propose a lightweight hybrid CNN–Transformer network (SFSIN) that effectively extracts strip-like features in RSIs using dynamic snake convolution (DSConv) and strip-like feature superpixel interaction (SFSI) modules, achieving parameter efficiency.
2. We introduce the CBAMUpConv module, which integrates upsampling convolution with spatial and channel attention mechanisms, significantly enhancing reconstruction performance while maintaining computational efficiency.

2. Related Work

2.1. Conventional Methods for SR

In the context of remote sensing, single-image super-resolution (SISR) refers to the process of reconstructing a high-resolution (HR) image from a single low-resolution (LR) observation, with the aim of revealing finer spatial details that may be lost during image acquisition. Traditional methods for SR include interpolation-based techniques such as bilinear, bicubic, and nearest-neighbor interpolation [23,24], as well as reconstruction-based approaches that use mathematical models or image priors. Interpolation-based methods are simple and computationally efficient, but often result in image blurring and loss of detail. Reconstruction-based approaches can provide better results in preserving edge and texture information, but their performance depends heavily on the accuracy of the previously used information and is computationally intensive [25,26]. While these classical approaches laid the foundation for SISR, they face significant limitations in balancing efficiency and image quality, especially when it comes to complex textures and high-frequency details in remote sensing images.

2.2. CNN-Based Models for SR

The application of deep learning to image SR began with Dong et al. [10] who introduced the SRCNN model for end-to-end mapping of LR to HR images. Although SRCNN improved speed and quality, its pre-upsampling module increased computational complexity and slowed convergence. This was fixed with VDSR [12], which fixed the gradient disappearing issue and improved the details. He et al. [27] leveraged residual networks to enable deeper architectures without sacrificing performance. Building on these advances, Lim et al. proposed EDSR [11], which refined SRResNet [28] by removing batch normalization layers, reducing memory usage during training by 40% while improving image quality. Attention mechanisms further improved SR models, as Zhang et al. [14] using a Residual Channel Attention Network (RCAN) to improve feature learning. Remote sensing image super-resolution (RSISR) quality is crucial for tasks such as object detection [29], instance segmentation [30], classification [31], etc. Liebel et al. [32] adapted SRCNN to outperform traditional interpolation methods, while Lei et al. [33] developed LGCNet to take into account the different scaling properties of RSIs and integrate cross-layer functions for improved reconstruction. Xu et al. [34] has further developed this with the Deep Memory Convolutional Network (DMCN), using a symmetric hourglass structure and multiple residual connections to increase performance. Ma et al. [35] introduced WTCRR, which combines wavelet transform with local and global residual connections to reduce artifacts and improve edge detail in RSIs.

2.3. *Transformer-Based Models for SR*

Transformers have inspired several adaptations for SR tasks. Chen et al. [9] introduced IPT, a pre-trained Transformer that excels in several low-level vision tasks, including SR. Liang et al. [8] followed with SwinIR, which uses the Swin Transformer [36] for SR, noise reduction, and artifact reduction. Fang et al. [37] proposed HNCT, a hybrid CNN–Transformer that provides high reconstruction quality and efficiency. Li et al. [21] introduced DLGSANet, leveraging dynamic local and global self-attention for state-of-the-art accuracy with fewer parameters. In RSISR, Lei et al. [38] introduced TransENet and integrated high and low-dimensional features, while He et al. [39] proposed DsTer, a dense spectral Transformer for 3D data processing. Tu et al. [40] developed SWCGAN, a generative adversarial network combining CNNs with the Swin Transformer, and Tang et al. [41] introduced HSTNet, capturing detailed contours using recursive information.

2.4. *Lightweight Models for SR*

To balance performance and computational efficiency, various lightweight SR models have been developed. Liu et al. [42] introduced RFDN, which uses a residual feature distillation mechanism to optimize feature extraction. Ahn et al. [43] proposed CARN, which uses a cascaded residual network structure for efficient SR. Lu et al. [44] introduced ESRT, which improves function representation and manages long-range dependencies with reduced computational costs. Zhang et al. [45] introduced ELAN, which combines shifted convolutions and multi-scale self-attention to efficiently extract local and global features, accelerated by attention mechanisms. Zhang et al. [46] introduced SPIN, a lightweight image SR model that improves feature extraction through superpixel token interaction while effectively reducing computational complexity. In the context of RSISR, lightweight models are essential for use in resource-constrained environments such as embedded devices. Wang et al. [47] proposed AMFFN, an attention-based multilayer feature fusion network that uses dynamic feature distillation modules and partial morphological residual blocks to efficiently extract key features, outperforming previous methods [10,48]. Wang et al. [49] also introduced CTN, which minimizes parameters by integrating multi-level context functions using context transition layers and contextual aggregation modules. Although these models achieve impressive efficiency, their designs primarily target natural images and do not explicitly address the unique challenges of reconstructing strip-like features in RSIs, such as roads and rivers, which require specialized mechanisms for curvilinear structure preservation. In contrast, our proposed model leverages the flexible deformation capabilities of convolutions and the long-range learning capability of Transformers coupled with superpixels to effectively reconstruct narrow, strip-like features, thereby striking a balance between parameter efficiency and performance.

3. Methodology

The architecture of the proposed strip-like feature superpixel interaction network (SFSIN) consists of three key phases: morphological feature extraction, deep feature extraction using strip-like feature superpixel interaction (SFSI) blocks, and image reconstruction through the CBAMUpConv module, as shown in Figure 2. Each of these components has been carefully designed to address specific challenges in RSISR, particularly in capturing strip-like features that are prevalent in RSIs.

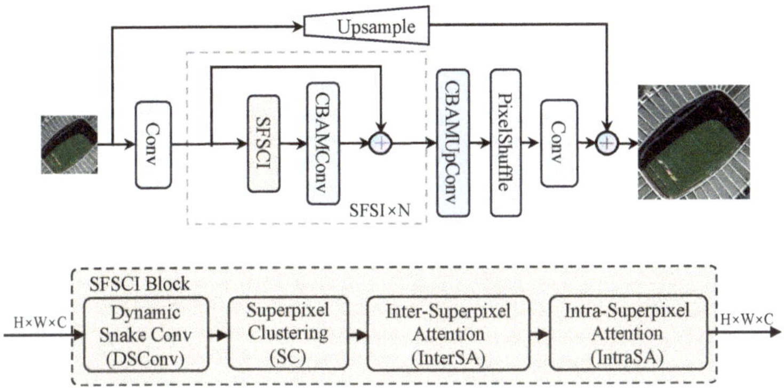

Figure 2. The network architecture of SFSIN. It consists of SFSI blocks for strip-like feature extraction and CBAM modules for improving spatial and channel attention.

In the following subsections, we will go into detail about the design and functionality of each module and how they contribute to the overall performance of the network.

3.1. Architecture

As depicted in Figure 2, SFSIN follows a three-phase design: (1) Morphological feature extraction captures low-level edges and corners; (2) SFSI blocks iteratively aggregate strip-like features through DSConv and superpixel attention; (3) CBAMUpConv reconstructs HR images by fusing multi-scale attentive features. This hierarchical approach ensures progressive refinement from local details to global structures.

Given an LR the quality of remote sensing image (RSI) $\mathbf{F}_S \in R^{H\times W\times C}$, the first phase applies a standard convolutional layer to extract morphological features, such as edges and corners, which are essential for preserving structural coherence in RSIs. This step ensures that foundational geometric patterns are retained before deeper feature extraction, resulting in $\mathbf{F}_S \in R^{H\times W\times C}$, where H and W represent the height and width of the image, and C denotes the number of feature channels. Morphological feature extraction is crucial for capturing basic structural information, which serves as the basis for subsequent deep feature learning.

Next, in the deep feature extraction phase, N blocks of SFSI are stacked to gradually capture deeper representations, which can be expressed as $\mathbf{F}_D \in R^{H\times W\times C}$, from the morphological features $\mathbf{F}_S$. Each SFSI block consists of the strip-like feature superpixel cross and intra interaction block (SFSCI), which includes dynamic snake convolution (DSConv), superpixel clustering (SC), inter-superpixel attention (InterSA), and intra-superpixel attention (IntraSA). These components are designed to effectively capture strip-like features and aggregate features from both local and global perspectives.

In addition, residual connections are used in each SFSI block to ensure stable training and better gradient propagation, allowing the model to learn deeper features without suffering from vanishing gradients.

This process can be expressed as follows:

$$\begin{aligned} \mathbf{x}_{sfsci_{(i)}} &= f_1(\mathbf{d}_{i-1}), \\ \mathbf{d}_i &= \mathbf{d}_{i-1} + f_2(\mathbf{x}_{sfsci_{(i)}}) \end{aligned} \tag{1}$$

where $\mathbf{d}_i$ denotes the features of the $i-th$ SFSI block, $\mathbf{x}_{sfsci_{(i)}}$ denotes the output functions of the $i-th$ SFSCI, f_1 and f_2 represent the SFSCI and CBAMConv operations, respectively.

The deep features $\mathbf{F}_D$ extracted from the final SFSI block are then passed to the image reconstruction module, which utilizes the CBAMUpConv module. The CBAMUpConv module integrates spatial and channel attention mechanisms to further refine feature maps before upsampling them through the PixelShuffle operation. This module ensures that important spatial patterns and channel-related information are highlighted, allowing the model to produce high-resolution images with minimal loss of detail. The final convolution layer aggregates the upsampled features into a high-resolution RSI $\mathbf{RSI}_{HR} \in R^{H_{out} \times W_{out} \times 3}$.

This process is summarized by the following equation:

$$\mathbf{RSI}_{HR} = f_{\text{lastconv}}(f_{\text{ps}}(f_{\text{cbamup}}(\mathbf{F}_D))) \tag{2}$$

where f_{cbamup} represents the CBAMUpConv module that applies attention mechanisms, f_{ps} denotes the PixelShuffle operation, and f_{lastconv} is the final convolutional layer that produces the high-resolution image.

3.2. *Strip-like Feature Superpixel Cross and Intra Interaction Module*

The core component of SFSIN is the strip-like feature superpixel cross and intra interaction (SFSCI), which is responsible for extracting and refining strip-like features in RSIs. As shown in Figure 2, the SFSCI module consists of four key components: dynamic snake convolution (DSConv), superpixel clustering (SC), inter-superpixel attention (InterSA), and intra-superpixel attention (IntraSA).

Each of these components plays a unique role in addressing the challenges presented by the unique geometries and feature patterns in RSIs. The DSConv module is specifically designed for effective strip-like feature extraction from RSIs. The SC module groups similar pixels into superpixels, which helps reduce computational complexity while maintaining the integrity of important boundaries within the image. The InterSA module captures long-range dependencies by using superpixels as mediators, while the IntraSA module focuses on refining details within each superpixel. These two attention mechanisms are integrated to improve feature representation at both global and local levels and enable more accurate reconstruction of the model.

In summary, this module extracts strip-like features from RSIs, generates superpixels, and then aggregates features from both global and local perspectives of the superpixels. The following subsections provide a detailed description of these components.

3.2.1. Dynamic Snake Convolution

RSIs often contain strip-like structures that are difficult to detect for standard convolution operations due to their fixed receptive fields. Dynamic snake convolution (DSConv) is introduced to adjust the receptive fields for convolution along these curvilinear structures, thereby providing a more flexible and effective method for detecting such features.

Specifically, given a standard 9 × 9 2D convolution kernel K with the center coordinate at $K_i = (x_i, y_i)$, by introducing offsets Δ, the convolution kernel extends along the $x-axis$ and $y-axis$, allowing it to follow the curvature of strip-like features. For the $x-axis$, the position of each grid in K is given by $k_{i\pm c} = (x_{i\pm c}, y_{i\pm c})$, where $c = \{0,1,2,3,4\}$ represents the horizontal distance from the center grid. The choice of each grid position $k_{i\pm c}$ in the convolution kernel K is an accumulation process. Starting from the center position K_i, the position of a grid K_{i+1} further from the center depends on the position of the previous grid K_i, where the offset is $\Delta = \{\delta | \delta \in [-1,-1]\}$ accumulates to ensure continuity along the strip-like features. The flexibility provided by DSConv ensures that important structural details are captured, which is critical to improving the accuracy of RSISR. This method not only increases the model's ability to capture these complex shapes but also alleviates the limitations of deformable convolutions, which, while more flexible than standard convolutions, still have problems with highly curvilinear features.

The process can be expressed as follows:

$$K_{i\pm c} = \begin{cases} (x_{i+c}, y_{i+c}) = (x_i + c, y_i + \sum_i^{i+c} \Delta y), \\ (x_{i-c}, y_{i-c}) = (x_i - c, y_i + \sum_{i-c}^{i} \Delta y), \end{cases} \tag{3}$$

Likewise, the process for the $y-axis$ is given by

$$K_{j\pm c} = \begin{cases} (x_{j+c}, y_{j+c}) = (x_j + \sum_j^{j+c} \Delta x, y_j + c), \\ (x_{j-c}, y_{j-c}) = (x_j + \sum_{j-c}^{j} \Delta x, y_j - c), \end{cases} \tag{4}$$

3.2.2. Superpixel Clustering

To efficiently handle the complexity of RSIs, superpixel clustering (SC) is used to group similar pixels into superpixels. This method significantly reduces computational complexity while preserving the integrity of important boundaries within the image.

The SC method used in SFSIN is based on the soft superpixel segmentation (SSN) approach [20], which avoids the fixed patch sizes usually used in standard approaches. This aggregation helps maintain structural coherence, particularly for strip-like features, while reducing boundary artifacts. Furthermore, by leveraging superpixels, InterSA and IntraSA (introduced in the following sections) reduce the computational complexity typically associated with traditional self-attention mechanisms while effectively capturing global and local relationships within the image.

Specifically, the feature map is first divided into a regular grid and superpixels are initialized into $\mathbf{s} \in \mathbf{R}^{M\times C}$, where M denotes the number of superpixels. Given a pixel $\mathbf{p} \in \mathbf{R}^{N\times C}$ (note that $N = H\times W$ is the number of pixels), it belongs to one of the M superpixels. The relationship between pixels and superpixels is then iteratively refined through soft associations.

For the $t-th$ iteration, the process of updating superpixel centers is given as follows:

$$\mathbf{Q}_{pi}^t = e^{-\mathbf{D}(\mathbf{I}_p, \mathbf{S}_i^{t-1})} = e^{-||\mathbf{I}_p - \mathbf{S}_i^{t-1}||^2} \tag{5}$$

where $\mathbf{Q}_{pi}^t$ denotes the soft association between pixel p and superpixel i during the $t-th$ iteration. $\mathbf{D}$ represents the distance between the pixel and the superpixel center. $\mathbf{I}_p$ denotes the $p-th$ pixel of the original image, and $\mathbf{S}_i^{t-1}$ denotes the center of the $i-th$ superpixel during the $(t-1)-th$ iteration.

It is important to note that, by reducing the number of elements the model must process and focusing on meaningful groups of pixels, SC enables more efficient feature extraction and reduces noise in the final reconstructed image. This is particularly useful in remote sensing, where image complexity is high, and boundary preservation is critical.

We then update the superpixel centers using the following formula:

$$\mathbf{S}_i^t = \frac{1}{\mathbf{Z}_i^t} \sum_{p=1}^{n} \mathbf{Q}_{pi}^t \mathbf{I}_p \tag{6}$$

where the notation $\mathbf{S}_i^t$ denotes the center of the $i-th$ superpixel during the $t-th$ iteration. While $\mathbf{Z}_i^t = \sum_p \mathbf{Q}_{pi}^t$ represents the normalization constant along the columns. After T iterations, we obtain the final relationship matrix $\mathbf{Q}^T$.

3.2.3. Inter-Superpixel Attention

RSIs often require capturing relationships between distant regions because linear and strip-like features can span large areas. Inter-superpixel attention (InterSA) addresses this problem by treating superpixels as proxies for individual pixels, allowing the model to more effectively capture feature interaction over long distances.

InterSA uses a self-attention mechanism to calculate relationships between superpixels, which is crucial for capturing long-term dependencies in RSIs. These dependencies provide valuable context for accurately reconstructing strip-like features.

This cross-attention mechanism allows the model to understand the connections between different parts of the image, especially for objects that are spatially distant but semantically connected. InterSA thereby improves the accuracy of feature reconstruction for these spatially extended structures.

Figure 3 illustrates the InterSA mechanism, which computes attention between superpixels to model long-range dependencies (e.g., connecting disjoint road segments).

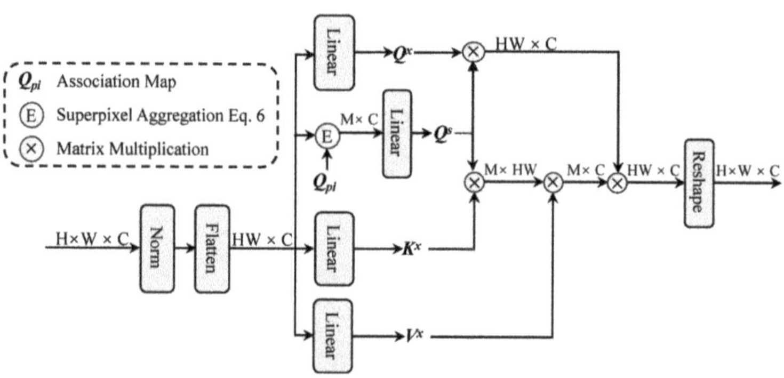

Figure 3. The inter-superpixel attention module (InterSA).

Given flattened pixels $\mathbf{p} \in \mathbf{R}^{HW \times C}$ and superpixels $\mathbf{s} \in \mathbf{R}^{M \times C}$, where M is the number of superpixels.

First, we use linear mappings to calculate the query: $\mathbf{Q}^s \in \mathbf{R}^{M \times D}$, key: $\mathbf{K}^x \in \mathbf{R}^{HW \times D}$, and value: $\mathbf{V}^x \in \mathbf{R}^{HW \times C}$ as follows:

$$\mathbf{Q}^s = \mathbf{s}\mathbf{W}_q^s, \mathbf{K}^x = \mathbf{x}\mathbf{W}_k^x, \mathbf{V}^x = \mathbf{x}\mathbf{W}_v^x \tag{7}$$

where $\mathbf{s}$ represents superpixels and $\mathbf{x}$ represents ordinary pixels, $\mathbf{W}_q^s \in \mathbf{R}^{C \times D}$, $\mathbf{W}_k^x \in \mathbf{R}^{C \times D}$, $\mathbf{W}_v^x \in \mathbf{R}^{C \times C}$ are the weight matrices for query, key, and value.

We then calculate the updated superpixel features as follows:

$$\mathbf{s}_u = \mathrm{softmax}(\mathbf{Q}^s(\mathbf{K}^x)^T / \sqrt{D})\mathbf{V}^x \tag{8}$$

where $\sqrt{D}$ is a scaling factor introduced to prevent the gradient from disappearing. We then pass the aggregated pixels to the individual pixels, specifically using $\mathbf{W}_q^x \in \mathbf{R}^{C \times D}$ to obtain the pixel queries, $\mathbf{Q}^s$ as the key, and $\mathbf{s}_u$ as the value. Finally, the updated superpixel features are mapped back to pixel-level features. Through this process, our model learns the global characteristics of RSIs.

3.2.4. Intra-Superpixel Attention

Intra-superpixel attention (IntraSA) focuses on refining local details within each superpixel. While InterSA captures long-range dependencies, IntraSA ensures that the model also accurately captures fine-grained information within each superpixel.

An intuitive approach to improving resolution in SR tasks is to exploit the complementarity of similar pixels within superpixels. However, this presents challenges such as a different number of pixels within each superpixel, which can increase computational complexity and memory consumption.

To mitigate this, as shown in Figure 4, IntraSA uses a top-N selection mechanism that selects the most relevant pixels within each superpixel for self-attention. This reduces the computational effort while ensuring that important local features (e.g., parking lot markings) are not missed.

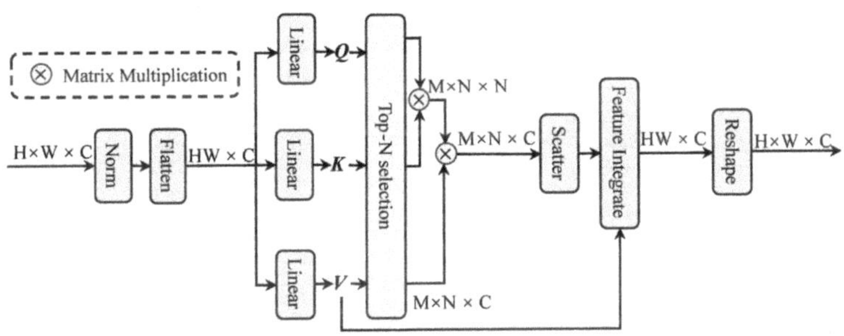

Figure 4. The intra-superpixel attention module (IntraSA).

It then calculates the relationships between these selected pixels within the superpixel using the self-attention mechanism defined by Equations (7) and (8). The calculated pixels are then distributed again to their respective positions in the image. While top-N selection alleviates the problems mentioned above, it also means that some similar pixels within a superpixel may not be considered. Therefore, we use the value key to capture all features before the pixel attention operation and integrate them back into the original image with distributed pixels.

3.3. *Convolutional Block Attention Module with Upsampling Convolution*

In the image reconstruction phase, standard upsampling convolutions and PixelShuffle methods often miss important spatial and channel information, resulting in suboptimal image quality. To address this limitation, we propose a novel CBAMUpConv module, which, to the best of our knowledge, is the first to integrate both spatial and channel attention mechanisms into the upsampling process, as presented in Figure 5.

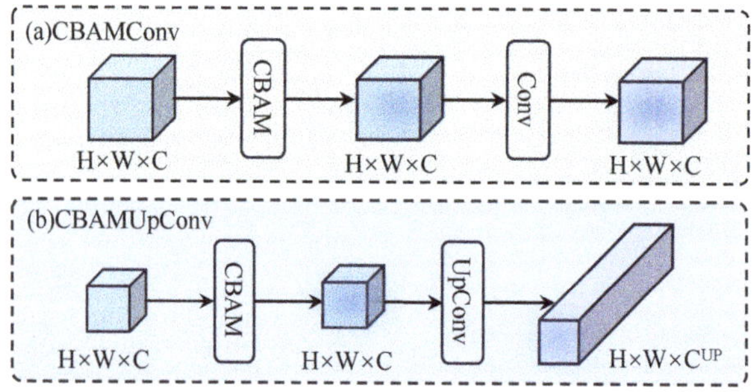

Figure 5. Variants of the CBAM attention mechanism: (**a**) spatial and channel attention in deep feature extraction and (**b**) spatial and channel attention in the reconstruction module.

Figure 5 details the two variants of the CBAM attention mechanism integrated into SFSIN:

Figure 5a applies spatial and channel attention during deep feature extraction. Here, the spatial attention gate prioritizes critical regions (e.g., edges of strip-like structures), while the channel attention suppresses redundant feature maps, enhancing discriminability.

Figure 5b illustrates the novel CBAMUpConv module used in the reconstruction phase. Unlike traditional upsampling, CBAMUpConv sequentially refines features through channel attention (highlighting informative maps) and spatial attention (focusing on structural details) before PixelShuffle. This dual mechanism ensures preservation of both high-frequency details (e.g., road boundaries) and low-frequency contexts (e.g., terrain textures), significantly reducing artifacts in the final HR output (see Section 4.2.2).

Our CBAMUpConv module applies attention mechanisms directly to the deep features $\mathbf{F}_d \in \mathbf{R}^{H \times W \times C}$, which were extracted from the SFSI blocks. By leveraging spatial attention, the model is able to prioritize the most important areas within the image, while channel attention ensures that the most relevant feature channels are highlighted, enabling more accurate and detailed reconstructions.

In a further step, the CBAMUpConv module expands the number of feature channels to $H \times W \times C^{up}$, where $C^{up} = C \times upscale^2$, and upscale corresponds to the model parameter, which can take values of 2, 3, or 4.

This design represents a novel contribution to the field as, to our knowledge, it is the first time that channel and spatial attention mechanisms have been explicitly combined in an upsampling convolution module specifically tailored to image reconstruction tasks.

In summary, the CBAMUpConv module introduces a novel approach to upsampling by integrating attention mechanisms into the upsampling convolution process. This combination of spatial attention and channel attention ensures that important features are preserved while reducing computational effort. The module improves the model's ability to produce high-quality, high-resolution reconstructions, especially in resource-limited environments.

4. Experiments

In this section, we present a comprehensive evaluation of our proposed SFSIN model, focusing on the contribution of each module through ablation studies. Furthermore, we evaluate the performance of the model at different scales in the RSISR tasks to demonstrate its robustness and adaptability to different levels of degradation.

4.1. Experimental Settings

4.1.1. Dataset and Evaluation

We use the AID dataset [50], a benchmark in RSI, which consists of 10,000 images from 30 different scene categories such as urban areas, forests, and water bodies. Each image is originally 600 × 600 pixels in size, providing a high-resolution foundation for SR tasks. The dataset is split into 8000 images for training (80%), 1000 for validation (10%), and 1000 for testing (10%), ensuring balanced performance evaluation.

To simulate real-world scenarios where image resolution varies significantly, we down-sample the original high-resolution images by bicubic interpolation with scaling factors ×2, ×3, and ×4. These different levels of degradation allow us to test the adaptability of our method to different reconstruction challenges. For quantitative evaluation, we use PSNR and SSIM [51], which are widely accepted for measuring the perceptual and structural quality of the reconstructed images. These metrics are calculated on the Y channel of the YCbCr color space because this contains most of the luminance information that is critical to visual fidelity.

4.1.2. Implementation Details

We design two variants of SFSIN with different complexity, called SFSIN-S and SFSIN. The SFSIN model includes eight SFSCI residual groups, each containing a DSConv module, and considers CBAM attention before the pixel shuffle operation. For SFSIN-S, DSConv modules are used only in the first four residual groups, which reduces the number of parameters while maintaining performance. All other settings remain consistent with SFSIN.

4.1.3. Training Settings

We train both models with 64 × 64 patches, a size chosen to ensure a balance between computational efficiency and the ability to capture important patterns in RSIs. Each model is trained with a batch size of 40. The initial learning rate is set to 2×10^{-4}, and a gradual learning rate decay is applied in epochs [250, 400, 450, 475, 500]. We believe that it effectively stabilizes training and prevents overadaptation. After 600 epochs, the training is complete.

To further improve the generalization and robustness of the model, we apply data augmentation techniques including random rotations of 90°, 180°, and 270°as well as horizontal reflections. These extensions simulate various angles and transformations that RSIs may encounter in real-world scenarios. The models are implemented in PyTorch and trained on a system equipped with two Intel Xeon Gold 6133 CPUs, an NVIDIA RTX 4090 GPU and 1007.5 GB memory running Ubuntu 20.04 LTS.

4.2. Comparison with Other Lightweight Methods

Finally, we compare our proposed models SFSIN-S and SFSIN with ten state-of-the-art lightweight models, including CNN-based methods such as AWSRN-M [52], RFDN [42], LatticeNet [53], and MAFFSRN-L [54] as well as Transformer-based approaches such as ESRT [44], SPIN [46] and ELAN-light [45]. In addition, we evaluate remote sensing-specific algorithms such as LGCNet [33], CTNet [49], and AMFFN [47].

To visually compare the performance of these models, we present the PSNR training curves in Figure 6. This figure illustrates how quickly and effectively each ×2 scale model converges to the AID dataset and the final reconstruction quality achieved after 600 epochs.

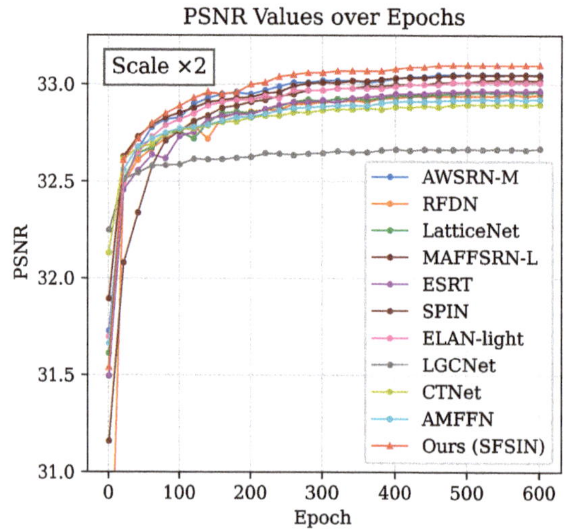

Figure 6. Comparison of PSNR training curves between the proposed method and other lightweight methods on the AID dataset (×2).

As shown in Figure 6, this analysis highlights the strength of our proposed attention mechanisms and DSConv modules in enabling more accurate and efficient RSISR. SFSIN's ability to consistently achieve the best PSNR across almost all epochs highlights its robustness in dealing with complex textures and strip-like features in RSIs. Furthermore, it is noteworthy that, while other models exhibit significant fluctuations and instability in their PSNR curves, our model maintains remarkably stable performance, further demonstrating its reliability and consistency.

This stability stems from two key design choices: (1) The residual connections in SFSCI blocks (Section 3.1) mitigate gradient vanishing, and (2) CBAMUpConv's attention mechanisms (Section 3.3) balance feature learning across scales. These results validate the synergy between architectural components in SFSIN.

4.2.1. Quantitative Evaluation

As shown in Table 1, our proposed SFSIN model consistently outperforms other methods at all scales, demonstrating its superiority in handling RSISR. On the ×2 scale, SFSIN achieves a PSNR of 33.10 dB and an SSIM of 0.8715, significantly outperforming the best-performing baseline methods. In particular, SFSIN shows a PSNR gain of 0.43 dB over LGCNet and a 0.2 dB improvement over CTNet, highlighting its ability to accurately reconstruct detailed structures in RSIs.

To further address the computational efficiency across different scales, we measured the inference time of all models at ×2, ×3, and ×4 scales under the same hardware configuration (NVIDIA RTX 4090, Intel Xeon Gold 6133). As shown in Table 1, the inference time generally increases with the scaling factor due to the higher-resolution output, but our SFSIN maintains a favorable trade-off between speed and performance. At the ×3 scale, SFSIN consumes 35.8 ms, outperforming heavier models like AWSRN-M (48.9 ms) and MAFFSRN-L (42.3 ms) while achieving the highest PSNR/SSIM. For the ×4 scale, where computational complexity is the highest, SFSIN-S (lightweight version) achieves a competitive inference time of 33.6 ms, demonstrating its efficiency in resource-constrained scenarios. In contrast, ultra-light models like LGCNet (193k params) are faster (22.3 ms at ×4) but sacrifice reconstruction quality, while SFSIN balances speed and accuracy across all scales.

Table 1. Quantitative comparison with state-of-the-art methods. The best and second best results are highlighted in red and blue, respectively.

Method	×2 Scale				×3 Scale				×4 Scale			
	Params (k)	PSNR	SSIM	Time (ms)	Params (k)	PSNR	SSIM	Time (ms)	Params (k)	PSNR	SSIM	Time (ms)
AWSRN-M [52]	1,064	33.05	0.8703	45.2	1,143	30.22	0.7835	48.9	1,254	28.55	0.7188	52.7
RFDN [42]	626	32.95	0.8676	35.8	633	30.14	0.7801	38.6	643	28.48	0.7157	41.3
LatticeNet [53]	756	32.96	0.8679	38.2	765	30.16	0.7810	40.5	777	28.48	0.7157	43.2
MAFFSRN-L [54]	791	33.05	0.8703	38.9	807	30.20	0.7826	42.3	830	28.54	0.7184	45.8
ESRT [44]	678	32.97	0.8680	36.5	770	30.12	0.7787	39.8	752	28.47	0.7143	42.1
SPIN [46]	497	33.02	0.8693	29.7	569	30.21	0.7828	32.5	555	28.54	0.7188	34.9
ELAN-light [45]	582	33.01	0.8693	33.2	590	30.19	0.7826	35.7	601	28.52	0.7183	38.4
LGCNet [33]	193	32.67	0.8612	18.7	193	29.82	0.7685	20.5	193	28.17	0.7023	22.3
CTNet [49]	402	32.90	0.8667	25.4	402	30.06	0.7779	27.8	413	28.42	0.7135	30.1
AMFFN [47]	298	32.93	0.8671	22.3	305	30.09	0.7784	24.6	314	28.43	0.7135	26.9
Ours (SFSIN-S)	642	33.08	0.8708	28.1	714	30.23	0.7837	31.2	700	28.58	0.7205	33.6
Ours (SFSIN)	784	33.10	0.8715	32.5	856	30.25	0.7844	35.8	842	28.57	0.7203	36.2

This improvement is due to SFSIN's ability to retain strip-like features in RSIs, a task that LatticeNet and CTNet struggle with. By using DSConv, our model can adaptively focus on these structures, while CBAM improves the feature extraction process by selectively prioritizing informative regions. The synergy between these components leads to more accurate reconstructions, especially for complex textures.

The smaller variant SFSIN-S also delivers competitive results, especially in resource-constrained scenarios where model complexity is a key factor. SFSIN-S achieves second-best performance in most cases, providing a balance between computational efficiency and reconstruction quality. For example, SFSIN-S achieves a PSNR of 30.23 dB on the ×3 scale, outperforming several state-of-the-art models and exhibiting only a small performance penalty compared to the full SFSIN model.

It is worth noting that, on the ×4 scale, SFSIN-S slightly outperforms SFSIN in terms of PSNR, which is likely due to its better generalization and efficiency in handling larger upsampling factors.

The quantitative comparison highlights the effectiveness of our proposed method, especially in extracting strip-like features such as linear elements, which are crucial for remote sensing tasks. These results confirm the strength of our DSConv and attention mechanisms in addressing the unique challenges of RSISR.

4.2.2. Visual Quality Analysis

In addition to quantitative improvements, our SFSIN model excels in the quality of visual reconstruction, especially in demanding remote sensing scenarios. In Figure 7, SFSIN demonstrates its ability to preserve thin structures that are often blurred or distorted by methods such as RFDN and LatticeNet. For clarity, the red box highlights correspond to the HR images.

For example, when reconstructing the RSI "church_110" at the ×2 scale, RFDN and LatticeNet — constrained by their reliance on fixed convolutional kernels — fail to adapt to the complex curvilinear patterns of rooftops and fences, leading to blurred edges and fragmented structures. In contrast, our SFSIN model effectively preserves these critical features and produces a result that is much closer to the high-resolution ground truth.

Similarly, in the "stadium_283" example (×3 scale), SFSIN accurately restores the linear markings on the stadium, while RFDN and LGCNet produce blurred or fragmented lines. This improvement is attributed to DSConv's adaptive receptive fields (Section 3.2.1) and InterSA's long-range dependency modeling (Section 3.2.3), which jointly preserve structural coherence.

For "parking_226" and "viaduct_210" (×4 scale), CBAMUpConv's attention-driven upsampling (Section 3.3) minimizes aliasing artifacts in thin area, whereas other methods fail to maintain such details.

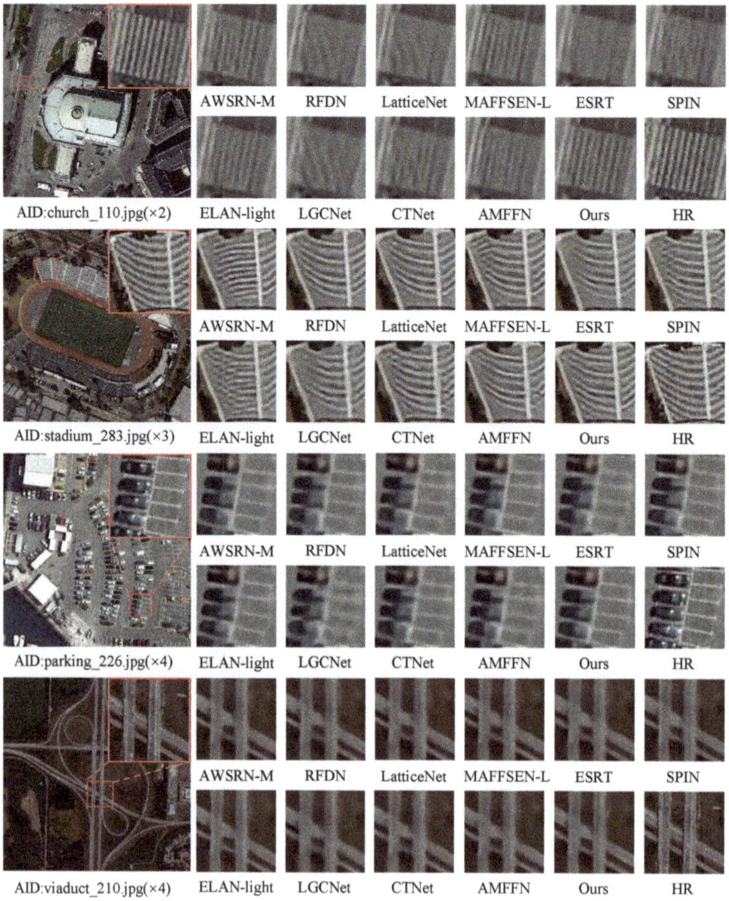

Figure 7. Visual comparison of RSISR (×2, ×3, ×4) in demanding scenarios.

In summary, these improvements are attributed to SFSIN's hybrid design, which combines DSConv's adaptive receptive fields, superpixel-based attention (InterSA/IntraSA), and CBAMUpConv's targeted feature refinement during upsampling. SFSIN's ability to adaptively capture and highlight strip-like structures directly addresses the unique requirements of RSISR and further validates its effectiveness across different image types and scales.

4.3. Ablation Studies

To thoroughly evaluate the contribution of the DSConv and CBAM modules in our proposed SFSIN model, we performed ablation experiments on the AID dataset over the scaling factors ×2, ×3, and ×4. All models were trained under identical settings to ensure a fair comparison. The results presented in Table 2 illustrate the incremental improvements each module brings and reveal important insights into the effectiveness of these components in addressing the challenges of RSISR.

Table 2. Impact of different modules on model performance.

Component				×2 Scale		×3 Scale			×4 Scale		
DSConv	CBAM-Conv	CBAM-UpConv	Params (k)	PSNR	SSIM	Params (k)	PSNR	SSIM	Params (k)	PSNR	SSIM
0			497	33.02	0.8693	569	30.21	0.7828	555	28.54	0.7188
1			781	33.06	0.8704	853	30.21	0.7831	839	28.55	0.7194
0	✓	✓	500	33.05	0.8699	572	30.21	0.7832	558	28.55	0.7196
1	✓		783	33.08	0.8708	855	30.23	0.7836	841	28.55	0.7195
1	✓	✓	586	33.09	0.8710	588	30.24	0.7840	594	28.56	0.7200
2	✓	✓	620	33.10	0.8712	633	30.24	0.7842	629	28.56	0.7200
3	✓	✓	660	33.11	0.8713	668	30.25	0.7843	665	28.57	0.7203
4	✓	✓	701	33.11	0.8714	704	30.25	0.7843	700	28.58	0.7205
5	✓	✓	730	33.11	0.8714	738	30.25	0.7843	736	28.57	0.7204
6	✓	✓	752	33.12	0.8715	769	30.26	0.7844	771	28.58	0.7207
7	✓	✓	784	33.11	0.8714	805	30.25	0.7843	807	28.57	0.7204
8	✓	✓	813	33.10	0.8715	836	30.25	0.7844	842	28.57	0.7203

4.3.1. Impact of DSConv

The DSConv module is introduced as a fundamental component in SFSIN and is used to capture the strip-like features prevalent in RSIs. By leveraging its efficiency in integrating both local and global spatial information, DSConv plays a crucial role in improving feature extraction.

As can be seen in Table 2, the inclusion of DSConv consistently improves PSNR and SSIM across all scales. For example, the model with DSConv at ×2 scale shows significant improvement in both PSNR (from 33.02 to 33.06) and SSIM (from 0.8693 to 0.8704). These results confirm that DSConv is particularly effective in preserving and reconstructing strip-like structures and other linear features that are crucial in RSIs. The improved performance across all scales highlights DSConv's robustness in dealing with various levels of degradation, making it an essential part of the SFSIN architecture.

To achieve a balance between model performance and complexity, we further investigated the optimal number of DSConv modules in the SFSI residual groups. We gradually increased the number of DSConv modules from one to eight and evaluated their impact on performance. As shown in Table 2, both PSNR and SSIM improve as the number of DSConv modules increases and reach their peak when six modules are used. At this point, the model achieves the highest PSNR and near optimal SSIM, suggesting that six DSConv modules provide the best compromise between capturing fine-grained details and controlling model complexity. In particular, when only four DSConv modules are used, the model still achieves a competitive PSNR while minimizing the number of parameters, making it a viable option for resource-constrained environments. This configuration forms the basis of our SFSIN-S variant, which maintains strong performance with fewer parameters and demonstrates the flexibility of our approach in adapting to different computing requirements.

4.3.2. Impact of SC, InterSA, and IntraSA

To validate the necessity of each subcomponent in SFSCI, we conducted ablation experiments on ×2, ×3, and ×4 scales. As shown in Table 3, removing SC, InterSA, or IntraSA leads to noticeable performance degradation. Specifically, SC contributes most significantly to global structure preservation, while InterSA and IntraSA enhance long-range dependency modeling and local detail refinement, respectively. This underscores the necessity of integrating superpixel clustering and cross/intra-attention mechanisms.

Table 3. Ablation study of SFSCI subcomponents across scales.

Configuration	×2 Scale			×3 Scale			×4 Scale		
	Params (k)	PSNR	SSIM	Params (k)	PSNR	SSIM	Params (k)	PSNR	SSIM
Full SFSCI	784	33.10	0.8715	856	30.25	0.7844	842	28.57	0.7203
Without SC	760	32.89	0.8672	832	30.04	0.7801	818	28.36	0.7160
Without InterSA	772	32.92	0.8681	844	30.07	0.7810	830	28.39	0.7169
Without IntraSA	768	32.95	0.8690	840	30.10	0.7829	826	28.42	0.7178

4.3.3. Impact of CBAMConv and CBAMUpConv

Next, we evaluate the effectiveness of the attention mechanisms CBAMConv and CBAMUpConv, which we innovatively integrate into the reconstruction phase of our model. CBAMConv is integrated with the SFSI module to improve feature extraction by capturing both local and global features, while CBAMUpConv is integrated with the reconstruction module to facilitate PixelShuffle during the upsampling process, as described in Section 3.3 .

The results in Table 2 clearly show the significant impact of the CBAM module. For example, using the DSConv module alone on the $\times 2$ scale results in a PSNR of 33.06 and an SSIM of 0.8704. However, when combined with the CBAMConv module, the PSNR increases to 33.08 and the SSIM improves to 0.8708. This performance increase highlights that, with the introduction of the DSConv and CBAMConv modules in the feature extraction process, SFSIN selectively improves key spatial and channel features and strengthens the strip-like features that the DSConv module extracts.

More importantly, the results show even more significant improvements when integrating the DSConv, CBAMConv, and CBAMUpConv modules, demonstrating the synergy between attention in feature extraction and reconstruction, as the PSNR increases to 33.10 and SSIM improves to 0.8715. This shows that attention applied to both deep feature extraction and reconstruction ensures better feature preservation and more accurate SR results.

5. Conclusion and Future Work

In this paper, we introduced the strip-like feature superpixel interaction network (SFSIN), a lightweight hybrid network that leverages the SFSCI modules with dynamic snake convolutions to effectively capture strip-like features. Superpixel clustering further improves the representation of local and global structures. The integration of the CBAMConv and CBAMUpConv modules improves the model's ability to learn rich features, resulting in superior performance at various scaling factors, especially in preserving details and reducing blur.

A limitation of CBAMUpConv is its sensitivity to highly textured or degraded inputs. Future work will integrate noise suppression modules (e.g., pre-denoising networks) to improve robustness in such scenarios. Furthermore, we plan to extend SFSIN for multispectral and hyperspectral images, thereby expanding its applicability in the real world. Finally, optimizing the model for real-time use in resource-constrained environments, such as on-board satellite systems, will be a key focus.

Author Contributions: Conceptualization, Y. L. (Yanxia Lyu); Methodology, Y. L. (Yanxia Lyu); Software, Y. L. (Yuhang Liu); Validation, Y. L. (Yuhang Liu); Formal analysis, Y. L. (Yanxia Lyu); Investigation, Z.H.; Resources, X.S.; Data curation, Z.H.; Writing—original draft, Y. L. (Yuhang Liu); Writing—review & editing, Q.Z.; Visualization, Q.Z.; Supervision, X.S.; Project administration, X.S.; Funding acquisition, X.S. All authors have read and agreed to the published version of the manuscript.

Funding: This research work was supported in part by the National Natural Science Foundation of China under Grant No. 72371067, Hebei National Science Foundation under Grant No. F2021501020, the Fundamental Research Funds for Central Universities under Grant No. N2323020, and the Funded by Science Research Project of Hebei Education Department under Grant No. QN2024167.

Data Availability Statement: The AID dataset [50] used in this study is publicly available at https://huggingface.co/datasets/blanchon/AID (accessed on 10 April 2025). The images were split into training (80%), validation (10%), and testing (10%) sets, as detailed in Section 4.1.

Conflicts of Interest: The authors declare that they have no known competing financial interests or personal relationships that could have appeared to influence the work reported in our work.

References

1. Turner, W.; Spector, S.; Gardiner, N.; Fladeland, M.; Sterling, E.; Steininger, M. Remote sensing for biodiversity science and conservation. *Trends Ecol. Evol.* **2003**, *18*, 306–314. [CrossRef]
2. Herold, M.; Liu, X.; Clarke, K.C. Spatial metrics and image texture for mapping urban land use. *Photogramm. Eng. Remote Sens.* **2003**, *69*, 991–1001. [CrossRef]
3. Thenkabail, P.S.; Lyon, J.G.; Huete, A. Advances in hyperspectral remote sensing of vegetation and agricultural crops. In *Fundamentals, Sensor Systems, Spectral Libraries, and Data Mining for Vegetation*; CRC Press: Boca Raton, FL, USA, 2018; pp. 3–37.
4. Joyce, K.E.; Belliss, S.E.; Samsonov, S.V.; McNeill, S.J.; Glassey, P.J. A review of the status of satellite remote sensing and image processing techniques for mapping natural hazards and disasters. *Prog. Phys. Geogr.* **2009**, *33*, 183–207. [CrossRef]
5. Shen, H.; Zhang, L.; Huang, B.; Li, P. A MAP approach for joint motion estimation, segmentation, and super resolution. *IEEE Trans. Image Process.* **2007**, *16*, 479–490. [CrossRef]
6. Köhler, T.; Huang, X.; Schebesch, F.; Aichert, A.; Maier, A.; Hornegger, J. Robust multiframe super-resolution employing iteratively re-weighted minimization. *IEEE Trans. Comput. Imaging* **2016**, *2*, 42–58. [CrossRef]
7. Dosovitskiy, A. An image is worth 16x16 words: Transformers for image recognition at scale. *arXiv* **2020**, arXiv:2010.11929.
8. Liang, J.; Cao, J.; Sun, G.; Zhang, K.; Van Gool, L.; Timofte, R. Swinir: Image restoration using swin transformer. In Proceedings of the IEEE/CVF International Conference on Computer Vision, Montreal, BC, Canada, 11–17 October 2021; pp. 1833–1844.
9. Chen, H.; Wang, Y.; Guo, T.; Xu, C.; Deng, Y.; Liu, Z.; Ma, S.; Xu, C.; Xu, C.; Gao, W. Pre-trained image processing transformer. In Proceedings of the IEEE/CVF Conference on Computer Vision and Pattern Recognition, Nashville, TN, USA, 19–25 June 2021; pp. 12299–12310.
10. Dong, C.; Loy, C.C.; He, K.; Tang, X. Image super-resolution using deep convolutional networks. *IEEE Trans. Pattern Anal. Mach. Intell.* **2015**, *38*, 295–307. [CrossRef]
11. Lim, B.; Son, S.; Kim, H.; Nah, S.; Mu Lee, K. Enhanced deep residual networks for single image super-resolution. In Proceedings of the IEEE Conference on Computer Vision and Pattern Recognition Workshops, Honolulu, HI, USA, 21–26 July 2017; pp. 136–144.
12. Kim, J.; Lee, J.K.; Lee, K.M. Accurate image super-resolution using very deep convolutional networks. In Proceedings of the IEEE Conference on Computer Vision and Pattern Recognition, Las Vegas, NV, USA, 27–30 June 2016; pp. 1646–1654.
13. Zhang, Y.; Tian, Y.; Kong, Y.; Zhong, B.; Fu, Y. Residual dense network for image super-resolution. In Proceedings of the IEEE conference on computer vision and pattern recognition, Salt Lake City, UT, USA, 18–22 June 2018; pp. 2472–2481.
14. Zhang, Y.; Li, K.; Li, K.; Wang, L.; Zhong, B.; Fu, Y. Image super-resolution using very deep residual channel attention networks. In Proceedings of the European Conference on Computer Vision (ECCV), Munich, Germany, 8–14 September 2018; pp. 286–301.
15. Dong, C.; Loy, C.C.; Tang, X. Accelerating the super-resolution convolutional neural network. In Proceedings of the Computer Vision–ECCV 2016: 14th European Conference, Amsterdam, The Netherlands, 11–14 October 2016; Proceedings, Part II 14; Springer: Berlin/Heidelberg, Germany, 2016; pp. 391–407.
16. Liu, Z.; Sun, M.; Zhou, T.; Huang, G.; Darrell, T. Rethinking the value of network pruning. *arXiv* **2018**, arXiv:1810.05270.
17. Yu, F. Multi-scale context aggregation by dilated convolutions. *arXiv* **2015**, arXiv:1511.07122.
18. Dai, J.; Qi, H.; Xiong, Y.; Li, Y.; Zhang, G.; Hu, H.; Wei, Y. Deformable convolutional networks. In Proceedings of the IEEE International Conference on Computer Vision, Venice, Italy, 22–29 October 2017; pp. 764–773.
19. Qi, Y.; He, Y.; Qi, X.; Zhang, Y.; Yang, G. Dynamic snake convolution based on topological geometric constraints for tubular structure segmentation. In Proceedings of the IEEE/CVF International Conference on Computer Vision, Paris, France, 4–6 October 2023; pp. 6070–6079.
20. Jampani, V.; Sun, D.; Liu, M.Y.; Yang, M.H.; Kautz, J. Superpixel sampling networks. In Proceedings of the European Conference on Computer Vision (ECCV), Munich, Germany, 8–14 September 2018; pp. 352–368.
21. Li, X.; Dong, J.; Tang, J.; Pan, J. Dlgsanet: Lightweight dynamic local and global self-attention networks for image super-resolution. In Proceedings of the IEEE/CVF International Conference on Computer Vision, Paris, France, 4–6 October 2023; pp. 12792–12801.
22. Woo, S.; Park, J.; Lee, J.Y.; Kweon, I.S. Cbam: Convolutional block attention module. In Proceedings of the European Conference on Computer Vision (ECCV), Munich, Germany, 8–14 September 2018; pp. 3–19.

23. Zhang, L.; Wu, X. An edge-guided image interpolation algorithm via directional filtering and data fusion. *IEEE Trans. Image Process.* **2006**, *15*, 2226–2238. [CrossRef]
24. Hung, K.W.; Siu, W.C. Robust soft-decision interpolation using weighted least squares. *IEEE Trans. Image Process.* **2011**, *21*, 1061–1069. [CrossRef] [PubMed]
25. Lu, X.; Yuan, H.; Yuan, Y.; Yan, P.; Li, L.; Li, X. Local learning-based image super-resolution. In Proceedings of the 2011 IEEE 13th International Workshop on Multimedia Signal Processing, Hangzhou, China, 17-19 October 2011; IEEE: Piscataway, NJ, USA, 2011; pp. 1–5.
26. Kim, K.I.; Kwon, Y. Single-image super-resolution using sparse regression and natural image prior. *IEEE Trans. Pattern Anal. Mach. Intell.* **2010**, *32*, 1127–1133. [PubMed]
27. He, K.; Zhang, X.; Ren, S.; Sun, J. Deep residual learning for image recognition. In Proceedings of the IEEE Conference on Computer Vision and Pattern Recognition, Las Vegas, NV, USA, 27–30 June 2016; pp. 770–778.
28. Ledig, C.; Theis, L.; Huszár, F.; Caballero, J.; Cunningham, A.; Acosta, A.; Aitken, A.; Tejani, A.; Totz, J.; Wang, Z.; et al. Photo-realistic single image super-resolution using a generative adversarial network. In Proceedings of the IEEE Conference on Computer Vision and Pattern Recognition, Honolulu, HI, USA, 21–26 July 2017; pp. 4681–4690.
29. Wang, J.; Yang, W.; Guo, H.; Zhang, R.; Xia, G.S. Tiny object detection in aerial images. In Proceedings of the 2020 25th International Conference on Pattern Recognition (ICPR), Milan, Italy, 10–15 January 2021; IEEE: Piscataway, NJ, USA, 2021, pp. 3791–3798.
30. Wang, L.; Li, R.; Zhang, C.; Fang, S.; Duan, C.; Meng, X.; Atkinson, P.M. UNetFormer: A UNet-like transformer for efficient semantic segmentation of remote sensing urban scene imagery. *ISPRS J. Photogramm. Remote Sens.* **2022**, *190*, 196–214. [CrossRef]
31. Chen, K.; Chen, B.; Liu, C.; Li, W.; Zou, Z.; Shi, Z. Rsmamba: Remote sensing image classification with state space model. *IEEE Geosci. Remote. Sens. Lett.* **2024**, *21*, 8002605. [CrossRef]
32. Liebel, L.; Körner, M. Single-image super resolution for multispectral remote sensing data using convolutional neural networks. *Int. Arch. Photogramm. Remote Sens. Spat. Inf. Sci.* **2016**, *41*, 883–890. [CrossRef]
33. Lei, S.; Shi, Z.; Zou, Z. Super-resolution for remote sensing images via local–global combined network. *IEEE Geosci. Remote Sens. Lett.* **2017**, *14*, 1243–1247. [CrossRef]
34. Xu, W.; Guangluan, X.; Wang, Y.; Sun, X.; Lin, D.; Yirong, W. High quality remote sensing image super-resolution using deep memory connected network. In Proceedings of the IGARSS 2018-2018 IEEE International Geoscience and Remote Sensing Symposium, Valencia, Spain, 22–27 July 2018; IEEE: Piscataway, NJ, USA, 2018; pp. 8889–8892.
35. Ma, W.; Pan, Z.; Guo, J.; Lei, B. Achieving super-resolution remote sensing images via the wavelet transform combined with the recursive res-net. *IEEE Trans. Geosci. Remote Sens.* **2019**, *57*, 3512–3527. [CrossRef]
36. Liu, Z.; Lin, Y.; Cao, Y.; Hu, H.; Wei, Y.; Zhang, Z.; Lin, S.; Guo, B. Swin transformer: Hierarchical vision transformer using shifted windows. In Proceedings of the IEEE/CVF International Conference on Computer Vision, Montreal, BC, Canada, 11–17 October 2021; pp. 10012–10022.
37. Fang, J.; Lin, H.; Chen, X.; Zeng, K. A hybrid network of cnn and transformer for lightweight image super-resolution. In Proceedings of the IEEE/CVF Conference on Computer Vision and Pattern Recognition, New Orleans, LA, USA, 18–24 June 2022; pp. 1103–1112.
38. Lei, S.; Shi, Z.; Mo, W. Transformer-based multistage enhancement for remote sensing image super-resolution. *IEEE Trans. Geosci. Remote Sens.* **2021**, *60*, 1–11. [CrossRef]
39. He, J.; Yuan, Q.; Li, J.; Xiao, Y.; Liu, X.; Zou, Y. DsTer: A dense spectral transformer for remote sensing spectral super-resolution. *Int. J. Appl. Earth Obs. Geoinf.* **2022**, *109*, 102773. [CrossRef]
40. Tu, J.; Mei, G.; Ma, Z.; Piccialli, F. SWCGAN: Generative adversarial network combining swin transformer and CNN for remote sensing image super-resolution. *IEEE J. Sel. Top. Appl. Earth Obs. Remote Sens.* **2022**, *15*, 5662–5673. [CrossRef]
41. Shang, J.; Gao, M.; Li, Q.; Pan, J.; Zou, G.; Jeon, G. Hybrid-scale hierarchical transformer for remote sensing image super-resolution. *Remote Sens.* **2023**, *15*, 3442. [CrossRef]
42. Liu, J.; Tang, J.; Wu, G. Residual feature distillation network for lightweight image super-resolution. In Proceedings of the Computer Vision–ECCV 2020 Workshops, Glasgow, UK, 23–28 August 2020; proceedings, part III 16; Springer: Berlin/Heidelberg, Germany, 2020; pp. 41–55.
43. Ahn, N.; Kang, B.; Sohn, K.A. Fast, accurate, and lightweight super-resolution with cascading residual network. In Proceedings of the European Conference on Computer Vision (ECCV), Munich, Germany, 8–14 September 2018; pp. 252–268.
44. Lu, Z.; Li, J.; Liu, H.; Huang, C.; Zhang, L.; Zeng, T. Transformer for single image super-resolution. In Proceedings of the IEEE/CVF Conference on Computer Vision and Pattern Recognition, New Orleans, LA, USA, 18–24 June 2022; pp. 457–466.
45. Zhang, X.; Zeng, H.; Guo, S.; Zhang, L. Efficient long-range attention network for image super-resolution. In Proceedings of the European Conference on Computer Vision, Tel Aviv, Israel, 23–27 October 2022; Springer: Berlin/Heidelberg, Germany, 2022; pp. 649–667.
46. Zhang, A.; Ren, W.; Liu, Y.; Cao, X. Lightweight image super-resolution with superpixel token interaction. In Proceedings of the IEEE/CVF International Conference on Computer Vision, Paris, France, 2–3 October 2023; pp. 12728–12737.

47. Wang, X.; Wu, Y.; Ming, Y.; Lv, H. Remote sensing imagery super resolution based on adaptive multi-scale feature fusion network. *Sensors* **2020**, *20*, 1142. [CrossRef]
48. Vaswani, A. Attention is all you need. In *Advances in Neural Information Processing Systems*; Curran Associates Inc.: Red Hook, NY, USA, 2017.
49. Wang, S.; Zhou, T.; Lu, Y.; Di, H. Contextual transformation network for lightweight remote-sensing image super-resolution. *IEEE Trans. Geosci. Remote Sens.* **2021**, *60*, 1–13. [CrossRef]
50. Xia, G.S.; Hu, J.; Hu, F.; Shi, B.; Bai, X.; Zhong, Y.; Zhang, L.; Lu, X. AID: A benchmark data set for performance evaluation of aerial scene classification. *IEEE Trans. Geosci. Remote Sens.* **2017**, *55*, 3965–3981. [CrossRef]
51. Wang, Z.; Bovik, A.C.; Sheikh, H.R.; Simoncelli, E.P. Image quality assessment: From error visibility to structural similarity. *IEEE Trans. Image Process.* **2004**, *13*, 600–612. [CrossRef]
52. Wang, C.; Li, Z.; Shi, J. Lightweight image super-resolution with adaptive weighted learning network. *arXiv* **2019**, arXiv:1904.02358.
53. Luo, X.; Xie, Y.; Zhang, Y.; Qu, Y.; Li, C.; Fu, Y. Latticenet: Towards lightweight image super-resolution with lattice block. In Proceedings of the Computer Vision–ECCV 2020: 16th European Conference, Glasgow, UK, 23–28 August 2020; Proceedings, Part XXII 16; Springer: Berlin/Heidelberg, Germany, 2020; pp. 272–289.
54. Muqeet, A.; Hwang, J.; Yang, S.; Kang, J.; Kim, Y.; Bae, S.H. Multi-attention based ultra lightweight image super-resolution. In Proceedings of the Computer Vision–ECCV 2020 Workshops, Glasgow, UK, 23–28 August 2020; Proceedings, Part III 16; Springer: Berlin/Heidelberg, Germany, 2020; pp. 103–118.

mathematics

MDPI

Article

Advanced Trans-EEGNet Deep Learning Model for Hypoxic-Ischemic Encephalopathy Severity Grading

Dong-Her Shih [1], Feng-I Chung [2,*], Ting-Wei Wu [1], Shuo-Yu Huang [1] and Ming-Hung Shih [3]

[1] Department of Information Management, National Yunlin University of Science and Technology, Douliu 64002, Taiwan; shihdh@yuntech.edu.tw (D.-H.S.); wutingw@yuntech.edu.tw (T.-W.W.); m11123035@yuntech.edu.tw (S.-Y.H.)
[2] Center for General Education, National Chung Cheng University, Chiayi 621301, Taiwan
[3] Department of Electrical and Computer Engineering, Iowa State University, 2520 Osborn Drive, Ames, IA 50011, USA; mshih@iastate.edu
* Correspondence: albertchung@lib.ccu.edu.tw

Abstract: Hypoxic-ischemic encephalopathy (HIE) is a brain injury condition that poses a significant risk to newborns, potentially causing varying degrees of damage to the central nervous system. Its clinical manifestations include respiratory distress, cardiac dysfunction, hypotension, muscle weakness, seizures, and coma. As HIE represents a progressive brain injury, early identification of the extent of the damage and the implementation of appropriate treatment are crucial for reducing mortality and improving outcomes. HIE patients may face long-term complications such as cerebral palsy, epilepsy, vision loss, and developmental delays. Therefore, prompt identification and treatment of hypoxic-ischemic symptoms can help reduce the risk of severe sequelae in patients. Currently, hypothermia therapy is one of the most effective treatments for HIE patients. However, not all newborns with HIE are suitable for this therapy, making rapid and accurate assessment of the extent of brain injury critical for treatment. Among HIE patients, hypothermia therapy has shown better efficacy in those diagnosed with moderate to severe HIE within 6 h of birth, establishing this time frame as the golden period for treatment. During this golden period, an accurate assessment of HIE severity is essential for formulating appropriate treatment strategies and predicting long-term outcomes for the affected infants. This study proposes a method for addressing data imbalance and noise interference through data preprocessing techniques, including filtering and SMOTE. It then employs EEGNet, a deep learning model specifically designed for EEG classification, combined with a Transformer model featuring an attention mechanism that excels at capturing long-term sequential features to construct the Trans-EEGNet model. This model outperforms previous methods in computation time and feature extraction, enabling rapid classification and assessment of HIE severity in newborns.

Keywords: neonatal hypoxic-ischemic encephalopathy (HIE); transformer; electroencephalogram (EEG); deep learning

MSC: 68T05; 68T35; 68Q32

1. Introduction

Hypoxic-ischemic encephalopathy (HIE) is one of the most common causes of neonatal brain disease. In high-income countries, three to five out of every 1000 newborns are affected by HIE [1]. Newborns with HIE face risks of mortality and cerebral palsy; even if they survive, they may suffer from long-term neurological conditions such as epilepsy, sensorineural hearing loss, vision loss, and developmental delays [2]. The initial symptoms of HIE include brain hypoxia and impaired blood supply, which subsequently lead to other neurological injuries. HIE is a progressive condition that develops over time [1].

Clinical and imaging studies have shown that hypothermia therapy has a neuroprotective effect on the brain. Currently, therapeutic hypothermia (TH) has become the standard treatment for newborns with moderate to severe HIE [3]. However, the window for hypothermia therapy is time limited, with the optimal treatment initiation within 6 h after birth [2]. Current diagnostic methods primarily rely on clinical diagnosis and other clinical markers to assess the severity of brain injury post-birth [1]. However, related studies indicate that diagnosis based on the neonatal clinical status and the degree of metabolic acidosis is insufficiently accurate in predicting the long-term prognosis of newborns [4].

In research on the grading of HIE using electroencephalograms (EEGs), Stevenson et al. [5] proposed a method that extracts non-stationary features based on time-frequency distribution (TFD). This method generates TFDs over short epochs (64 s, 50% overlap) and extracts instantaneous amplitude and frequency features. Combined with more standard quantitative EEG features, these features are used to classify HIE severity using a multi-class linear discriminant classifier.

Regarding the classification of HIE, Matić et al. [6] proposed a tensor-based method that adaptively segments continuous EEG data and extracts three features from each segment to construct a tensor. This tensor is then dimensionally reduced using a multi-dimensional decomposition method and classified using a least-squares support vector machine (SVM). Subsequently, Matić et al. [7] introduced a detection method based on dynamic inter-burst intervals (dIBIs), combined with an SVM classifier, to quantify the EEG of neonates with HIE. Ahmed et al. [8] proposed a supervised learning approach using a Gaussian Mixture Model (GMM) and SVM to assess the severity of HIE. Raurale et al. [9] employed convolutional neural networks (CNNs) and introduced a classification framework that combines quadratic time-frequency distributions with CNNs.

Given the complexity and time-consuming nature of continuous EEG monitoring and interpretation, which can only be assessed by specialized neurophysiologists, the use of computational algorithms for automatic EEG grading can overcome the challenges of conducting extensive and continuous EEG monitoring for all suspected HIE neonates in the neonatal intensive care unit (NICU). This allows neonatologists to assess brain function in a simple and timely manner [9]. Convolutional neural networks (CNNs) have succeeded significantly in various medical imaging tasks [10]. Thus, this study aims to classify the severity of HIE using novel deep learning models. The main objectives of this study include improving the accuracy of EEG-based grading, supporting clinical decision-making, advancing EEG-based analysis, and further promoting broader applications in the field of medical imaging.

Previous studies on HIE classification have primarily utilized basic neural network architectures [9]. However, as a time-series data type, EEG signals contain crucial information for accurate classification in both temporal and spatial dependencies between time points and different electrodes [11]. This study plans to use a Transformer model known for capturing long-range dependencies with an inbuilt attention mechanism that effectively extracts temporal features [12]. On the other hand, EEGNet is a neural network designed explicitly for EEG analysis, featuring depthwise separable convolutional structures, which have demonstrated superior classification performance over other models in previous studies. This model offers advantages in EEG feature extraction while maintaining high computational efficiency [13]. Therefore, this study will integrate the Transformer and EEGNet models to propose an advanced Trans-EEGNet deep learning model, aiming to develop a framework for grading the severity of HIE that surpasses existing methods in computation time and feature extraction.

2. Literature Review

2.1. Neonatal Hypoxic-Ischemic Encephalopathy (HIE)

Neonatal hypoxic-ischemic encephalopathy (HIE) is clinically defined as a condition affecting fetuses at a gestational age greater than 36 weeks, caused by hypoxia and asphyxia due to abnormal umbilical blood flow [14]. HIE typically occurs during labor, making it an unpredictable emergency [15]. The progression of HIE can be divided into two stages: the first stage involves brain injury caused by hypoxia and ischemia, known as primary energy failure [2], characterized by reduced cerebral blood flow and oxygen supply [3]. As secondary energy failure and the accumulation of reactive metabolites occur, the condition worsens, leading to the second stage, which results in delayed brain injury [2]. Pathophysiologically, HIE encompasses a series of processes caused by excitotoxicity and oxidative injury, ultimately leading to cell death [3]. These pathological features indicate the extent of brain damage in HIE, and the severity of the damage is reflected in the grading system for HIE.

For grading, HIE is typically classified into mild, moderate, and severe categories based on the Modified Sarnat Encephalopathy Grade (MSEG) [16]. According to the study by Horn et al. [17], infants with mild HIE may exhibit abnormal alertness, average activity levels, and exaggerated Moro reflexes while maintaining normal autonomic function. Symptoms of moderate HIE include lethargy, reduced activity, hypotonia, diminished primitive reflexes, constricted pupils, bradycardia, or hyperventilation. When HIE progresses to the severe stage, symptoms may include coma, lack of spontaneous activity, severe muscle weakness, absence of primitive reflexes, unresponsive pupils, or episodes of apnea.

Neonatal hypoxic-ischemic encephalopathy (HIE) is one of the leading causes of neonatal mortality and disability worldwide, accounting for 23% of global infant mortality [14]. In a small study involving 28 full-term infants born between 1980 and 1982, those with severe perinatal asphyxia and moderate or severe encephalopathy exhibited multi-organ dysfunction involving the lungs, central nervous system, kidneys, heart, as well as metabolic and hematologic systems [18]. Over the past two decades, the incidence of neonatal brain injury has not significantly decreased in developed countries [14]. In high-income countries, the incidence of HIE is approximately two cases per 1000 live births, while in low- and middle-income countries, the incidence is higher [19].

Before the widespread adoption of therapeutic hypothermia, studies on the outcomes of infants with perinatal asphyxia and HIE indicated that the disability rate for infants with moderate encephalopathy ranged from 6% to 21%. In contrast, for those with severe encephalopathy, the disability rate was as high as 42% to 100% [18]. Infants with severe HIE have a very high mortality rate, and even those who survive without functional deficits often face challenges with cognitive deficits. Even in the absence of severe disabilities, these children may exhibit mild motor dysfunction and tend to enroll in school later than their peers. Moreover, compared to children who were healthy at birth, infants with moderate and severe HIE show a significantly higher need for educational support [18].

The most effective emerging therapy for infants with HIE is moderate therapeutic hypothermia. Hypothermia therapy can reduce free radical and glutamate levels, decrease oxygen demand, and inhibit apoptosis, making it an effective treatment method [20]. Shankaran et al. [21] demonstrated that reducing brain temperature by 2 °C to 5 °C can provide neuroprotection for neonates. Brain cooling has improved various pathological processes that cause brain injury, including excitatory amino acids, cerebral energy state, cerebral blood flow, metabolism, nitric oxide production, and apoptosis. For full-term infants with severe acidosis at birth or requiring continuous ventilation for resuscitation, therapeutic hypothermia should be administered if moderate or severe encephalopathy is detected within the first 6 h after birth [3]. Hypothermia therapy has transformed the clinical management of HIE and is now considered the standard treatment for moderate to severe HIE in high-income countries [15].

2.2. Research on Convolutional Neural Networks in Electroencephalography

Ranjani and Supraja [22] proposed a method based on Deep Convolutional Neural Networks (DCNNs) for classifying electroencephalogram (EEG) signals related to autism and epilepsy. This method first converts EEG signals into power spectral density energy diagrams (PSDEDs) and then automatically applies DCNNs to extract features from the PSDED. Using a fully connected layer, the signals are classified into autism, epilepsy, and regular groups. Experimental results indicate that the proposed model performs well in terms of classification.

Wang et al. [23] introduced an EEG emotion recognition method combining CNNs with a spatiotemporal attention mechanism. The method first uses CNNs to extract local features from EEG signals and then applies the spatiotemporal attention mechanism to focus on emotional regions. The experimental results demonstrate that this approach effectively enhances the accuracy of EEG-based emotion recognition.

Li et al. [24] proposed a motor imagery EEG classification algorithm based on a CNN-LSTM feature fusion network. This method utilizes a parallel connection of CNNs and LSTM to capture the spatiotemporal features of EEG signals simultaneously. Subsequently, intermediate features are extracted through convolutional layers, and a flattening layer is added to merge all features into a fully connected layer, thereby improving classification accuracy.

Li et al. [25] proposed a multi-scale one-dimensional convolution model (MS-FTSCNN) designed to capture and integrate EEG signal frequency and temporal and spatial domain features. This method effectively fuses features from the three domains to enhance emotion recognition accuracy. Additionally, through one-dimensional convolution and reduced network parameters, the model can more precisely process the frequency domain features of emotion-related EEG signals. A summary of related research is presented in Table 1.

Table 1. Related research on EEG and CNN.

Subject	Method	Author
Classifying autism and epilepsy using EEG signals	Proposed a method for classifying autism and epilepsy using deep convolutional neural networks (DCNNs).	[22]
Emotion recognition and classification through the EEG signals	A method for EEG emotion recognition using the hybrid spatiotemporal feature fusion neural network is proposed.	[23]
Classification of motor imagery tasks through electroencephalography	A motion imagination EEG classification algorithm based on the CNN-LSTM feature fusion network is proposed.	[24]
Emotion recognition and classification through electroencephalography	A multi-scale one-dimensional convolutional model, MS-FTSCNN, was proposed to capture and integrate the frequency, temporal, and spatial domain features of EEG signals. This model effectively combines the three types of features, thereby improving the accuracy of emotion recognition.	[25]

2.3. *Related Research on Attention Mechanisms*

2.3.1. Multi-Head Attention

Xie et al. [11] proposed a Transformer-based framework that combines deep learning networks with spatiotemporal information for raw EEG classification. This framework first uses convolutional neural networks (CNNs) to extract spatiotemporal features and then encodes these features into continuous representations through multi-head attention. Finally, a classifier categorizes the encoded representations into different classes. Experimental results indicate that this framework outperforms traditional deep learning methods in raw EEG classification.

Xin et al. [26] introduced an Attention-based Waveform Convolutional Neural Network (AMWCNN) for epilepsy EEG classification. This method decomposes EEG signals into different frequency components using a waveform convolution layer to extract features and then employs a multi-head attention mechanism to emphasize essential features in the EEG, thereby improving classification performance.

Wei et al. [27] proposed a Transformer Capsule Network (TC-Net) for EEG-based emotion recognition. TC-Net incorporates a novel patch-merging strategy within the EEG Transformer architecture to enhance the capture of local features. It also integrates an Emotion Capsule module to refine features for emotion state classification. This method effectively extracts global information from EEG signals and achieves state-of-the-art performance on emotion recognition datasets DEAP and DREAMER.

Mulkey et al. [28] presented a deep learning approach based on Vision Transformers for predicting delirium in critically ill elderly patients. This method converts EEG signals into two-dimensional images and trains a Vision Transformer model on these images to learn delirium-related patterns from EEG data. Table 2 summarizes the related research.

Table 2. Related research on multi-head attention mechanism.

Subject	Method	Author
Classification judgment through electroencephalogram	Proposed a method of combining the Transformer and CNN to classify motor imagination tasks	[11]
	An attention mechanism-based waveform convolutional neural network (AMWCNN) is proposed for epilepsy EEG classification.	[26]
	The TC-Net model was proposed, which combines a Transformer for extracting EEG features with an emotion capsule module for refining features, enabling emotion recognition classification.	[27]
	A Vision Transformer was used to analyze EEG data and predict whether elderly individuals have delirium.	[28]

2.3.2. Single-Head Attention

Merity et al. [29] explored the application of single-head attention in RNN models. The study found that single-head attention can significantly reduce the consumption of computational resources and memory when capturing different parts of the input compared to multi-head attention. While Transformer models typically use multi-head attention to enhance feature extraction capabilities, incorporating single-head attention in specific model layers can maintain model performance while improving inference speed and memory efficiency. The results indicate that single-head attention performs well even in resource-constrained environments.

Michel et al. [30] validated the practical effectiveness of multi-head and single-head attention in Transformer models. The study pointed out that although Transformer models use multi-head attention to capture different parts of the input, removing many attention heads during training does not significantly impact model performance. The research found that single-head attention in specific layers can maintain model performance while improving computational speed and memory efficiency. Therefore, the study concluded that the advantages of multi-head attention are primarily in training stability, while single-head attention remains effective in feature extraction.

Liu et al. [31] empirically compared multi-head and single-head attention during Transformer training. The study revealed that incorporating appropriate initialization, regularization, and multi-layer single-head attention in the model effectively captures dependencies across multiple positions, offering efficiency advantages over multi-head attention. After improving stability, deep single-head Transformers achieved better performance. The research demonstrated that using multi-layer scaled dot-product attention helps extract richer features, thereby enhancing the model's overall performance. Table 3 summarizes the related research.

Table 3. Related research on single-head attention mechanism.

Subject	Result	Author
The role of single-head attention in RNN models was explored	Compared with multi-head attention, single-head attention still has good performance in resource-constrained environments	[29]
The actual performance of multi-head attention and single-head attention in Transformer models was validated	Many attention heads often focus on similar features, leading to redundancy. Study Shows Comparable or Better Performance with Fewer Attention Heads	[30]
The effectiveness of multi-head attention and single-head attention in Transformer models was validated.	Through adaptive model initialization techniques, the single-head attention Transformer model can surpass traditional multi-head attention models in terms of stability and performance.	[31]

3. Materials and Methods

3.1. Dataset

The dataset used in this study consists of 77 multi-channel electroencephalogram (EEG) recordings, each lasting for 1 h. Each recording is graded based on the severity of background abnormalities. Two neonatal EEG experts independently scored each segment, and in cases of disagreement, they jointly reviewed the EEG to reach a consensus. The grading system evaluates various attributes of the EEG, including amplitude and frequency, continuity, sleep–wake cycle, symmetry and synchrony, and characteristics of abnormal waveforms. According to the HIE classification criteria proposed by Murray et al. [32], the EEG recordings are categorized into four levels: normal or mildly abnormal (Grade 1), moderately abnormal (Grade 2), severely abnormal (Grade 3), and inactive (Grade 4), as shown in Table 4.

Table 4. HIE classification.

EEG Grade (Description)	Background	IBI(s)	Features of the EEG	Sleep-Wake Cycle
0 (normal)	Continuous	—	Normal physiologic features (e.g., anterior slow waves)	—
1 (mild abnormalities)	Continuous	—	Slightly abnormal activity (e.g., mild asymmetry, mild voltage depression)	Or poorly defined
2 (moderate abnormalities)	Discontinuous	<10	Or clear asymmetry or asynchrony	Not clearly defined
3 (major abnormalities)	Discontinuous	10–60	Severe attenuation of background patterns	Or absent
4 (inactive)	Severe discontinuous	>60	Or background activity of <10 µV	Absent

3.1.1. Research Subject

The data for this study was collected from 53 term neonates diagnosed with hypoxic-ischemic encephalopathy (HIE) in the neonatal intensive care unit of Cork University Maternity Hospital, Ireland. A total of 53 EEG recordings were collected from these infants. The recording of these EEG data received approval from the Cork Research Ethics Committee at the Cork University Teaching Hospitals. After obtaining written informed consent from guardians or parents, the Cork Research Ethics Committee approved the release of the anonymized dataset, which is publicly available at https://zenodo.org/records/7477575#.Y--W-nZBy5d (accessed on 10 January 2023).

3.1.2. Data Acquisition

This study focused on patients clinically determined to be at risk of seizures, at a gestational age between 36 and 44 weeks, and admitted to the neonatal intensive care unit (NICU). After obtaining written consent from guardians or parents, EEG recordings were conducted between January 2011 and February 2017. The data were collected from eight neonatal centers across Ireland, the Netherlands, Sweden, and the United Kingdom. From this cohort, 284 neonates with a clinical diagnosis of hypoxic-ischemic encephalopathy (HIE) and at least 6 h of valid EEG recordings were selected, while 18 were excluded due to comorbid diagnoses.

472 neonates were initially recruited for the study, with 284 ultimately selected. Their inclusion was primarily due to the presence of clinically confirmed HIE symptoms and valid EEG recordings. The remaining 188 neonates were excluded from the study. Of these, 18 were excluded due to comorbid diagnoses, 68 infants were reserved for a validation set for future EEG algorithm development, and 17 were excluded because EEG recordings were not conducted within 48 h after birth. Among the remaining 181 neonates, 54 with consent for data sharing were included, with their EEGs recorded at Cork University Maternity Hospital in Ireland. After thorough inspection of the EEG quality, one neonate with a low-quality recording was excluded. The final sample consisted of 53 neonates, with a median gestational age of 40 weeks and a male proportion of 62%, of which 58% received therapeutic hypothermia. Figure 1 shows the EEG diagram of HIE.

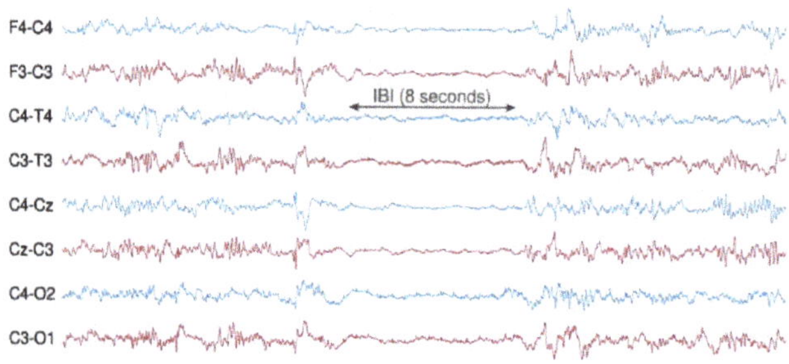

Figure 1. EEG diagram of HIE.

3.2. Pre-Processing

This study first addressed the issues of outliers and missing values in the dataset through data cleaning, resulting in a refined dataset comprising 76 hourly records. Among these, 46 records were classified as HIE Grade 1 (mild abnormalities), 12 as HIE Grade 2 (moderate abnormalities), and 9 each as HIE Grade 3 (significant abnormalities) and Grade 4 (inactive) (Figure 2). The following sections will provide a detailed explanation of the preprocessing methods used in this study. Section 3.2.1 will describe the methods for handling the imbalanced dataset, while Section 3.2.2 will introduce the filtering techniques.

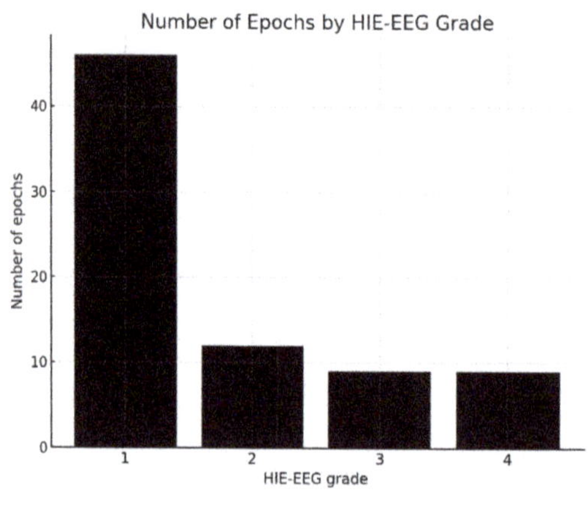

Figure 2. Bar chart of HIE graded distribution of original data.

3.2.1. Handling Imbalanced Datasets

Handling imbalanced datasets is a common challenge in machine learning, as the efficiency of predictive models can significantly decrease when data are imbalanced [33]. When dealing with medical data, imbalanced datasets are a common challenge. Traditional oversampling methods may lead to overfitting, as repeated data cannot provide additional information to the model. SMOTE (Synthetic Minority Over-sampling Technique) addresses this issue by generating new synthetic samples, enriching the distribution of the minority class, and reducing the risk of overfitting. In medical datasets, minority classes often contain critical features. By creating new samples based on the distribution of the original minority data, SMOTE preserves data diversity and enhances the model's generalization capability. Thabtah et al. [34] highlighted that SMOTE (Synthetic Minority Over-sampling Technique) performs better than under-sampling methods, especially in larger datasets with unclear decision boundaries.

The Safe-level SMOTE method assigns a safety level to each positive sample before generating synthetic instances. The generated synthetic instances are closer to samples with the highest safety levels, ensuring that all synthetic samples are created only within safe regions. This approach can improve the predictive performance of classifiers for the minority class [35]. Given that previous studies have successfully used Safe-level SMOTE to address the class imbalance in EEG datasets related to adult anxiety states, this study intends to use Safe-level SMOTE to resolve the imbalance issue in the dataset.

The main steps of Safe-level SMOTE involve first calculating the Safe-level value for each minority class sample, which is defined by the number of its k-nearest neighbors that belong to the minority class. Next, for each minority class sample, one of its k-nearest neighbors that belongs to the minority class is selected as a reference point to generate new synthetic samples. Finally, these steps are repeated for all minority class samples in the dataset until the minority class reaches the desired proportion. Safe-level SMOTE is particularly suitable for applications such as medical data analysis or financial fraud detection, where misclassification costs are high. It focuses on generating synthetic samples in safe regions of the feature space, enabling more accurate classification of minority classes.

After applying the Safe-level SMOTE method and processing the data, the study balanced the number of samples across the four levels, resulting in 184 hourly records. HIE Grade 1 remained at 46 records, while SMOTE-balanced HIE Grades 2, 3, and 4 each contained 46 records, as illustrated in the bar chart below (Figure 3).

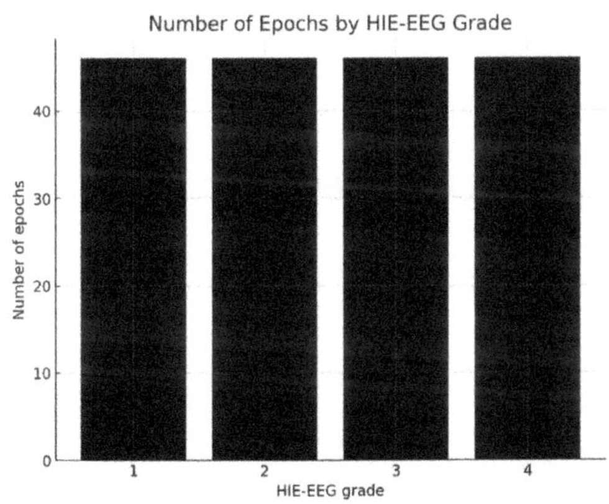

Figure 3. Bar chart of HIE grade distribution after SMOTE.

3.2.2. Filtering

Due to electroencephalogram (EEG) data characteristics, multi-electrode recordings and high-frequency sampling generate a large number of data, leading to substantial noise and outliers. Many of these data points may be irrelevant to the task, causing the model to learn patterns from this noise. Focusing on essential features during training is challenging, leading to overfitting in EEG signal analysis [36]. As a result, the trained model may need more generalization capability, resulting in suboptimal performance when testing on new data. Reducing the sampling frequency is a standard method for avoiding overfitting [37].

Pan et al. [38] noted that the computational complexity of neural networks increases as the input data dimension grows. Downsampling filtering methods based on reducing the sampling frequency can significantly decrease the subsequent computational complexity of the model. Therefore, this study downsampled the data to 40 Hz. Since each record has a total duration of one hour, with an original sampling frequency of 200 Hz, the raw data comprised 720,000-time steps. After downsampling to 40 Hz, each time step is 0.03 s, reducing the number of time steps to 120,000 per record.

3.2.3. Data Segmentation

Each one-hour record was segmented into five-minute segments with a 50% overlap in time steps, resulting in 23 five-minute segments per hour of data, as illustrated in the figure below. After oversampling, 184 one-hour records were obtained, which, after segmentation, yielded 4232 five-minute data segments (Figure 4).

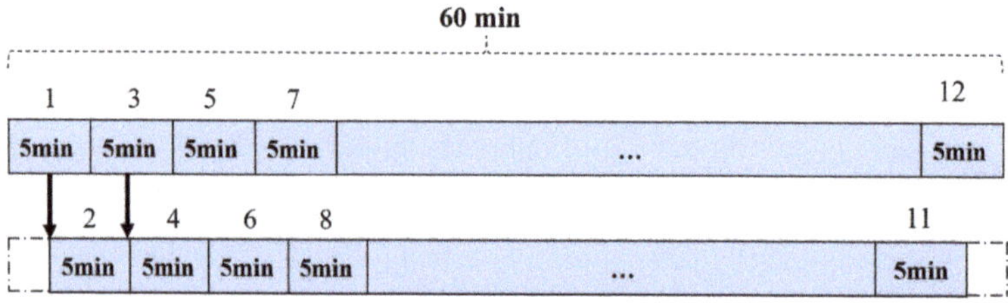

Figure 4. Schematic diagram of one-hour data segmentation.

In the Trans-EEGNet model, 10-fold cross-validation will be used to evaluate the model. The training-to-validation ratio is set at 8:2. The training set is divided into ten subsets. For each training fold, a portion of the subsets is randomly selected as the validation set, while the remaining subsets are used as the training set for model training. Upon completion of training, the average value from the 10-fold cross-validation will be used as the result for each performance evaluation, which will then be compared to the baseline system (Figure 5).

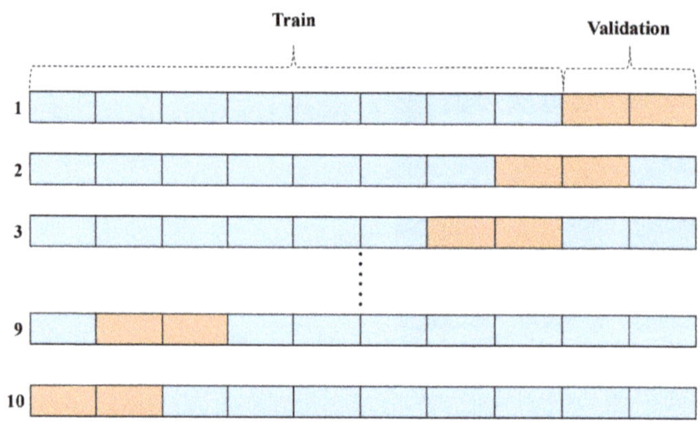

Figure 5. Ten-fold cross validation (The blue part is the training set, and the orange part is the testing set).

3.3. *Research Methods*

3.3.1. EEGNet

EEGNet is one of the most popular and successful deep learning architectures in BCI (brain–computer interface) applications. It utilizes separable and depthwise convolution to build EEG classification models and incorporates well-known EEG feature extraction concepts from the BCI field [39]. EEGNet is a CNN-based compact network inspired by the Xception architecture. It replaces traditional square convolutions with depthwise separable convolution structures, encapsulating temporal and spatial filters and significantly reducing the number of parameters. The depthwise separable convolution layers learn the temporal patterns for each channel and the correlations between different channels [40].

The effectiveness of EEGNet has been demonstrated in various BCI tasks [13]. Compared to other deep learning architectures commonly used for BCI classification, EEGNet requires fewer trainable parameters while achieving higher decoding accuracy and shorter training times [41]. EEGNet's strength lies in its ability to learn diverse and interpretable features across various BCI tasks [13].

The basic architecture of EEGNet is primarily divided into two blocks. In Block 1, there are two sequentially arranged convolutional layers. The first layer captures feature maps of different frequency bands from the input EEG signals with a kernel size of (1, Fs/2), where Fs represents the sampling frequency. The next layer performs depthwise convolution with a kernel size of (C, 1), where C is the number of channels. This layer is not fully connected to the previous feature maps, reducing the number of trainable parameters and explicitly enabling the network to learn spatial filters for each temporal filter. The output of Block 1 is frequency-specific spatial feature maps [40].

In Block 1, two convolution steps are performed: first, a 2D convolution layer (Conv2D), followed by a depthwise convolution layer (DepthwiseConv2D). Batch normalization is applied after both the Conv2D and DepthwiseConv2D layers. The Conv2D layer focuses on extracting feature maps of different frequency bands from the input EEG signals, with a kernel size of (1, Fs/2), where Fs represents the sampling frequency. The subsequent depthwise convolution layer uses the same kernel size (C, 1), where C is the number of channels. This layer is not fully connected to the previous feature maps, which reduces the number of trainable parameters and enables precise learning of the spatial features for each temporal filter. One advantage of depthwise convolution is reducing the parameters required for model training [40]. Not all feature maps are fully connected to the depthwise convolution layer, allowing spatial features to be learned from combining Conv2D and depthwise convolution layers, directly corresponding to each temporal filter. This approach is inspired by the Filter Bank Common Spatial Pattern (FBCSP) technique and controls the number of spatial filters by adjusting depth parameters, which need to be learned during training.

Block 2 involves separable convolution. In this block, pointwise convolution is added after applying depthwise convolution to the output of Block 1. This approach reduces the number of parameters and decouples the relationships within and between feature maps [40]. By using separable convolution, the model's parameter requirements can be further reduced, allowing for better summarization of each feature map. The combination of pointwise and depthwise convolution aids in optimally integrating these feature maps and helps to represent feature maps based on time scales.

In Block 3, a Softmax function processes the features from the previous block for classification tasks, allowing either binary or multi-class classification depending on the nature of the dataset [40] (Figure 6).

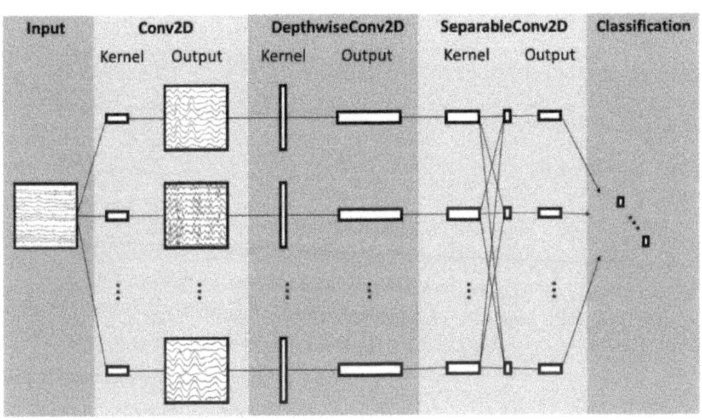

Figure 6. EEGNet architecture.

3.3.2. Transformer

The attention mechanism was initially proposed in natural language processing (NLP), with the self-attention mechanism becoming a core component of the Transformer model. The Transformer architecture has achieved outstanding performance in translation tasks within NLP [42]. This model follows an encoder–decoder structure, modeling through the stacking of self-attention and pointwise fully connected layers. The model multiplies the input vectors with three different weight matrices to generate query vectors (Q), key vectors (K), and value vectors (V).

The Transformer is the first sequence transduction model that relies entirely on the attention mechanism to capture long-range dependencies without the need for complex recurrent neural networks (RNNs) or convolutional neural networks (CNNs). Therefore, in EEG research, the Transformer has an advantage in effectively extracting both spatial and temporal dependencies from EEG signals, thereby enhancing performance in classification tasks [11]. Using the Transformer to model long-range dependencies can compensate for the shortcomings of CNNs in extracting global features [42].

3.3.3. The Proposed Advanced Trans-EEGNet Deep Learning Model

The EEGNet model used in this study is a CNN-based EEG classification model with excellent local feature extraction capabilities [13]. Due to its structure, which is specifically designed for the characteristics of EEG signals, EEGNet can effectively extract features such as amplitude, phase, and phase differences across different frequency bands of EEG data, as well as relationships between adjacent time points. Additionally, EEGNet requires fewer training parameters, resulting in a faster convergence speed.

This study also employs the attention mechanism from the Transformer to extract global features. This mechanism captures long-range dependencies between different time points and dynamically weights the input features, allowing the model to focus on the critical features required for classification tasks. Its advantage lies in its ability to extract the average amplitude, average phase, and average phase difference of EEG signals over different time intervals. It can reveal long-range dependencies, effectively handling the complex time-series information in EEG signals.

Moreover, the single-head attention mechanism, when handling sustained states and memory layers, can avoid excessive matrix multiplication operations due to its simplified computation method, significantly reducing memory usage and computational resource consumption. These layers reduce computational and memory requirements without adversely affecting the model's overall performance (Figure 7).

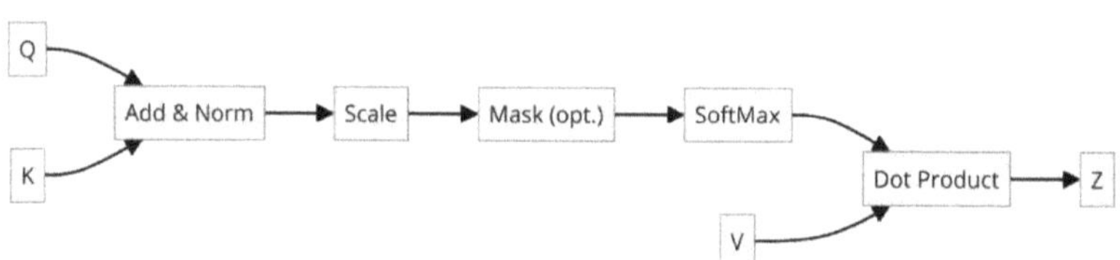

Figure 7. Scaled dot product architecture.

This study combines EEGNet with the attention mechanism of the Transformer, integrating the advantages of EEGNet in local feature extraction [13] with the strengths of the attention mechanism in global feature extraction [43]. This enables more effective capture of both local and global features in EEG data, further improving classification accuracy. The attention mechanism's ability to capture long-range dependencies within input sequences is beneficial for analyzing the time-series information in EEG signals. Therefore, combining these two models can enhance the capability to process EEG signals.

Although EEGNet has high computational efficiency, the Transformer model is less efficient computationally, and applying self-attention mechanisms directly to frameworks like convolutional networks may only sometimes achieve the expected performance improvements [44]. Kuang and Michoski [45] noted that multi-head attention mechanisms can encounter issues of redundancy and over-parameterization when capturing information from different subspaces, with some attention heads learning similar features. This may negate the lightweight advantage of the original EEGNet model. EEGNet is a lightweight and compact model, with its primary benefit being the reduction in parameter count and increased computational efficiency. Introducing an overly complex multi-head attention mechanism could have adverse effects.

Based on this, this study proposes a novel hybrid model that combines EEGNet with a single-head attention mechanism (scaled dot-product attention). This approach retains the computational efficiency of EEGNet while leveraging the attention mechanism to capture global features, thereby improving the classification performance of EEG data. Specifically, the contribution of this study lies in integrating EEGNet's advantage in local feature extraction with the attention mechanism's ability to capture global features and using single-head attention to avoid the redundancy and over-parameterization issues associated with multi-head attention mechanisms. This reduces model training time and memory usage, maintaining the model's lightweight nature and efficiency.

In summary, this study proposes a novel EEG classification model that combines EEGNet with a scaled dot-product attention mechanism. The model effectively captures both local and global features while maintaining high computational efficiency. The detailed structure of the model is shown in Figure 8.

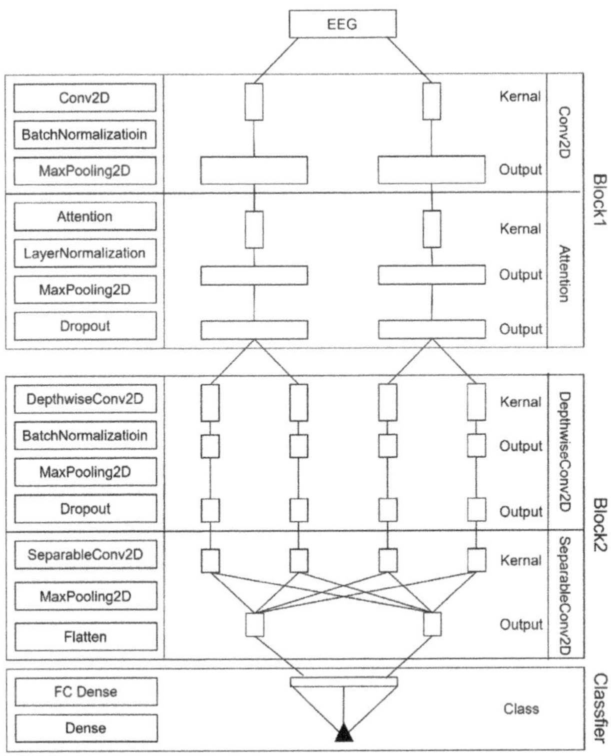

Figure 8. Proposed Trans-EEGNet model.

Trans-EEGNet adopts the three-layer convolution architecture proposed by EEGNet and adds an attention layer composed of Scaled Dot-product Attention. Its formula is as follows:

$$\mathrm{Attention}(\mathrm{Q},\mathrm{K},\mathrm{V}) = softmax\left(\frac{\mathrm{QK}^{\mathrm{T}}}{\sqrt{\mathrm{d_k}}}\right)\mathrm{V} \tag{1}$$

Q, K, and V represent the query vector (Q), key vector (K), and value vector (V), respectively. The *softmax* function is applied to compute the attention weights, converting the raw attention scores into attention weights, thereby creating a valid probability distribution that sums to 1. The overall model is divided into two blocks, with a detailed explanation of each layer's architecture provided below.

First, the initial block of the model performs preliminary feature extraction through a 2D convolution. The number of convolutional kernels is 32, with a size of (1, 64), and the activation function used is the Exponential Linear Unit (ELU). The padding mode is set to "valid", meaning no padding is applied to the input data during the convolution operation. As a result, the convolutional kernels only compute over the valid portions of the input data without extending beyond the data boundaries. The advantage of using the ELU activation function lies in its ability to produce small negative values instead of zeros for negative inputs, thus helping to avoid the vanishing gradient problem. This improves the model's learning capability and accelerates convergence. Its definition is as follows:

$$\begin{cases} x & , if\ x > 0 \\ \alpha(e^x - 1) & , if\ x \leq 0 \end{cases} \tag{2}$$

The Exponential Linear Unit (ELU) function features negative outputs with a smooth transition around zero, aiding faster convergence and improved model performance. In contrast, the ReLU function outputs zero for negative inputs, leading to the "dead neuron" problem. ELU's exponential form in the negative region retains non-zero gradients, effectively mitigating this issue. By combining the efficiency of ReLU with the smoothness of Sigmoid/Tanh, ELU demonstrates clear advantages in addressing dead zones and accelerating model convergence.

On the other hand, the output feature map is smaller than the input feature map, which reduces the computational load. This layer mainly focuses on extracting features in the time domain. After the convolution operation, batch normalization is applied to the output feature maps to accelerate model convergence and improve stability. Subsequently, a MaxPooling2D layer with a size of (2, 2) is used to further reduce the feature maps' dimensions and computational complexity while retaining essential features.

After the initial feature extraction, this study introduces a scaled dot-product attention mechanism in the second layer. By incorporating the attention mechanism at an earlier stage, its ability to extract global features is fully leveraged. It avoids an excessive increase in the computational complexity of subsequent layers, thus achieving a balance between model performance and complexity. When applying the attention mechanism, it is necessary to reshape the feature maps into a one-dimensional form to calculate the relationships between different feature positions. Specifically, the feature maps are first padded to a four-dimensional shape with ((0, 0), (16, 17)) padding and then reshaped into a one-dimensional sequence through a Reshape layer before being processed by the attention mechanism. The attention mechanism typically requires input in a sequential format to compute the relationships between different positions.

In this layer, layer normalization is used, which stabilizes the feature distribution without relying on batch size. Since Trans-EEGNet is a deep learning model that integrates an attention mechanism with a three-layer convolutional architecture, it has a higher complexity and many learnable parameters. To prevent the model from overfitting to the training data during the training process and to maintain generalization ability, dropout regularization is employed. During training, the Dropout layer randomly drops some neurons and connections to reduce the model's reliance on specific weights [45].

EEGNet is composed of three convolutional network types: 2D convolutional networks (Conv2D), depthwise convolutional networks (DepthwiseConv2D), and separable convolutional networks (SeparableConv2D) [13]. Therefore, the DepthwiseConv2D and SeparableConv2D convolutional layers are constructed in the second block of the model.

The depthwise convolutional network focuses on capturing frequency feature maps across different channels of EEG signals and ultimately outputs spatial feature maps characterized by frequency (time). Zero padding fills the blank areas in the attention mechanism's output with zeros, adjusting the dimensions for subsequent convolution operations. The depthwise convolution layer then processes the resulting output. In this depthwise convolution, 16 convolutional kernels of size (3, 3) are used, with the activation function being the Exponential Linear Unit (ELU). This convolution method effectively extracts local features while maintaining computational efficiency. Depthwise convolution reduces the computational load by performing convolutions separately for each input channel, extracting features from each channel.

In the second layer of the second block, SeparableConv2D is used for computation. Separable convolution includes a depthwise convolution followed by a pointwise convolution layer. The output of the depthwise convolution is first zero-padded to align with the subsequent separable convolution operation, and then the result is processed through the separable convolution. This layer uses 8 convolutional kernels of size (8, 4), with ELU as the activation function. Due to the characteristics of the EEGNet architecture, which separates the spatial and temporal feature extraction layers, this layer requires fewer parameters. It can capture relationships within and between feature maps, outputting feature maps that emphasize the relationships between channels (spatial). On the other hand, separable convolution effectively extracts both local and cross-channel features while maintaining computational efficiency [46].

Finally, the outputs from all convolutional and pooling layers are flattened and passed through a fully connected layer (Dense) with 64 neurons, using the ELU activation function. The output layer (Dense) uses the Softmax activation function, providing the final classification result with 4 neurons. The fully connected layer efficiently classifies the extracted features, while the Softmax activation function converts the outputs into a probability distribution, making it suitable for multi-class classification. The Softmax function transforms input values into probabilities such that their sum equals 1, and its formula is as follows:

$$\sigma(x)_j = \frac{e^{x_j}}{\sum_{i=1}^{C} e^{x_i}} \quad where\ J = 1, \ldots..c \tag{3}$$

$\sigma(x_i)$ represents the output of the Softmax function, which is the probability value of the input x_i after normalization, and c denotes the number of classes. With this design, our model can efficiently extract and combine time-frequency features from EEG signals and enhance its performance through the attention mechanism. Combining deep convolution, separable convolution, and the attention mechanism, this network architecture exhibits muscular flexibility and adaptability when processing EEG data.

3.3.4. Majority Voting

She et al. [47] pointed out that recording a full hour of EEG data provides more stable and reliable observations in monitoring HIE. In contrast, shorter recordings may be influenced by transient physiological fluctuations or interference signals, leading to less accurate data. However, directly handling an entire hour of data in model training consumes significant computational resources, especially for deep learning models. Splitting the data into smaller segments can reduce the amount of data input into the model each time, thereby decreasing the computational load and improving the efficiency of model training and inference [48]. Therefore, this study trains the model by segmenting one hour of EEG data into five-minute segments and, after training, integrates the output using a voting mechanism.

This study adopts a majority voting mechanism to ensure the final classification result's reliability. Specifically, the labels for all 23 five-minute segments are collected, and the frequency of each label is counted. The label with the highest occurrence is selected as the final output for the one-hour data. This voting mechanism combines multiple prediction results, offsetting potential errors from individual predictions, thereby enhancing the robustness of the classification outcome. Through this voting mechanism, the model's classification accuracy is significantly improved, and it can produce a comprehensive classification result for the one-hour EEG data (Figure 9).

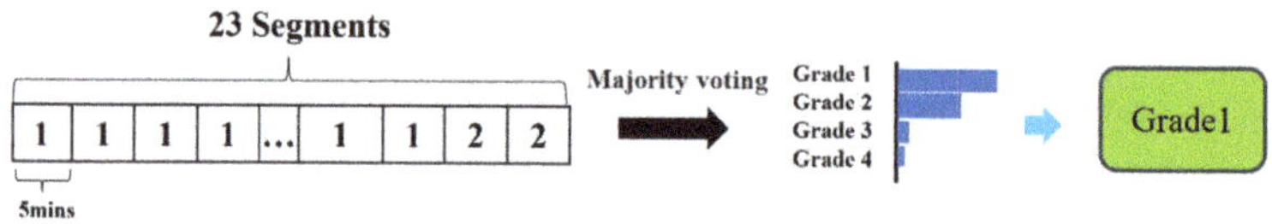

Figure 9. Post-processing voting diagram.

4. Experimental Design

4.1. Experimental Process

The detailed research process is as follows:

1. Apply filtering to the data, reducing the original frequency from 200 Hz to 40 Hz.
2. Use Safe-level SMOTE to handle the imbalanced data classes, balancing the number of samples across all classes to reduce the potential impact of class imbalance on the classification task.
3. Segment the one-hour EEG data (5 min per segment with a 50% overlap, resulting in 23 segments per hour).
4. Randomly split the data into training and validation sets and perform 10-fold cross-validation.
5. Adjust model parameters.
6. Each model outputs 23 classification results for every hourly segment, and the final classification result is determined through a majority voting mechanism.
7. Evaluate the model using standard metrics such as accuracy, specificity, sensitivity, precision, F-score, and the Kappa value.
8. Compare the proposed model with other existing methods to validate its effectiveness (Figure 10).

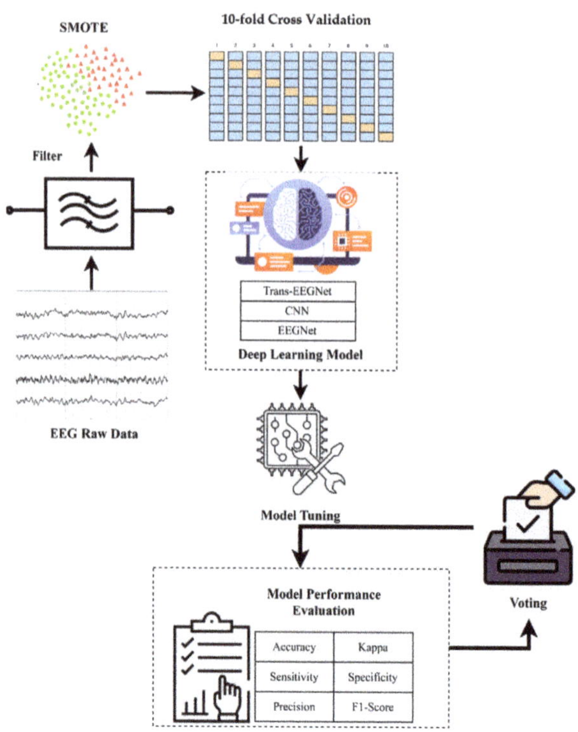

Figure 10. Research process flow chart.

4.2. Baseline System

This study aims to evaluate the performance of the Trans-EEGNet model by comparing it with other deep learning and machine learning methods. The following introduces the two baseline systems, CNNs and EEGNet, which will be used for performance comparison.

First, the CNN (Convolutional Neural Network) is a well-established neural network algorithm that has been proven to be a solid foundation for various state-of-the-art models in EEG classification research [49]. Therefore, this study includes a comparison with the CNN to demonstrate the performance improvements of Trans-EEGNet. The other baseline system is EEGNet, a compact convolutional neural network architecture designed explicitly for EEG data. EEGNet uses depthwise separable convolution operations to extract EEG features, creating a model optimized for EEG characteristics [50]. By comparing with this foundational EEGNet architecture, we can assess whether Trans-EEGNet performs better in classification tasks.

4.3. Experimental Setup

4.3.1. Hyperparameters and Environment Setup

The same hyperparameters are used for the baseline systems and the proposed model for consistency in experiments. The hyperparameters include 10-fold cross-validation (k = 10). Through a systematic grid search process, the optimal hyperparameters for the model were determined as follows: a batch size of 64, 20 epochs, a dropout rate of 0.25, and a learning rate of 0.0001. These parameters were selected to balance training efficiency and generalization capability, minimizing overfitting while ensuring adequate model convergence. The chosen dropout rate aids in regularization, while the finely tuned learning rate facilitates gradual optimization, contributing to the model's overall performance and stability during training. Table 5 displays the hardware environment settings. In the experiment, the training time for the CNN model ranged from 10 to 20 min, while the EEGNet model required 5 to 15 min, and the Trans-EEGNet model took 30 to 60 min. After training, all three models completed inference tasks within approximately one to three seconds.

Table 5. Specifications of Experimental Equipment.

Name	Model/Version
Operating System	Windows 10 22H2
Processor	Intel Core i7-13700
Memory	ADATA DDR4-3200 64 G
SSD	Kingston KC3000 1 TB
Graphics Card	Nvidia GeForce RTX 3060

4.3.2. Evaluation Metrics

This study uses accuracy, specificity, sensitivity/recall, precision, the F-score, Kappa value, and Matthews Correlation Coefficient (MCC) to evaluate the performance of the classifier model.

Accuracy is used to measure the proportion of correctly predicted samples out of the total number of samples. It is defined as follows:

$$\text{Accuracy}(\text{Acc}) = \frac{TP + TN}{TP + TN + FP + FN} \tag{4}$$

TP (True Positive) means the number of "positive classes" correctly predicted by the model, and *TN* (True Negative) means the number of "negative classes" correctly predicted by the model.

Specificity is the true negative part of the correct identification. The equation is

$$\text{Specificity}(\text{SPE}) = \frac{TP + TN}{TP + FP} \times 100 \tag{5}$$

Sensitivity measures the proportion of correctly predicted positive samples to the total number of positive samples. It is defined as

$$\text{Sensitivity}(\text{SEN}) = \frac{TP}{TP + TN} \times 100 \tag{6}$$

Precision is used to measure the proportion of actual positive instances classified as positive instances, defined as

$$\text{Precision}(\text{Prec}) = \frac{TP}{TP + FP} \tag{7}$$

The F-score is an extension of classification accuracy, which combines precision and recall. The calculation of F-score is defined as

$$\text{F-score} = 2 \times \frac{Precision \times Sensitivity}{Precision + Sensitivity} \tag{8}$$

Kappa is used to evaluate the consistency of the classification model. It is defined as the consistency ratio between the actual classification results and the random classification results. Cohen's Kappa provides a more reliable performance measure in machine learning, where using accuracy alone can be biased when dealing with imbalanced data. Its formula is:

$$k = \frac{p_o - p_e}{1 - p_e} \tag{9}$$

k is Cohen′s Kappa coefficient, ranging from 1 to -1. p_o is the observed agreement, expressed as the proportion of the annotator or model predictions that are consistent with the real labels in the actual situation, p_e stands for Expected Agreement, which represents the probability that the prediction result of the model or annotator is consistent with the real label under completely random conditions.

The Matthews Correlation Coefficient (MCC) is used to evaluate the consistency between the actual classification results and random classification results, especially when dealing with imbalanced datasets. By considering true positives, true negatives, false positives, and false negatives, it provides a comprehensive and balanced measure of classification performance. The formula is as follows:

$$MCC = \frac{TP \times TN - FP \times FN}{\sqrt{(TP + FP)(TP + FN)(TN + FP)(TN + FN)}} \tag{10}$$

5. Experimental Results and Discussion

5.1. Experimental Performance

5.1.1. Comparison with Baseline Model

First, the performance results of each model, including the mean and standard deviation, will be compared. The stability of deep learning models can be assessed by evaluating their performance's standard deviation (STD) and mean. Achieving high consistency in performance evaluation indicates that the model's performance is less affected by variations in the data.

The standard deviation reflects a model's degree of performance variation across different cross-validation folds. A minor standard deviation indicates more consistent performance across different datasets, demonstrating model stability and ensuring accurate predictions on new data in real-world applications. If the standard deviation is large, it suggests significant performance variation across datasets, which may indicate overfitting issues. Therefore, standard deviation plays a crucial role in evaluating model performance.

The mean represents the average performance of the model across all cross-validation folds, providing an overview of the model's overall performance. In most cases, models with a higher mean performance score perform better, making it an essential criterion for model selection and tuning. This study uses standard deviation to assess the model's stability and utilizes the mean to comprehensively evaluate various performance metrics, quantifying the model's actual performance across different datasets.

As shown in Table 6, the performance metrics of Trans-EEGNet are as follows: accuracy 0.9549 ± 0.0160, sensitivity 0.9587 ± 0.0140, specificity 0.9841 ± 0.0050, F-score 0.9623 ± 0.0145, precision 0.9607 ± 0.0149, and Kappa value 0.9841 ± 0.0050. The performance of EEGNet is accuracy 0.8819 ± 0.0278, sensitivity 0.8871 ± 0.0276, specificity 0.9588 ± 0.0097, F-score 0.8883 ± 0.0273, precision 0.8975 ± 0.0252, and Kappa value 0.8383 ± 0.0352. The performance of CNN is accuracy 0.6937 ± 0.1973, sensitivity 0.6836 ± 0.2221, specificity 0.9048 ± 0.0692, F-score 0.6609 ± 0.2108, precision 0.7253 ± 0.2108, and Kappa value 0.5821 ± 0.2667.

Table 6. Model performance comparison.

	Accuracy	**Sensitivity**	**Specificity**	**Loss**
Trans-EEGNet	0.9549 ± 0.0160	0.9587 ± 0.0140	0.9841 ± 0.0050	0.1423 ± 0.0531
EEGNet	0.8819 ± 0.0278	0.8871 ± 0.0276	0.9588 ± 0.0097	0.8855 ± 0.4580
CNN	0.6937 ± 0.1973	0.6836 ± 0.2221	0.9048 ± 0.0692	0.5829 ± 0.2371
	F-Score	Precision	Kappa	
Trans-EEGNet	0.9623 ± 0.0145	0.9607 ± 0.0149	0.9366 ± 0.0185	
EEGNet	0.8883 ± 0.0273	0.8975 ± 0.0252	0.8383 ± 0.0352	
CNN	0.6609 ± 0.2108	0.7253 ± 0.2108	0.5821 ± 0.2667	

Based on the average performance results from 10-fold cross-validation, Trans-EEGNet achieved the best performance across all metrics. Accuracy represents the proportion of all data correctly classified and is a crucial indicator of overall model performance. Sensitivity reflects the model's ability to capture true positive samples; a high sensitivity indicates that the model can identify most positive samples, making it helpful in determining if the model mistakenly classifies actual positive samples as negative. Specificity measures the proportion of negative samples correctly identified by the model; a high specificity indicates that the model seldom misclassifies actual negative samples as positive.

Precision refers to the proportion of true positive samples among those predicted as positive by the model. High precision means that the model's positive predictions are more reliable, meaning that most samples predicted as positive are indeed positive. F-score combines precision and sensitivity to evaluate the model's balanced ability to correctly classify positive samples and avoid misclassifying negative samples as positive. Cohen's Kappa measures the consistency of a classification model, considering not only accuracy but also the possibility of random agreement. A high Kappa value indicates high consistency in the model's classification results. It is significantly better than random guessing, making it a good indicator for assessing the model's prediction accuracy, consistency, and reliability.

Among all the evaluation metrics mentioned above, Trans-EEGNet achieved the best performance, indicating more excellent reliability and accuracy in the classification task. Additionally, according to Anguita et al. [51], when performing cross-validation, using a lower loss as the model's performance evaluation criterion can help achieve better generalization performance and minimize the error range between the model and the predicted data. The results in the table show that Trans-EEGNet's generalization and adaptability are superior to those of the other two baseline models.

In summary, the Trans-EEGNet model offers a more comprehensive approach to classification and performs better across all metrics compared to other baseline models. Therefore, this study selects the proposed Trans-EEGNet model for HIE classification and serves as the basis for the subsequent voting mechanism.

To further verify the model's statistical significance, an analysis of variance (ANOVA) was conducted, as shown in Table 7. The table shows that the model's p-value (6.67×10^{-5}) is far smaller than 0.05, indicating that the model is statistically significant. Additionally, the F-value (14.02) is relatively large, suggesting that the variance between models is significantly greater than within groups. This further confirms the effectiveness of Trans-EEGNet in extracting EEG features.

Table 7. Model ANOVA analysis result.

Source	Sum of Squares	Degrees of Freedom	F-Value	p-Value
Model	14.02	2	14.02	6.67×10^{-5}
Residual		27		

Since the ANOVA analysis results indicated that the variance between models is significantly greater than within groups, this study used a multiple comparison test (Tukey's HSD) to compare the performance differences between different models. Table 8 presents the results of the multiple comparison test. The results show that Trans-EEGNet is significantly superior to the other models in all comparisons, indicating that this model has a significant advantage in classifying EEG data. Additionally, significant differences were observed between all three models.

Table 8. Tukey's HSD test.

Group 1	Group 2	Mean Difference	p-adj	Lower	Upper	Significant
CNN	EEGNet	0.1872	0.0028	−0.2463	0.0724	Yes
CNN	Trans-EEGNet	0.2602	0.0001	−0.3683	0.1944	Yes
EEGNet	Trans-EEGNet	0.122	0.0051	−0.2089	0.035	Yes

Table 8 presents the results of Tukey's HSD test for each model. This test evaluates the performance of two machine learning models in each comparison and examines the significance of the mean differences between the models. In the table, Group 1 and Group 2 represent the two model combinations being compared. The Mean Difference indicates the difference in mean absolute error (MAE) between the two models. P-adj is the adjusted p-value used to test whether the mean difference is significant. Lower and Upper represent the lower and upper bounds of the 95% confidence interval. Significant indicates whether to reject the null hypothesis; if it is "Yes", it means that there is a significant difference between the means of the two groups.

Tukey's HSD test results show that the mean differences between CNN and EEGNet, CNN and Trans-EEGNet, and EEGNet and Trans-EEGNet all reach a significant level (p-value smaller than 0.05). This indicates that there are statistically significant differences in performance among these models.

Mean Absolute Error (MAE) directly indicates the model's prediction accuracy, with smaller values indicating higher accuracy. The Mean Difference compares the relative performance difference between the two models. When comparing model performance, the conclusions should be based on the actual performance metric of the models, namely MAE. According to the test results, the Trans-EEGNet model exhibits significantly lower MAE in these comparisons, indicating that its prediction performance is superior to the other models.

5.1.2. Majority Voting Result

This study uses the output of Trans-EEGNet as the input for the majority voting mechanism, with the classification results of Trans-EEGNet shown in Figure 11. A total of 437 five-minute data samples were classified. As observed in Figure 11, the classification performance for Grade 3 is excellent, with the vast majority of samples correctly classified and only one sample misclassified as Grade 4. The classification performance for Grade 4 is also good, with most samples correctly classified and only three samples misclassified as Grade 3. However, the classification errors for Grade 1 and Grade 2 are relatively higher, with most misclassifications categorized as Grade 3. The final classification accuracy reached only 0.7849, as shown in Table 9.

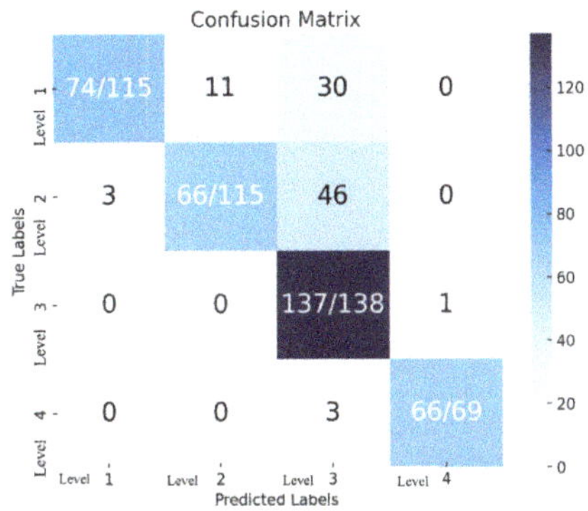

Figure 11. Trans-EEGNet classification confusion matrix.

Table 9. Trans-EEGNet classification performance.

	Accuracy	Recall	F1 Score	MCC
Trans-EEGNet	0.7849	0.7917	0.8007	0.8300

To improve the classification accuracy, this study combines the 23 five-minute segments within each hour using a majority voting mechanism for classification integration, aiming for better classification performance.

In the 437 five-minute data samples test set, the 23 consecutive segments for each subject were combined into one-hour data. The model classified these 23 segments, and the results were processed through a majority voting mechanism to obtain the outcome. As shown in Table 10, the performance results show significant improvement compared to the original output, with accuracy increasing from 0.7849 to 0.8421. As illustrated in Figure 12, the classification accuracy for the one-hour data of 19 subjects is better than the direct output from Trans-EEGNet.

Table 10. Trans-EEGNet majority voting results.

	Accuracy	Recall	F1 Score	MCC
Trans-EEGNet (Majority)	0.8421	0.8500	0.8597	0.8300

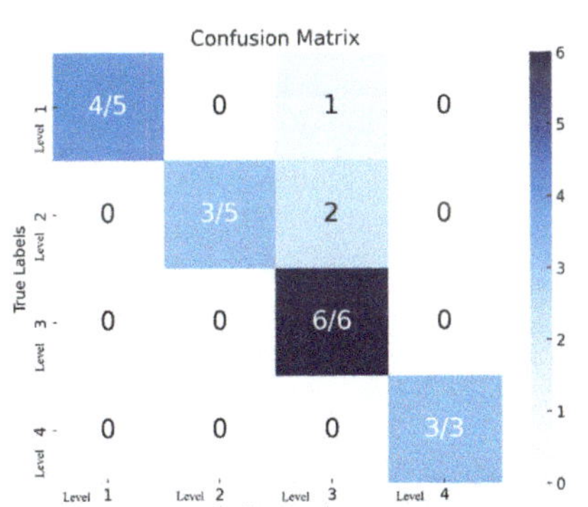

Figure 12. Confusion matrix of majority voting results.

5.2. Discussion

5.2.1. Cross-Validation Visualization Results

In terms of performance evaluation, we compared the performance metrics of three models, Trans-EEGNet, EEGNet, and CNN, and presented the results for each fold using line charts. The results show that Trans-EEGNet outperforms the other two models in all metrics, including accuracy, sensitivity, specificity, F-score, precision, and Kappa value. Trans-EEGNet has a more minor standard deviation, indicating less performance variation across different datasets and demonstrating higher stability. Moreover, the loss values for each fold were significantly lower than those of the other models, further proving its stability. As a result, Trans-EEGNet also achieved good results when classifying the new test set (Figures 13–18).

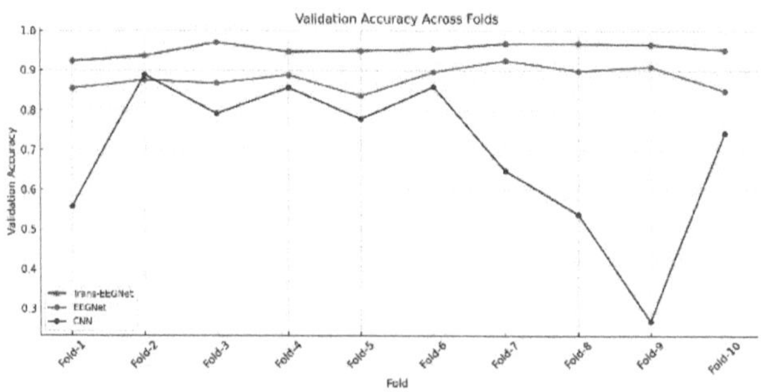

Figure 13. Line chart of Accuracy in cross-validation.

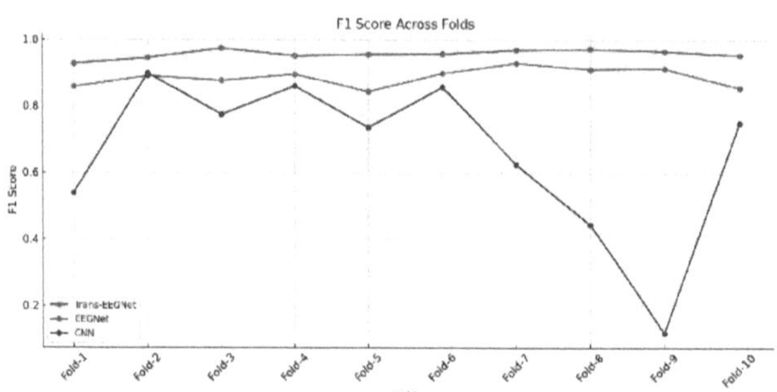

Figure 14. Line chart of F1 score in cross-validation.

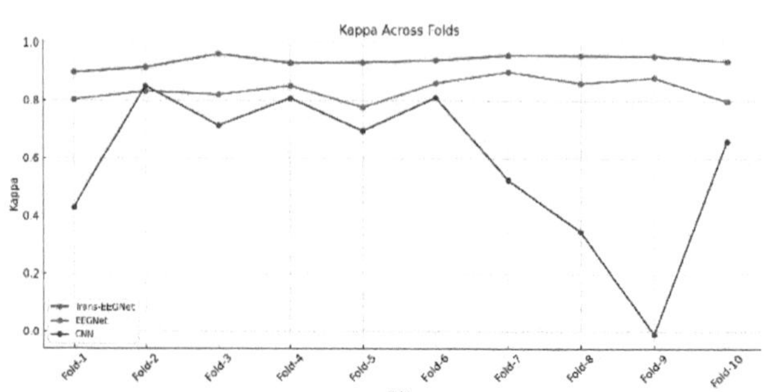

Figure 15. Line chart of Kappa in cross-validation.

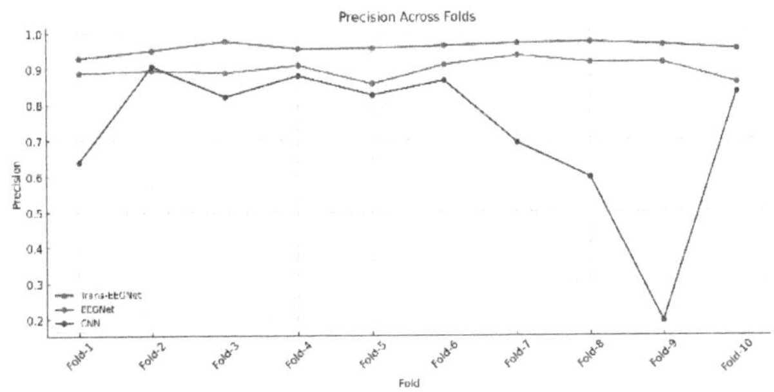

Figure 16. Line chart of Precision in cross-validation.

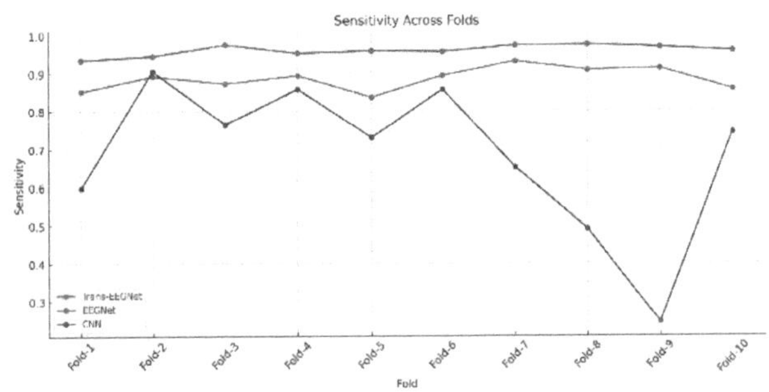

Figure 17. Line chart of Sensitivity in cross-validation.

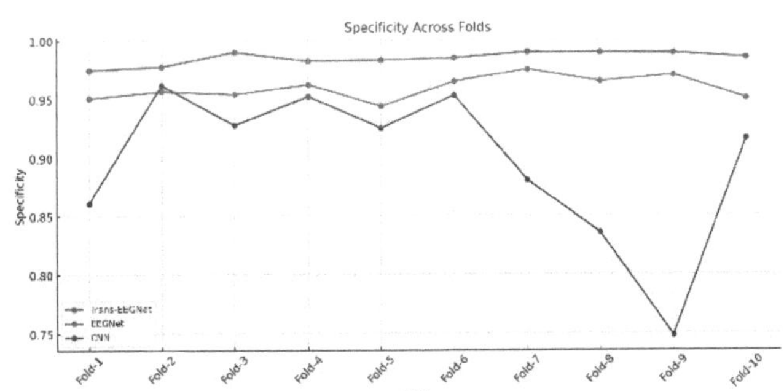

Figure 18. Line chart of Specificity in cross-validation.

5.2.2. Voting Mechanism

According to the study by Padfield et al. [52], data segmentation and overlapping sampling can effectively increase the diversity of data samples, thereby improving the training performance of models. Therefore, in the post-processing phase, this study adopted a majority voting mechanism to integrate the predictions of different time segments. Specifically, each hour of EEG data was divided into five-minute segments, generating 23 segments with a 50% overlap. This overlapping approach helps increase the diversity of data samples, allowing the model to capture feature variations across different periods better while reducing the bias that may arise from a single segment.

After classifying each segment, the classification results of all segments were counted, and the most frequently occurring class was selected as the final prediction. This majority voting mechanism combines multiple prediction results to offset potential errors from individual predictions, thus enhancing the robustness and accuracy of the classification results. In the test set of 437 five-minute samples, the final classification results obtained by applying majority voting to the 23 consecutive samples of each subject showed a significant improvement in accuracy, from 0.7849 to 0.8421. This demonstrates that the majority voting method is highly effective in enhancing the accuracy and robustness of the final classification.

5.2.3. Comparison of Research Results on HIE Topics

In the research on HIE grading, previous scholars have proposed various methods to address this issue. Stevenson et al. [5] proposed the TFDfeat method, which first converts EEG signals into a quadratic time-frequency distribution to extract features related to time and frequency, making it particularly suitable for handling dynamic changes in non-stationary data. This method combines these features with traditional spectral power features and uses a multi-class linear discriminant classifier (MLDC) for classification. The final decision for more extended periods is made by combining the classification results of shorter segments through a majority voting approach.

Ahmed et al. [8] proposed the GSVfeat method, which combines generative and discriminative models using Gaussian Mixture Models (GMMs) to describe the statistical characteristics of the data. This method first extracts features from short segments of EEG and then generates supervisors using GMM to represent the features of the entire segment. A support vector machine (SVM) is used for grading. This approach effectively handles data with complex feature distributions but has a higher computational burden and a more complex model structure.

Raurale et al. [53] proposed the IBIfeat method, which focuses on identifying EEG inter-beat interval (IBI) features. The duration and stability of these intervals play a critical role in HIE grading. This method uses specific algorithms to detect and quantify the intervals within the signal and then uses a multilayer perceptron (MLP) for classification. Raurale et al. [9] later proposed the CNN1d method, which uses a one-dimensional convolutional neural network (CNN) to process EEG data. The neural network automatically learns features from the data and captures signal characteristics through multiple convolutional layers. The final classification is determined through a fully connected layer and a Softmax layer, with results from each time segment combined using a voting mechanism.

Performance comparisons from previous studies indicate that neural networks outperform traditional machine learning methods in EEG classification. Neural networks can automatically extract features from EEG data without relying on manually labeled features to find the optimal classification boundaries. Raurale et al. [1] further proposed a method that combines EEG signals transformed through quadratic time-frequency distribution with CNNs for feature extraction. The preprocessing through quadratic time-frequency distribution enhances the prominence of features in EEG, and combined with the feature learning capability of CNN, this approach achieved better classification accuracy.

Compared to previous studies, the Trans-EEGNet proposed in this research combines EEGNet with a single-head attention mechanism. EEGNet is a CNN architecture specifically designed for EEG data, capable of automatically extracting features. Its lightweight design helps to reduce computational costs and improve training efficiency. The single-head attention mechanism addresses the limitation of CNNs being overly focused on local features. By contrast, earlier studies did not use attention mechanisms, making them relatively weaker in capturing long-range dependencies or multi-dimensional data relationships. This makes Trans-EEGNet more comprehensive in its feature extraction capabilities.

Due to privacy concerns, most EEG medical data are not publicly available. In their study, Raurale et al. [1] used the ANSeR dataset, a neonatal seizure recognition algorithm dataset, to compare previous methods. This dataset was collected with written consent from the parents of the newborns, but the consent did not include permission for data sharing or public release. Therefore, this study cannot directly compare its results with those of Raurale et al.'s research. All the results are shown in Table 11.

Table 11. Related research on HIE classification.

Method	Accuracy	Kappa	Author
TFDfeat	77.8%	0.68	[5]
GSVfeat	77.8%	0.81	[8]
IBIfeat	77.8	0.68	[53]
CNN1d	81.5%	0.73	[9]
QTFD+CNN	88.9%	0.84	[1]
Trans-EEGNet	95%	0.93	This Study

5.2.4. Limitations and Future Research

This study successfully improved the classification capability of EEG data, but it also has some limitations that need further refinement in future research. For EEG data, factors such as brain anatomy, head size, electrode placement, and inherent differences between subjects greatly limit the generalizability of EEG analysis. In other words, even if a model achieves good training results on a particular dataset, its generalization ability to other datasets may need to be improved [54].

As machine learning models become increasingly complex, their interpretability has become crucial in clinical settings. Integrating explainable artificial intelligence (XAI) techniques with digital health data is advancing steadily in precision medicine, addressing the need for transparency and comprehensibility in clinical applications. Moreover, explainable machine learning algorithms demonstrate how to analyze complex patterns, providing critical insights for predictions tailored to individual patients. Another model interpretability technique, Grad-CAM (Gradient-weighted Class Activation Mapping), visualizes the reasoning behind deep learning model predictions. Generating heat maps through weighted feature maps highlights the areas of interest in the model, aiding in understanding its decision-making process. Grad-CAM can be integrated with any convolution-based architecture, such as Xception and ResNet. In medical imaging, Grad-CAM can pinpoint abnormal regions, assisting doctors in comprehending the basis of the model's judgments [55,56]. Explainable AI can articulate the rationale behind its diagnoses or predictions, making it easier for doctors to understand and accept AI system recommendations rather than relying solely on "accuracy" metrics. In medical data, explainable AI is crucial in enhancing system transparency and credibility, supporting medical decision-making, uncovering data biases, and advancing clinical research [56]. In the future, these technologies could be further combined to identify and interpret feature patterns associated with hypoxic-ischemic encephalopathy (HIE), facilitating more precise diagnosis and treatment decisions.

The first limitation concerns the dataset. The dataset used in this study comes from a specific environment and subjects, which may limit the model's generalization ability in other settings and among different subjects. Therefore, future research should consider incorporating more data from diverse backgrounds and conditions to enhance the model's applicability and stability.

Furthermore, although Trans-EEGNet combines EEGNet with a single-head attention mechanism, improving classification performance, it also increases the model's complexity and computational cost, which could be a limitation in resource-constrained applications. Future research could explore more efficient model architectures, such as lightweight deep learning models like CapsNet, to reduce computational requirements.

The convolutional layers in EEGNet have been optimized, but the introduction of Transformer has rendered the model architecture more hybridized. This design significantly enhances the ability to extract local and global features but also increases computation complexity, further extending processing time. In Trans-EEGNet, additional fusion layers are required to integrate the features of the Transformer and EEGNet and the parameters and computations of these layers also impact computational efficiency. Transformers typically have more parameters than traditional convolutional neural networks (such as the CNN and EEGNet). This is particularly evident when handling attention mechanisms and large feature matrices, where the additional weight matrices demand more memory and computational resources.

Additionally, this study only used EEG data for classification without considering the integration of other biological signals, such as the electrocardiogram (ECG) and electromyography (EMG). Multimodal data fusion can provide richer information, enhancing classification accuracy and robustness. Future research could explore combining EEG data with other biological signals for analysis to obtain more comprehensive medical classification results.

Lastly, this study primarily focused on analyzing and classifying offline data without addressing the challenges of real-time applications. Real-time applications require handling issues such as data latency, computational resource limitations, and constraints on computation time. Future research could focus on effectively deploying and operating the Trans-EEGNet model in real-time systems to achieve more efficient real-time classification.

6. Conclusions

The Trans-EEGNet model proposed in this study achieves efficient feature extraction and classification of EEG signals by combining CNN and Transformer layers. The results of 10-fold cross-validation confirm the model's effectiveness and stability. Comparisons with baseline models further demonstrate that Trans-EEGNet exhibits superior performance in grading hypoxic-ischemic encephalopathy (HIE), providing strong support for future clinical applications. Inspired by deep learning and attention mechanisms, this study aims to use EEGNet for local feature extraction and a Transformer for global feature extraction. The proposed Trans-EEGNet integrates the strengths of both models, enhancing the ability to model and predict temporal features of EEG signals.

In summary, this study's main contribution is the proposal of a hybrid model that combines EEGNet with a Transformer. This model achieves better grading results through the synergistic effect of feature extraction and long-term dependency learning. The designed experiments validate the model's effectiveness, showing that Trans-EEGNet significantly outperforms other models.

Additionally, through the majority voting mechanism, this study effectively enhances the classification performance of the Trans-EEGNet model, especially in handling EEG time-series data, allowing better management of challenges posed by transient noise and variations. This approach improves the model's robustness and provides more reliable technical support for clinical applications. Future work will focus on interpreting the obtained long-term dependency representations and exploring the application of this method to other biological time-series signals, such as the electrocardiogram (ECG).

Author Contributions: Conceptualization, D.-H.S. and M.-H.S.; Formal analysis, S.-Y.H.; Investigation, F.-I.C. and T.-W.W.; Methodology, D.-H.S., F.-I.C. and S.-Y.H.; Resources, D.-H.S. and M.-H.S.; Software, F.-I.C. and S.-Y.H.; Supervision, D.-H.S.; Validation, D.-H.S. and T.-W.W.; Visualization, M.-H.S.; Writing—original draft, S.-Y.H.; Writing—review and editing, F.-I.C., T.-W.W. and M.-H.S. All authors have read and agreed to the published version of the manuscript.

Funding: This research received no external funding.

Data Availability Statement: The Cork Research Ethics Committee approved the release of the anonymized dataset, which is publicly available at https://zenodo.org/records/7477575#.Y--W-nZBy5d (accessed on 10 January 2023).

Conflicts of Interest: The authors declare no conflicts of interest.

References

1. Raurale, S.A.; Boylan, G.B.; Mathieson, S.R.; Marnane, W.P.; Lightbody, G.; O'Toole, J.M. Grading hypoxic-ischemic encephalopathy in neonatal EEG with convolutional neural networks and quadratic time–frequency distributions. *J. Neural Eng.* **2021**, *18*, 046007. [CrossRef] [PubMed]
2. Walsh, B.H.; Murray, D.M.; Boylan, G.B. The use of conventional EEG for the assessment of hypoxic ischaemic encephalopathy in the newborn: A review. *Clin. Neurophysiol.* **2011**, *122*, 1284–1294. [CrossRef] [PubMed]
3. Shankaran, S. Therapeutic hypothermia for neonatal encephalopathy. *Curr. Treat. Options Neurol.* **2012**, *14*, 608–619. [CrossRef] [PubMed]

4. Murray, D.M.; Ryan, C.A.; Boylan, G.B.; Fitzgerald, A.P.; Connolly, S. Prediction of seizures in asphyxiated neonates: Correlation with continuous video-electroencephalographic monitoring. *Pediatrics* **2006**, *118*, 41–46. [CrossRef]
5. Stevenson, N.J.; Korotchikova, I.; Temko, A.; Lightbody, G.; Marnane, W.P.; Boylan, G.B. An automated system for grading EEG abnormality in term neonates with hypoxic-ischaemic encephalopathy. *Ann. Biomed. Eng.* **2013**, *41*, 775–785. [CrossRef]
6. Matic, V.; Cherian, P.J.; Koolen, N.; Naulaers, G.; Swarte, R.M.; Govaert, P.; Van Huffel, S.; De Vos, M. Holistic approach for automated background EEG assessment in asphyxiated full-term infants. *J. Neural Eng.* **2014**, *11*, 066007. [CrossRef]
7. Matić, V.; Cherian, P.J.; Jansen, K.; Koolen, N.; Naulaers, G.; Swarte, R.M.; Govaert, P.; Van Huffel, S.; De Vos, M. Improving reliability of monitoring background EEG dynamics in asphyxiated infants. *IEEE Trans. Biomed. Eng.* **2015**, *63*, 973–983. [CrossRef]
8. Ahmed, R.; Temko, A.; Marnane, W.; Lightbody, G.; Boylan, G. Grading hypoxic–ischemic encephalopathy severity in neonatal EEG using GMM supervectors and the support vector machine. *Clin. Neurophysiol.* **2016**, *127*, 297–309. [CrossRef]
9. Raurale, S.A.; Boylan, G.B.; Lightbody, G.; O'Toole, J.M. Grading the severity of hypoxic-ischemic encephalopathy in newborn EEG using a convolutional neural network. In Proceedings of the 2020 42nd Annual International Conference of the IEEE Engineering in Medicine & Biology Society (EMBC), Montreal, QC, Canada, 20–24 July 2020; IEEE: New York, NY, USA, 2020; pp. 6103–6106.
10. Greenspan, H.; Van Ginneken, B.; Summers, R.M. Guest editorial deep learning in medical imaging: Overview and future promise of an exciting new technique. *IEEE Trans. Med. Imaging* **2016**, *35*, 1153–1159. [CrossRef]
11. Xie, J.; Zhang, J.; Sun, J.; Ma, Z.; Qin, L.; Li, G.; Zhou, H.; Zhan, Y. A transformer-based approach combining deep learning network and spatial-temporal information for raw EEG classification. *IEEE Trans. Neural Syst. Rehabil. Eng.* **2022**, *30*, 2126–2136. [CrossRef]
12. Sun, J.; Xie, J.; Zhou, H. EEG classification with transformer-based models. In Proceedings of the 2021 IEEE 3rd Global Conference on Life Sciences and Technologies (LifeTech), Nara, Japan, 9–11 March 2021.
13. Lawhern, V.J.; Solon, A.J.; Waytowich, N.R.; Gordon, S.M.; Hung, C.P.; Lance, B.J. EEGNet: A compact convolutional neural network for EEG-based brain–computer interfaces. *J. Neural Eng.* **2018**, *15*, 056013. [CrossRef] [PubMed]
14. Millar, L.J.; Shi, L.; Hoerder-Suabedissen, A.; Molnár, Z. Neonatal hypoxia ischaemia: Mechanisms, models, and therapeutic challenges. *Front. Cell. Neurosci.* **2017**, *11*, 78. [CrossRef] [PubMed]
15. Marlow, N.; Shankaran, S.; Rogers, E.E.; Maitre, N.L.; Smyser, C.D.; Guidelines, N.B.S.; Publications Committee. Neurological and developmental outcomes following neonatal encephalopathy treated with therapeutic hypothermia. In *Seminars in Fetal and Neonatal Medicine*; WB Saunders: Philadelphia, PA, USA, 2021; Volume 26, p. 101274.
16. Thompson, C.M.; Puterman, A.S.; Linley, L.L.; Hann, F.M.; van Molteno, C.D.; Malan, A.F. The value of a scoring system for hypoxic ischaemic encephalopathy in predicting neurodevelopmental outcome. *Acta Paediatr.* **1997**, *86*, 757–761. [CrossRef]
17. Horn, A.R.; Swingler, G.H.; Myer, L.; Linley, L.L.; Raban, M.S.; Joolay, Y.; Harrison, M.C.; Chandrasekaran, M.; Rhoda, N.R.; Robertson, N.J. Early clinical signs in neonates with hypoxic ischemic encephalopathy predict an abnormal amplitude-integrated electroencephalogram at age 6 hours. *BMC Pediatr.* **2013**, *13*, 52. [CrossRef] [PubMed]
18. Natarajan, G.; Pappas, A.; Shankaran, S. Outcomes in childhood following therapeutic hypothermia for neonatal hypoxic-ischemic encephalopathy (HIE). In *Seminars in Perinatology*; WB Saunders: Philadelphia, PA, USA, 2016; Volume 40, pp. 549–555.
19. O'Toole, J.M.; Mathieson, S.R.; Raurale, S.A.; Magarelli, F.; Marnane, W.P.; Lightbody, G.; Boylan, G.B. Neonatal EEG graded for severity of background abnormalities in hypoxic-ischaemic encephalopathy. *Sci. Data* **2023**, *10*, 129. [CrossRef] [PubMed]
20. Allen, K.A.; Brandon, D.H. Hypoxic Ischemic Encephalopathy: Pathophysiology and Experimental Treatments. *Newborn Infant Nurs. Rev.* **2011**, *11*, 125–133. [CrossRef]
21. Shankaran, S.; Laptook, A.R.; Ehrenkranz, R.A.; Tyson, J.E.; McDonald, S.A.; Donovan, E.F.; Fanaroff, A.A.; Poole, W.K.; Wright, L.L.; Jobe, A.H.; et al. Whole-body hypothermia for neonates with hypoxic–ischemic encephalopathy. *N. Engl. J. Med.* **2005**, *353*, 1574–1584. [CrossRef]
22. Ranjani, M.; Supraja, P. Classifying the autism and epilepsy disorder based on EEG signal using deep convolutional neural network (DCNN). In Proceedings of the 2021 International Conference on Advance Computing and Innovative Technologies in Engineering (ICACITE), Greater Noida, India, 4–5 March 2021; IEEE: New York, NY, USA, 2021; pp. 880–886.
23. Wang, X.; Wang, Z. CNN with self-attention in EEG classification. In Proceedings of the International Conference on Human-Computer Interaction, Virtual, 26 June–1 July 2022; Springer Nature: Cham, Switzerland, 2022; pp. 512–526.
24. Li, H.; Ding, M.; Zhang, R.; Xiu, C. Motor imagery EEG classification algorithm based on CNN-LSTM feature fusion network. *Biomed. Signal Process. Control* **2022**, *72*, 103342. [CrossRef]
25. Li, F.; Hao, K.; Wei, B.; Hao, L.; Ren, L. MS-FTSCNN: An EEG emotion recognition method from the combination of multi-domain features. *Biomed. Signal Process. Control* **2024**, *88*, 105690. [CrossRef]
26. Xin, Q.; Hu, S.; Liu, S.; Zhao, L.; Zhang, Y.D. An attention-based wavelet convolution neural network for epilepsy EEG classification. *IEEE Trans. Neural Syst. Rehabil. Eng.* **2022**, *30*, 957–966. [CrossRef]
27. Wei, Y.; Liu, Y.; Li, C.; Cheng, J.; Song, R.; Chen, X. TC-Net: A transformer capsule network for EEG-based emotion recognition. *Comput. Biol. Med.* **2023**, *152*, 106463. [CrossRef] [PubMed]
28. Mulkey, M.A.; Huang, H.; Albanese, T.; Kim, S.; Yang, B. Supervised deep learning with vision transformer predicts delirium using limited lead EEG. *Sci. Rep.* **2023**, *13*, 7890. [CrossRef] [PubMed]
29. Merity, S. Single headed attention RNN: Stop thinking with your head. *arXiv* **2019**, arXiv:1911.11423.
30. Michel, P.; Levy, O.; Neubig, G. Are Sixt. Heads Really Better Than One? *arxiv* **2019**, arXiv:1905.10650.

31. Liu, L.; Liu, J.; Han, J. Multi-head or single-head? An empirical comparison for transformer training. *arXiv* **2021**, arXiv:2106.09650.
32. Murray, D.M.; Boylan, G.B.; Ryan, C.A.; Connolly, S. Early EEG findings in hypoxic-ischemic encephalopathy predict outcomes at 2 years. *Pediatrics* **2009**, *124*, e459–e467. [CrossRef]
33. Amin, A.; Anwar, S.; Adnan, A.; Nawaz, M.; Howard, N.; Qadir, J.; Hawalah, A.; Hussain, A. Comparing oversampling techniques to handle the class imbalance problem: A customer churn prediction case study. *IEEE Access* **2016**, *4*, 7940–7957. [CrossRef]
34. Thabtah, F.; Hammoud, S.; Kamalov, F.; Gonsalves, A. Data imbalance in classification: Experimental evaluation. *Inf. Sci.* **2020**, *513*, 429–441. [CrossRef]
35. Daud, S.N.S.S.; Sudirman, R.; Shing, T.W. Safe-level SMOTE method for handling the class imbalanced problem in electroencephalography dataset of adult anxious state. *Biomed. Signal Process. Control* **2023**, *83*, 104649.
36. Rakhmatulin, I.; Dao, M.S.; Nassibi, A.; Mandic, D. Exploring convolutional neural network architectures for EEG feature extraction. *Sensors* **2024**, *24*, 877. [CrossRef]
37. Saqib, M.; Zhu, Y.; Wang, M.; Beaulieu-Jones, B. Regularization of deep neural networks for EEG seizure detection to mitigate overfitting. In Proceedings of the 2020 IEEE 44th Annual Computers, Software, and Applications Conference (COMPSAC), Madrid, Spain, 13–17 July 2020.
38. Pan, Y.; Dong, F.; Wu, J.; Xu, Y. Downsampling of EEG signals for deep learning-based epilepsy detection. *IEEE Sens. Lett.* **2023**, *7*, 7007104. [CrossRef]
39. Saideepthi, P.; Gaur, P.; Chowdhury, A.; Nyati, K.; Dwivedi, T.; Sharma, S.; Pachori, R.B. Sliding window along with EEGNet based prediction of EEG motor imagery. *IEEE Sens. J.* **2023**, *23*, 17703–17713. [CrossRef]
40. Peng, R.; Zhao, C.; Jiang, J.; Kuang, G.; Cui, Y.; Xu, Y.; Du, H.; Shao, J.; Wu, D. TIE-EEGNet: Temporal information enhanced EEGNet for seizure subtype classification. *IEEE Trans. Neural Syst. Rehabil. Eng.* **2022**, *30*, 2567–2576. [CrossRef] [PubMed]
41. Deng, X.; Zhang, B.; Yu, N.; Liu, K.; Sun, K. Advanced TSGL-EEGNet for motor imagery EEG-based brain-computer interfaces. *IEEE Access* **2021**, *9*, 25118–25130. [CrossRef]
42. Li, C.; Huang, X.; Song, R.; Qian, R.; Liu, X.; Chen, X. EEG-based seizure prediction via Transformer guided CNN. *Measurement* **2022**, *203*, 111948. [CrossRef]
43. Vaswani, A.; Shazeer, N.; Parmar, N.; Uszkoreit, J.; Jones, L.; Gomez, A.N.; Kaiser, Ł.; Polosukhin, I. Attention is all you need. *Adv. Neural Inf. Process. Syst.* **2017**, *30*, 5998–6008.
44. Dosovitskiy, A.; Beyer, L.; Kolesnikov, A.; Weissenborn, D.; Zhai, X.; Unterthiner, T.; Dehghani, M.; Minderer, M.; Heigold, G.; Houlsby, N.; et al. An image is worth 16x16 words: Transformers for image recognition at scale. *arXiv* **2020**, arXiv:2010.11929.
45. Kuang, D.; Michoski, C. KAM-A kernel attention module for emotion classification with EEG data. In *International Workshop on Interpretability of Machine Intelligence in Medical Image Computing*; Springer Nature: Cham, Switzerland, 2022; pp. 93–103.
46. Srivastava, N.; Hinton, G.; Krizhevsky, A.; Sutskever, I.; Salakhutdinov, R. Dropout: A simple way to prevent neural networks from overfitting. *J. Mach. Learn. Res.* **2014**, *15*, 1929–1958.
47. She, H.-Q.; Sun, Y.-F.; Chen, L.; Xiao, Q.-X.; Luo, B.-Y.; Zhou, H.-S.; Zhou, D.; Chang, Q.-Y.; Xiong, L.-L. Current analysis of hypoxic-ischemic encephalopathy research issues and future treatment modalities. *Front. Neurosci.* **2023**, *17*, 1136500. [CrossRef]
48. Ismael, A.M.; Alçin, Ö.F.; Abdalla, K.H.; Şengür, A. Two-stepped majority voting for efficient EEG-based emotion classification. *Brain Inform.* **2020**, *7*, 9. [CrossRef]
49. Wang, Z.; Wang, Y.; Zhang, J.; Hu, C.; Yin, Z.; Song, Y. Spatial-temporal feature fusion neural network for EEG-based emotion recognition. *IEEE Trans. Instrum. Meas.* **2022**, *71*, 2507212. [CrossRef]
50. Song, X.; Yan, D.; Zhao, L.; Yang, L. LSDD-EEGNet: An efficient end-to-end framework for EEG-based depression detection. *Biomed. Signal Process. Control* **2022**, *75*, 103612. [CrossRef]
51. Anguita, D.; Ghelardoni, L.; Ghio, A.; Oneto, L.; Ridella, S. The 'K' in K-fold Cross Validation. In Proceedings of the ESANN 2012, Bruges, Belgium, 25–27 April 2012; Volume 102, pp. 441–446.
52. Padfield, N.; Ren, J.; Qing, C.; Murray, P.; Zhao, H.; Zheng, J. Multi-segment majority voting decision fusion for MI EEG brain-computer interfacing. *Cogn. Comput.* **2021**, *13*, 1484–1495. [CrossRef]
53. Raurale, S.A.; Nalband, S.; Boylan, G.B.; Lightbody, G.; O'Toole, J.M. Suitability of an inter-burst detection method for grading hypoxic-ischemic encephalopathy in newborn EEG. In Proceedings of the 2019 41st Annual International Conference of the IEEE Engineering in Medicine and Biology Society (EMBC), Berlin, Germany, 23–27 July 2019; IEEE: New York, NY, USA, 2019; pp. 4125–4128.
54. Lashgari, E.; Liang, D.; Maoz, U. Data augmentation for deep-learning-based electroencephalography. *J. Neurosci. Methods* **2020**, *346*, 108885. [CrossRef]
55. Veselov, D.; Andriyanov, N.; Trung, L. Detection of Intracranial Hemorrhage by Artificial Intelligence and Deep Learning Methods. In Proceedings of the 2024 X International Conference on Information Technology and Nanotechnology (ITNT), Samara, Russian, 20–24 May 2024; IEEE: New York, NY, USA, 2024; pp. 1–6.
56. Allen, B. The promise of explainable ai in digital health for precision medicine: A systematic review. *J. Pers. Med.* **2024**, *14*, 277. [CrossRef]

mathematics

MDPI

Article

Advanced Trans-BiGRU-QA Fusion Model for Atmospheric Mercury Prediction

Dong-Her Shih [1], Feng-I. Chung [2], Ting-Wei Wu [1,*], Bo-Hao Wang [1] and Ming-Hung Shih [3]

[1] Department of Information Management, National Yunlin University of Science and Technology, Douliu 64002, Taiwan; shihdh@yuntech.edu.tw (D.-H.S.); bohau888@gmail.com (B.-H.W.)
[2] Center for General Education, National Chung Cheng University, Chiayi 621301, Taiwan; albertchung@lib.ccu.edu.tw
[3] Department of Electrical and Computer Engineering, Iowa State University, 2520 Osborn Drive, Ames, IA 50011, USA; mshih@iastate.edu
* Correspondence: wutingw@yuntech.edu.tw

Abstract: With the deepening of the Industrial Revolution and the rapid development of the chemical industry, the large-scale emissions of corrosive dust and gases from numerous factories have become a significant source of air pollution. Mercury in the atmosphere, identified by the United Nations Environment Programme (UNEP) as one of the globally concerning air pollutants, has been proven to pose a threat to the human environment with potential carcinogenic risks. Therefore, accurately predicting atmospheric mercury concentration is of critical importance. This study proposes a novel advanced model—the Trans-BiGRU-QA hybrid—designed to predict the atmospheric mercury concentration accurately. Methodology includes feature engineering techniques to extract relevant features and applies a sliding window technique for time series data preprocessing. Furthermore, the proposed Trans-BiGRU-QA model is compared to other deep learning models, such as GRU, LSTM, RNN, Transformer, BiGRU, and Trans-BiGRU. This study utilizes air quality data from Vietnam to train and test the models, evaluating their performance in predicting atmospheric mercury concentration. The results show that the Trans-BiGRU-QA model performed exceptionally well in terms of Mean Absolute Error (MAE), Root Mean Square Error (RMSE), and R-squared (R^2), demonstrating high accuracy and robustness. Compared to other deep learning models, the Trans-BiGRU-QA model exhibited significant advantages, indicating its broad potential for application in environmental pollution prediction.

Keywords: atmospheric mercury; air pollution; transformer; bidirectional gated recurrent unit (BiGRU); quick attention (QA)

MSC: 68T05; 68T35; 68Q32

1. Introduction

Since the 20th century, the development of the Industrial Revolution has driven the rapid rise in the chemical industry, with its emissions of corrosive gases and dust becoming a significant source of air pollution. As industrialization and urbanization accelerate, air pollution has become increasingly severe in developing countries and cities [1], and the long-term emission of pollutants has had profound negative impacts on the human living environment [2]. Among these pollutants, the element mercury (Hg) has been listed by the United Nations Environment Programme (UNEP) as one pollutant that requires severe global attention. Yuan et al. [3] further pointed out that mercury is one of the most toxic metal elements. Its derivatives pose significant health risks to humans.

Mercury (Hg) exhibits potential carcinogenicity under certain conditions, with particularly pronounced neurotoxic effects on the human nervous system [4]. The long-range atmospheric dispersion of mercury emissions exacerbates the global pollution problem [5].

Therefore, predicting atmospheric mercury concentrations is significant for identifying risks in advance and reducing environmental impacts. Studies have analyzed the spatiotemporal variations, gaseous distributions, and potential sources of atmospheric mercury around the Taiwan Strait, revealing that mercury in the atmosphere, carried by airflows, may affect the air quality in Taiwan [3]. Wang et al. [6] conducted a two-year study on the spatiotemporal variations and long-distance transport of atmospheric mercury in northern coastal China, finding that the concentration of gaseous elemental mercury (GEM) exhibited significant seasonal variation, peaking in winter. In Ho Chi Minh City, Vietnam, the total gaseous mercury (TGM) concentration was significantly influenced by the monsoon, and local mercury pollution was closely related to urban areas [7]. Pang et al. [8] pointed out that small-scale gold mining significantly elevated atmospheric mercury concentrations in the surrounding environment and mining areas, causing severe health damage to residents and miners.

With the accelerated process of industrialization, air pollution problems in numerous cities have become increasingly severe. Previous studies have explored the correlation between mercury (Hg) and other air pollutants by integrating different air pollution components, revealing a close relationship between gaseous mercury (Hg) and carbon monoxide (CO), as well as positive correlations with $PM_{2.5}$, PM_{10}, and nitrogen dioxide (NO_2) [9]. Additionally, other research has successfully employed Long Short-Term Memory (LSTM) neural networks from deep learning to predict air quality in the Beijing–Tianjin–Hebei region of China, achieving significant results [10]. Wen et al. [11] effectively predicted dioxin concentrations by combining deep-learning models with time series data, noting that airflow, temperature, and temporal factors significantly impacted the concentrations. Samad et al. [2] accurately predicted $PM_{2.5}$, PM_{10}, and NO_2 concentrations using variables collected from monitoring stations combined with deep learning models. Yuan et al. [3] pointed out that mercury threatens human life. Since the 20th century, the public has gradually become aware of the significant impacts of mercury on the ecological environment and human health, prompting the adoption of preventive measures to mitigate mercury poisoning and emissions.

Regarding the uniqueness of atmospheric mercury data, the existing literature predominantly focuses on analyzing the environmental impact of various mercury forms and their distribution in the atmosphere. However, research on the interdependence between atmospheric mercury and other air pollution components is relatively limited, particularly in univariate and multivariate fusion. Studies that explore the predictive performance of various deep learning models in this regard are even scarcer. Additionally, due to the insufficient number and uneven distribution of air monitoring stations in Taiwan, relying solely on data from these stations to represent regional air pollution levels has certain limitations [12]. Therefore, the air pollution data prediction and simulation model proposed in this study is essential, providing a scientific basis for a more comprehensive understanding and prediction of atmospheric mercury concentrations.

Previous research results have shown that applying deep learning techniques enables more accurate predictions of regional air quality [2,9,10]. In air pollution studies, many researchers have collected and combined air pollution data with a single machine-learning model to assess environmental benefits. Studies have indicated that combining a single machine-learning model with others can further enhance the performance of predictive data [1]. Among these models, the Transformer architecture has demonstrated excellent performance in the data training and preprocessing phases, with its self-attention mechanism enabling the model to simultaneously process all positions in the input sequence and more effectively capture long-range dependencies, thereby understanding internal data relationships. Additionally, this model can perform data preprocessing and weight training through fine-tuning, avoiding repetitive training, and maintaining the stability of node information. The BiGRU model improves accuracy by considering both past and future data points, making predictions more precise. The Quick Attention model, due to its high computational efficiency and simple structure, allows the model to focus more on extracting relevant features from the data.

Mercury has long been proven to pose a threat to human life. In the twentieth century, the public gradually became aware of its significant impact on ecosystems and living environments. However, the current number of monitoring stations still needs to be improved, making research on mercury prediction relatively scarce compared to other air pollutants. Therefore, this study aims to utilize relevant data collected from Vietnam to predict mercury levels, addressing the gap in mercury prediction research.

This study proposes a novel advanced Trans-BiGRU-QA (Transformer-bidirectional gated recurrent unit-Quick Attension) hybrid model for predicting atmospheric mercury concentration. To evaluate its training effectiveness, it compares its performance with those of various machine learning models, including GRU, LSTM, RNN, Transformer, BiGRU, and Trans-BiGRU. The performance of the models are assessed based on the Minimum Error Value (MAE), Root Mean Square Error (RMSE), and coefficient of determination (R^2). The study utilizes an air variable dataset collected from Vietnam, which includes five features: total gaseous mercury (TGM), temperature, relative humidity, $PM_{2.5}$, and carbon dioxide. These features are used to predict the hourly atmospheric mercury concentration.

2. Literature Review

2.1. Air Pollution

In urban industrialization, the combustion of fossil fuels has not only had a severe impact on human health, but the greenhouse gases generated by industrial activities have also exacerbated the global warming trend [12]. Air pollution poses environmental challenges and exposes adults, pregnant women, school-aged children, and fetuses to potential health risks [13]. In addition to being affected by domestic sources such as vehicles, industrial zones, and factories, Taiwan's air quality is also impacted by the influx of pollutants from abroad, contributing to land pollution. Table 1 summarizes air pollution-related studies, covering research areas, methods, results, and author years. It classifies them by research field, discussing the significance of atmospheric mercury and the application of machine learning models in data prediction.

Table 1. Summary of research on air pollution.

Field	Method	Result	Refs.
Importance of Atmospheric Mercury	Interaction between different air pollution variables and mercury	Strong positive correlation between carbon monoxide (CO) and gaseous mercury (Hg)	[9]
Using Machine Learning Models for Data Prediction	LSTM model predicting air quality in the Beijing–Tianjin–Hebei region	MAE: 25.26 R^2: 0.37	[10]
	Predicting air quality using RIDGE, SVR, RFR, ETR, and XGBOOST	$PM_{2.5}$: 0.67 (R^2) PM_{10}: 0.54 (R^2) NO_2: 0.69 (R^2)	[2]
	Performance of LSTM, CNN, SVM, and RF models with non-temporal inputs (TSs)	CNN-TS: 0.412 (MAE) CNN-TS: 0.252 (MSE)	[11]
	Predicting Air Quality Index through LSTM-GRU	R^2: 0.69 MAE: 36.12 RMSE: 57.77	[14]
	Predict O_3 and NO_2 concentrations through Res-GCN-BiLSTM	O_3 R^2: 0.85 RMSE: 10.60 NO_2 R^2: 0.88 RMSE: 9.05	[15]

As shown in previous studies, Wang et al. [9] investigated the interaction between various air pollution variables and mercury, revealing a robust positive correlation between carbon monoxide (CO) and gaseous mercury (Hg), as well as positive correlations with nitrogen dioxide (NO_2), $PM_{2.5}$, and PM_{10}. Xu et al. [10] employed the LSTM model to predict air quality in the Beijing–Tianjin–Hebei region of China, with results showing that the LSTM model outperformed the ARIMA regression model. For the Shijiazhuang site, the prediction results indicated that the LSTM model achieved a Mean Absolute Error (MAE) of 25.26 and an R^2 of 0.37. Samad et al. [2] used machine learning techniques to simulate accurate monitoring station data to predict $PM_{2.5}$, PM_{10}, and NO_2 concentrations. The results demonstrated that the best model achieved an R^2 of 0.67 for $PM_{2.5}$, 0.54 for PM_{10}, and 0.69 for NO_2. Wen et al. [11] used a deep learning model combined with time series (TS) techniques to accurately predict dioxin concentrations, with their proposed CNN-TS hybrid model being the best-performing model, achieving the best MAE of 0.412 and the best MSE of 0.252. They also found significant correlations between temperature, airflow, temporal dimensions, and dioxin levels. In summary, the air pollution-related studies presented in Table 1 indicate that air pollution poses a threat to the environment in Taiwan and has severe health implications for humans. In studies on air pollution forecasting using hybrid models, Sarkar et al. [14] used an LSTM-GRU model to predict the Air Quality Index, while Wu et al. [15] developed a Res-GCN-BiLSTM model to forecast NO_2 and O_3 levels. Both achieved excellent predictive performance.

2.2. Atmospheric Mercury

Mercury (Hg) is a potent neurotoxin. Both Pang et al. [8] and Skalny et al. [4] pointed out that mercury can lead to cardiovascular diseases in adults and cause severe damage to fetal neurocognitive functions. Additionally, mercury is believed to increase the risk of cancer. Mercury affects daily human life and poses serious health threats [1,4]. In previous studies, it was revealed that the critical components of atmospheric mercury include gaseous elemental mercury (GEM), particle-bound mercury (PBM), and gaseous oxidized mercury (GOM). The sum of GEM and GOM is defined as total gaseous mercury (TGM) [16]. Gaseous elemental mercury (GEM) accounts for up to 90% of atmospheric mercury. Luo et al. [17] further indicated that mercury can combine with air to form toxic atmospheric mercury, which is transported globally through airflows and deposited in remote areas.

Table 2 summarizes studies related to atmospheric mercury, covering research areas, methods, results, and author years. The literature on atmospheric mercury is categorized into two areas: seasonal variations of mercury components and regional impacts. Wang et al. [6] explored the two-year spatiotemporal variations and long-distance transport of atmospheric mercury forms in northern coastal China, revealing that the concentration of gaseous elemental mercury (GEM) exhibited significant seasonal variation. Yuan et al. [3] collected mercury (Hgp) and total gaseous mercury (TGM) samples from six coastal and island regions on both sides of the central Taiwan Strait, indicating that atmospheric mercury could affect Taiwan's air quality. Pang et al. [8] simulated the global health impact of atmospheric mercury emissions from small-scale artisanal gold mining (ASGM). Nguyen et al. [7] monitored the concentration of total gaseous mercury (TGM) during the monsoon season in Ho Chi Minh City, Vietnam. Their results showed that tropical cyclone monsoons interacted with TGM concentrations, potentially altering the levels of TGM.

Previous studies, such as those by Wang et al. [6], Yuan et al. [3], and Nguyen et al. [7], primarily focused on collecting atmospheric mercury variables through sensing equipment and analyzing their impact on regional environments. However, relatively little literature has explored the combined prediction of atmospheric mercury concentration with other air pollutants. Since mercury has already infiltrated daily human life, predicted air pollution and analyzed the composition of mercury has become increasingly urgent.

Table 2. Summary of research on atmospheric mercury.

Field	Method	Result	Refs.
Seasonal Variation in Mercury Components	Collected gaseous oxidized mercury (GOM) and elemental mercury (Hg) for sampling analysis	Concentration of gaseous elemental mercury (GEM) varies seasonally	[6]
Regional Impact of Mercury Components	Collected mercury (Hgp) and TGM samples in the Taiwan Strait	Atmospheric mercury may affect air quality in Taiwan	[3]
	Simulation of ASGM impact on residents and miners	Global public faces 1.5 times the risk of ASGM miners	[8]
	Monitoring total gaseous mercury concentration (TGM) in Ho Chi Minh City, Vietnam	Tropical cyclone monsoons interact with TGM concentration and may alter TGM levels	[7]

3. Methodology

3.1. Transformer

The Transformer model is a powerful neural network architecture often used for analyzing sequential data. It uses a mechanism called "attention" to focus on the most relevant parts of input data across long sequences. This allows it to capture dependencies across distant time steps more effectively than traditional models, making it ideal for tasks that require understanding complex patterns in data. It has been widely applied in fields such as Natural Language Processing (NLP) [18], computer vision [19], and speech recognition [20], demonstrating unparalleled computational performance. In recent years, many studies have begun applying the Transformer model to time series data analysis with remarkable success [21]. The core technology of the Transformer model—Self-Attention—effectively avoids the issues of forgetting and redundant computations that Recurrent Neural Networks (RNNs) may encounter when processing long sequences. Additionally, the Transformer model offers the advantage of parallel computation, significantly enhancing computational speed, and its attention mechanism dramatically improves the model's interpretability [22].

Figure 1 illustrates the architecture of the Transformer model [23]. The model consists of several components: Input Embedding, Output Embedding, Positional Encoding, the Encoder (on the left), the Decoder (on the right), Linear transformations, and a SoftMax normalization layer. Each layer of the Transformer model contains vital elements, including the Multi-Head Attention mechanism, Feedforward Neural Network, and Masked Multi-Head Attention mechanism.

In the Transformer architecture, the encoder maps the input sequence into a continuous representation, which is then passed to the decoder. The decoder receives the output from the encoder and the output from the decoder at the previous time step, ultimately generating the output sequence. The input embedding layer maps each token in the input sequence to real-valued vectors, enabling the model to manipulate and learn the representation of the input sequence. Positional encoding introduces the positional information of the sequence into the model by adding positional encodings to the embedding vectors, ensuring the model can distinguish variables at different positions. The output embedding layer maps the continuous-valued vectors generated by the model back to discrete symbols, which are used in subsequent tasks, such as generating class labels in text classification and machine translation.

The Multi-Head Attention mechanism extends the standard attention mechanism, allowing the model to focus on different parts of the input sequence across various representation subspaces. After the Self-Attention layer, the representation at each position is passed through a Feedforward Neural Network (FFN), which includes a ReLU activation function. This helps the model capture the nonlinear relationships at each position. The Masked Multi-Head Attention mechanism operates similarly to Multi-Head Attention but is designed to prevent the model from attending to future information during certain computations, ensuring that future data are not leaked at the current time step.

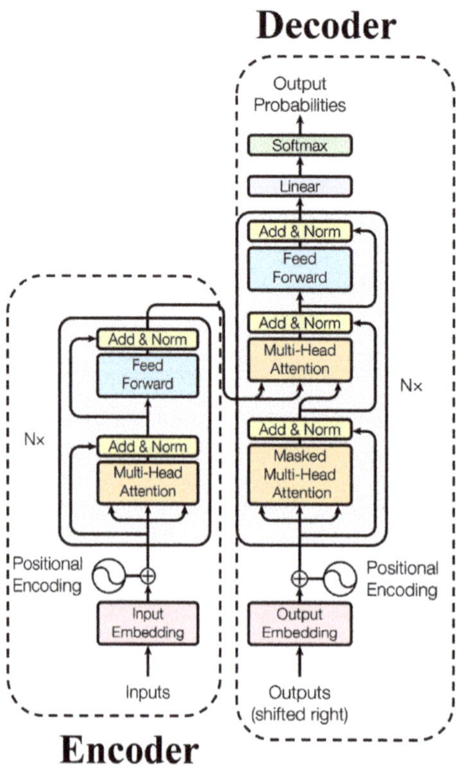

Figure 1. Architecture diagram of the transformer model.

Linear transformation is responsible for linearly projecting the input into a higher-dimensional space, enabling the network to learn features and representations more effectively. Finally, the crucial SoftMax normalization function is applied to classify the input into different categories by calculating the probability distribution across classes [23], providing a robust and reliable classification process.

The data undergo dimensional enhancement in the decoder before entering the Masked Multi-Head Attention layer in the decoder stage. This layer performs the decoding operation, where the query (Q) comes from the decoder's input, while the output of the encoder provides the key (K) and value (V). After training, the Feedforward Neural Network connects to and processes the data via the Add and norm layer. Before the final output, the data pass through another Add and norm layer, and the final computation result is produced [23].

The Transformer model is a Self-Attention structure comprising Scaled Dot-Product Attention and the Multi-Head Attention mechanism. Scaled Dot-Product Attention is the fundamental Self-Attention unit, where the input consists of queries (Q) and keys (K) with a dimension of d_k, and values (V) with a dimension of d_v. In the model proposed by Vaswani et al. [23], the Scaled Dot-Product Attention calculates the output by computing a weighted sum of all keys. Specifically, each key is scaled by $\sqrt{d_k}$, and then, the SoftMax normalization function is applied to compute the weight values.

$$Attention(Q, K, V) = softmax\left(\frac{QK^T}{\sqrt{d_k}}\right)V \tag{1}$$

The Multi-Head Self-Attention mechanism involves multiple attention layers executing in parallel. Instead of applying a single attention function using keys, values, and queries with a dimensionality of d_{model}, the model benefits from using different learned linear projections of the queries, keys, and values into subspaces of dimensions d_k and d_k, and performing attention operations h times. Each query, key, and value operate in parallel within the attention function. The Multi-Head Self-Attention mechanism allows the model to simultaneously focus on different information and subspaces from various positions in the input sequence [23]. The equation for Multi-Head Self-Attention is as follows:

$$MultiHead(Q,K,V) = Concat(head_1, \ldots, head_h)W^O, \ where\ head_i = Attention\left(QW_i^Q, KW_i^K, VW_i^V\right) \tag{2}$$

where the set of Multi-Head Attention (projections) is the parameter matrix $W_i^Q \in R^{d_{model} * d_k}$, $W_i^K \in R^{d_{model} * d_k}$, $W_i^K \in R^{d_{model} * d_v}$, and $W^O \in R^{hd_v * d_{model}}$.

3.2. Gated Recurrent Unit (GRU) and Bidirectional Gated Recurrent Unit (BiGRU)

Figure 2 illustrates the architecture of the Gated Recurrent Unit (GRU) model [24]. As shown in Figure 2, the GRU is a variant of the Long Short-Term Memory (LSTM) model. This model addresses the issues of gradient explosion and gradient vanishing in Recurrent Neural Networks (RNNs) while retaining the predictive performance of LSTM. GRU's structure is more streamlined than that of LSTM, making training more accessible and improving the model training efficiency [25]. The GRU model has only two gates: the update gate and the reset gate, which reduces the computational complexity by eliminating one set of the matrix multiplications found in LSTM. As a result, the GRU model consumes less time when training with large datasets [26]. The following equations describe the architecture of the GRU model:

$$z_t = \sigma(W_z \cdot [h_{t-1}, x_t]) \tag{3}$$

$$r_t = \sigma(W_r \cdot [h_{t-1}, x_t]) \tag{4}$$

$$\widetilde{h_t} = tanh(W \cdot [r_t * h_{t-1}, x_t]) \tag{5}$$

$$h_t = (1 - z_t) * h_{t-1} + z_t * \widetilde{h_t} \tag{6}$$

$$y_t = \sigma(W_o h_t) \tag{7}$$

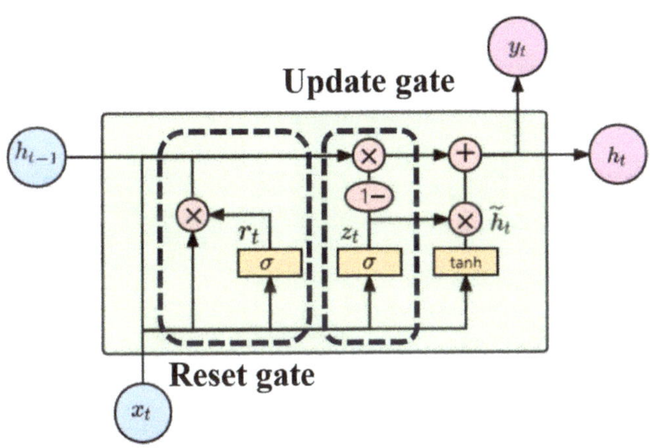

Figure 2. Architecture of the GRU model.

Equation (3) is the equation of the update gate. Update gates are used to control the ratio of past information to current information. $[h_{t-1}, X_t]$ uses the sigmoid function to determine z_t, and z_t allows for memory and forgetting. W_z is the weight matrix of the update gate [24,25]. σ is the sigmoid activation function, which compresses the output to the (0,1) interval and is used for gating structures (update gates and reset gates).

Equation (4) to Equation (6) are the equations of the reset gate. As shown in Equation (4) to Equation (6), tanh is the activation function, which compresses the output to the (−1,1) interval and is used to calculate candidate hidden states. The reset gate is used to forget the previous state information to obtain the post-reset data, and X_t and tanh are used in a scale of [−1,1] to retrieve $\widetilde{h}_t$. x_t and y_t are the input and output of time t, respectively [24,25]. h_{t-1} and h_t are the state output of the hidden layer unit at time $t-1$ and time t, respectively [24]. $(1 - z_t) * h_{t-1}$ is used to forget the previous information in order to facilitate $z_t * \widetilde{h}_t$ to store new data. h_{t-1} is the neuron output at the previous moment, and x_t is the input at the current moment [25]. In the GRU model's architecture equation, r_t and z_t correspond to the outputs of the reset gate and update gate. W_r, W_z, W, and W_o are the weight matrices of the reset gate, update gate, hidden layer unit, and output layer, respectively [24].

In summary, the reset gate r_t allows the model to selectively ignore information from the previous time step, enabling a more flexible capture of short-term dependencies. The update gate z_t controls the proportion of past and new information in the hidden state at the current time step, allowing the model to capture both long-term and short-term dependencies flexibly. The candidate hidden state $\widetilde{h}_t$ is calculated using the current input and partial information from the previous time step, allowing the hidden state to reflect both current information and past influences.

Figure 3 illustrates the architecture of the Bidirectional Gated Recurrent Unit (BiGRU) model [22]. BiGRU is an advanced type of neural network that processes data in both directions, forward and backward. This bidirectional approach allows it to capture information from both the past and future of a data sequence, making it particularly effective for tasks like time series predictions where context from all sides is valuable. As shown in Figure 3, the BiGRU model is a machine-learning model composed of a forward GRU and a backward GRU. The BiGRU model effectively extracts deep features from data by simultaneously performing time series computations in both forward and backward directions. This bidirectional computation mitigates the disadvantage in the standard GRU model, where the input data sequence depends solely on the results from the final time step. Consequently, this approach significantly improves the model's prediction accuracy [24,27].

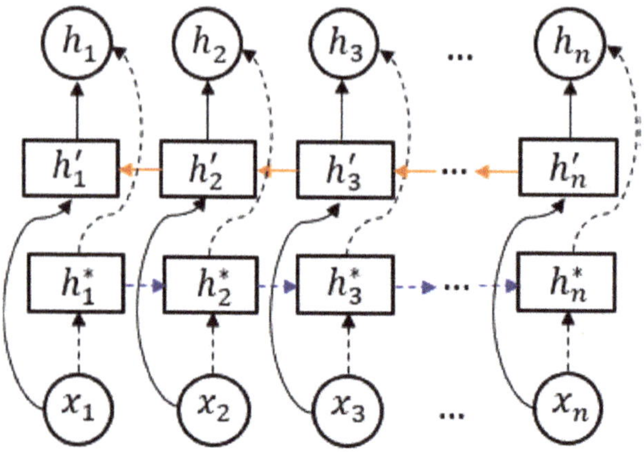

Figure 3. Architecture of the BiGRU model.

In summary, BiGRU processes sequences in both the forward and backward directions, enabling the model to extract more comprehensive information from context [28]. This is particularly effective for tasks that require contextual understanding, such as language comprehension and trend detection in time series forecasting. The forward and backward GRUs include reset and update gates, which control information filtering and updating. Consequently, BiGRU is well-suited for tasks that demand full contextual information, such as natural language processing, time series prediction, and speech recognition.

3.3. *Quick Attention*

Quick Attention (QA) is a simplified and efficient type of attention mechanism that helps the model prioritize important features in data without excessive computational demand. By quickly highlighting essential information, it enhances the model's ability to focus on the most relevant data points, improving prediction accuracy while keeping the processing time low [29]. Figure 4 illustrates its architecture. As shown in the figure, the Quick Attention model performs feature learning by applying a 1 × 1 × C convolution operation on the feature map, enabling the model to focus on extracting relevant features and enhancing global and local feature capture [29]. In the architecture of the Quick Attention model, the input feature map is duplicated twice, followed by 1 × 1 × C convolution operations. The results are then passed through a sigmoid function to compute the attention weights. Finally, the weighted features are added to the original input features, generating the final attention feature map as the output.

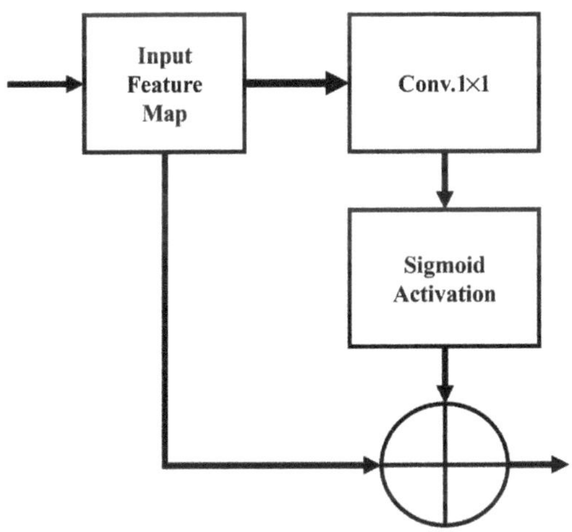

Figure 4. Architecture of the Quick Attention model.

The Quick Attention model focuses on learning essential features, effectively reducing the interference of noisy features and improving the model's stability and prediction accuracy [30]. The following equations describe the architecture of the Quick Attention model:

$$QA(x) = \sigma\left(f(x)^{1\times 1}\right) + x \tag{8}$$

Equation (8) is the architectural equation of the Quick Attention model. As shown in Equation (8), x is the input feature image, and σ is the sigmoid function. In the Quick Attention model, the feature map $f(x)^{1\times 1}$ is a 1 × 1 convolutional layer with a stride of 1 and the same number of filters as the input, ensuring that the output retains the same dimensionality as the input. The input feature image is structured as W × H × C (width × height × channels), and it is duplicated twice before feature analysis begins [29].

Quick Attention simplifies the computational process compared to standard Multi-Head Self-Attention, significantly reducing resource consumption, especially for long sequences. By using attention weights to selectively focus on essential features within a sequence, Quick Attention minimizes the interference of irrelevant features, enhancing the model's predictive accuracy. It balances focused attention and lower computational cost, making it ideal for applications requiring rapid inference or where resources are limited.

3.4. The Proposed Trans-BiGRU-QA Hybrid Model

Figure 5 presents the architecture of the proposed Trans-BiGRU-QA hybrid model in this study. The orange section highlights the Transformer model. The Transformer model performs exceptionally well in data training and preprocessing, with its Self-Attention mechanism capable of simultaneously processing all positions within the input sequence. This mechanism effectively captures long-range dependencies, enabling a better understanding of the internal relationships within the data [23]. Since the original Transformer model's Input Embedding and Positional Encoding are designed to convert signals in Natural Language Processing (NLP) tasks into vectors, and the dataset in this study consists of floating-point data (float); these components were removed. Additionally, considering the scope of the Transformer model's application in this study, the output from the decoder (Transformer Outputs) is not utilized during the initial training phase.

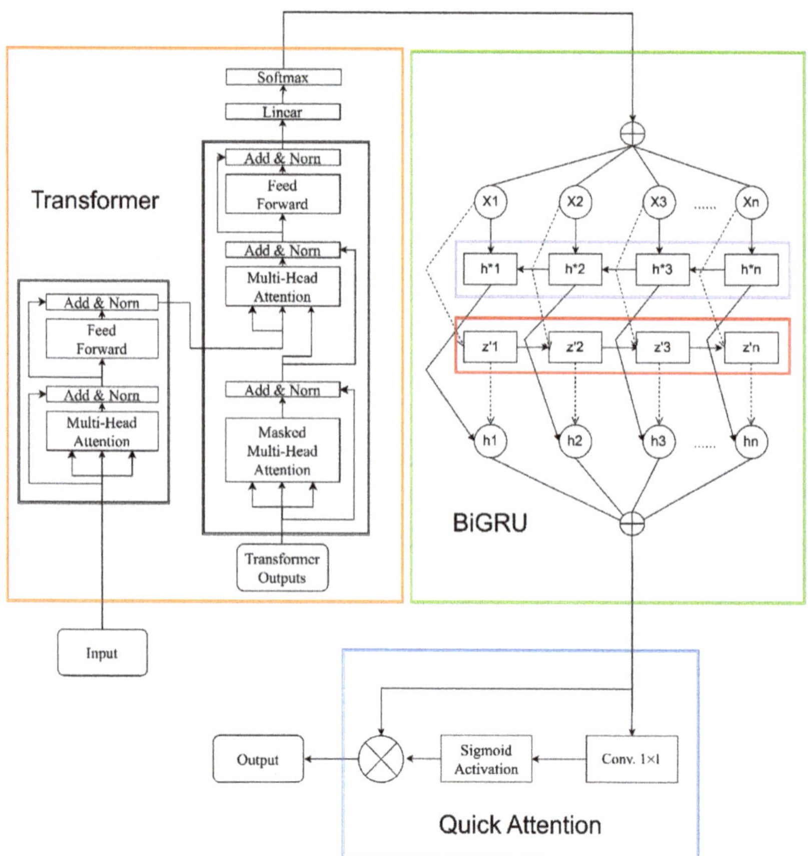

Figure 5. Architecture of the proposed Trans-BiGRU-QA hybrid model.

The hybrid model proposed in this study aims to leverage the advantages of the Multi-Head Attention mechanism to capture long-range dependencies better, thus selecting the Transformer model as the first part of the hybrid structure. The BiGRU model, represented in the green box, is integrated as the middle block. The BiGRU extracts both forward and backward deep features simultaneously, enabling the model to capture deeper data characteristics comprehensively [24,27]. Finally, the Quick Attention mechanism, shown in the blue box, is incorporated at the end of the model to enhance the learning of essential features, thereby improving prediction accuracy and model stability. Since the data predictions in this study are not related to image prediction, the final addition operation in the Quick Attention model is modified to a multiplication-sum operation. By combining the Self-Attention mechanism of the Transformer model, the BiGRU model, and the Quick Attention mechanism, this study aims to improve training speed and prediction accuracy, validating the superiority of the proposed Trans-BiGRU-QA hybrid model.

The hybrid model proposed in this study consists of an input layer (Input) and an output layer (Output), internally integrating the Transformer model, BiGRU model, and Quick Attention mechanism. First, data enter through the input layer and are immediately passed to the encoder part of the Transformer model. Within the encoder, the Multi-Head Attention mechanism processes the data, which learns the internal relationships within the input sequence. The training effectiveness in deep learning is further enhanced through residual connections and normalization (Add & Norm) combined with the Feedforward Neural Network. Once the Feedforward Neural Network training is complete, the data are transmitted via the Add & Norm layer to the decoder. During decoding, the decoder compares the optimal features from the previous time step with the current features, decoding data through the Masked Multi-Head Attention layer. Subsequently, the data pass again through the Add & Norm layer and are processed by the Feedforward Neural Network. Before generating the final output, a linear transformation (Linear) and normalization (SoftMax) are applied to improve the accuracy of the data training further.

Subsequently, the data undergo a summation operation and are passed to the BiGRU model. In the BiGRU model, the input (X) is processed through both forward and backward layers, ultimately generating the output (h). The hidden layers of the BiGRU model consist of X1, X2, X3, . . ., up to Xn. The forward GRU layer (red box) and the backward GRU layer (purple box) extract deep features from the current and the next time step, respectively. For example, taking X1 as a reference, the input X1 is simultaneously passed to the forward GRU layer (z′1) and the backward GRU layer (h1). Since X1 is the first step in the sequence, the forward GRU layer z′1 only receives information from X1, and the backward GRU layer h1 only processes information from X1. These two GRU layers calculate their respective hidden states and combine them to generate the final output h1, which includes the optimal deep features from both the forward and backward GRU layers. This process continues through the sequence, and the final hidden states h1, h2, h3, . . ., up to hn are summed and then passed into the Quick Attention mechanism for further processing.

In the Quick Attention (QA) mechanism, the input feature data are duplicated twice and processed through a $1 \times 1 \times C$ convolution for feature learning. Following this, the sigmoid function is applied to compute the attention weights. The original input features are then combined with the generated results through an element-wise multiplication operation, ultimately producing the Attention data as the final output of the model. The Quick Attention model, through the $1 \times 1 \times C$ convolutional feature learning, focuses on extracting key features, thereby enhancing the model's ability to capture essential data characteristics [29]. QA is a lightweight and efficient attention mechanism that maintains computational efficiency while focusing on a sequence's most representative and relevant parts. BiGRU inherently has bidirectional memory, allowing it to consider a sequence's preceding and succeeding context. However, more than BiGRU alone may still be required in practical applications to capture key features. By integrating QA, the model can quickly focus on critical instantaneous or periodic information within time series data, enhancing

BiGRU's feature-learning capabilities and enabling it to capture essential patterns and characteristics in the data more effectively.

In the Trans-BiGRU-QA model architecture proposed in this study, each component plays a distinct and crucial role in predicting atmospheric mercury concentrations: Transformer: Leveraging its self-attention mechanism, the Transformer effectively captures long-range dependencies within time series data. This is especially important for predicting atmospheric mercury concentrations, as fluctuations in concentration may be related to specific events at past time points. Its Multi-Head Attention mechanism allows the model to learn various patterns or trends in the data from multiple perspectives. For mercury concentration prediction, this means the model can capture both short-term fluctuations and long-term trends, thereby enhancing prediction accuracy.

BiGRU considers both the preceding and succeeding relationships within a sequence, making it particularly effective at capturing contextual information related to changes in mercury concentration. Compared to traditional LSTM, the GRU structure is more straightforward and has fewer parameters, yet it maintains sequential solid modeling capabilities. This makes BiGRU an efficient and stable choice, helping to improve model efficiency, reduce the risk of overfitting, and enhance stability in sequence prediction tasks.

In the Trans-BiGRU-QA model, QA filters and enhances vital features. The QA mechanism focuses on critical information, such as significant variation points or periodic patterns based on the feature distribution of atmospheric mercury concentrations, rather than processing all data points equally. Its lightweight design enables faster attention operations, avoiding the high computational cost of traditional Self-Attention mechanisms. This efficiency advantage of QA is precious when handling large-scale environmental data.

3.5. Evaluation Metrics

To evaluate the accuracy of the prediction models, this study employed multiple evaluation metrics to determine the precision and relative advantages of the experimental models. Specifically, Mean Absolute Error (MAE), Root Mean Square Error (RMSE), and the coefficient of determination (R^2) were used to assess the performance of deep learning models in predicting atmospheric mercury levels. RMSE provides an immediate reflection of the deviation between actual and predicted values, while MAE measures the absolute difference between the actual and predicted values [31]. Additionally, the R^2 coefficient is used to evaluate the model's and the dataset's fit, exploring the correlation between the actual and predicted values [31,32].

MAE directly measures the model's prediction accuracy, assessing the degree of deviation between predicted and actual observed values. In atmospheric mercury concentration prediction, MAE helps to understand the model's average error in daily data fluctuations, reflecting its accuracy under typical conditions. RMSE, as the square root of the Mean Squared Error (MSE), is more sensitive to larger error values. When the model exhibits significant prediction deviations for specific samples, RMSE magnifies these outlier errors, indicating the model's performance in handling high-error cases. R^2 provides an intuitive understanding of the model's fit to the data. In complex and variable data such as mercury concentration, R^2 helps determine whether the model effectively captures the main trends in concentration changes

Through the combined evaluation of MAE, RMSE, and R^2, the model's effectiveness in predicting atmospheric mercury concentration can be assessed from various perspectives. MAE and RMSE provide insight into the range of errors, while R^2 reflects the model's ability to explain the variance in the data. Using these metrics together allows for a more comprehensive understanding of the model's strengths and weaknesses, facilitating targeted adjustments and optimizations to enhance reliability in practical applications.

The following are the equations for calculating the Mean Absolute Error (MAE), Root Mean Square Error (RMSE), and the coefficient of determination (R^2):

$$\text{MAE} = \frac{1}{\text{N}} \sum_{i=1}^{n} |\hat{y} - y| \tag{9}$$

$$\text{RMSE} = \sqrt{\frac{1}{\text{N}} \sum_{i=1}^{n} (\hat{y} - y)^2} \tag{10}$$

4. Data Description

The data used in this study came from the Vietnam air pollution dataset. Table 3 summarizes the attributes of this dataset. As shown in Table 3, the dataset contains 1272 data entries spanning from 13 September 2022 to 21 June 2023. The dataset includes six input variables, $X_1(t)$ to $X_6(t)$, which are in the following order: Temperature (Temp), Relative Humidity (RH), Fine Particulate Matter ($PM_{2.5}$), Carbon Dioxide (CO_2), Total Gaseous Mercury (TGM), and the current Atmospheric Mercury Concentration (Hg(t)). The output variable, Y_{t+1}, represents the atmospheric mercury concentration at the next time step (Hg(t + 1)).

Table 3. Summary of data attributes.

Variable	Name	Description	Data Type	Update Frequency	Unit
$X_1(t)$	Temp	Physical quantity representing air temperature	Float	Hourly	°C
$X_2(t)$	RH	Predicted probability of rainfall in meteorology	Float	Hourly	%
$X_3(t)$	$PM_{2.5}$	Fine particulate matter harmful to human health	Float	Hourly	ug/m^3
$X_4(t)$	CO_2	Major greenhouse gas contributing to global warming	Float	Hourly	ppm
$X_5(t)$	TGM	Chemical component affecting human health	Float	Hourly	ng/m^3
$X_6(t)$	Hg(t)	Current atmospheric mercury index	Float	Hourly	ng/m^3
Y_{t+1}	Hg(t + 1)	Predicted atmospheric mercury index for the next hour	Float	Hourly	ng/m^3

Additionally, this study summarized the air variables used in previous research in Table 3 to further explore the relationship between the air prediction variables and atmospheric mercury index in this study. Such analysis will help reveal the impact of different air pollutants on the atmospheric mercury concentration and enhance the accuracy of the model's predictions.

The data type used in this study was floating-point (Float), with the data being updated hourly daily. According to the publicly available Air Quality Index data provided by Taiwan's Environmental Protection Agency's Air Quality Monitoring Network (https://airtw.moenv.gov.tw/, accessed on 1 July 2023), the existing publicly available data are updated hourly and daily. Therefore, this study utilized the existing input variables $X_1(t)$ to $X_6(t)$ to predict the atmospheric mercury index for the next hour using the model, allowing for an analysis of the distribution of mercury in the air. Some indirect factors can also directly influence the concentration of mercury in the atmosphere and air pollution, including:

- Volatility of Mercury: Mercury exists in various forms in the environment and can enter the human body through air, food, and water. The primary sources of mercury emissions are industrial activities, waste incineration, and coal-fired power generation. Mercury typically remains in the air as particulate-bound mercury and gaseous mercury [33]. The temperature is one of the critical factors influencing mercury volatility. Under high-temperature conditions, mercury tends to volatilize more easily [34]. Higher temperatures may increase the volatility of certain mercury compounds, thereby exacerbating mercury pollution [34,35]. Mercury's high volatility and low water solubility significantly contribute to air pollution [36].

- Effect of Humidity in the Atmosphere: Mercury is a heavy metal element with intense volatility [36]. The relative humidity can influence the volatility of mercury, as higher humidity levels cause water molecules in the air to bind with mercury atoms, forming mercury hydrates. This process reduces the volatility of mercury [37,38]. In environments with high relative humidity, mercury pollution can worsen due to the decreased ability of mercury to volatilize effectively, leading to its accumulation in the atmosphere.
- Mercury and Fine Particulate Matter: Mercury pollution threatens the environment and human health [3,4]. Fine particulate matter ($PM_{2.5}$) is one of the central air pollutants and can bind with mercury, prolonging the time mercury remains suspended in the air. In environments with higher concentrations of fine particulate matter, the pollution level of mercury increases as the particles enhance mercury's persistence in the atmosphere [37,38].
- Mercury and Carbon Dioxide: The interaction between mercury and carbon dioxide is an often-unnoticed environmental issue. Carbon dioxide can combine with mercury to form compounds, increasing the amount of mercury in the environment. Mercury–carbon dioxide compounds are insoluble in water, and their presence raises mercury levels in the environment, exacerbating mercury pollution [37]. With global climate change, mercury pollution may pose even more significant environmental hazards [39,40].

The interactions between mercury and factors such as volatility, humidity effects, fine particulate matter, and carbon dioxide reveal that mercury can indirectly influence atmospheric mercury concentrations through these air variables. This, in turn, contributes to air pollution and poses risks to human health and the living environment [33,36–38].

4.1. Feature Engineering

Feature engineering is constructing features (input variables), selecting them based on domain knowledge, modifying them, or enhancing the efficiency of machine learning methods [41]. The feature engineering process in this study consists of five stages: feature adjustment, feature transformation, feature normalization, dimensionality reduction, and feature importance assessment.

This study employed feature engineering methods, including feature adjustment, feature normalization, and feature importance assessment, to conduct data preprocessing and feature comparison. Feature adjustment aims to modify the data to reduce skewness appropriately [41] and eliminate abnormal data, such as missing or erroneous values, which may distort training performance [42]. Feature normalization enhances the model's training efficiency and convergence speed by scaling all features to a uniform numerical range [41]. Finally, feature importance assessment is used to measure the contribution of each feature in the machine learning model's prediction process and evaluate its impact on the model's predictive results.

4.1.1. Feature Adjustment

Feature adjustment involves the appropriate transformation or modification of data to reduce skewness. This process includes mathematically correcting heavily skewed or unevenly distributed data, bringing them closer to a normal distribution. Thus, positive or negative skewness in the distribution can be effectively corrected, making the data more symmetric [41]. Incorrect or missing data and other anomalies may distort the training performance [42]. Even if the dataset does not contain explicit errors, there may still be anomalous elements that differ from other patterns within the dataset. Advanced methods for detecting outliers in data samples extend beyond measuring average time intervals; they can fit the observed data within a set period to a curve, allowing for direct comparisons [43]. In this study, the dataset's missing data handling and outlier detection were performed using SPSS 25. Missing values were imputed through linear interpolation, while outlier detection commonly utilized Cook's Distance to assess anomalies in the data. Cook's Distance is a statistical measure used to evaluate the degree of change in the parameter estimates of a regression model when a particular observation is removed.

Cook's Distance is calculated as follows:

$$D_i = \frac{\sum_{j=1}^{n}\left(\hat{y}_j - \hat{y}_{j(i)}\right)^2}{\rho \cdot MSE} \tag{11}$$

D_i represents the Cook's Distance for the i-th observation, where $\hat{y}_j$ is the predicted value of the j-th observation when all data points are included, and $\hat{y}_{j(i)}$ is the predicted value of the j-th observation after removing the i-th observation. ρ denotes the number of estimated parameters in the model (including the intercept). The Mean Squared Error (MSE) is used to standardize Cook's Distance, allowing for the comparability of distances across different models. Cook's Distance can be viewed as a measure of the overall change in model predictions after removing a particular observation, with standardization by MSE to ensure consistency across models.

Before conducting deep learning training, this study performed outlier detection and data cleaning. During the data cleaning process, missing values, anomalies, and duplicate data were removed to ensure that the data fell within normal ranges. This process also minimized the impact of outliers on the model's prediction accuracy, ensuring that the dataset was clean and reliable for training.

4.1.2. Feature Normalization

Feature normalization involves scaling all features to the exact numerical range to improve model training effectiveness and speed up convergence [41]. Data normalization transforms data into a specific range, such as scaling it between −1 and 1, or between 0 and 1. Normalization becomes especially important when the numerical ranges of different features in the dataset vary significantly. When there are no missing values or anomalies in the dataset, Min-max scaling is a beneficial normalization technique [44]. This study applied Min-max scaling to normalize the air pollution dataset. The equation for Min-max normalization is as follows:

$$X' = \frac{x - min}{max - min} \tag{12}$$

Equation (12) is the equation for data normalization. X' is the normalized data, x is the denormalized data, and min and max have the same values used previously in the normalization process.

4.1.3. Feature Importance Evaluation

Feature importance assessment measures the contribution of each feature during the model prediction process and evaluates its impact on the machine learning model's predictive outcomes. Through this process, researchers can identify the features that significantly influence model performance, enabling model optimization and selecting the best features [45]. This study used Pearson correlation coefficients and SHAP values to assess feature importance. First, the Pearson correlation coefficient was used to observe the relationships among the five variables: Atmospheric Mercury (TGM), Temperature (Temp), Relative Humidity (RH), $PM_{2.5}$, and Carbon Dioxide (CO_2). Second, SHAP values were applied to quantify each feature's contribution to the prediction outcomes, helping to identify which features are most critical to the model's overall performance.

4.2. Sliding Window

In this study, the variables of the data attributes in Table 3 were added to $\mathbf{X}_t = \{X_1(t), X_2(t), \ldots, X_6(t)\}$. The details of the variables in the sliding window of this study are shown in Figure 6.

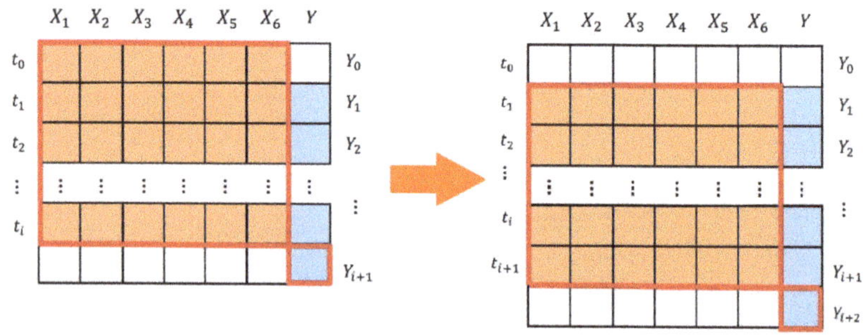

Figure 6. Sliding window with a width of $i + 1$.

Figure 6 illustrates the sliding window equation with a width of $i + 1$. As shown in Figure 6, the process begins from the left side, where there is no output data for the initial value t_0; so, it is excluded, and the first output is set as Y_{i+1}. The input variables, X_1 to X_6, are the predictive features, including Temperature (Temp), Relative Humidity (RH), Fine Particulate Matter ($PM_{2.5}$), Carbon Dioxide (CO_2), Total Gaseous Mercury (TGM), and Current Atmospheric Mercury (Hg(t)). The output variable, Y, represents the next hour's Atmospheric Mercury Index (Hg(t + 1)). In the prediction process, t_i represents the time the prediction is made, with iii indicating the corresponding data point. For instance, at t_0, the input variables $X_1(t)$ to $X_6(t)$ are used to predict the next hour's atmospheric mercury index (Y_{i+1}), which corresponds to the prediction for the next state, t_1. Once the prediction for (Y_{i+1}) is completed, the process moves forward to predict the next hour's atmospheric mercury index (Y_{i+2}), as shown from left to right in the figure. In this study, the input air variables and current atmospheric mercury levels were combined to predict the next atmospheric mercury value, thereby analyzing the gas distribution of mercury over time.

The window size is carefully selected to balance between capturing a comprehensive history of the time series data and keeping the dataset manageable for efficient processing in this study. A smaller window size might be more responsive but could miss longer-term patterns, while a larger window size captures more historical context at the cost of increased computational load and potential overfitting. In this study, the window size was optimized based on validation tests to maximize predictive accuracy without compromising the model's responsiveness to recent data changes.

At the beginning of the prediction series, where there are insufficient data to fill the window, specific strategies were implemented to avoid inaccuracies. Our approach was padding, where initial values are filled with zeros or the first available data point, ensuring consistent window size without introducing abrupt changes. Alternatively, predictions may start only after the window is fully populated, which provides stable and reliable input data for the model without needing artificial adjustments.

5. Experiment and Discussion

5.1. Experimental Process

Figure 7 illustrates the experimental workflow of this study. At the beginning of the research, atmospheric mercury air data underwent feature engineering, which included feature adjustment, feature normalization, and feature importance assessment for data preprocessing and feature comparison. (1). Feature Adjustment: Outlier detection and data cleaning is the first step. Outlier detection aims to modify the data by reducing skewness and effectively correcting skewed distributions, making the data more symmetric. Data cleaning removes erroneous data and missing values to enhance the effectiveness of data training. (2). Feature Normalization: This step scales all features to a uniform numerical range to improve the model's training performance. The Min-max method is applied to optimize the model's training efficiency. (3). Feature Importance Assessment: The final step involves evaluating the importance of features by exploring their relationships using a Pearson correlation matrix. SHAP values are then used to quantify each feature's contribution to the prediction, highlighting the most significant features for the model's performance. This comprehensive process ensures that the data are well-prepared for the predictive modeling phase and that the most important features are identified to enhance model accuracy.

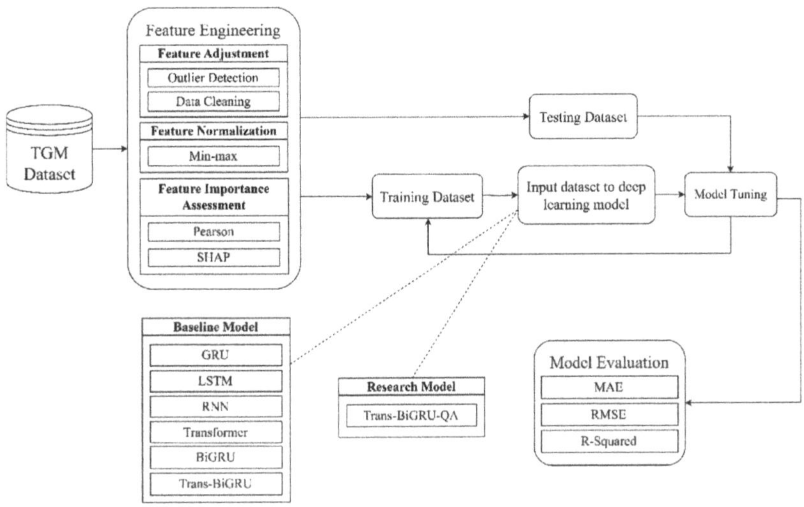

Figure 7. Flowchart of the experimental process.

Next, the data were split into training and testing sets, and the datasets were fed into baseline models for training. The baseline models included Gated Recurrent Unit (GRU), Long Short-Term Memory (LSTM), Recurrent Neural Network (RNN), Transformer, Bidirectional Gated Recurrent Unit (BiGRU), and the hybrid Transformer and Bidirectional Gated Recurrent Unit model (Trans-BiGRU). These models were compared with the proposed Trans-BiGRU-QA hybrid model through benchmarking tests. Model hyperparameter tuning and data validation were conducted during the training process. The model performance was evaluated using metrics such as Mean Absolute Error (MAE), Root Mean Square Error (RMSE), and the coefficient of determination R^2 (R-Squared). Each baseline and hybrid model was run ten times, and the average MAE and RMSE were used as the final evaluation metrics. The standard deviation (STD) was calculated to assess the stability of the models. This study employed grid search to optimize the proposed model's hyperparameter settings to identify the best hyperparameters and achieve the most accurate predictions. This process ensures that the model is finely tuned for optimal performance in predicting atmospheric mercury concentrations.

The dataset used in this study came from Vietnam and is related to air pollution. The original dataset consists of 1272 records, covering from 13 September 2022 to 21 June 2023. Table 4 summarizes the descriptive statistics for all variables. The table includes the count of data entries for each variable (Count), minimum value (Min), median value (Median), mean value (Mean), maximum value (Max), and standard deviation (STD). The detailed statistical results are presented in Table 4. This descriptive analysis not only provides an overview of the distribution and variability of the variables but also offers valuable insights into the data, enhancing their value for model training and evaluation.

Table 4. Descriptive statistics of all variables.

Variables	Count	Min	Median	Mean	Max	STD
TGM	1272	1.297	2.031	2.134	4.66	0.558
Temp	1272	23.262	28.445	29.104	38.735	3.04
RH	1272	34.354	77.025	74.306	94.254	12.718
$PM_{2.5}$	1272	1.003	32.938	35.057	264.416	19.347
CO_2	1272	390.312	421.638	426.938	529.913	22.038
$Hg(t)$	1272	1.297	2.031	2.135	4.66	0.558

To enhance the accuracy of data predictions, it is necessary to split the entire dataset into subsets and establish separate models based on different conditions during the data processing phase. This approach relies on large datasets to provide sufficient data for training and testing each model [46]. In this study, a 70:30 ratio divided the dataset for training and testing. After feature adjustment in the feature engineering process, the total number of available data entries was 1245. The training dataset covered from 13 September 2022 to 10 January 2023, representing 70% of the total data. The testing datasets spanned from 11 January 2023 to 21 June 2023, representing 30% of the total data.

5.2. Experimental Parameter Settings

5.2.1. Environment Setup

This study used PyCharm as the development environment and Python version 3.11 as the programming language. The libraries used for machine learning model analysis included Pandas, Numpy, Matplotlib, and Scikit-learn. The hardware configuration for the experiments is outlined in Table 5. This setup ensured compatibility with the required libraries and provided the necessary computational resources for executing the machine-learning models efficiently.

Table 5. Specifications of the experimental equipment.

Name	Model/Version
Operating System	Windows 10 22H2
Processor	Intel Core i7-13700
Memory	ADATA DDR4-3200 64G
SSD	Kingston KC3000 1TB
Graphics Card	Nvidia GeForce RTX 3060

5.2.2. Hyperparameter Experiment Setup

To perform model tuning, this study employed grid search to find the optimal parameters during the training of the learning model. The experimental steps were as follows: (1). Extract the raw data. (2). Partition of the raw data into training and testing sets. (3). Adjust or create machine learning model objects. (4). In Scikit-learn, set up and instantiate the grid search method. (5). Fit the grid search model to the data, identifying the best parameters and model for prediction [31]. Various combinations were tested during the parameter selection process, and the best-performing parameters were chosen as the final result. This approach ensured that the most influential parameter configuration was selected for accurate and efficient model predictions.

The learning rate is a crucial parameter that affects the convergence speed of the model. If the learning rate is too large, it may cause the model to fail to converge; if the learning rate is too low, while it may more stably find the global optimum, the convergence speed will be slower, and it might not reach the optimal value within an acceptable number of training epochs [31]. Epochs refer to the number of times the entire dataset is passed through the model during training, while batch size determines the number of samples fed into the model before each weight update. Balancing these parameters is critical to achieving efficient and accurate model training.

Additionally, the Num_head parameter in the Transformer model determines the number of attention heads in the Multi-Head Attention mechanism. The Multi-Head mechanism enables the model to focus on different parts of the input, and increasing the number of heads can improve the model's ability to capture diverse spatiotemporal features [47]. The Key_dim defines the dimension of each attention head responsible for processing the internal information within the model, and it influences both the complexity and the processing capability of the model [47].

Table 6 summarizes the reference literature for the GRU, LSTM, RNN, Transformer, BiGRU, and Trans-BiGRU models, providing a detailed comparison of their hyperparameter settings, including Batch_size, Epoch, Learning rate, Num_head, and Key_dim.

Table 6. Summary of hyperparameter tuning.

Model	Batch_Size	Epoch	Learning Rate	Num_Head	Key_Dim
GRU	128	30	0.001	-	-
LSTM	[1, 100]	-	[0, 0.01]	-	-
RNN	100	[100, 500]	0.01	-	
Transformer	32	8	1×10^{-4}	4	8
BiGRU	128	100	0.005	-	-
Trans-BiGRU	150	150	0.005	4	8

5.2.3. Parameter Settings of the Proposed Trans-BiGRU-QA Hybrid Model

This study's proposed Trans-BiGRU-QA hybrid model integrates the characteristics of the Transformer model, BiGRU model, and Quick Attention mechanism. This study's batch size was set to 32, the epochs to 100, and the learning rate to 0.0001.

In the hybrid Trans-BiGRU-QA model, the fully connected layer (Dense layer) was set to 64 neurons. Additionally, since this study introduced the Quick Attention mechanism to enhance the extraction of data features, the fully connected layer in the Quick Attention model (Dense_layer—QA) was set to 32 neurons. The BiGRU layer, responsible for capturing both forward and backward deep learning features, was set to 64 neurons in the BiGRU model. In the Transformer model, the default values for the Multi-Head mechanism (Num_head) and the size of each head (Key_dim) were set to 4 and 64, respectively. In the initial design phase, default hyperparameters were used for experimentation, and future experiments will employ grid search to optimize and progressively determine the best model parameter settings. Table 7 outlines the detailed parameter settings for the Trans-BiGRU-QA hybrid model.

Table 7. Parameter settings of the Trans-BiGRU-QA hybrid model.

Model	Batch_Size	Epoch	Learning Rate	Dense_Layer
Trans-BiGRU-QA	32	100	0.0001	64
	Dense_layer(QA)	BiGRU layer	Num_head	Key_dim
	32	64	4	64

In the Trans-BiGRU-QA model, the results obtained from grid search hyperparameter tuning include several fields, each representing different hyperparameter configurations within the model. Batch size indicates the number of samples used in each parameter update, while epoch refers to the total number of complete learning cycles over the entire training dataset. Learning rate controls the step size during each parameter update; a smaller learning rate, such as 0.0001, enhances training stability, reducing the risk of overshooting the optimal solution, which is particularly suitable for complex deep learning models. The dense layer denotes the number of units in the fully connected layer. Num_head represents the number of heads in the Multi-Head Attention mechanism within Quick Attention. At the same time, Key_dim specifies the dimensionality of the Key vector for each head in the attention mechanism, set to 64 in this paper, meaning that each head's Key vector contained 64 dimensions.

5.3. Experimental Results

5.3.1. Performance Comparison of Each Model

To evaluate the accuracy of the predictive models, this study employed several performance metrics to compare the precision of each model. Table 8 presents a performance comparison using Mean Absolute Error (MAE), Root Mean Square Error (RMSE), and R-squared (R^2) as critical evaluation criteria for the predictive models. Standard deviation (STD) is an essential indicator for assessing model performance, particularly in deep-learning model evaluations. Standard deviation is often used to measure the variability of results across multiple experimental runs, allowing researchers to assess the stability of model performance. A more minor standard deviation indicates more stable model performance. In this study, the standard deviation was used to evaluate the stability of each model. The MAE, RMSE, and R-squared values in Table 8 represent the average of ten runs for each model. The table also includes the average MAE and RMSE values and their respective standard deviations for each model.

Table 8. Performance comparison of each model.

	MAE ± SD	**RMSE ± SD**	$\mathbf{R^2}$
GRU	$0.0567 \pm 7.63 \times 10^{-4}$	$0.0860 \pm 3.82 \times 10^{-4}$	0.69
LSTM	$0.0939 \pm 4.10 \times 10^{-4}$	$0.1260 \pm 2.72 \times 10^{-4}$	0.34
RNN	$0.0930 \pm 46.44 \times 10^{-4}$	$0.1197 \pm 34.38 \times 10^{-4}$	0.33
Transformer	$0.0644 \pm 19.54 \times 10^{-4}$	$0.0909 \pm 22.14 \times 10^{-4}$	0.66
BiGRU	$0.0574 \pm 39.94 \times 10^{-4}$	$0.0865 \pm 38.49 \times 10^{-4}$	0.69
Trans-BiGRU	$0.0543 \pm 18.29 \times 10^{-4}$	$0.0817 \pm 22.44 \times 10^{-4}$	0.67
Trans-BiGRU-QA	$0.0509 \pm 15.80 \times 10^{-4}$	$0.0787 \pm 19.14 \times 10^{-4}$	0.72

Based on the performance comparison in Table 8, the results for each model are as follows:

- GRU model: MAE = $0.0567 \pm 7.63 \times 10^{-4}$, RMSE = $0.0860 \pm 3.82 \times 10^{-4}$, R-squared = 0.69.
- LSTM model: MAE = $0.0939 \pm 4.10 \times 10^{-4}$, RMSE = $0.1260 \pm 2.72 \times 10^{-4}$, R-squared = 0.34.
- RNN model: MAE = $0.0930 \pm 46.44 \times 10^{-4}$, RMSE = $0.1197 \pm 34.38 \times 10^{-4}$, R-squared = 0.33.
- Transformer model: MAE = $0.0644 \pm 19.54 \times 10^{-4}$, RMSE = $0.0909 \pm 22.14 \times 10^{-4}$, R-squared = 0.66.
- BiGRU model: MAE = $0.0574 \pm 39.94 \times 10^{-4}$, RMSE = $0.0865 \pm 38.49 \times 10^{-4}$, R-squared = 0.69.
- Trans-BiGRU model: MAE = $0.0543 \pm 18.29 \times 10^{-4}$, RMSE = $0.0817 \pm 22.44 \times 10^{-4}$, R-squared = 0.67.
- For the proposed Trans-BiGRU-QA hybrid model, the results are: MAE = $0.0509 \pm 15.80 \times 10^{-4}$, RMSE = $0.0787 \pm 19.14 \times 10^{-4}$, and R-squared = 0.72.

Compared to baseline models such as GRU, LSTM, and RNN, the Trans-BiGRU-QA model demonstrates significant advantages across the evaluation metrics MAE, RMSE, and R-squared. The lowest MAE and RMSE indicate that the Trans-BiGRU-QA model excels in average deviation and performance on high-error samples, capturing the finer fluctuations in atmospheric mercury concentration more accurately. The lower MAE and RMSE suggest that this model exhibits more minor prediction deviations in typical and anomalous cases than the other baseline models. The highest R-squared value signifies that the Trans-BiGRU-QA model can better explain the total variance in concentration data, indicating a more precise capturing of overall trends. This is particularly important for analyzing long-term dependencies in time series data. However, the computational time for this hybrid model may be longer than that of the other baseline models.

After multiple runs, the evaluation metrics (MAE, RMSE, and R^2) showed minimal variation, indicating that the model is not sensitive to the randomness of the training data and exhibits stable performance. Consistently outperforming baseline models across multiple runs suggests a low variability in model performance. This demonstrates that the Trans-BiGRU-QA model architecture and training process are relatively stable.

These results indicate that the Trans-BiGRU-QA hybrid model outperforms the other models in both performance and stability, as reflected by the lower MAE and RMSE values, the higher R-squared, and the more minor standard deviations. This shows that the proposed model is more accurate and consistent in predicting atmospheric mercury concentrations.

The performance of LSTM, RNN, and GRU in predicting the atmospheric mercury concentration (as measured by MAE, RMSE, and R^2) is inferior to that of the Trans-BiGRU-QA model, likely due to their relatively limited ability to capture long-term dependencies. In contrast, the Self-Attention mechanism in the Transformer component enables Trans-BiGRU-QA to capture distant dependencies within the data, providing the model an advantage in forecasting long-term trends. Additionally, LSTM and RNN are typically unidirectional, meaning they process sequences in a single direction, from past to future. In contrast, BiGRU is bidirectional and can consider the past and future contexts within a sequence.

Moreover, LSTM, RNN, and GRU lack an Attention mechanism, which limits their ability to selectively adjust the influence of different time points or features, leading to a poorer performance when handling data with high diversity and randomness. The Quick Attention (QA) mechanism in Trans-BiGRU-QA plays a crucial role by enabling the model to focus on features closely related to changes in atmospheric mercury concentration, reducing the impact of noise on prediction outcomes and thereby enhancing model accuracy and stability.

The Mean Absolute Error (MAE) measures the absolute difference between the actual and predicted values. At the same time, the Root Mean Square Error (RMSE) reflects the deviation between the actual results and predictions in real time [31]. According to the equations for MAE and RMSE, the smaller the values, the better the model's performance. The proposed Trans-BiGRU-QA hybrid model, which incorporates the Quick Attention mechanism, had experimental results where the MAE and RMSE were smaller than those of other single models and more accurate than those of the Trans-BiGRU hybrid model.

Including the Quick Attention mechanism enhances the model's prediction accuracy, as evidenced by the R-squared value, which reaches 0.72. This proves that the Trans-BiGRU-QA hybrid model is the best-performing model in this study, providing both a superior accuracy and stability compared to the other models.

LSTM and GRU have their strengths in time series modeling, particularly excelling at capturing short-term contextual dependencies. However, when long-term dependencies exist within a sequence, these models may need help to retain the influence of earlier information, presenting limitations in capturing distant dependencies. While LSTM and GRU can model contextual dependencies within sequences, more than a unidirectional structure is needed to consider past and future information as effectively as BiGRU. By utilizing bidirectional memory, BiGRU can more comprehensively capture both long-term and short-term dependencies within a sequence, which enhances coherence in mercury concentration prediction tasks.

In the Trans-BiGRU-QA model, the Quick Attention mechanism further enhances feature selection capability. It quickly focuses on information highly relevant to mercury concentration changes, suppressing noise and minimizing the influence of non-essential data on prediction outcomes. Quick Attention intensifies focus on specific features, increasing the model's attention to critical data points, leading to a superior performance across evaluation metrics such as MAE, RMSE, and R^2. This design improves prediction accuracy and strengthens the model's ability to interpret long-term dependency data, demonstrating robust performance in atmospheric mercury concentration forecasting.

Figure 8 and Table 8 present the bar chart of MAE and RMSE for each model. To compare the predictive performance and accuracy of single models versus the hybrid model, this study plotted a bar chart displaying the MAE and RMSE values for a clear and intuitive comparison of each model's performance. The bar chart, from left to right, shows the MAE and RMSE data for the GRU, LSTM, RNN, Transformer, BiGRU, Trans-BiGRU, and Trans-BiGRU-QA models.

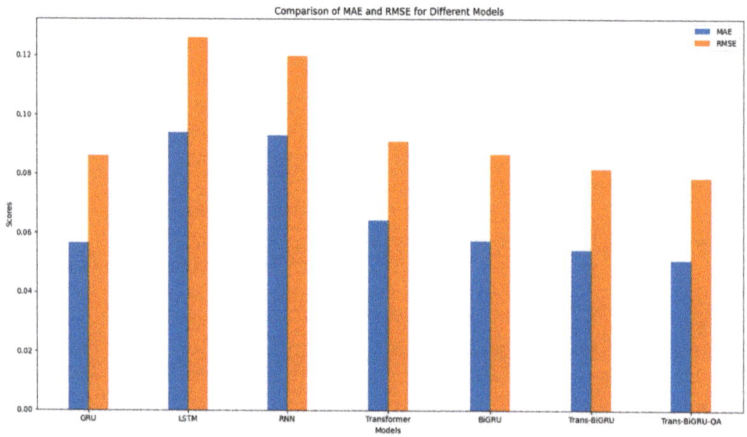

Figure 8. Bar chart of MAE and RMSE for each model.

As Figure 7 depicts, the proposed Trans-BiGRU-QA hybrid model exhibits significantly lower MAE and RMSE values than the other single and hybrid models. This result further confirms the superior predictive accuracy of the Trans-BiGRU-QA hybrid model, establishing it as the best-performing model in the study.

Figures 9–12 show the scatter plots of the predicted and actual values for the GRU, LSTM, RNN, Transformer, BiGRU, Trans-BiGRU, and Trans-BiGRU-QA models, respectively. These scatter plots compare the predictive performance of each model and identify outliers, providing a visual representation of the relationship between predicted values and actual values. In the plots, the X-axis represents the actual values, and the Y-axis represents the predicted values. Each point represents a sample, comparing the actual value with the model's prediction. The closer the points are to the diagonal line, the more accurate the model's predictions are. Points that deviate significantly from the diagonal indicate less accurate predictions or potential outliers.

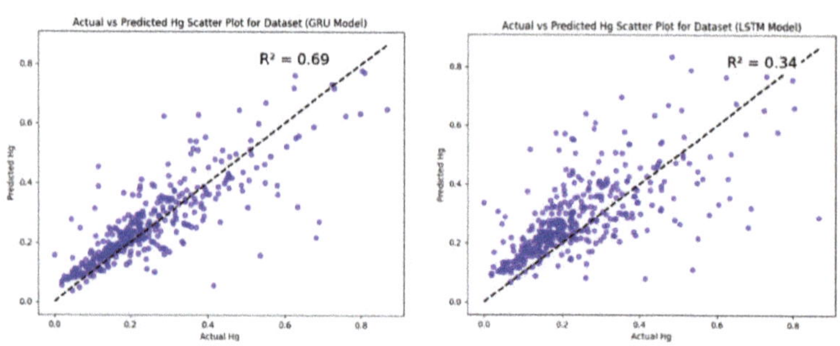

(**a**) (**b**)

Figure 9. GRU (**a**) and LSTM (**b**) model predictions, respectively.

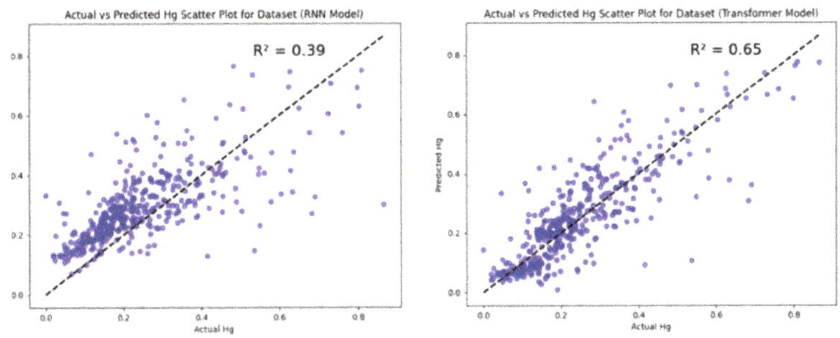

(a) (b)

Figure 10. RNN (**a**) and Transformer (**b**) model predictions, respectively.

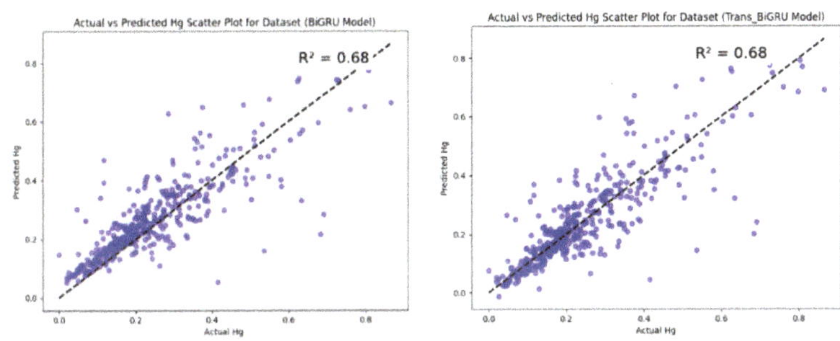

(a) (b)

Figure 11. BiGRU (**a**) and Tran-BiGRU (**b**) model predictions, respectively.

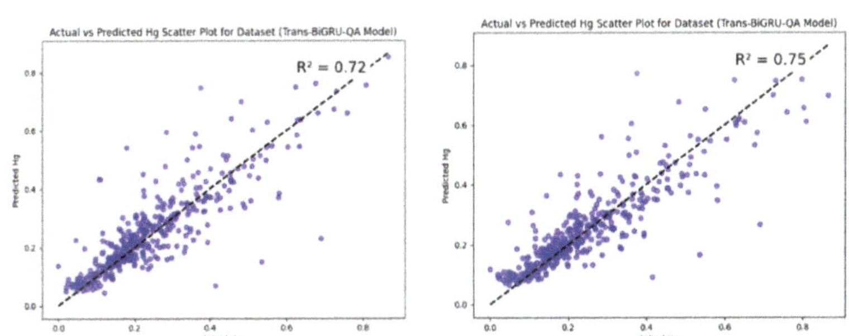

(a) (b)

Figure 12. Trans-BiGRU-QA model predictions (**a**,**b**).

Figures 9–12 show that the GRU model demonstrates a relatively dense distribution of the actual and predicted values, indicating a good predictive accuracy. In contrast, the LSTM and RNN models show more dispersed distributions, reflecting a poorer performance in matching the actual values with the predictions.

The scatter points for the Transformer, BiGRU, and Trans-BiGRU models are more closely grouped and show a more stable predictive performance compared to the LSTM and RNN models. These models exhibit a more consistent alignment between the predicted and actual values, though there is still room for improvement in their predictive precision.

As shown in Figure 12a, the proposed Trans-BiGRU-QA hybrid model demonstrates a points distribution that aligns closely with the diagonal line, indicating a higher predictive accuracy. The model achieved an R-squared value of 0.72, confirming its superior performance compared to the other models.

This study employed grid search to further optimize the hyperparameters of the Trans-BiGRU-QA hybrid model during the training process. Figure 12b displays the scatter plot of data predictions after applying the optimized hyperparameters using grid search. Figure 12b shows that, after hyperparameter optimization, the model's predictive accuracy improved further, with the R-squared value increasing to 0.75. This demonstrates an even stronger model performance, highlighting the effectiveness of grid search in fine-tuning the Trans-BiGRU-QA model for optimal results.

Figure 13 shows the line chart of the actual vs. predicted values for the Trans-BiGRU-QA model.

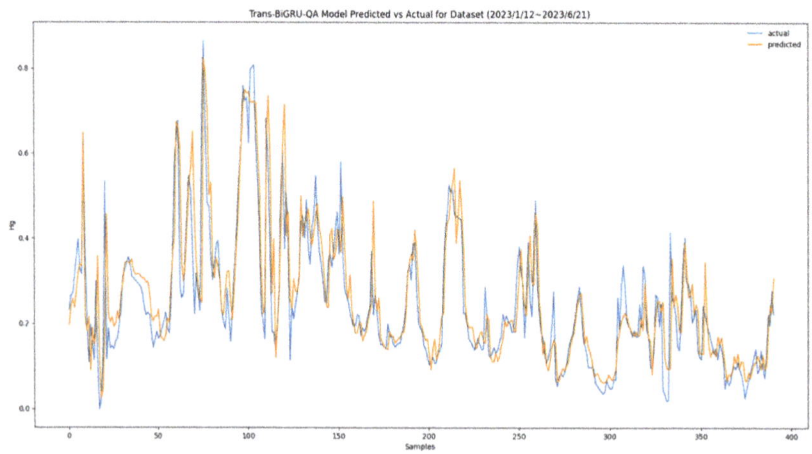

Figure 13. Trans-BiGRU-QA model prediction and actual data line chart.

5.3.2. Statistical Analysis of the Performance of the Proposed Model

Table 9 presents the Analysis of Variance (ANOVA) results for the models. According to the table: The sum_sq under Model represents the total variance the Model explains, i.e., the Model's sum of squares. The sum_sq under Residual represents the residual sum of squares, indicating the variance not explained by the Model. Df refers to the degrees of freedom, where the Model's df is 6, indicating the presence of 7 model groups, while the Residual's df is 63.

Table 9. Analysis of variance (ANOVA) for each model.

	Sum-sq	DF	F	PR (>F)
Model	0.020227	6.0	442.999226	1.590326×10^{-49}
Residual	0.000479	63.0	NaN	NaN

The F-value is a statistic that tests whether the variance between groups is significantly greater than within groups. The F-value for this Model is 442.999226, indicating that the variance between groups is significantly more significant than within groups.

The *p*-value (PR (>F)) represents the probability of observing an extreme F-value if the null hypothesis is true. In this case, the *p*-value is 1.590326×10^{-49}, much smaller than 0.05, suggesting that the null hypothesis can be rejected. This means there is a statistically significant difference between the model groups.

The ANOVA results demonstrate that the differences between the models are statistically significant, given the very low *p*-value. Consequently, it is appropriate to proceed with Tukey's HSD Test to compare the specific differences between the models.

Table 10 presents the results of Tukey's HSD Test for the models. The table summarizes the Mean Absolute Error (MAE) after running each model ten times. The models compared included GRU, LSTM, RNN, Transformer, BiGRU, Trans-BiGRU, and the proposed Trans-BiGRU-QA model. The comparisons between two machine learning models are shown in the Group1 and Group2 columns.

Table 10. Summary of Tukey's HSD test results for each model.

Group 1	Group 2	Mean Diff.	P-Adj	Lower	Upper	Reject
BiGRU	GRU	−0.00165	0.9	−0.00518	0.00188	False
BiGRU	LSTM	0.03761	0.001	0.03407	0.04114	True
BiGRU	RNN	0.03616	0.001	0.03263	0.03969	True
BiGRU	Trans-BiGRU	0.00223	0.9	−0.00131	0.00576	False
BiGRU	Trans-BiGRU-QA	−0.00587	0.001	−0.00941	−0.00234	True
BiGRU	Transformer	−0.00473	0.002	−0.00826	−0.00119	True
GRU	LSTM	0.03926	0.001	0.03572	0.04279	True
GRU	RNN	0.03781	0.001	0.03427	0.04134	True
GRU	Trans-BiGRU	0.00388	0.622	−0.00017	0.00794	False
GRU	Trans-BiGRU-QA	−0.00421	0.013	−0.00825	−0.00016	True
GRU	Transformer	−0.00308	0.239	−0.00713	0.00098	False
LSTM	RNN	−0.00145	0.9	−0.00548	0.00258	False
LSTM	Trans-BiGRU	−0.03538	0.001	−0.03942	−0.03135	True
LSTM	Trans-BiGRU-QA	−0.04346	0.001	−0.04749	−0.03942	True
LSTM	Transformer	−0.04233	0.001	−0.04637	−0.03830	True
RNN	Trans-BiGRU	−0.03393	0.001	−0.03796	−0.02989	True
RNN	Trans-BiGRU-QA	−0.04201	0.001	−0.04605	−0.03798	True
RNN	Transformer	−0.04088	0.001	−0.04491	−0.03684	True
Trans-BiGRU	Trans-BiGRU-QA	−0.00808	0.001	−0.1211	−0.00404	True
Trans-BiGRU	Transformer	−0.00695	0.001	−0.01098	−0.0029	True
Trans-BiGRU-QA	Transformer	0.00113	0.9	−0.00290	0.00517	False

Mean diff. represents the mean difference between the two models being compared. P-adj is the adjusted p-value used to test whether the mean difference is statistically significant. Lower and Upper represent the lower and upper limits of the 95% confidence interval. Reject indicates whether the null hypothesis (that the means are equal) is rejected. If the Reject column shows "True", the mean difference between the two models is statistically significant.

According to the results of Tukey's Test, when compared to the other baseline models, the Trans-BiGRU-QA model consistently demonstrates a significant performance advantage. The model has a significantly lower MAE in all comparisons, confirming its predictive performance is noticeably better than the other models. This further validates the superiority of the Trans-BiGRU-QA hybrid model in this study.

5.3.3. Robustness Analysis

Model robustness refers to a model's ability to maintain reliable performance and consistency across different datasets, environments, or training conditions [48]. A robust model can withstand small data fluctuations or variations in testing sets while maintaining high predictive accuracy. This study conducted a model robustness analysis to ensure that machine learning models perform stably in practical applications. By studying and improving model robustness, the credibility and reliability of machine learning systems can be enhanced, promoting more widespread research into trustworthy machine learning. A robust model can effectively handle data variability, reduce the risk of overfitting, and increase model trustworthiness [48]. Robust models possess a strong generalization ability, allowing them to adapt to data changes while maintaining a stable performance and increasing confidence in the model's results.

In this study, the standard deviation (STD) was used to assess the robustness of each model. In deep learning models, performance stability is typically evaluated by calculating multiple experimental results' mean and standard deviation. A more minor standard deviation indicates excellent stability in the model's performance. Therefore, the standard deviation is a crucial measure to evaluate the robustness of the models.

Table 11 compares the robustness of each machine learning model, showing the overall average Mean Absolute Error (MAE) and Root Mean Square Error (RMSE) along with their corresponding standard deviations. Lower MAE and RMSE values indicate smaller prediction errors, while the standard deviation reflects the variability in performance across multiple experiments. A smaller standard deviation means the model's performance remains stable across different training and testing conditions, indicating a stronger robustness.

Table 11. Comparison of robustness across models.

	MAE	RMSE
GRU	$0.0567 \pm 7.63 \times 10^{-4}$	$0.0860 \pm 3.82 \times 10^{-4}$
LSTM	$0.0939 \pm 4.10 \times 10^{-4}$	$0.1260 \pm 2.72 \times 10^{-4}$
RNN	$0.0930 \pm 46.44 \times 10^{-4}$	$0.1197 \pm 34.38 \times 10^{-4}$
Transformer	$0.0644 \pm 19.54 \times 10^{-4}$	$0.0909 \pm 22.14 \times 10^{-4}$
BiGRU	$0.0574 \pm 39.94 \times 10^{-4}$	$0.0865 \pm 38.49 \times 10^{-4}$
Trans-BiGRU	$0.0543 \pm 18.29 \times 10^{-4}$	$0.0817 \pm 22.44 \times 10^{-4}$
Trans-BiGRU-QA	$0.0509 \pm 15.80 \times 10^{-4}$	$0.0787 \pm 19.14 \times 10^{-4}$

As shown in Table 11, the proposed Trans-BiGRU-QA model achieves the best results in both MAE and RMSE, followed by the Trans-BiGRU and GRU models, demonstrating a good robustness and low error rates. On the other hand, the LSTM and RNN models have higher standard deviations and more significant errors, indicating poor robustness. The Transformer model shows moderate error levels, but its more significant standard deviation suggests some volatility in prediction performance. The BiGRU model achieves low error rates, but its higher standard deviation implies that its robustness may fluctuate in some instances.

From this robustness analysis, it is clear that the Trans-BiGRU-QA model demonstrates the best robustness and accuracy, with the GRU model being a close second. The Trans-BiGRU-QA and Trans-BiGRU models are recommended for those prioritizing low error and high stability.

5.4. Ablation Experiment

The purpose of ablation experiments is to investigate the contribution of various structural configurations to the performance of a new model. Different variant model structures are typically constructed and compared using the same training data when evaluating different combinations in deep learning models and their impact on overall performance [49]. Ablation experiments allow for assessing how specific features or components of a model contribute to the overall performance. This process typically involves modifying the model or progressively removing specific components, followed by observing the resulting changes in performance. This helps to understand better how each model component influences the outcome.

Table 12 presents the comparison results from the ablation experiments for the hybrid model in this study. According to Table 12, this study follows Sheikholeslami et al.'s [49] ablation experiment methodology, using Mean Absolute Error (MAE), Root Mean Square Error (RMSE), and R-squared to evaluate the performance of the Trans-BiGRU-QA hybrid model and the contribution of each of its components.

Table 12. Comparison of hybrid model experiments.

	MAE	RMSE	R^2	Equation
Trans-BiGRU-QA	0.0509	0.0787	0.72	$C_m(M)$
Trans-BiGRU	0.0543	0.0817	0.67	$C_m(M, \{C\})$
BiGRU-QA	0.0580	0.0871	0.68	$C_m(M, \{A\})$
Trans-QA	0.0578	0.0840	0.71	$C_m(M, \{B\})$
BiGRU	0.0574	0.0865	0.69	$C_m(M, \{A, C\})$

The equations for the ablation experiments, Equations (13) and (14), are provided as follows:

$$C_m(M) = C_m(A,\ B,\ C) \tag{13}$$

$$C_m(M,\ \{B\}) \tag{14}$$

As shown in Equation (13), the total sum of the Trans-BiGRU-QA model is defined as C_m, with models A, B, and C defined as three different model combinations for cross-testing. Model A refers to the Transformer model, model B refers to the BiGRU model, and model C refers to the Quick Attention model. Model M is the Trans-BiGRU-QA model [49]. Since this study used a model that integrates all three models, the equation for all combined models was defined as $C_m(M) = C_m(A,\ B,\ C)$, as shown in Equation (14).

Since this study removed model B (BiGRU) for an ablation test, the equation during the testing phase was $C_m(M,\ \{B\})$ [46]. Each testing phase's MAE, RMSE, and R-squared were executed ten times, and the average was taken as the final test value.

This study's ablation research wasdivided into five testing phases to assess whether the novel Trans-BiGRU-QA fusion model effectively improves training performance. The first phase tested the predictive structure of the Trans-BiGRU-QA fusion model, referred to as $C_m(M)$. The second phase removed the Quick Attention model and generated the second phase $C_m(M, \{C\})$ (Trans-BiGRU). The third phase removed the Transformer model to generate $C_m(M, \{A\})$ (BiGRU-QA). The fourth phase removed the BiGRU model to generate the fourth phase $C_m(M, \{B\})$ (Trans-QA). Finally, both the Transformer and Quick Attention models were removed for an individual test of the BiGRU model, generating the fifth phase $C_m(M, \{A, C\})$ (BiGRU).The results indicate that the proposed Trans-BiGRU-QA fusion model is the best, with an MAE of 0.0509, an RMSE of 0.0787, and an R-squared of 0.72.

5.5. SHAP

SHAP (SHapley Additive exPlanations) is a tool (Python library) used to explain the predictions of machine learning models. Its primary goal is to help this study understand the factors influencing the prediction process and the decision-making of the model and to explain the outcomes of machine learning model predictions [50]. SHAP's application mainly covers four areas: explaining model predictions, evaluating feature importance, improving the model, and enhancing model trust and transparency.

Explaining model predictions: SHAP quantifies the contribution of each feature to the model's prediction, helping to interpret the logic behind the model's predictions. Feature importance evaluation: SHAP assesses the average impact of each feature on the dataset's predictions, allowing this study to identify the most critical features for overall model performance. Model improvement: Adjusting the model structure or features based on SHAP values can enhance model stability or prediction accuracy. Increasing trust and transparency: SHAP boosts trust in the model's decision-making process by making the typically black-box nature of machine learning models more understandable. SHAP makes the model's prediction process more interpretable and transparent, clarifying the internal operations that are otherwise difficult to comprehend [50].

As an essential tool for analyzing machine learning model predictions, SHAP can quantify the contribution of each feature to the prediction results. In a SHAP plot, the *X*-axis represents the magnitude of SHAP values, which indicates the impact of each feature on the model output—the larger the value, the more significant the impact. The *Y*-axis lists all the features: TGM, CO_2, Temp, $PM_{2.5}$, and RH. Each point's color represents the magnitude of the feature value, ranging from blue (low feature value) to red (high feature value).

Figure 14 displays the SHAP plot for the input variables. According to Figure 12b:

- TGM has the greatest influence on the model output, followed by CO_2, Temperature (temperature), $PM_{2.5}$, and RH (Relative Humidity).
- For TGM, CO_2, and Temp, higher feature values have a positive impact on the model output, driving the predicted results in an upward direction.

- In contrast, $PM_{2.5}$ and RH have relatively minor influences, and the shading indicates a low impact on the prediction output, suggesting that variations in these features contribute less to the model output than TGM and other primary features.

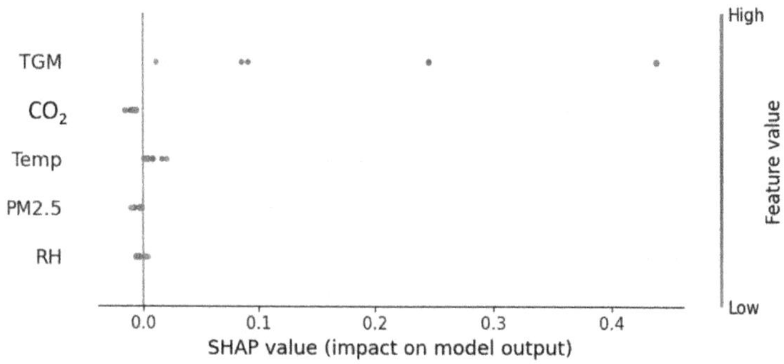

Figure 14. SHAP plot of input variables.

5.6. Discussion

5.6.1. Discussion of Ablation Experiments

Based on the results of the ablation experiments, the proposed Trans-BiGRU-QA hybrid model demonstrated the best performance, with an MAE of 0.0509, RMSE of 0.0787, and an R-squared of 0.72. The ablation experiments confirmed that integrating Transformer, BiGRU, and Quick Attention within the proposed architecture significantly enhances the model's predictive performance.

During the ablation experiments, different model components were gradually removed, allowing the observation of changes in model performance. This process provided insights into the contribution of each component to the overall model performance. The results indicate that integrating these structural elements effectively improves the model's predictive capabilities. Furthermore, removing any single part resulted in a decline in model performance, which further validated each component's critical role in enhancing the model's overall effectiveness. This confirms that the combination of Transformer, BiGRU, and Quick Attention is essential for achieving optimal predictive accuracy in the hybrid model.

When the Quick Attention mechanism was removed, the model reverted to Trans-BiGRU, resulting in an MAE of 0.0543, RMSE of 0.0817, and decreased the R-squared value to 0.67. This decline in performance indicates that the Quick Attention mechanism plays a significant role in enhancing the model's capabilities. The Quick Attention mechanism helps the model extract key features more effectively, thereby improving the prediction accuracy. Therefore, the contribution of this mechanism within the overall hybrid model is substantial and cannot be overlooked.

When the Transformer model was removed, the model became BiGRU-QA, resulting in an MAE of 0.0580, RMSE of 0.0871, and a decrease in the R-squared value to 0.68. This further decline in performance demonstrates that the Transformer model plays a crucial role in improving overall predictive performance. The Transformer model effectively captures long-distance dependencies and key features in the data, which has a significant impact on the model's prediction accuracy. Thus, its importance within the model structure is substantial and cannot be overlooked.

When the BiGRU component was removed, the model became Trans-QA, resulting in an MAE of 0.0578, RMSE of 0.0840, and an R-squared value of 0.71. This indicates a decline in performance, though the impact is less severe compared to the removal of the Transformer model or the Quick Attention mechanism. This suggests that BiGRU also contributes to improving the model's performance. The BiGRU model can extract forward and backward information from sequential data, thus enhancing prediction accuracy.

However, its contribution is slightly less significant than that of the Transformer model and the Quick Attention mechanism in the overall model structure.

When testing with a single BiGRU model, the results show an MAE of 0.0574, an RMSE of 0.0865, and an R-squared value of 0.69. The model's performance significantly declined, indicating that a single model cannot achieve the predictive accuracy of the hybrid model. The hybrid model effectively combines the strengths of different models, significantly improving prediction accuracy and stability. In contrast, a single model's performance is more limited, as it cannot fully exploit the complex features in the data.

Through ablation experiments, this study demonstrated the impact of different combinations on the overall performance of the hybrid model. The results indicate that integrating the three models—Transformer, BiGRU, and Quick Attention—within the Trans-BiGRU-QA hybrid model significantly enhances the model's predictive capabilities. The experimental findings further confirm that the proposed hybrid model offers a notable advantage in data prediction performance, effectively improving prediction accuracy and stability.

5.6.2. Robustness

This study evaluated each model's stability by calculating the mean and standard deviation across multiple experiments. The standard deviation reflects the variability in model performance; a smaller standard deviation indicates that the model performs more consistently across different training and testing scenarios. The experimental results show that the LSTM model demonstrated the best stability, followed by the GRU model.

The proposed Trans-BiGRU-QA model exhibited a significant advantage in predictive performance, with an MAE of 0.0509 (standard deviation: $\pm 15.80 \times 10^{-4}$) and an RMSE of 0.0787 (standard deviation: $\pm 19.14 \times 10^{-4}$). This model achieved the lowest prediction error in the experiments, highlighting its superior accuracy.

In contrast, the LSTM and RNN models showed weaker predictive performance. Although their standard deviations were relatively small, indicating a degree of stability, their overall effectiveness was not ideal. For instance, the LSTM model had an MAE of 0.0939 (standard deviation: $\pm 4.10 \times 10^{-4}$) and an RMSE of 0.1260 (standard deviation: $\pm 2.72 \times 10^{-4}$). This suggests that, while the LSTM and RNN models were stable across multiple experiments, they suffered from more significant prediction errors and lacked the predictive accuracy required for more precise results.

The Transformer model exhibited moderate error levels, but its more significant standard deviation indicates that its predictions may experience more significant fluctuations under certain conditions. While the BiGRU model had a relatively low error, it showed a higher standard deviation, suggesting that its stability might vary under some conditions.

The robustness experiments concluded that the proposed Trans-BiGRU-QA model, as well as the Trans-BiGRU model, both performed exceptionally well in terms of stability and low error rates. The analysis of the different models' robustness demonstrated that integrating multiple models can lead to a better performance and stability compared to single models. The Trans-BiGRU-QA hybrid model developed in this study is a significant contribution, effectively managing data variability, reducing overfitting, and enhancing the reliability of the prediction results.

5.6.3. Limitations

This study's total number of data points was 1245, obtained after removing outliers and handling missing values. During the data collection process for Vietnam's air quality data, factors such as equipment malfunctions, power outages, or human errors led to missing or abnormal values. The final dataset used for analysis underwent a thorough cleaning and processing.

However, models are prone to overfitting when the training dataset is limited. This means that, while a model may perform well on the training data, it may still perform poorly on the test set. The primary reason is that the model may need to learn the underlying patterns in the data effectively instead of memorizing specific features present in the training set.

The limited data quantity can restrict the prediction accuracy of the models, potentially causing the performance of various models to be quite similar. This challenge underscores the urgent need for larger and more representative datasets for training. With such datasets, models can better generalize to unseen data and achieve improved predictive accuracy, addressing this issue and improving the overall performance of our models. Atmospheric mercury monitoring stations are relatively scarce, and currently, most can only collect relevant concentration data within limited areas. This results in spatial and temporal data sparsity, making it challenging to comprehensively reflect mercury concentration variations across more significant regions. Additionally, environmental conditions, equipment aging, and maintenance quality can affect atmospheric mercury measurement equipment, impacting the accuracy and consistency of the data. If the data contains a high noise level or outliers, the accuracy of model predictions may be compromised.

5.6.4. Integration and Application

The outstanding performance of the Trans-BiGRU-QA model in predicting atmospheric mercury concentrations demonstrates its feasibility for future implementation in early warning systems or environmental monitoring networks. The model must handle real-time data streams from various monitoring points in an early warning system. Trans-BiGRU-QA can be deployed on edge servers, directly receiving updated data from the source and performing real-time predictions. Based on the model's predictions, specific mercury concentration thresholds can be set to trigger alerts. When the model's predicted values exceed these thresholds, the system automatically initiates warning mechanisms and activates response protocols.

Trans-BiGRU-QA can be configured as a distributed model deployed across different monitoring stations for single-point predictions and integrated analysis. As predictions from multiple monitoring points are aggregated, the system can identify spatial trends in mercury concentration, aiding in tracking the sources and spread pathways of mercury pollution.

In the future, the Trans-BiGRU-QA model could incorporate a broader range of meteorological variables, such as atmospheric pressure, rainfall, and hours of sunlight. These factors directly influence the mercury's transport, transformation, and deposition, enabling the model to capture the impact of environmental conditions on concentration levels accurately. Additionally, an ensemble model could be considered to strengthen the prediction framework. By combining models, the bias of a single model can be reduced, leading to more robust predictions. The final prediction could be determined through methods like weighted averaging or voting.

5.6.5. Application to an Additional Dataset

To verify the applicability of the proposed Trans-BiGRU-QA model used in this study, this study further used another EU27&UK gas dataset for verification. The verification dataset was taken from the Zenodo open dataset. These data come from the natural gas data of the entire 27 EU countries and the United Kingdom. The characteristics of natural gas data include the country's total natural gas emissions and some factors that affect the natural gas supply, transmission, consumption structure and consumption change drivers, etc. The data source is (https://zenodo.org/records/11175364, accessed on 31 October 2024), the number of data items is 67,986, and the data period is from 1 January 2016 to 30 April 2024. This study used its input variables to forecast the volume of natural gas heating for homes for the next day. Table 13 is a summary table of each data attribute.

Table 13. Summary of data attributes in the gas dataset.

Variable	Name	Description	Data Type
$XG_0(t)$	TOTAL	All natural gas supplies	integer
$XG_1(t)$	RU	Russian natural gas supply	float
$XG_2(t)$	LNG	LNG supply	float
$XG_3(t)$	PRO	Amount of natural gas produced	float
$XG_4(t)$	AZ	Azerbaijan's natural gas supplies	float
$XG_5(t)$	DZ	Algeria's natural gas supplies	integer
$XG_6(t)$	NO	Norwegian natural gas supplies	float
$XG_7(t)$	LY	Libyan natural gas supply	float
$XG_8(t)$	TR	Natural gas supplies in the Netherlands	float
$XG_9(t)$	RU_from_storage	Natural gas supplies from Russian storage	float
$XG_{10}(t)$	LNG_from_storage	Natural gas supply from LNG storage	float
$XG_{11}(t)$	PRO_from_storage	Natural gas supply from production storage	integer
$XG_{12}(t)$	AZ_from_storage	Natural gas supplies from Azerbaijan storage	integer
$XG_{13}(t)$	DZ_from_storage	Natural gas supplies from Algerian storage	integer
$XG_{14}(t)$	NO_from_storage	Natural gas supplies from Norwegian storage	float
$XG_{15}(t)$	RS_from_storage	Natural gas supplies from Russian storage	float
$XG_{16}(t)$	LY_from_storage'	Natural gas supplies from Libyan storage	float
$XG_{17}(t)$	TR_from_storage	Natural gas supplies from Turkish storage	float
$XG_{18}(t)$	house_heating	Natural gas heating for homes	float
$YG_1(t+1)$	house_heating	Natural gas heating for homes (next day)	float

The research results of all models are shown in Table 14. The Trans-BiGRU-QA model proposed in this study shows the best performance in terms of evaluation indices. Although another Trans-BiGRU model also has good performance, its performance is still not as good as the Trans-BiGRU-QA model proposed in this study.

Table 14. Comparison of hybrid models in the gas dataset.

	MAE	RMSE	R^2
Trans-BiGRU-QA	0.0614	0.0888	0.69
Trans-BiGRU	0.0621	0.0904	0.65
BiGRU-QA	0.0682	0.1003	0.66
Trans-QA	0.0627	0.0945	0.68
BiGRU	0.0754	0.1005	0.67

These results show that, compared to other basic or hybrid models, the Trans-BiGRU-QA model proposed in this study still has the best performance when processing the EU27&UK gas dataset, further supporting the applicability of the Trans-BiGRU-QA model method proposed in this study. This also shows the significant role of the Trans-BiGRU-QA model proposed in this study in predicting performance and is worthy of further exploration and application in future research and practice.

6. Conclusions

This study proposed an advanced Trans-BiGRU-QA hybrid model for atmospheric mercury (TGM) forecasting, comparing its performance against other machine learning models, including GRU, LSTM, RNN, Transformer, BiGRU, and Trans-BiGRU. The evaluation metrics included the Mean Absolute Error (MAE), Root Mean Square Error (RMSE), and R-squared, providing a comprehensive and rigorous assessment of each model's strengths and weaknesses. The study utilized a dataset of air variables collected in Vietnam, incorporating five key features—atmospheric mercury concentration (TGM), temperature (Temp), relative humidity (RH), $PM_{2.5}$, and carbon dioxide (CO_2)—to predict hourly atmospheric mercury levels.

In air pollution research, machine learning models are commonly used to integrate air pollution data to assess environmental impacts. This study demonstrates that the hybrid model can significantly improve prediction accuracy through the performance evaluation, statistical analysis, and robustness analysis of the models. The Self-Attention mechanism in the Transformer model enables it to process all positions in input sequences simultaneously, effectively capturing long-term dependencies. When combined with BiGRU, which extracts deep features through forward and backward time series processing, and the Quick Attention mechanism, the model focuses more precisely on critical features in the data.

The proposed Trans-BiGRU-QA hybrid model showed exceptional performance in forecasting atmospheric mercury levels. Leveraging feature engineering and sliding window techniques, the model accurately predicts future trends in atmospheric mercury. When compared to baseline models like GRU, LSTM, RNN, Transformer, BiGRU, and Trans-BiGRU, the results indicate that Trans-BiGRU-QA is the best-performing hybrid model, with superior MAE, RMSE, and R-squared values. This hybrid model offers technical support for real-time predictions, advancing the application of deep learning techniques in air pollution forecasting and providing valuable tools for meteorologists and air quality experts.

Author Contributions: Conceptualization, D.-H.S.; formal analysis, B.-H.W.; investigation, D.-H.S., F.-I.C., and T.-W.W.; methodology, D.-H.S. and B.-H.W.; project administration, D.-H.S.; Resources, D.-H.S. and M.-H.S.; software, F.-I.C. and B.-H.W.; supervision, D.-H.S.; validation, T.-W.W. and M.-H.S.; visualization, M.-H.S.; writing—original draft, T.-W.W. and B.-H.W.; writing—review and editing, F.-I.C. and M.-H.S. All authors have read and agreed to the published version of the manuscript.

Funding: This research received no external funding.

Data Availability Statement: The data are not publicly available due to privacy or ethical restrictions.

Acknowledgments: The authors thank Ly Sy Phu Nguyen, Vietnam National University, Linh Trung Ward, Thu Duc District, Ho Chi Minh City 700000, Vietnam, for the dataset provided. Atmospheric mercury concentration monitoring is primarily conducted in Ho Chi Minh City.

Conflicts of Interest: The authors declare no conflicts of interest.

References

1. Yan, R.; Liao, J.; Yang, J.; Sun, W.; Nong, M.; Li, F. Multi-hour and multi-site air quality index forecasting in Beijing using CNN, LSTM, CNN-LSTM, and spatiotemporal clustering. *Expert Syst. Appl.* **2021**, *169*, 114513. [CrossRef]
2. Samad, A.; Garuda, S.; Vogt, U.; Yang, B. Air pollution prediction using machine learning techniques—An approach to replace existing monitoring stations with virtual monitoring stations. *Atmos. Environ.* **2023**, *310*, 119987. [CrossRef]
3. Yuan, C.-S.; Jhang, Y.-M.; Ie, I.-R.; Lee, C.-E.; Fang, G.-C.; Luo, J. Exploratory Investigation on Spatiotemporal Variation and Source Identification of Atmospheric Speciated Mercury Surrounding the Taiwan Strait. *Atmos. Pollut. Res.* **2021**, *12*, 54–64. [CrossRef]
4. Skalny, A.V.; Aschner, M.; Sekacheva, M.I.; Santamaria, A.; Barbosa, F.; Ferrer, B.; Aaseth, J.; Paoliello, M.M.; Rocha, J.B.; Tinkov, A.A. Mercury and cancer: Where are we now after two decades of research? *Food Chem. Toxicol.* **2022**, *164*, 113001. [CrossRef]
5. Wu, Q.; Tang, Y.; Wang, S.; Li, L.; Deng, K.; Tang, G.; Liu, K.; Ding, D.; Zhang, H. Developing a statistical model to explain the observed decline of atmospheric mercury. *Atmos. Environ.* **2020**, *243*, 117868. [CrossRef]
6. Wang, C.; Wang, Z.; Zhang, X. Two years measurement of speciated atmospheric mercury in a typical area of the north coast of China: Sources, temporal variations, and influence of regional and long-range transport. *Atmos. Environ.* **2020**, *228*, 117235. [CrossRef]
7. Nguyen, L.S.P.; Pham, T.D.H.; Truong, M.T.; Tran, A.N. Characteristics of total gaseous mercury at a tropical megacity in Vietnam and influence of tropical cyclones. *Atmos. Pollut. Res.* **2023**, *14*, 101813. [CrossRef]
8. Pang, Q.; Gu, J.; Wang, H.; Zhang, Y. Global health impact of atmospheric mercury emissions from artisanal and small-scale gold mining. *iScience* **2022**, *25*, 104881. [CrossRef] [PubMed]

9. Wang, C.; Wang, Z.; Zhang, Y.; Zhang, X. Sustained high atmospheric Hg level in Beijing during wet seasons suggests that anthropogenic pollution is continuing: Identification of potential sources. *Environ. Res.* **2022**, *214*, 113814. [CrossRef] [PubMed]
10. Xu, N.; Li, L.; Dong, H.; Huang, F. Prediction of Air Quality in the Beijing-Tianjin-Hebei Region Based on LSTM Model. *Acad. J. Comput. Inf. Sci.* **2023**, *6*, 113–118. [CrossRef]
11. Wen, C.; Lin, X.; Ying, Y.; Ma, Y.; Yu, H.; Li, X.; Yan, J. Dioxin emission prediction from a full-scale municipal solid waste incinerator: Deep learning model in time-series input. *Waste Manag.* **2023**, *170*, 93–102. [CrossRef]
12. Sarkar, N.; Gupta, R.; Keserwani, P.K.; Govil, M.C. Air Quality Index prediction using an effective hybrid deep learning model. *Environ. Pollut.* **2022**, *315*, 120404. [CrossRef]
13. Wu, C.-L.; He, H.-D.; Song, R.-F.; Zhu, X.-H.; Peng, Z.-R.; Fu, Q.-Y.; Pan, J. A hybrid deep learning model for regional O_3 and NO_2 concentrations prediction based on spatiotemporal dependencies in air quality monitoring network. *Environ. Pollut.* **2023**, *320*, 121075. [CrossRef]
14. Wu, Z.; Zeng, Y. Air pollution distribution under climate change: Application of geographical artificial intelligence technology. *Civ. Eng. Water Conserv.* **2023**, *50*, 16–23.
15. Wang, S. Air pollution warning for special education. *Taiwan Educ. Rev. Mon.* **2018**, *7*, 121–124. Available online: https://www.airitilibrary.com/Article/Detail?DocID=P20130114001-201807-201807160019-201807160019-121-124 (accessed on 11 November 2024).
16. Fu, X.W.; Zhang, H.; Yu, B.; Wang, X.; Lin, C.-J.; Feng, X.B. Observations of atmospheric mercury in China: A critical review. *Atmos. Meas. Tech.* **2015**, *15*, 9455–9476. [CrossRef]
17. Luo, Q.; Ren, Y.; Sun, Z.; Li, Y.; Li, B.; Yang, S.; Zhang, W.; Wania, F.; Hu, Y.; Cheng, H. Characterization of atmospheric mercury from mer-cury-added product manufacturing using passive air samplers. *Environ. Pollut.* **2023**, *337*, 122519. [CrossRef]
18. Kalyan, K.S.; Rajasekharan, A.; Sangeetha, S. Ammus: A survey of transformer-based pretrained models in natural language processing. *arXiv* **2021**, arXiv:2108.05542.
19. Han, K.; Wang, Y.; Chen, H.; Chen, X.; Guo, J.; Liu, Z.; Tang, Y.; Xiao, A.; Xu, C.; Xu, Y.; et al. A survey on vision transformer. *IEEE Trans. Pattern Anal. Mach. Intell.* **2022**, *45*, 87–110. [CrossRef]
20. Chen, M.; Tan, X.; Ren, Y.; Xu, J.; Sun, H.; Zhao, S.; Qin, T.; Liu, T.-Y. Multispeech: Multi-speaker text to speech with transformer. *arXiv* **2020**, arXiv:2006.04664.
21. Wen, Q.; Zhou, T.; Zhang, C.; Chen, W.; Ma, Z.; Yan, J.; Sun, L. Transformers in time series: A survey. *arXiv* **2022**, arXiv:2202.07125.
22. Gao, Y.; Miyata, S.; Matsunami, Y.; Akashi, Y. Spatio-temporal interpretable neural network for solar irradiation prediction using transformer. *Energy Build.* **2023**, *297*, 113461. [CrossRef]
23. Vaswani, A.; Shazeer, N.; Parmar, N.; Uszkoreit, J.; Jones, L.; Gomez, A.N.; Kaiser, L.; Polosukhin, I. Attention is all you need. In Proceedings of the Advances in Neural Information Processing Systems: Annual Conference on Neural Information Processing Systems 2017, Long Beach, CA, USA, 4–9 December 2017.
24. Mao, X.; Ren, N.; Dai, P.; Jin, J.; Wang, B.; Kang, R.; Li, D. A variable weight combination prediction model for climate in a greenhouse based on BiGRU-Attention and LightGBM. *Comput. Electron. Agric.* **2024**, *219*, 108818. [CrossRef]
25. Zhao, L.; Li, Z.; Qu, L.; Zhang, J.; Teng, B. A hybrid VMD-LSTM/GRU model to predict non-stationary and irregular waves on the east coast of China. *Ocean Eng.* **2023**, *276*, 114136. [CrossRef]
26. Busari, G.A.; Lim, D.H. Crude oil price prediction: A comparison between AdaBoost-LSTM and AdaBoost-GRU for improving forecasting performance. *Comput. Chem. Eng.* **2021**, *155*, 107513. [CrossRef]
27. Tang, J.; Hou, H.J.; Chen, H.G.; Wang, S.J.; Sheng, G.H.; Jiang, C.X. Concentration prediction method based on Seq2Seg network improved by BI-GRU for dissolved gas in transformer oil. *Electr. Power Autom. Equip.* **2022**, *42*, 196–202.
28. Ji, Y.; Huang, Y.; Zeng, J.; Ren, L.; Chen, Y. A physical–data-driven combined strategy for load identification of tire type rail transit vehicle. *Reliab. Eng. Syst. Saf.* **2025**, *253*, 110493. [CrossRef]
29. Wazir, S.; Fraz, M.M. HistoSeg: Quick attention with multi-loss function for multi-structure segmentation in digital histology images. In Proceedings of the 12th International Conference on Pattern Recognition Systems (ICPRS), Saint-Etienne, France, 7–10 June 2022; pp. 1–7.
30. Soydaner, D. Attention mechanism in neural networks: Where it comes and where it goes. *Neural Comput. Appl.* **2022**, *34*, 13371–13385. [CrossRef]
31. Huang, Q.; Cui, Z. Study on prediction of ocean effective wave height based on hybrid artificial intelligence model. *Ocean Eng.* **2023**, *289*, 116137. [CrossRef]
32. Sari, Y.; Arifin, Y.F.; Novitasari, N.; Faisal, M.R. Deep learning approach using the GRU-LSTM hybrid model for Air temperature prediction on daily basis. *Int. J. Intell. Syst. Appl. Eng.* **2022**, *10*, 430–436.
33. Ie, I.-R.; Yuan, C.-S.; Lee, C.-E.; Chiang, K.-C.; Chen, T.-W.; Soong, K.-Y. Chemical significance of atmospheric mercury at fishing port compared to urban and suburb in an offshore island. *Atmos. Pollut. Res.* **2022**, *13*, 101538. [CrossRef]
34. Gustin, M.L.; Lindberg, S.E.; Poissant, L. A review of mercury volatilization from soil and sediment. *Environ. Sci. Technol.* **2000**, *34*, 4322–4337.
35. Lindberg, S.E.; Poissant, L.; Gustin, M.L. The influence of temperature on the volatilization of mercury from contaminated soil. *J. Geophys. Res. Atmos.* **1999**, *104*, 21879–21888. [CrossRef]
36. Horowitz, H.M.; Jacob, D.J.; Zhang, Y.; Dibble, T.S.; Slemr, F.; Amos, H.M.; Schmidt, J.A.; Corbitt, E.S.; Marais, E.A.; Sunderland, E.M. A new mechanism for atmospheric mercury redox chemistry: Implications for the global mercury budget. *Atmos. Meas. Tech.* **2017**, *17*, 6353–6371. [CrossRef]

37. Zhang, C.; Zhang, Y.; Wang, D. The influence of relative humidity on the volatilization of mercury from contaminated soil. *Environ. Sci. Technol.* **2012**, *46*, 10342–10347.
38. Li, J.; Liu, X.; Yu, H. The effect of relative humidity on mercury volatilization from water. *Water Res.* **2014**, *58*, 104–111. [CrossRef] [PubMed]
39. Kannan, S.; Vijayan, P. The impact of carbon dioxide on mercury methylation in aquatic systems. *Environ. Sci. Pollut. Res.* **2016**, *23*, 12135–12142.
40. Wu, Y.; Zhang, Y.; Zhang, C. The influence of carbon dioxide on the partitioning and mobility of mercury in environmental systems. *Environ. Sci. Technol.* **2017**, *51*, 7808–7816.
41. Aamir, M.; Zaidi, S.M.A. DDoS attack detection with feature engineering and machine learning: The framework and performance evaluation. *Int. J. Inf. Secur.* **2019**, *18*, 761–785. [CrossRef]
42. Zhu, L.; Husny, Z.J.B.M.; Samsudin, N.A.; Xu, H.; Han, C. Deep learning method for minimizing water pollution and air pollution in urban environment. *Urban Clim.* **2023**, *49*, 101486. [CrossRef]
43. Martínez, J.; Saavedra, Á; García-Nieto, P.; Piñeiro, J.; Iglesias, C.; Taboada, J.; Sancho, J.; Pastor, J. Air quality parameters outliers detection using functional data analysis in the Langreo urban area (Northern Spain). *Appl. Math. Comput.* **2014**, *241*, 1–10. [CrossRef]
44. Ali, P.J.M.; Faraj, R.H. Data normalization and standardization: A technical report. *Mach. Learn. Tech. Rep.* **2014**, *1*, 1–6.
45. Molnar, C. *Interpretable Machine Learning*; Lulu.com: Morrisville, NC, USA, 2020.
46. Catalano, M.; Galatioto, F.; Bell, M.; Namdeo, A.; Bergantino, A.S. Improving the prediction of air pollution peak episodes generated by urban transport networks. *Environ. Sci. Policy* **2016**, *60*, 69–83. [CrossRef]
47. Wang, S.; Shi, J.; Yang, W.; Yin, Q. High and low frequency wind power prediction based on Transformer and BiGRU-Attention. *Energy* **2024**, *288*, 129753. [CrossRef]
48. Freiesleben, T.; Grote, T. Beyond generalization: A theory of robustness in machine learning. *Synthese* **2023**, *202*, 1–28. [CrossRef]
49. Sheikholeslami, S.; Meister, M.; Wang, T.; Payberah, A.H.; Vlassov, V.; Dowling, J. Autoablation: Automated parallel ablation studies for deep learning. In Proceedings of the 1st Workshop on Machine Learning and Systems, Online, 26 April 2021; pp. 55–61.
50. Xiao, W.; Wang, C.; Liu, J.; Gao, M.; Wu, J. Optimizing Faulting Prediction for Rigid Pavements Using a Hybrid SHAP-TPE-CatBoost Model. *Appl. Sci.* **2023**, *13*, 12862. [CrossRef]

mathematics

Article

Fortify the Guardian, Not the Treasure: Resilient Adversarial Detectors

Raz Lapid [1,2], Almog Dubin [2] and Moshe Sipper [1,*]

1 Department of Computer Science, Ben-Gurion University, Beer-Sheva 8410501, Israel; razla@post.bgu.ac.il
2 DeepKeep, Tel-Aviv 6701203, Israel; almog@deepkeep.ai
* Correspondence: sipper@bgu.ac.il

Abstract: Adaptive adversarial attacks, where adversaries tailor their strategies with full knowledge of defense mechanisms, pose significant challenges to the robustness of adversarial detectors. In this paper, we introduce RADAR (Robust Adversarial Detection via Adversarial Retraining), an approach designed to fortify adversarial detectors against such adaptive attacks while preserving the classifier's accuracy. RADAR employs adversarial training by incorporating adversarial examples—crafted to deceive both the classifier and the detector—into the training process. This dual optimization enables the detector to learn and adapt to sophisticated attack scenarios. Comprehensive experiments on CIFAR-10, SVHN, and ImageNet datasets demonstrate that RADAR substantially enhances the detector's ability to accurately identify adaptive adversarial attacks without degrading classifier performance.

Keywords: robustness; adversarial attacks; adaptive adversarial attacks; deep learning

MSC: 68T07

1. Introduction

Rapid advances in deep learning systems and their applications in various fields, such as finance, healthcare, and transportation, have greatly enhanced human capabilities [1–5]. However, these systems continue to be vulnerable to adversarial attacks, where unintentional or intentionally designed inputs—known as *adversarial examples*—can mislead the decision-making process [6–16]. These malicious inputs, known as adversarial examples, are typically generated by applying subtle perturbations to legitimate data samples—perturbations that are often imperceptible to human observers but can significantly alter the output of the model. Such adversarial attacks pose severe threats to the reliability and trustworthiness of deep learning technologies, particularly in critical applications where erroneous decisions can have serious consequences [17,18].

Extensive research efforts have been dedicated to developing robust machine learning classifiers that are resilient to adversarial attacks. One popular and effective way relies on adversarial training, which involves integrating adversarial examples within the training process, to improve the classifier's resistance to attack [19,20].

The development of adversarial detectors has become a crucial area of research [21–25]. Adversarial detectors are specialized mechanisms or algorithms designed to identify and filter out adversarial examples before they can adversely affect the decision-making process of machine learning models. By analyzing input data for signs of tampering or abnormal patterns indicative of adversarial manipulation, these detectors aim to enhance the security and robustness of AI systems, thereby maintaining their integrity in the face of malicious attacks.

This paper presents a novel approach to adversarially train detectors, combining the strengths of both classifier robustness and detector sensitivity to adversarial examples.

Adversarial detectors (Figure 1), which aim to distinguish adversarial examples from benign ones, have gained momentum recently, but their robustness is unclear. The purpose of adversarial detection is to enhance the robustness of machine learning systems by identifying and mitigating adversarial attacks—thereby preserving the reliability and integrity of the classifiers in critical applications.

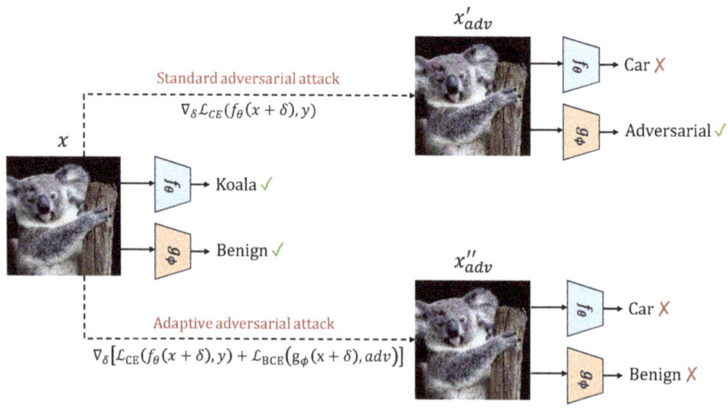

Figure 1. General scheme of adversarial attacks. x: original image. x'_{adv}: standard adversarial attack. x''_{adv}: adaptive adversarial attack, targeting both f_θ (classifier) and g_ϕ (detector). The attacker's goal is to fool the classifier into misclassifying the image and simultaneously deceive the detector into reporting the attack as benign (i.e., failing to detect the adversarial manipulation). The classifier f_θ and the detector g_ϕ share the same input but operate independently, with separate parameters and architectures. The classifier is trained to perform standard classification, while the detector is explicitly trained to identify adversarial instances.

Several studies have found that these detectors—even when combined with robust classifiers that have undergone adversarial training—can be fooled by designing tailored attacks; this engenders a cat-and-mouse cycle of attacking and defending [26,27]. It is therefore critical to thoroughly assess the robustness of adversarial detectors and ensure that they are able to withstand adaptive adversarial attacks.

The attacker's goal is to fool the classifier into misclassifying the image *and*, at the same time, fool the the detector into reporting the attack as benign (i.e., fail to recognize an attack). The attacker, in essence, carries out a two-pronged attack, targeting both the "treasure" and the treasure's "guardian".

An *adaptive* adversarial attack is *aware of the defenses*—and attempts to bypass them. To our knowledge, research addressing such attacks is lacking.

We thus face a crucial problem: How can adversarial detectors be made robust? This question underscores the need for a comprehensive understanding of the interplay between adversarial training strategies and the unique characteristics of adversarial detectors.

We hypothesize that adversarially training adversarial detectors will lead to their improvement in terms of both robustness and accuracy, thus creating a more resilient defense mechanism against sophisticated adversarial attacks. This supposition forms the basis of our investigation and serves as a guiding principle for the experiments and analyses presented in this paper.

There are two major motivations for our work here:

1. Contemporary adversarial detectors are predominantly evaluated within constrained threat models, assuming attackers lack information about the adversarial detector itself. However, this approach likely does not align with real-world scenarios, where sophisticated adversaries possess partial knowledge of the defense mechanisms.

We believe it is necessary to introduce a more realistic evaluation paradigm that considers the potential information available to an attacker. Such a paradigm will improve—perhaps significantly—the reliability of adversarial detection mechanisms.
2. Our fundamental assumption is that adversarial training of the *adversarial detector*—in isolation—has the potential to render the resultant system significantly more challenging for adversaries to thwart. Unlike conventional approaches, where increasing the robustness of the *classifier* often leads to decreased accuracy, our approach focuses solely on enhancing the capabilities of the detector, thereby avoiding such trade-offs. By bolstering the detector through adversarial training, we introduce a distinct tier of defense that adversaries must contend with, amplifying the overall adversarial resilience of the system.

The main innovation in this paper is the introduction of a novel approach to adversarial robustness by focusing on strengthening adversarial detectors rather than the classifiers themselves. Traditional methods enhance classifier robustness through adversarial training, which often leads to a compromise between robustness and clean accuracy. Our method maintains the classifier's original performance on clean data by leaving it unaltered and instead fortifies the adversarial detector against adaptive attacks.

This approach is particularly advantageous in scenarios where preserving the classifier's clean accuracy is critical. By not retraining the classifier, we avoid the typical trade-offs associated with adversarial training. Our fortified detectors demonstrate improved resilience against sophisticated adaptive attacks, offering a robust defense without sacrificing the classifier's performance on benign inputs. **We suggest a paradigm shift: instead of defending the classifier, strengthen the adversarial detector**. Thus, we ask the following:

(Q) *How can adversarial detectors be made robust?*

To our knowledge, problem **(Q)** remains open in the literature. Our contributions are the following:

- Paradigm shift: Unlike existing approaches that focus on robustifying classifiers, we introduce a novel paradigm of robustifying adversarial detectors, eliminating the trade-off between clean and robust classification.
- We introduce **RADAR**, a pioneering adversarial training technique specifically designed to enhance the resilience of adversarial detectors, demonstrating its effectiveness through extensive evaluations on three datasets and across six detection architectures.
- Our study provides comprehensive insights into the generalizability and efficacy of adversarial training strategies across diverse data distributions and model architectures, reinforcing the critical role of robust adversarial detectors in securing machine learning systems.

The next section describes previous work on adversarial training. Section 3 delineates our methodology, followed by the experimental framework in Section 4. We describe our results in Section 5, ending with conclusions in Section 6.

2. Previous Work

The foundation of adversarial training was laid by Madry et al. [19], who demonstrated its effectiveness on the MNIST [28] and CIFAR-10 [29] datasets. Their approach used Projected Gradient Descent (PGD) attacks to generate adversarial examples and incorporate them into the training process alongside clean (unattacked) data.

Subsequent work by Kurakin et al. [30] explored diverse adversarial training methods, highlighting the trade-off between robustness and accuracy. These early pioneering works laid the groundwork for the field of adversarial training and showcased its potential for improving classifier robustness.

Adversarial training has evolved significantly since its inception. Zhang et al. [31] introduced MixUp training, probabilistically blending clean and adversarial samples during training, achieving robustness without significant accuracy loss.

Tramer and Boneh [32] investigated multi-attack adversarial training, aiming for broader robustness against diverse attack types.

A number of works explored formal verification frameworks to mathematically certify classifier robustness against specific attacks, demonstrating provably robust defense mechanisms [33–36].

Zhang et al. [37] provided theoretical insights into the robustness of adversarially trained models, offering a deeper understanding of the underlying mechanisms and limitations. Their work elucidated the trade-offs between robustness, expressiveness, and generalization in adversarial training paradigms, contributing to a more comprehensive theoretical framework for analyzing and designing robust classifiers.

In the pursuit of improving robustness against adversarial examples, Xie et al. [38] proposed a novel approach using feature denoising. Their work identified noise within the extracted features as a vulnerability during adversarial training. To address this, they incorporated denoising blocks within the network architecture of a convolutional neural network (CNN). These blocks leverage techniques such as non-local means filters to remove the adversarial noise, leading to cleaner and more robust features. Their approach achieved significant improvements in adversarial robustness on benchmark datasets, when compared with baseline adversarially trained models. This work highlights feature denoising as a promising defense mechanism that complements existing adversarial training techniques. Pinhasov et al. [39] introduced a novel method to combat adversarial attacks on deepfake detectors. The authors leveraged eXplainable Artificial Intelligence (XAI) [40] to generate interpretability maps, revealing the decision-making process of the deepfake detector. By analyzing these maps, their system could identify vulnerabilities exploited by adversarial attacks.

Building on the limitations of standard adversarial training, requiring a large amount of labeled data, Carmon et al. [41] explored leveraging unlabeled data for improved robustness. Their work demonstrates that incorporating unlabeled data through semi-supervised learning techniques, such as self-training, can significantly enhance adversarial robustness. This approach bridges the gap in sample complexity, achieving high robust accuracy with the same amount of labeled data needed for standard accuracy. Their findings were validated empirically on datasets such as CIFAR-10, achieving state-of-the-art robustness against various adversarial attacks. This research highlights the potential of semi-supervised learning as a cost-effective strategy to improve adversarial training and achieve robust models.

Despite its successes, adversarial training faces several challenges. Transferability of adversarial examples remains a concern [42,43], because attacks often lack effectiveness across different classifiers and architectures. The computational cost of generating and training on adversarial examples can be significant, especially for large models and datasets. Moreover, adversarial training can lead to a reduction in clean data accuracy, requiring effective optimization strategies to mitigate this trade-off [44]. Additionally, carefully crafted evasive attacks can sometimes bypass adversarially trained classifiers, highlighting the need for further research and diversification of defense mechanisms.

There are but a few examples of works that compare adversarial attacks that take into account full knowledge of the defense, i.e., adaptive attacks. He et al. [45] showed promising results, at the cost of multiple model inferences coupled with multiple augmented neighborhood images. Klingner et al. [46] demonstrated a detection method based on edge extraction of features, such as depth estimation and semantic segmentation, and comparison with natural image edges based on the SSIM metric. We believe the underlying assumption of adversarial examples containing abnormal edges might not hold in un-natural settings.

Another notable work is that of Yang et al. [47], which introduces an adversarial detection method utilizing a conditional generative adversarial network (CGAN) and an encoder to reconstruct input images. By comparing the discrepancies between the original and reconstructed images, their ContraNet detects adversarial examples based on reconstruction errors. While this approach demonstrates competitive performance, it introduces significant computational overhead due to the use of the CGAN and encoder components, potentially limiting its applicability in real-time or resource-constrained scenarios.

Previous research has explored using sentiment analysis for adversarial example detection [48], focusing on the impact of adversarial perturbations on deep neural networks' hidden-layer feature maps under attack.

All of the above compared their work with some adaptive power like PGD, yet did not show state-of-the-art adaptive attacks, which optimize under the constraint imposed by the classifier decision boundary, like SPGD and OPGD [49]. Only a few methods were compared under these powerful optimizers. Yang et al. [47] presented a novel encoder-generator architecture that compared the generated image label with the original image label. We believe this was a step in the right direction, yet with a computationally expensive generator that had difficulties differentiating semantically close classes. We compared our results with theirs and others [50–52], which already have some comparison with SPGD or OPGD.

3. Methodology

Before delineating the methodology, we note that the overall framework comprises three distinct components:

1. **Classifier**, which is not modified (i.e., no learning);
2. **Detector**, with a "standard" loss function (to be discussed);
3. **Attacker**, with an adaptive loss function (to be discussed).

3.1. Threat Model

We assume a strong adversary, with full access to both the classifier f and the adversarial detector g. The attacker possesses comprehensive knowledge of the internal workings, parameters, and architecture of both models.

The attacker has two goals:

1. Manipulate the classifier's prediction such that it outputs a class label different from the correct label.
2. Deceive the detector into predicting that the adversarial image is benign.

Goal 1: Manipulate the classifier's prediction such that it outputs a class different from the correct class label y. Specifically, the attacker seeks a perturbation δ that causes misclassification, i.e., $f(x+\delta) \neq y$, while keeping the perturbation within an acceptable limit defined by the l_p norm constraint, $\|\delta\|_p \leq \epsilon$. Here, f is the classifier function, x is the original input, and ϵ is the maximum allowable perturbation magnitude. This problem can be formulated as

$$\underset{k=0,1,\ldots K-1}{\arg\max}\ f_k(x+\delta) \neq y,\ (x,y) \in \mathcal{D},\ \text{ s.t. } \|\delta\|_p \leq \epsilon, \tag{1}$$

where K is the total number of classes in the classification task, $f_k(x+\delta)$ denotes the classifier's output (e.g., probability or logit) for class k when input $x+\delta$ is provided, and $\mathcal{D}$ represents the dataset of input-label pairs.

We can solve this problem using the following optimization objective:

$$\underset{\delta:\|\delta\|_p \leq \epsilon}{\arg\max}\ \mathcal{L}_{\text{CE}}(f_\theta(x+\delta), y), \tag{2}$$

where $\mathcal{L}_{\text{CE}}$ is the cross-entropy loss.

Goal 2: The attacker's second goal is to deceive the detector g into predicting that the adversarial image is benign. The attacker aims to find a perturbation δ such that $g(x+\delta) \neq \texttt{adv}$, indicating that the input is not detected as adversarial, while still satisfying the perturbation constraint, $\|\delta\|_p \leq \epsilon$. The detector g outputs a prediction indicating whether an input is benign (ben) or adversarial (adv). This objective can be formalized as

$$\arg\max_{k=\texttt{ben},\texttt{adv}} g_k(x+\delta) \neq \texttt{adv}, \; x \in \mathcal{D}, \text{ s.t. } \|\delta\|_p \leq \epsilon, \tag{3}$$

where $g_k(x+\delta)$ represents the detector's output for label k, and k can be either ben or adv. All other variables were as previously defined.

We can solve this problem using the following optimization objective:

$$\arg\max_{\delta:\|\delta\|_p \leq \epsilon} \mathcal{L}_{\text{BCE}}(g_\phi(x+\delta), \texttt{adv}), \tag{4}$$

where $\mathcal{L}_{\text{BCE}}$ is the binary cross-entropy loss and ϵ is the allowed perturbation norm.

Combining the two goals, the attacker's overall goal is defined as

$$\arg\max_{\delta:\|\delta\|_p \leq \epsilon} \mathcal{L}_{\text{CE}}(f_\theta(x+\delta), y) + \mathcal{L}_{\text{BCE}}(g_\phi(x+\delta), \texttt{adv}). \tag{5}$$

By adjusting δ within the perturbation constraint, $\|\delta\|_p \leq \epsilon$, the attacker aims to achieve the following two objectives:

1. **Misclassification by the classifier**: By maximizing the cross-entropy loss $\mathcal{L}_{\text{CE}}(f\theta(x+\delta), y)$, the attacker increases the discrepancy between the classifier's prediction $f_\theta(x+\delta)$ and the true label y, causing the classifier to misclassify the perturbed input $x+\delta$.
2. **Evade detection**: By maximizing the binary cross-entropy loss $\mathcal{L}_{\text{BCE}}(g\phi(x+\delta), \texttt{adv})$ with respect to the label adv, the attacker forces the detector's output $g_\phi(x+\delta)$ away from correctly identifying the input as adversarial. This results in the detector misclassifying the adversarial input $x+\delta$ as benign.

Through careful adjustment of δ, the attacker simultaneously degrades the classifier's accuracy and circumvents the detector's ability to recognize adversarial inputs.

3.2. Problem Definition

We now formalize the problem of enhancing the robustness of an adversarial detector (g) through adversarial training. The setup involves a classifier (f) and an adversarial detector (g), both initially trained on a clean dataset $\mathcal{D}$ containing pairs (x, y), where x is an input data point and y is the ground-truth label. We denote with θ and ϕ the weight parameters of the classifier and the detector, respectively. Note that $\mathcal{D}$ is the clean dataset—adversarial examples are represented by $x+\delta$.

Adversarial training is formulated as a minimax game, as follows:

$$\min_\theta \left\{ \mathbb{E}_{(x,y)\sim\mathcal{D}} \left[\max_{\delta:\|\delta\|_p \leq \epsilon} \mathcal{L}_{\text{CE}}(f_\theta(x+\delta), y) \right] \right\}. \tag{6}$$

This minimax game pits the classifier against an adversary: the adversary maximizes the classifier's loss on perturbed inputs, while the classifier minimizes that loss across all such perturbations, ultimately becoming robust to attacks.

Our main objective is to improve the robustness of detector g using adversarial training by iteratively updating ϕ based on adversarial examples. Formally, the optimization objective for the adversarial training of the detector is

$$\min_\phi \left\{ \mathbb{E}_{(x,y)\sim\mathcal{D}} \left[\max_{\delta:\|\delta\|_p \leq \epsilon} \mathcal{L}_{\text{BCE}}(g_\phi(x+\delta), \texttt{adv}) \right] \right\}. \tag{7}$$

With regard to the classifier, we have a minimax game for the detector.

However, the above equation does not take into account the classifier, f. Therefore, we added the classifier outputs to our (almost) final objective, as follows:

$$\min_{\phi}\left\{\mathbb{E}_{(x,y)\sim\mathcal{D}}\left[\max_{\delta:\|\delta\|_p\leq\epsilon}\left(\mathcal{L}_{\mathrm{CE}}(f_\theta(x+\delta),y)+\mathcal{L}_{\mathrm{BCE}}(g_\phi(x+\delta),\mathtt{adv})\right)\right]\right\}. \tag{8}$$

Here, the objective incorporates both the classifier and the detector in a unified adversarial training framework. The goal is to simultaneously minimize the classification error *and* enhance the detector's robustness.

However, a potential conflict arises with this combined objective. The cross-entropy loss ($\mathcal{L}_{\mathrm{CE}}$) for the classifier and the binary cross-entropy loss ($\mathcal{L}_{\mathrm{BCE}}$) for the detector inherently contradict each other. The attacker's objective is to simultaneously induce misclassification in the classifier and deceive the detector into labeling adversarial examples as benign. This dual objective creates opposing forces in the optimization process. Specifically, the attacker's optimization of $\mathcal{L}_{\mathrm{CE}}$ aims to increase the classification error by adjusting δ so that the predicted class probabilities do not align with the true labels. Conversely, the optimization of $\mathcal{L}_{\mathrm{BCE}}$ seeks to reduce the detector's ability to differentiate between clean and adversarial examples, driving g_ϕ to misclassify adversarial inputs as benign. This opposition can lead to conflicting gradient directions, where optimizing for one objective may detract from progress on the other, thereby complicating the optimization process and potentially preventing either objective from being fully achieved.

This dual optimization can result in non-convergent behavior for several reasons. First, the gradients derived from $\mathcal{L}_{\mathrm{CE}}$ and $\mathcal{L}_{\mathrm{BCE}}$ often point in opposing directions. For example, a gradient step that reduces classification accuracy might enhance the detector's ability to identify adversarial examples. This phenomenon occurs because reducing classification accuracy involves adding perturbations to the input data, which in turn makes these perturbations more detectable by the adversarial detector. Consequently, the detector's task of distinguishing between clean and perturbed inputs becomes easier. This tug-of-war can impede the optimization process, preventing the simultaneous realization of both objectives. Lastly, the optimization landscapes of $\mathcal{L}_{\mathrm{CE}}$ and $\mathcal{L}_{\mathrm{BCE}}$ can dynamically shift as δ is updated.

To address this challenge, we employ the selective and orthogonal approaches proposed by Bryniarski et al. [49].

Selective Projected Gradient Descent (SPGD) [49] optimizes only with respect to a constraint that has not been satisfied yet—while not optimizing against a constraint that has been optimized. The loss function used by SPGD is

$$\mathcal{L}_{\mathrm{CE}}(f_\theta(x+\delta),y)\cdot\mathbb{1}[f_\theta(x)=y]+\mathcal{L}_{\mathrm{BCE}}(g_\phi(x+\delta),\mathtt{adv})\cdot\mathbb{1}[g_\phi(x+\delta)=\mathtt{adv}]. \tag{9}$$

Rather than minimizing a convex combination of the two loss functions, the idea is to optimize either the left-hand side of the equation, if the classifier's prediction is still y, meaning the optimization has not been completed, or optimize the right-hand side of the equation, if the detector's prediction is still $\mathtt{adv}$.

This approach ensures that updates consistently enhance the loss on either the classifier or the adversarial detector, with the attacker attempting to "push" the classifier away from the correct class y and also "push" the detector away from raising the adversarial "flag".

Orthogonal Projected Gradient Descent (OPGD) [49] focuses on modifying the update direction to ensure it remains orthogonal to the constraints imposed by previously satisfied objectives. This orthogonal projection ensures that the update steers the input towards the adversarial objective without violating the constraints imposed by the classifier's decision boundary, allowing for the creation of adversarial examples that bypass the detector. Thus, the update rule is slightly different, as follows:

$$\mathcal{L}_{\text{update}}(x,y) = \begin{cases} \nabla\mathcal{L}_{\text{CE}}(f_\theta(x+\delta),y) - \text{proj}_{\nabla\mathcal{L}_{\text{BCE}}(g_\phi(x+\delta),\text{adv})}\nabla\mathcal{L}_{\text{CE}}(f_\theta(x+\delta),y) & \text{if } \; f_\theta(x) = y \\ \nabla\mathcal{L}_{\text{BCE}}(g_\phi(x+\delta),\text{adv}) - \text{proj}_{\nabla\mathcal{L}_{\text{CE}}(f_\theta(x+\delta),y)}\nabla\mathcal{L}_{\text{BCE}}(g_\phi(x+\delta),\text{adv}) & \text{if } \; g_\phi(x) = \text{adv}. \end{cases} \tag{10}$$

In essence, we have set up a minimax game: the attacker wants to maximize loss with respect to the image, while the defender wants to minimize loss with respect to the detector's parameters.

Since optimization is customarily viewed as minimizing a loss function, we will consider that the attacker uses minimization instead of maximization. A failed attack would thus be observed though a large loss value (which we will indeed observe in Section 5).

All aforementioned objectives are intractable and thus approximated using iterative gradient-based attacks, such as PGD. Algorithm 1 shows the pseudocode of our method for adversarially training an adversarial detector. Figure 2 illustrates **RADAR**.

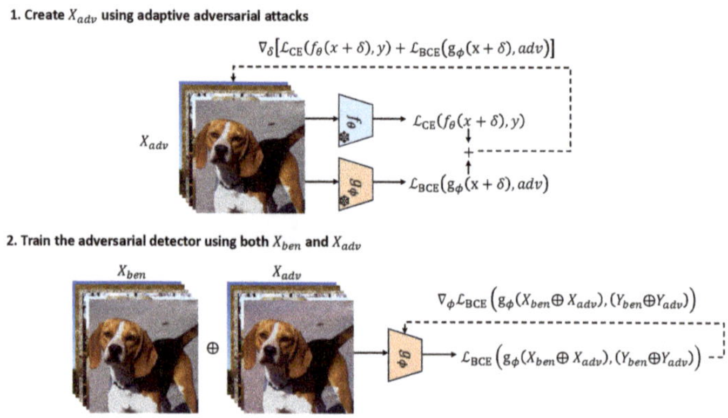

Figure 2. Overview of **RADAR**. (1) The process begins with the generation of adaptive adversarial instances, X_{adv}. (2) After completing the batch attack, we train the detector g_ϕ using both benign instances X_{ben} and adversarial instances X_{adv}. The ❄ symbol refers to the models being frozen.

Algorithm 1: RADAR

Input: dataset $\mathcal{D}$, classifier f_θ, detector, g_ϕ, detector's loss function $\mathcal{L}_{\text{BCE}}$, classifier's loss function $\mathcal{L}_{\text{CE}}$, batch size B, step size α, epsilon ϵ, number of steps I, number of epochs E, learning rate η

Output: adversarially trained g_ϕ

Set f to eval mode

for $e = 1, \ldots, E$ **do**

  for $X_{\text{ben}} \subseteq \mathcal{D}$, s.t. $|X_{\text{ben}}| = B$ **do**

    Set g to eval mode

    Compute adversarial examples X_{adv}:

$$X_{\text{adv}} \leftarrow \text{OPGD/SPGD}(f_\theta, g_\phi, X_{\text{ben}}, \epsilon, \alpha, I, \mathcal{L}_{\text{BCE}}, \mathcal{L}_{\text{CE}})$$

    Form a new batch:

$$X_{\text{mixed}} \leftarrow X_{\text{ben}} \oplus X_{\text{adv}}$$
$$Y_{\text{mixed}} \leftarrow \{\text{ben}\}_{i=1}^{|B|} \oplus \{\text{adv}\}_{i=1}^{|B|}$$

    Set g to train mode

    Compute average loss gradient for X_{mixed}:

$$\nabla_{\text{mixed}} \leftarrow \frac{1}{2|B|}\sum_{j=1}^{2|B|} \nabla_\phi\mathcal{L}_{\text{BCE}}(x_{\text{mixed}}, y_{\text{mixed}}; \phi)$$

    Update parameters:

$$\phi \leftarrow \phi - \eta\nabla_{\text{mixed}}$$

  end

end

---

4. Experimental Framework

Datasets and models. We used the VGG-{11, 13, 16} and ResNet-{18, 34, 50} architectures both for classification and for adversarial detection. Specifically, we employed these architectures in dual roles: as classifiers to perform the primary task of image classification and as adversarial detectors to identify adversarial examples. By leveraging the same architectures for both tasks, we ensured consistency in our experimental setup and enabled a comprehensive evaluation of their robustness and effectiveness in the context of adversarial training. We modified the classification head of the detector, $C \in \mathbb{R}^{K\times e}$, where K is the number of classes and e is the embedding space size, to $C \in \mathbb{R}^{2\times e}$, for binary classification (benign/adversarial), and added a sigmoid transformation at the end.

We utilized the CIFAR-10 [29], the SVHN [53], and a subset of the ImageNet [54] dataset to evaluate our proposed approach. For ImageNet, we randomly selected 50 classes from the original dataset, which contains over 14 million images and 1000 classes. This subset was used to maintain manageability and to focus our evaluation on a representative sample of the larger dataset, while still leveraging the diversity and complexity that ImageNet provides for benchmarking in image classification tasks. It is important to highlight that adversarial training for adversarial detectors incurs substantially higher computational costs compared with conventional adversarial training. As a result, this process is considerably more time-consuming when applied to large datasets. To ensure the feasibility of our experiments, we employed a reduced number of classes from ImageNet.

We used the definition of attack success rate presented by Bryniarski et al. [49] as part of their evaluation methodology. Attack efficacy is measured through Attack Success Rate at N, SR@N: proportion of deliberate attacks achieving their objectives subject to the condition that the defense's false-positive rate is configured to N%. The underlying motivation is that, in real-life scenarios, we must strike a delicate balance between security and precision. A 5% false positive is acceptable, while extreme cases might even use 50%. Our results proved excellent, so we set N to a low 5%, i.e., SR@5.

Throughout the training, the allowed perturbation was constrained by an ℓ_∞ norm, denoted as $\|\cdot\|_\infty$, with the maximum magnitude set to $\epsilon = \frac{16}{255}$. We employed an adversarial attack strategy, specifically utilizing 100 iterations of PGD with a step size parameter α set to 0.03. This approach was employed to generate adversarial instances and assess the resilience of the classifier under scrutiny. We then evaluated the classifiers on the attacked test set—the results are delineated in Table 1.

Table 1. Performance (accuracy percentage) of original classifiers on both clean and adversarial PGD-perturbed test sets.

Dataset	VGG-11		VGG-13		VGG-16		ResNet-18		ResNet-34		ResNet-50	
	Ben	Adv	Ben	Adv	Ben	Adv	Ben	Adv	Ben	Adv	Ben	Adv
CIFAR-10	92.40	0.35	94.21	0.19	94.00	5.95	92.60	0.14	93.03	0.21	93.43	0.26
SVHN	93.96	0.00	94.85	0.01	94.95	0.48	94.88	0.02	94.84	0.11	94.33	0.10
ImageNet	70.08	0.00	70.44	0.00	71.96	0.00	70.24	0.00	72.24	0.00	74.96	0.00

Afterwards, we split the training data into training (70%) and validation sets (30%). We trained 3 VGG-based and 3 ResNet-based adversarial detectors for 20 epochs using the Adam optimizer (with default β_1 and β_2 values), with a learning rate of 1×10^{-4} , a `CosineAnnealing` learning rate scheduler with $T_{\max} = 10$, and a batch size of 32. We tested the adversarial detectors on the test set that was composed of one-half clean images and one-half attacked images. They all performed almost perfectly.

Following the initial clean training phase, we implemented our proposed **RADAR** approach, which involves adversarial fine-tuning on the adversarial detectors. This process entailed attacking the detectors to an adaptive adversarial attack, specifically the OPGD attack. The adversarial fine-tuning was conducted over the course of 20 epochs, utilizing the same optimizer and the `ReduceLROnPlateau` learning rate scheduler, with the patience parameter set to 3 and a batch size of 32. Subsequently, the performance was evaluated on a test set consisting of an equal distribution of clean images and images subjected to OPGD attacks. Table 2 details the hyperparameters employed throughout the experiments.

Table 2. Summary of hyperparameters and implementation details used in the experiments.

Parameter	Value
Datasets	CIFAR-10, SVHN, ImageNet (50 classes)
Model architectures	VGG-11/13/16, ResNet-18/34/50
Optimizer	Adam ($\beta_1 = 0.9$, $\beta_2 = 0.999$)
Initial learning rate	1×10^{-4}
Learning rate scheduler (clean training)	Cosine annealing ($T_{\max} = 10$ epochs)
Learning rate scheduler (fine-tuning)	ReduceLROnPlateau (patience = 3, factor = 0.1)
Batch size	32
Number of epochs	20
Adversarial attack (PGD)	$\epsilon = 16/255$, $\alpha = 0.03$, 100 iterations
Adversarial attack (OPGD)	$\epsilon = 16/255$, 100 iterations

5. Results

Initially, we conducted an assessment of classifier performance following the generation of adversarial perturbations employing the PGD method.

The outcomes of this evaluation, presented in Table 1, highlight classifier performance on both clean and perturbed test sets. The results reveal significant vulnerability to adversarial manipulations. For instance, on the CIFAR-10 dataset, the VGG-11 classifier drops from 92.40% accuracy on clean data to 0.35% on adversarial examples. Other classifiers on CIFAR-10 show similar trends, with clean accuracy values between 92.40% and 94.21% and adversarial accuracy values below 6%. A similar pattern is observed on the SVHN dataset, where the VGG-11 classifier's accuracy falls from 93.96% on clean data to 0.00% on adversarial attacks. Other SVHN classifiers also exhibit significant performance drops, with adversarial accuracy values near 0%. On the ImageNet dataset, all classifiers reach 0% accuracy when attacked. These findings illustrate the stark vulnerability of standard classifiers to adversarial perturbations, underscoring the need for more robust defense mechanisms.

After standard training involving the use of PGD-generated adversarial images, Table 3 shows the performance outcomes of the adversarial detectors, as assessed through the ROC-AUC metric, before the deployment of **RADAR**. The table summarizes the average ROC-AUC ($AUC_{Avg.}$) and individual ROC-AUC scores for PGD (AUC_{PGD}), OPGD (AUC_{OPGD}), and SPGD (AUC_{SPGD}) attacks. For the CIFAR-10 dataset, the VGG-16 detector achieved the highest average ROC-AUC score of 0.46, which is slightly worse than tossing a coin. All detectors performed perfectly against PGD attacks, but their performance dropped significantly against OPGD and SPGD, with most detectors showing a score close to 0.00. The SVHN and ImageNet datasets displayed a similar trend. All models achieved perfect detection against PGD attacks, but their effectiveness plummeted for OPGD and SPGD attacks, with only ResNet-50 showing minimal detection capability.

Table 3. Without RADAR: Performance of detectors on several classifiers and datasets. In this and subsequent tables, boldface marks best performance. Note: for ROC-AUC, higher is better.

Detector	$AUC_{Avg.}$	CIFAR-10			SVHN			ImageNet		
		AUC_{PGD}	AUC_{OPGD}	AUC_{SPGD}	AUC_{PGD}	AUC_{OPGD}	AUC_{SPGD}	AUC_{PGD}	AUC_{OPGD}	AUC_{SPGD}
VGG-11	0.33	1.00	0.00	0.00	1.00	0.00	0.00	1.00	0.00	0.00
VGG-13	0.33	1.00	0.00	0.00	1.00	0.00	0.00	1.00	0.00	0.00
VGG-16	**0.46**	1.00	0.61	0.59	1.00	0.00	0.00	1.00	0.00	0.00
ResNet-18	0.33	1.00	0.00	0.00	1.00	0.00	0.00	1.00	0.00	0.00
ResNet-34	0.33	1.00	0.00	0.00	1.00	0.00	0.00	1.00	0.00	0.00
ResNet-50	0.37	1.00	0.15	0.14	1.00	0.03	0.05	1.00	0.00	0.00
Avg.	0.36	1.00	0.13	0.12	1.00	0.00	0.00	1.00	0.00	0.00

Table 4 presents results regarding the adversarial detectors' performance, based on the SR@5 metric, prior to using **RADAR**. Notably, the VGG-16 detector exhibits the best performance with a significantly lower SR@5$_{Avg.}$ value of 0.78. It performs particularly well against OPGD and SPGD attacks on CIFAR-10, achieving SR@5 values of 0.37 and 0.40, respectively. This indicates a higher robustness compared with other detectors. In contrast, detectors such as VGG-11, VGG-13, ResNet-18, and ResNet-34 show higher SR@5$_{Avg.}$ values of around 0.97 for both datasets. ResNet-50 performs better than most with an average SR@5 of 0.88 on CIFAR-10 but still falls short of VGG-16. On the ImageNet dataset, the detectors also fail to withstand the attacks, achieving SR@5 values of 0.98 and 0.99 for OPGD and SPGD, respectively.

Table 4. Without RADAR: Performance of detectors on several classifiers and datasets. VGG-16 is the most robust detector in terms of SR@5. Note: for SR@5, lower is better.

Detector	SR@5$_{Avg.}$	CIFAR-10		SVHN		ImageNet	
		SR@5$_{OPGD}$	SR@5$_{SPGD}$	SR@5$_{OPGD}$	SR@5$_{SPGD}$	SR@5$_{OPGD}$	SR@5$_{SPGD}$
VGG-11	0.98	0.97	0.97	0.98	0.99	0.99	1.00
VGG-13	0.99	0.97	0.99	0.99	0.99	1.00	1.00
VGG-16	0.78	0.37	0.40	0.99	0.99	0.97	0.99
ResNet-18	0.98	0.96	0.97	0.99	0.99	0.99	1.00
ResNet-34	0.98	0.96	0.97	0.99	0.99	0.99	1.00
ResNet-50	0.93	0.81	0.83	0.96	0.94	0.97	0.99
Avg.	0.90	0.84	0.85	0.98	0.98	0.98	0.99

We then deployed **RADAR**. The outcomes on the efficacy of adversarial detectors, measured by ROC-AUC and SR@5 metrics after integrating **RADAR**, are presented in Tables 5 and 6. Table 7 shows the accuracy percentages of all the classifiers on clean and adversarially perturbed test sets across the CIFAR-10, SVHN, and ImageNet datasets after applying **RADAR**. Notably, we constructed an equal distribution of clean and adversarially perturbed test sets, effectively doubling the original test set size to ensure a balanced evaluation. Accuracy was computed as follows: If the detector identified the input as adversarial, the classifier's prediction was disregarded; otherwise, the classifier's prediction was considered. The observed accuracy drop in Table 7, particularly noticeable in smaller models, can be attributed to their limited number of parameters, making adaptation to both adaptive and standard adversarial attacks more challenging. Note that the benign accuracy for all classifiers across CIFAR-10, SVHN, and ImageNet remained unchanged.

Table 5. With RADAR: Performance of employing **RADAR** with OPGD on several classifiers and datasets.

Detector	AUC$_{Avg.}$	CIFAR-10			SVHN			ImageNet		
		AUC$_{PGD}$	AUC$_{OPGD}$	AUC$_{SPGD}$	AUC$_{PGD}$	AUC$_{OPGD}$	AUC$_{SPGD}$	AUC$_{PGD}$	AUC$_{OPGD}$	AUC$_{SPGD}$
VGG-11	0.98	0.99	0.95	0.94	1.00	1.00	1.00	1.00	1.00	1.00
VGG-13	0.99	0.99	0.99	0.99	1.00	1.00	1.00	1.00	0.99	0.99
VGG-16	0.99	1.00	0.99	0.99	1.00	1.00	1.00	1.00	0.99	0.99
ResNet-18	0.98	0.99	0.96	0.96	1.00	0.99	1.00	0.95	1.00	1.00
ResNet-34	0.99	0.99	0.99	1.00	1.00	1.00	1.00	0.98	1.00	1.00
ResNet-50	0.99	0.99	0.99	0.99	1.00	1.00	0.99	0.99	1.00	1.00
Avg.	0.99	0.99	0.98	0.98	1.00	0.99	0.99	0.98	0.99	0.99

For all datasets, **RADAR** maintains high accuracy on both PGD and OPGD samples. VGG-11 on CIFAR-10 retains an accuracy of 92.40% across all scenarios, while ResNet-50 on SVHN shows only a slight reduction from 94.33% to 94.32% on OPGD samples. In contrast, the ImageNet dataset reveals more significant accuracy drops under adversarial conditions, particularly for ResNet-18, which falls from 70.24% on benign samples to 61.05% on PGD samples.

Following **RADAR** integration, we observed significant improvements in adversarial detection performance across various classifiers and datasets, as shown in Table 5. Notably, on CIFAR-10, models such as VGG-13, VGG-16, ResNet-34, and ResNet-50 achieved high average ROC-AUC scores of 0.99, with ResNet-18 slightly lower at 0.98. For SVHN, all models achieved ROC-AUC scores of 1.00, except for ResNet-18 and ResNet-50, which scored 0.99 under specific attack conditions. Similarly, for the ImageNet dataset, models exhibited robust performance, with most achieving ROC-AUC scores of 1.00. Specifically, ResNet-50 scored consistently high at 1.00 or 0.99 across different attack types. We observed that ResNet-18 on ImageNet exhibits a lower AUC_{PGD} score (0.95) compared with other models. This drop is likely due to ResNet-18's shallower architecture, which may not capture the complex feature representations necessary for effective adversarial detection on high-resolution datasets like ImageNet. These results underscore **RADAR**'s ability to fortify adversarial detectors against various attack methods.

Table 6. With RADAR: Performance of detectors on several classifiers and datasets.

Detector	$SR@5_{Avg.}$	CIFAR-10		SVHN		ImageNet	
		$SR@5_{OPGD}$	$SR@5_{SPGD}$	$SR@5_{OPGD}$	$SR@5_{SPGD}$	$SR@5_{OPGD}$	$SR@5_{SPGD}$
VGG-11	0.02	0.04	0.06	0.00	0.00	0.00	0.00
VGG-13	0.00	0.00	0.00	0.00	0.00	0.00	0.00
VGG-16	0.00	0.00	0.00	0.00	0.00	0.00	0.00
ResNet-18	0.02	0.05	0.05	0.00	0.00	0.00	0.00
ResNet-34	0.00	0.00	0.00	0.00	0.00	0.00	0.00
ResNet-50	0.00	0.00	0.00	0.00	0.00	0.00	0.00
Avg.	0.00	0.01	0.02	0.00	0.00	0.00	0.00

Table 7. With RADAR: The accuracy percentage of the original classifiers is assessed on both clean and adversarially perturbed test sets, using both PGD and OPGD, subsequent to the application of **RADAR**. In instances where the adversarial detector indicates an adversarial sample (adv), the classifier's prediction is disregarded.

Dataset	VGG-11			VGG-13			VGG-16			ResNet-18			ResNet-34			ResNet-50		
	Ben	PGD	OPGD	Ben	PGD	OPGD	Ben	PGD	OPGD	Ben	PGD	OPGD	Ben	PGD	OPGD	Ben	PGD	OPGD
CIFAR-10	92.40	92.40	92.37	94.21	94.17	94.08	94.00	93.96	93.91	92.60	92.41	91.84	93.03	93.03	93.03	93.43	93.43	93.14
SVHN	93.96	93.96	93.95	94.85	94.85	94.85	94.95	94.95	94.94	94.88	94.88	94.86	94.84	94.83	94.82	94.33	94.33	94.32
ImageNet	70.08	68.89	68.73	70.44	69.87	69.83	71.96	71.96	71.96	70.24	61.05	68.63	72.24	68.18	72.18	74.96	74.63	74.96

The SR@5 metric further confirms the robustness of **RADAR**-enhanced detectors, as detailed in Table 6. Models like VGG-13, VGG-16, ResNet-34, and ResNet-50 achieved perfect SR@5 scores of 0.00 on all datasets, indicating successful detection of adversarial attacks. VGG-11 and ResNet-18 demonstrated slightly lower performance on CIFAR-10. **RADAR** significantly improves the robustness of adversarial detectors, as evidenced by high ROC-AUC scores and low SR@5 values across different models and datasets, including the challenging ImageNet dataset. This comprehensive performance across diverse datasets reinforces the efficacy of our proposed approach in enhancing adversarial detector resilience.

Figure 3 show the generalization performance of **RADAR**-trained detectors on classifiers they were not trained on. This table shows the ROC-AUC values of **RADAR**-trained detectors when evaluated on the different classifier models. Each cell in the table corresponds to the ROC-AUC value achieved by the detector–classifier pair. For example, the top-left cell in the top-right table indicates the performance of a VGG-11 detector model trained on a VGG-11 classifier model using the ImageNet dataset and subsequently evaluated on attacks utilizing a ResNet-50 classifier model. The results indicate consistently high generalization across different classifiers, with most detector–classifier pairs achieving ROC-AUC values of 0.99 or higher. This demonstrates the effectiveness of **RADAR**-trained detectors in maintaining high adversarial detection performance across diverse datasets and classifier architectures. These findings underscore the resilience of adversarial detectors trained with **RADAR**, showcasing their ability to maintain robust detection capabilities even when confronted with unseen classifiers. The high ROC-AUC values indicate that our approach effectively fortifies the detectors themselves, rather than relying solely on robust classifier training, thereby enhancing the overall security and reliability of the adversarial detection system.

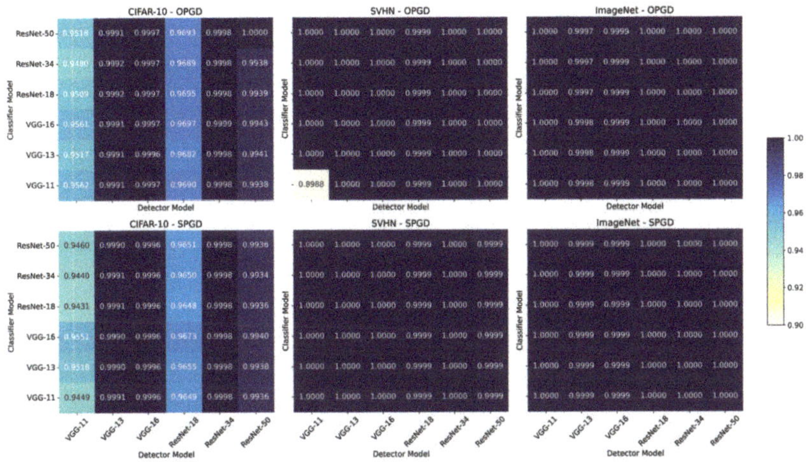

Figure 3. Generalization performance of adversarially trained detectors trained on CIFAR-10, SVHN, and ImageNet. Each adversarial detector was trained using each corresponding classifier; e.g., ResNet-50 adversarial detector was trained using ResNet-50 image classifier. This table shows the generalization of each detector to other classifiers, which it did not train with. A value represents the ROC-AUC of the respective detector–classifier pair for OPGD (top row) and SPGD (bottom row) with $\epsilon = \frac{16}{255}$.

A notable enhancement is observed across all detectors with respect to ROC-AUC and SR@5. Moreover, our findings suggest that adversarial training did not optimize solely for adaptability to specific adversarial techniques, but also demonstrated efficacy against conventional PGD attacks, which are different in nature, as illustrated in Figure 4.

Impact of adversarial training on optimization dynamics. Before the incorporation of adversarial training, the optimization process exhibited a trend of rapid convergence towards zero loss within a few iterations, as can be seen in the top rows of Figures 5–7.

Once we integrated adversarial training into the detector, we observed a distinct shift in the optimization behavior. Upon deploying **RADAR**, the optimization process displayed a tendency to plateau after a small number of iterations, with loss values typically higher by orders of magnitude, as compared with those observed prior to deployment. This plateau phase persisted across diverse experimental settings and datasets, indicating a fundamental change in the optimization landscape, induced by **RADAR**. This behavior can be seen as a robustness-enhancing effect, because the detector appears to resist rapid convergence towards trivial solutions, thereby enhancing its generalization capabilities. This showcases the efficacy of our method in bolstering the defenses of detection systems against adversarial threats—without sacrificing clean accuracy.

Robustness analysis with various epsilon values. The results of our experiments, depicted in Figures 8 and 9, provide a comprehensive evaluation of the robustness of the adversarial detectors against OPGD and SPGD attacks with different ϵ values.

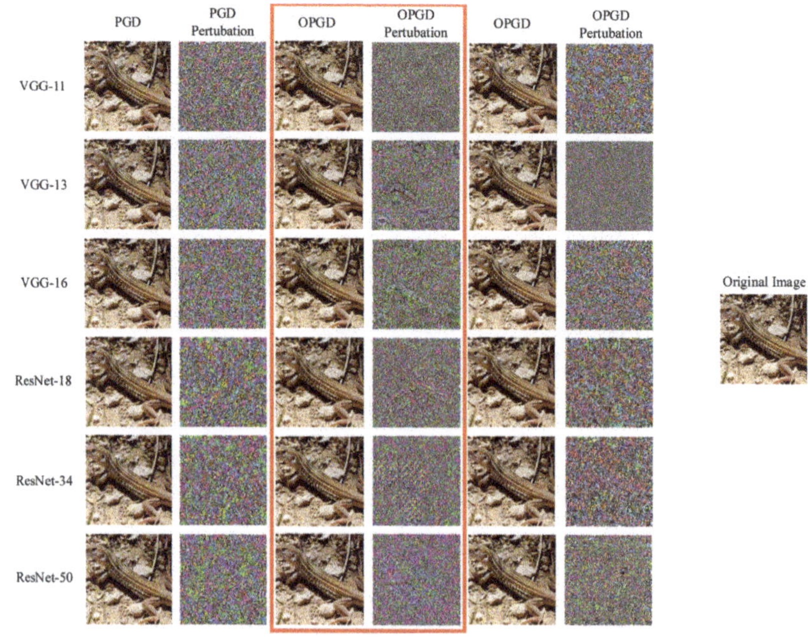

Figure 4. Comparison of perturbations generated by PGD and OPGD across adversarial detectors. The red box contains the manipulated images and the corresponding perturbation over the adversarially trained detectors. Each row represents one model architecture, while the columns show the adversarial image generated by PGD, the corresponding perturbation from PGD, the adversarial image generated by OPGD, and the corresponding perturbation from OPGD. The original image is shown on the right for reference. Note: PGD only attacks a classifier, while OPGD attacks both a classifier and a detector.

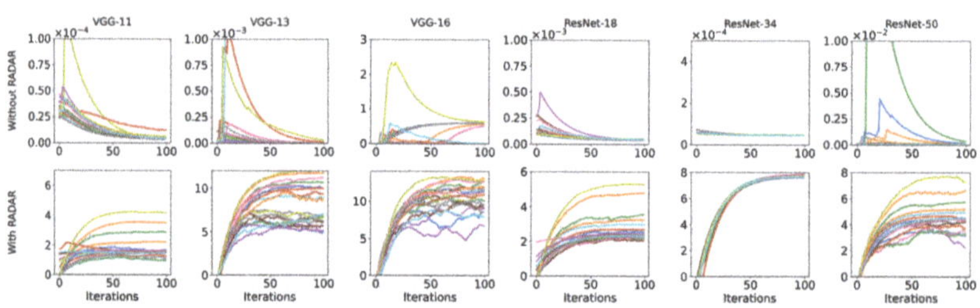

Figure 5. CIFAR-10. Binary cross-entropy loss metrics, from the point of view of an attacker, are presented here in the context of crafting an adversarial instance from the test set. These plots illustrate the progression of loss over 20 different images of orthogonal projected gradient descent (OPGD) with the main goal being to minimize the loss. The progression for each image is represented in a distinct color. Top: Prior to adversarial training, the loss converges to zero after a small number of iterations. Bottom: After adversarial training, the incurred losses are significantly higher by orders of magnitude (note the difference in scales) compared with those observed in their standard counterparts. This shows that the detector is now resilient, i.e., far harder to fool.

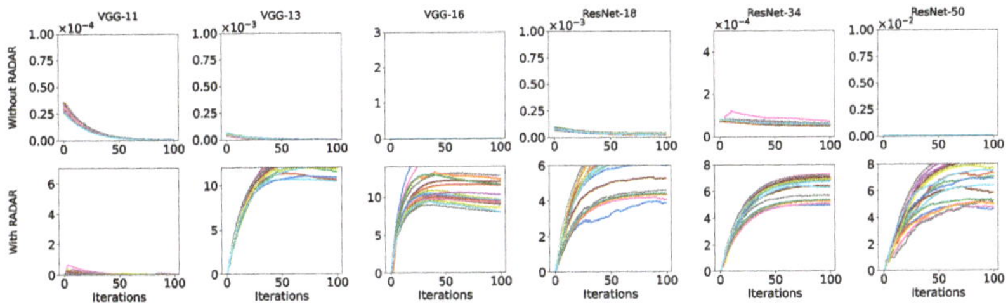

Figure 6. SVHN. Binary cross-entropy loss metrics, from the point of view of an attacker, are presented here in the context of crafting an adversarial instance from the test set. The progression for each image is represented in a distinct color.

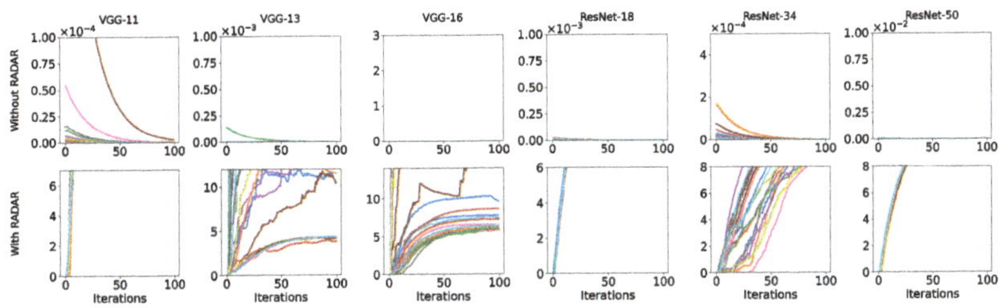

Figure 7. ImageNet. Binary cross-entropy loss metrics, from the point of view of an attacker, are presented here in the context of crafting an adversarial instance from the test set using OPGD. The progression for each image is represented in a distinct color.

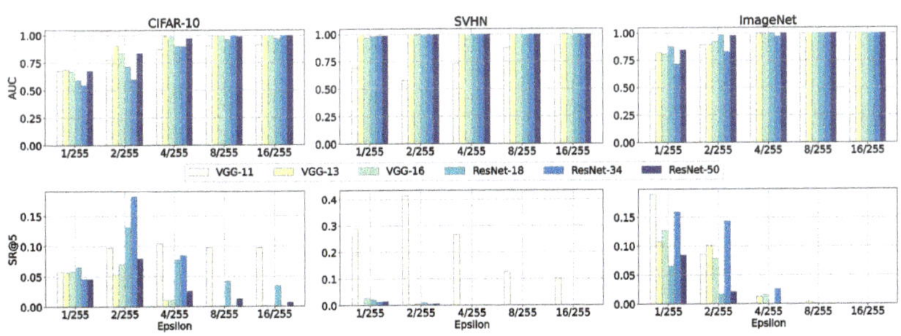

Figure 8. AUC and SR@5 scores across different epsilon values for CIFAR-10, SVHN, and ImageNet datasets using OPGD. The performance of the adversarial detectors is illustrated, highlighting how AUC and SR@5 vary across different perturbation magnitudes.

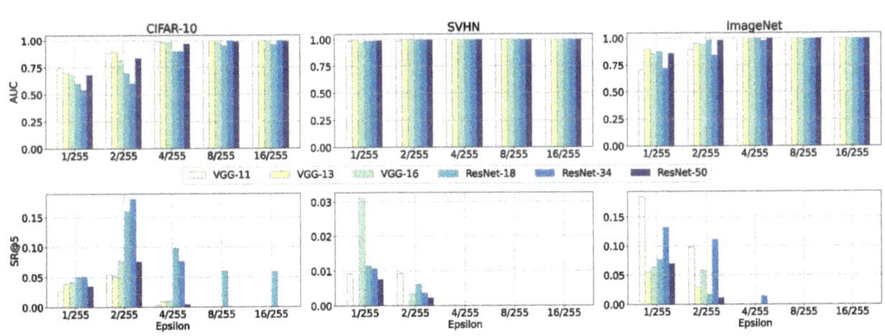

Figure 9. AUC and SR@5 scores across different epsilon values for CIFAR-10, SVHN, and ImageNet datasets using SPGD.

For the CIFAR-10, SVHN, and ImageNet datasets, increasing ϵ values generally results in increasing ROC-AUC scores and decreasing SR@5 rates using both OPGD and SPGD, indicating improved detection capabilities and decreased success of adversarial attacks.

Specifically, VGG-11 shows a significant drop in AUC and a corresponding rise in SR@5 as ϵ decreases, reflecting its susceptibility to lower magnitude perturbations. VGG-13 and VGG-16 exhibit similar patterns, though VGG-16 demonstrates slightly better robustness at lower ϵ values. This trend is consistent across both OPGD and SPGD attack evaluations.

The ResNet models, particularly ResNet-50, demonstrate superior resilience performance. Across various ϵ values, ResNet-50 consistently exhibits higher ROC-AUC scores and lower SR@5 rates compared with other models, signifying its robust ability to detect subtle adversarial examples. Notably, our method maintains consistently low SR@5 values across all datasets, underscoring its resilience. Specifically, experiments on the SVHN dataset consistently achieve an SR@5 of 0%. For CIFAR-10 and ImageNet, SR@5 ranges between 0% and 17% with OPGD and between 0% with 15% with SPGD, affirming the efficacy of our approach in enhancing adversarial detection capability. These results highlight the advantage of applying adversarial training directly to adversarial detectors rather than focusing solely on classifiers themselves.

Comparison with other detectors against adaptive attacks. Table 8 presents the robust accuracy ($\text{Acc}_{\text{robust}}$) of various defenses against OPGD and SPGD adaptive attacks at two perturbation levels, $\epsilon = 0.01$ and $\epsilon = 8/255$, and at two false-positive rates, 5% (FP@5) and 50% (FP@50). The defenses evaluated are ContraNet [55], Trapdoor [50], DLA [51], and SID [52]. **RADAR** consistently achieves the highest robust accuracy across both attack types and perturbation levels, maintaining nearly 100% accuracy in all scenarios. ContraNet also shows high performance, particularly at lower perturbation levels, but its accuracy decreases at higher perturbation levels. Trapdoor, DLA, and SID exhibit varying degrees of robustness, with significant decreases in accuracy at higher perturbation levels. For instance, Trapdoor's accuracy drops to almost 0% under both attack types at $\epsilon = 8/255$.

Table 8. Robust accuracy of different defenses under OPGD and SPGD attacks. The table presents the robust accuracy ($\text{Acc}_{\text{robust}}$) of various defenses when subjected to the adaptive attacks, OPGD and SPGD. The accuracy is evaluated at two perturbation levels, $\epsilon = 0.01$ and $\epsilon = 8/255$, and is reported for two false-positive rates (FP), 5% (FP@5) and 50% (FP@50).

Attack	Defense	$\epsilon = 0.01$		$\epsilon = 8/255$	
		$\text{Acc}_{\text{robust}} FP@5$	$\text{Acc}_{\text{robust}} FP@50$	$\text{Acc}_{\text{robust}} FP@5$	$\text{Acc}_{\text{robust}} FP@50$
OPGD	**RADAR**	99.2%	**99.3%**	**99.8%**	**99.9%**
	ContraNet [55]	93.7%	99.2%	89.8%	94.7%
	Trapdoor [50]	0.0%	7.0%	0.0%	8.0%
	DLA [51]	62.6%	83.7%	0.0%	28.2%
	SID [52]	6.9%	23.4%	0.0%	1.6%
SPGD	**RADAR**	**99.2%**	**99.1%**	**99.8%**	**99.9%**
	ContraNet [55]	93.7%	99.3%	89.7%	95.1%
	Trapdoor [50]	0.2%	49.5%	0.4%	37.2%
	DLA [51]	17.0%	55.9%	0.0%	13.5%
	SID [52]	8.9%	50.9%	0.0%	11.4%

Susceptibility of datasets and models to adversarial attacks. The susceptibility of machine learning models to adversarial attacks is influenced both by the characteristics of the datasets and by the architectures of the models employed. Datasets with higher complexity, such as those containing more classes, higher-resolution images, or greater intra-class variability, can lead to models that are more vulnerable to adversarial perturbations. For example, models trained on datasets like ImageNet may exhibit higher susceptibility compared with those trained on simpler datasets like CIFAR-10 or SVHN due to the increased complexity and diversity of the data, as shown in Table 1. Model architecture also plays a significant role in vulnerability to adversarial attacks. Deep neural networks with complex and highly non-linear decision boundaries can be more easily manipulated by small perturbations. Models with a larger number of parameters may overfit to the training data, making them less robust to unseen adversarial examples. However, larger and deeper models can also capture more complex patterns and representations, potentially enhancing their ability to generalize and resist certain types of adversarial attacks. This is evidenced in our experimental results (see Tables 5 and 6 and Figure 3), where deeper architectures demonstrate improved performance in detecting adversarial inputs.

Ablation Studies

In this section, we conduct comprehensive ablation studies to evaluate the impact of critical hyperparameters in our proposed loss function on the performance of our adversarial detectors on the validation set. Specifically, we focus on these five key parameters: (1) number of steps, (2) step size (α), (3) batch size, (4) learning rate, and (5) whether the model was pretrained through standard training. Each of these parameters plays a significant role in the training process and potentially influences the robustness and effectiveness of our adversarial detectors. To evaluate the effectiveness and trade-offs associated with these parameters, we conducted a series of experiments using the VGG-11 architecture on the CIFAR-10 dataset. The results are delineated in Figure 10.

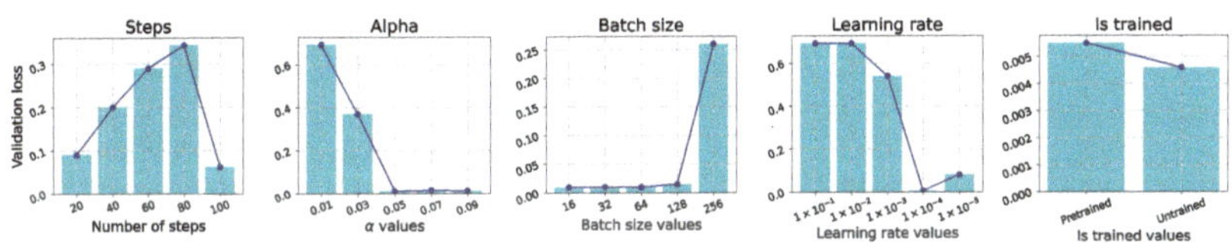

Figure 10. Ablation studies were conducted using VGG-11, varying the (1) number of steps, (2) step size α, (3) batch size, (4) learning rate, and (5) whether the model was pretrained through standard training, presented sequentially from left to right.

The results reveal that the number of steps significantly affects the model's performance. The detector's performance reaches its peak at 100 steps. This suggests that more iterations in the adversarial training process lead to better optimization and enhanced robustness of the adversarial detector. The choice of α also plays a critical role. Our findings show that a smaller α (0.05) yields the best performance, while increasing α increases effectiveness. This indicates that bigger perturbations during training are more effective in strengthening the detector's resilience to adversarial attacks. However, we want to detect attacks that are unrecognizable; thus we chose to use $\alpha = 0.03$.

Regarding batch size, the performance remains relatively stable across smaller batch sizes but shows a notable decline at the largest batch size tested (256).

Learning rate is another crucial factor. Initially, learning rates of 1×10^{-1} and 1×10^{-2} perform worse, but as the learning rate decreases, there is an improvement in performance. However, a learning rate that is too small (1×10^{-5}) results in under-performance, highlighting the need for a balanced learning rate to ensure effective training.

The "Is trained" graph reveals that pretrained models exhibit a slightly higher validation loss than untrained ones, suggesting slightly poorer performance. This may be due to untrained models' overfitting to the new adversarial data, while pretrained models—already informed by standard training—generalize better. Thus, pretraining appears to provide a foundation but may limit adaptability to newly introduced adversarial nuances.

Based on this ablation study, we selected the hyperparameters that yielded the best performance: a batch size of 32, a learning rate of 1×10^{-2}, 100 steps, and an α value of 0.03. These settings were found to optimize the robustness of our adversarial detector, providing a strong defense against adversarial attacks.

As illustrated in Figure 11, we conducted an in-depth analysis of the impact of excluding standard training and relying solely on adversarial training across three distinct datasets: CIFAR-10, SVHN, and ImageNet.

For CIFAR-10, the results demonstrate that standard training significantly boosts performance—particularly for ResNet models—at lower epsilon values (1/255 and 2/255). Accuracy for ResNet-18, for example, shows a clear advantage with standard training, highlighting its role in enhancing model robustness at smaller perturbations. However, as the epsilon values increase, the gap between models trained with and without standard training narrows, suggesting that adversarial training alone is sufficient to maintain robustness at higher perturbations.

In the case of SVHN, the benefits of standard training are evident in ResNet-based models but less pronounced compared with CIFAR-10. Accuracy trends show that while standard training does provide a marginal improvement—particularly noticeable for the ResNet architectures—models trained exclusively with adversarial training still achieve good performance. This suggests that, for simpler datasets, e.g., SVHN, the reliance on standard training might be reduced without significant loss in robustness, especially at mid to high epsilon values.

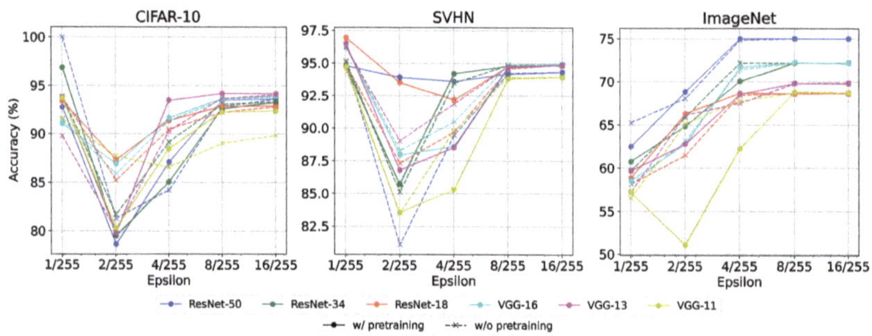

Figure 11. Comparison of classification accuracies of models utilizing adversarial detectors trained with standard pretraining followed by adversarial training (solid lines) versus detectors trained exclusively with adversarial training (dashed lines) across CIFAR-10, SVHN, and ImageNet datasets. The plot demonstrates the impact of increasing ϵ values on the accuracy of the classification models when using the respective adversarial detectors.

For ImageNet, results show a relatively modest impact with standard training compared with the other datasets. Performance improvement when incorporating standard training is not as pronounced, which may be attributed to the fact that all models in this evaluation were pretrained on ImageNet. This pretraining likely provided the models with a strong baseline robustness, diminishing the relative benefit of standard training in this specific case. As with the other datasets, when the epsilon values increase, the performance gap between models with and without standard training narrows further, suggesting that adversarial training alone is effective at higher perturbation strengths.

Overall, the analysis across these datasets indicates that while standard training contributes positively to model robustness, particularly at lower epsilon values, adversarial training alone can achieve comparable performance as the perturbation strength increases. The decision to incorporate standard training may therefore depend on the specific dataset and the computational resources available.

6. Conclusions

We presented a paradigmatic shift in the approach to adversarial training of deep neural networks, transitioning from fortifying classifiers to fortifying networks dedicated to adversarial detection. Our findings illuminate the prospective capacity to endow deep neural networks with resilience against adversarial attacks. Rigorous empirical inquiries substantiate the efficacy of our developed adversarial training methodology.

There is no trade-off between clean and adversarial classification because the classifier is not modified.

Our results bring forth a sense of optimism regarding the attainability of adversarially robust deep learning detectors. Notably, the significant robustness exhibited by our networks across the datasets examined manifested in increased accuracy against a diverse array of potent ℓ_∞-bound adversaries.

However, despite the promising results, our approach has a number of limitations that warrant further investigation. First, our adversarial training methodology primarily focuses on ℓ_∞-norm bounded attacks, which may limit its effectiveness against adversaries employing different norms, such as ℓ_2 or ℓ_1 attacks. This norm-specific robustness suggests that our detectors might not generalize well to all possible adversarial perturbations.

A further limitation lies in the dependency of **RADAR**'s effectiveness on the architecture of the detector: detectors with limited expressive capacity may fail to provide adequate gradient signals, thus hindering the robustness of the detection mechanism.

Additionally, the computational overhead associated with training and deploying the adversarial detector could pose challenges for resource-constrained applications. The necessity for extensive adversarial examples during training increases computational cost and may not be feasible for larger-scale systems.

Future research directions include extending our adversarial training approach to cover a wider range of attack norms and developing norm-agnostic detection mechanisms. Investigating the scalability of our methodology to larger and more complex datasets, as well as its applicability to different neural network architectures, remains an open question for now.

Our study not only contributes valuable insights into enhancing the resilience of deep neural networks against adversarial attacks but also underscores the importance of continued exploration in this domain. Therefore, we encourage researchers to persist in their endeavors to advance the frontier of adversarially robust deep learning detectors.

Author Contributions: Writing—original draft, A.D.; Methodology, R.L.; Software, R.L.; Writing—review & editing, R.L. and M.S.; Supervision, M.S.; Project administration, M.S. All authors have read and agreed to the published version of the manuscript.

Funding: This research was funded by the Israeli Innovation Authority through the Trust.AI consortium.

Data Availability Statement: Data are contained within the article.

Conflicts of Interest: Authors Raz Lapid and Almog Dubin were employed by the company Deep-Keep. The remaining authors declare that the research was conducted in the absence of any commercial or financial relationships that could be construed as a potential conflict of interest.

References

1. Huang, J.; Chai, J.; Cho, S. Deep learning in finance and banking: A literature review and classification. *Front. Bus. Res. China* **2020**, *14*, 13. [CrossRef]
2. Miotto, R.; Wang, F.; Wang, S.; Jiang, X.; Dudley, J.T. Deep learning for healthcare: Review, opportunities and challenges. *Brief. Bioinform.* **2018**, *19*, 1236–1246. [CrossRef] [PubMed]
3. Chen, L.; Pelger, M.; Zhu, J. Deep learning in asset pricing. *Manag. Sci.* **2024**, *70*, 714–750. [CrossRef]
4. Shamshirband, S.; Fathi, M.; Dehzangi, A.; Chronopoulos, A.T.; Alinejad-Rokny, H. A review on deep learning approaches in healthcare systems: Taxonomies, challenges, and open issues. *J. Biomed. Inform.* **2021**, *113*, 103627. [CrossRef]
5. Lv, Z.; Zhang, S.; Xiu, W. Solving the security problem of intelligent transportation system with deep learning. *IEEE Trans. Intell. Transp. Syst.* **2020**, *22*, 4281–4290. [CrossRef]
6. Goodfellow, I.J.; Shlens, J.; Szegedy, C. Explaining and harnessing adversarial examples. *arXiv* **2014**, arXiv:1412.6572.
7. Szegedy, C.; Zaremba, W.; Sutskever, I.; Bruna, J.; Erhan, D.; Goodfellow, I.; Fergus, R. Intriguing properties of neural networks. *arXiv* **2013**, arXiv:1312.6199.
8. Alter, T.; Lapid, R.; Sipper, M. On the Robustness of Kolmogorov-Arnold Networks: An Adversarial Perspective. *arXiv* **2024**, arXiv:2408.13809.
9. Tamam, S.V.; Lapid, R.; Sipper, M. Foiling Explanations in Deep Neural Networks. *arXiv* **2023**, arXiv:2211.14860.
10. Chen, Z.; Li, B.; Wu, S.; Jiang, K.; Ding, S.; Zhang, W. Content-based unrestricted adversarial attack. *Adv. Neural Inf. Process. Syst.* **2024**, *36*, 51719–51733 .
11. Lapid, R.; Langberg, R.; Sipper, M. Open Sesame! Universal Black-Box Jailbreaking of Large Language Models. In Proceedings of the ICLR 2024 Workshop on Secure and Trustworthy Large Language Models, Vienna, Austria, 11 May 2024.

12. Carlini, N.; Wagner, D. Towards evaluating the robustness of neural networks. In Proceedings of the 2017 IEEE Symposium on Security and Privacy (SP), San Jose, CA, USA, 22–26 May 2017; pp. 39–57.
13. Lapid, R.; Sipper, M. I See Dead People: Gray-Box Adversarial Attack on Image-To-Text Models. In Proceedings of the 5th Workshop on Machine Learning for Cybersecurity, part of ECMLPKDD 2023, Turin, Italy, 22 September 2023 .
14. Andriushchenko, M.; Croce, F.; Flammarion, N.; Hein, M. Square attack: A query-efficient black-box adversarial attack via random search. In Proceedings of the European Conference on Computer Vision. Springer, Glasgow, UK, 23–28 August 2020; pp. 484–501.
15. Lapid, R.; Haramaty, Z.; Sipper, M. An evolutionary, gradient-free, query-efficient, black-box algorithm for generating adversarial instances in deep convolutional neural networks. *Algorithms* **2022**, *15*, 407. [CrossRef]
16. Lapid, R.; Sipper, M. Patch of invisibility: Naturalistic black-box adversarial attacks on object detectors. *arXiv* **2023**, arXiv:2303.04238.
17. Finlayson, S.G.; Bowers, J.D.; Ito, J.; Zittrain, J.L.; Beam, A.L.; Kohane, I.S. Adversarial attacks on medical machine learning. *Science* **2019**, *363*, 1287–1289. [CrossRef]
18. Liu, M.; Zhang, Z.; Chen, Y.; Ge, J.; Zhao, N. Adversarial attack and defense on deep learning for air transportation communication jamming. *IEEE Trans. Intell. Transp. Syst.* **2023**, *25*, 973–986. [CrossRef]
19. Madry, A.; Makelov, A.; Schmidt, L.; Tsipras, D.; Vladu, A. Towards deep learning models resistant to adversarial attacks. *arXiv* **2017**, arXiv:1706.06083.
20. Zhao, W.; Alwidian, S.; Mahmoud, Q.H. Adversarial Training Methods for Deep Learning: A Systematic Review. *Algorithms* **2022**, *15*, 283. [CrossRef]
21. Lu, J.; Issaranon, T.; Forsyth, D. Safetynet: Detecting and rejecting adversarial examples robustly. In Proceedings of the IEEE International Conference on Computer Vision, Venice, Italy, 22–29 October 2017; pp. 446–454.
22. Grosse, K.; Manoharan, P.; Papernot, N.; Backes, M.; McDaniel, P. On the (statistical) detection of adversarial examples. *arXiv* **2017**, arXiv:1702.06280.
23. Gong, Z.; Wang, W. Adversarial and clean data are not twins. In Proceedings of the Sixth International Workshop on Exploiting Artificial Intelligence Techniques for Data Management, Seattle, WA, USA, 18 June 2023; pp. 1–5.
24. Lust, J.; Condurache, A.P. Gran: An efficient gradient-norm based detector for adversarial and misclassified examples. *arXiv* **2020**, arXiv:2004.09179.
25. Metzen, J.H.; Genewein, T.; Fischer, V.; Bischoff, B. On Detecting Adversarial Perturbations. In Proceedings of the International Conference on Learning Representations, San Juan, Puerto Rico, 2–4 May 2016.
26. Carlini, N.; Wagner, D. Adversarial examples are not easily detected: Bypassing ten detection methods. In Proceedings of the 10th ACM Workshop on Artificial Intelligence and Security, Dallas, TX, USA, 3 November 2017; pp. 3–14.
27. Grosse, K.; Papernot, N.; Manoharan, P.; Backes, M.; McDaniel, P. Adversarial examples for malware detection. In Proceedings of the Computer Security–ESORICS 2017: 22nd European Symposium on Research in Computer Security, Oslo, Norway, 11–15 September 2017; Proceedings, Part II 22; pp. 62–79.
28. LeCun, Y.; Bottou, L.; Bengio, Y.; Haffner, P. Gradient-based learning applied to document recognition. *Proc. IEEE* **1998**, *86*, 2278–2324. [CrossRef]
29. Krizhevsky, A. Learning Multiple Layers of Features from Tiny Images, 2009. Available online: https://www.cs.toronto.edu/~kriz/learning-features-2009-TR.pdf (accessed on 9 September 2024).
30. Kurakin, A.; Goodfellow, I.J.; Bengio, S. Adversarial Machine Learning at Scale. In Proceedings of the International Conference on Learning Representations, San Juan, Puerto Rico, 2–4 May 2016.
31. Zhang, H.; Cisse, M.; Dauphin, Y.N.; Lopez-Paz, D. mixup: Beyond empirical risk minimization. *arXiv* **2017**, arXiv:1710.09412.
32. Tramer, F.; Boneh, D. Adversarial training and robustness for multiple perturbations. In Proceedings of the 33rd Conference on Neural Information Processing Systems, Vancouver, BC, Canada, 8–14 December 2019; Volume 32 .
33. Cohen, J.; Rosenfeld, E.; Kolter, Z. Certified adversarial robustness via randomized smoothing. In Proceedings of the International Conference on Machine Learning. PMLR, Long Beach, CA, USA, 9–15 June 2019; pp. 1310–1320.
34. Lecuyer, M.; Atlidakis, V.; Geambasu, R.; Hsu, D.; Jana, S. Certified robustness to adversarial examples with differential privacy. In Proceedings of the 2019 IEEE Symposium on Security and Privacy (SP), San Francisco, CA, USA, 19–23 May 2019; pp. 656–672.
35. Li, L.; Xie, T.; Li, B. Sok: Certified robustness for deep neural networks. In Proceedings of the 2023 IEEE Symposium on Security and Privacy (SP), San Francisco, CA, USA, 22–25 May 2023; pp. 1289–1310.
36. Singh, G.; Gehr, T.; Mirman, M.; Püschel, M.; Vechev, M. Fast and effective robustness certification. *Adv. Neural Inf. Process. Syst.* **2018**, *31*, 10825–10836.
37. Zhang, H.; Yu, Y.; Jiao, J.; Xing, E.; El Ghaoui, L.; Jordan, M. Theoretically principled trade-off between robustness and accuracy. In Proceedings of the International Conference on Machine Learning, PMLR, Long Beach, CA, USA, 9–15 June 2019; pp. 7472–7482.
38. Xie, C.; Wu, Y.; Maaten, L.v.d.; Yuille, A.L.; He, K. Feature denoising for improving adversarial robustness. In Proceedings of the IEEE/CVF Conference on Computer Vision and Pattern Recognition, Long Beach, CA, USA, 15–20 June 2019; pp. 501–509.
39. Pinhasov, B.; Lapid, R.; Ohayon, R.; Sipper, M.; Aperstein, Y. Xai-based detection of adversarial attacks on deepfake detectors. *arXiv* **2024**, arXiv:2403.02955.

40. Došilović, F.K.; Brčić, M.; Hlupić, N. Explainable artificial intelligence: A survey. In Proceedings of the 2018 41st International Convention on Information and Communication Technology, Electronics and Microelectronics (MIPRO), Opatija, Croatia, 21–25 May 2018; pp. 0210–0215.
41. Carmon, Y.; Raghunathan, A.; Schmidt, L.; Duchi, J.C.; Liang, P.S. Unlabeled data improves adversarial robustness. In Proceedings of the Advances in Neural Information Processing Systems, Vancouver, BC, Canada, 8–14 December 2019; Volume 32.
42. Cheng, S.; Dong, Y.; Pang, T.; Su, H.; Zhu, J. Improving black-box adversarial attacks with a transfer-based prior. *Adv. Neural Inf. Process. Syst.* **2019**, *32*.
43. Dong, Y.; Cheng, S.; Pang, T.; Su, H.; Zhu, J. Query-efficient black-box adversarial attacks guided by a transfer-based prior. *IEEE Trans. Pattern Anal. Mach. Intell.* **2021**, *44*, 9536–9548. [CrossRef] [PubMed]
44. Yang, Y.Y.; Rashtchian, C.; Zhang, H.; Salakhutdinov, R.R.; Chaudhuri, K. A closer look at accuracy vs. robustness. *Adv. Neural Inf. Process. Syst.* **2020**, *33*, 8588–8601.
45. He, Z.; Yang, Y.; Chen, P.Y.; Xu, Q.; Ho, T.Y. Be Your Own Neighborhood: Detecting Adversarial Example by the Neighborhood Relations Built on Self-Supervised Learning, 2022. Available online: http://arxiv.org/abs/2209.00005 (accessed on 9 September 2024).
46. Klingner, M.; Kumar, V.R.; Yogamani, S.; Bär, A.; Fingscheidt, T. Detecting Adversarial Perturbations in Multi-Task Perception. In Proceedings of the 2022 IEEE/RSJ International Conference on Intelligent Robots and Systems (IROS), Kyoto, Japan, 23–27 October 2022. [CrossRef]
47. Yang, Y.; Gao, R.; Li, Y.; Lai, Q.; Xu, Q. What You See is Not What the Network Infers: Detecting Adversarial Examples Based on Semantic Contradiction. In Proceedings of the Proceedings 2022 Network and Distributed System Security Symposium. Internet Society, NDSS 2022, San Diego, CA, USA, 24–28 April 2022. [CrossRef]
48. Wang, Y.; Li, T.; Li, S.; Yuan, X.; Ni, W. New Adversarial Image Detection Based on Sentiment Analysis. *IEEE Trans. Neural Netw. Learn. Syst.* **2023**, *35*, 14060–14074. [CrossRef]
49. Bryniarski, O.; Hingun, N.; Pachuca, P.; Wang, V.; Carlini, N. Evading Adversarial Example Detection Defenses with Orthogonal Projected Gradient Descent. In Proceedings of the International Conference on Learning Representations, Vienna, Austria, 4 May 2021.
50. Shan, S.; Wenger, E.; Wang, B.; Li, B.; Zheng, H.; Zhao, B.Y. Gotta catch'em all: Using honeypots to catch adversarial attacks on neural networks. In Proceedings of the 2020 ACM SIGSAC Conference on Computer and Communications Security, Virtual Event USA, 9–13 November 2020; pp. 67–83.
51. Sperl, P.; Kao, C.Y.; Chen, P.; Lei, X.; Böttinger, K. DLA: Dense-layer-analysis for adversarial example detection. In Proceedings of the 2020 IEEE European Symposium on Security and Privacy (EuroS&P), Genoa, Italy, 7–11 September 2020; pp. 198–215.
52. Tian, J.; Zhou, J.; Li, Y.; Duan, J. Detecting adversarial examples from sensitivity inconsistency of spatial-transform domain. In Proceedings of the AAAI Conference on Artificial Intelligence, Virtual, 2–9 February 2021; Volume 35, pp. 9877–9885.
53. Netzer, Y.; Wang, T.; Coates, A.; Bissacco, A.; Wu, B.; Ng, A.Y. Reading digits in natural images with unsupervised feature learning. In Proceedings of the NIPS Workshop on Deep Learning and Unsupervised Feature Learning, Granada, Spain, 12–14 December 2011; Volume 2011, p. 7.
54. Deng, J.; Dong, W.; Socher, R.; Li, L.J.; Li, K.; Fei-Fei, L. Imagenet: A large-scale hierarchical image database. In Proceedings of the 2009 IEEE Conference on Computer Vision and Pattern Recognition, Miami, FL, USA, 20–25 June 2009; pp. 248–255.
55. Yang, Y.; Gao, R.; Li, Y.; Lai, Q.; Xu, Q. What you see is not what the network infers: Detecting adversarial examples based on semantic contradiction. *arXiv* **2022**, arXiv:2201.09650.

mathematics

MDPI

Article

Pre-Trained Language Model Ensemble for Arabic Fake News Detection

Lama Al-Zahrani * and Maha Al-Yahya

Information Technology Department, College of Computer and Information Sciences, King Saud University, P.O. Box 145111, Riyadh 4545, Saudi Arabia
* Correspondence: 442203072@student.ksu.edu.sa

Abstract: Fake news detection (FND) remains a challenge due to its vast and varied sources, especially on social media platforms. While numerous attempts have been made by academia and the industry to develop fake news detection systems, research on Arabic content remains limited. This study investigates transformer-based language models for Arabic FND. While transformer-based models have shown promising performance in various natural language processing tasks, they often struggle with tasks involving complex linguistic patterns and cultural contexts, resulting in unreliable performance and misclassification problems. To overcome these challenges, we investigated an ensemble of transformer-based models. We experimented with five Arabic transformer models: AraBERT, MARBERT, AraELECTRA, AraGPT2, and ARBERT. Various ensemble approaches, including a weighted-average ensemble, hard voting, and soft voting, were evaluated to determine the most effective techniques for boosting learning models and improving prediction accuracies. The results of this study demonstrate the effectiveness of ensemble models in significantly boosting the baseline model performance. An important finding is that ensemble models achieved excellent performance on the Arabic Multisource Fake News Detection (AMFND) dataset, reaching an F1 score of 94% using weighted averages. Moreover, changing the number of models in the ensemble has a slight effect on the performance. These key findings contribute to the advancement of fake news detection in Arabic, offering valuable insights for both academia and the industry

Keywords: fake news detection; Arabic; learning ensemble; LLM; AraBERT; MARBERT; AraELECTRA; AraGPT2; ARBERT

MSC: 68T07

1. Introduction

With the rise of online communication, the ability to share information has increased tremendously and surpassed authorized entities. Anyone, anywhere, can easily participate in generating and disseminating information. This comes with the significant consequence of the widespread proliferation of fake news. The sheer volume of information constantly streaming online makes manual verification nearly impossible. Traditional methods of addressing fake news involved employing journalists and editorial teams to verify information against reliable sources before publication. This process, however, proved costly and time consuming, especially when dealing with the vast volume of information requiring verification against a limited number of fact-checkers. This challenge has become particularly evident during critical events, such as the COVID-19 pandemic [1].

Recent research [2–6] has explored utilizing machine learning algorithms to address the shortcomings of manual fact-checking. However, these approaches often face challenges like overfitting, scalability limitations, and difficulties in generalizing to new situations. Additionally, due to their statistical nature, machine learning models might struggle to understand the contextual nuances of continuously evolving fake news content. While the development of deep learning models has been effective in predicting the validity of news, training these models from scratch can be time-consuming and requires large quantities of labeled data.

Pre-trained language (transformer-based) models (PLMs) are a type of language model trained using a self-supervised learning (SSL) approach on large-scale corpora [7]. These models can then be fine-tuned for specific downstream tasks such as text classification, named entity recognition, and text summarization. Pre-trained language models like BERT have demonstrated promising performance in various NLP tasks, including text classification [8]. These models require less data for training due to their prior exposure to large unlabeled datasets. The remarkable achievements of transformer-based approaches have encouraged the development of Arabic transformers such as Arabic Bidirectional Encoder Representations from Transformers (AraBERT) [9], the Arabic Generative Pre-trained Transformer version 2 (AraGPT2) [10], Arabic Efficiently Learning an Encoder that Classifies Token Replacements Accurately (AraELECTRA) [11], Arabic Bidirectional Encoder Representations from Transformers (ARBERT), and Multilingual Arabic Bidirectional Encoder Representations from Transformers (MARBERT) [12], which enabled significant progress in various NLP tasks. These techniques are widely used in text classification [13], where it has been employed to capture the relationship between labels in multilabel classification through attention. In the field of fake news detection, numerous efforts have been made to address the spread of fake news and enhance the accuracy of detection models. A recent survey [14] reviewed several studies that proposed solutions and developed fake news detection methods. A comparative analysis of these methods was reported in terms of feature-extraction techniques and classification accuracy. The study demonstrated the superior performance of contextually dependent-based models, particularly transformer models, which outperform other models consistently. Additionally, research suggests that combining multiple feature representation and classification models can yield better performance and reduce computational costs.

In the context of Arabic FND, pre-trained language models have shown significant progress recently, despite challenges like overfitting. Ensemble learning methods can address such issues by leveraging the strengths of multiple transformer models. Ensemble learning is a machine-learning technique that helps to improve the accuracy of poor-performing models by combining several models together into one optimal model [15]. This approach emerged with the introduction of machine learning and weak learners and continues to proliferate for improving deep learning networks to handle the complexity of data and to enhance accuracy for tasks like speech processing, image recognition, and text classification. By combining predictions from various models, this approach mitigates overfitting and utilizes the diverse knowledge acquired by each individual model [16]. According to a recent literature review [17], ensemble learning has been widely used in the field of fault diagnosis and classification. In their comparative analysis, the authors of [17] compare fault diagnosis models that used different ensemble methods, including bagging, boosting, stacking, and other ensemble models. The evaluation results demonstrate the promising results of ensemble learning strategies for fault diagnosis, outperforming using a single model.

In previous works, the focus has not been on utilizing ensemble learning techniques with Arabic transformer models specifically for the task of Arabic fake news detection (FND). While individual transformer models, such as AraBERT and MARBERT, have demonstrated strong performance in various natural language processing (NLP) tasks, their individual weaknesses and limitations—such as domain biases or overfitting—can hinder their ability to generalize effectively in fake news detection. Ensemble learning, which combines multiple models, has the potential to overcome these challenges by leveraging the diverse strengths of different transformers, thus providing a more robust and accurate solution. However, the use of ensemble techniques for Arabic FND has not been thoroughly investigated, particularly in the context of combining multiple transformer architectures.

This study aims to address this gap by developing an ensemble of state-of-the-art Arabic pre-trained transformer models with the goal of advancing Arabic fake news detection. By integrating multiple pre-trained models, such as AraBERT, MARBERT, and other transformer-based models, into an ensemble framework, we aim to enhance model performance by reducing individual model uncertainties and improving generalizations across various types of fake news. In addition, we combine several standard Arabic fake news datasets into a unified dataset, representing a wide range of domains, such as politics, health, and social issues, and experiment with various ensemble learning techniques including weighted averaging, hard voting, and soft voting. In particular, the contributions of this study are as follows:

- A novel ensemble strategy using State-of-the-Art Arabic Pre-Trained Models: We propose and evaluate an ensemble strategy that incorporates state-of-the-art Arabic pre-trained models (e.g., AraBERT and MARBERT) for fake news detection. The ensemble leverages techniques such as weighted averaging, hard voting, and soft voting to enhance the overall performance by combining the strengths of these models. The weights assigned to each model in the ensemble are not fixed or predefined. These weights are dynamically optimized through a search algorithm that identifies the best combination of models to maximize the performance metrics (e.g., accuracy) on the validation set.
- A Unified Arabic Multisource Fake News Dataset (AMFND): We create a comprehensive dataset called AMFND by merging several Arabic fake news datasets from different sources, enabling the model to generalize better across various types of misinformation and Arabic dialects. The dataset is curated from various online sources across different domains (e.g., politics, health, sports, and social issues). Unlike many fake news detection datasets that focus primarily on political misinformation, our approach ensures that the model is exposed to different types of fake news, each with distinct language patterns and structures.
- The employment of different fine-tuning strategies: we fine-tune our model using both the traditional 80/20 train–test split and cross-validation techniques, ensuring the model is thoroughly evaluated and tuned for generalizability across different fake news contexts.
- An extensive baseline comparison and performance evaluation: we rigorously compare the performance of the proposed ensemble models against a strong baseline, demonstrating significant improvements in fake news detection accuracy, precision, recall, and F1 score using the ensemble of pre-trained models.
- Given the unique linguistic challenges posed by Arabic fake news detection, such as the complexity of morphological structures and the scarcity of relevant datasets, applying ensemble techniques of pre-trained language models offers a novel contribution to the field. The ensemble method proposed in this paper leverages the strengths of multiple models to address the specific challenges within the Arabic context, which has been relatively underexplored compared to other languages.

2. Related Work

Fake news is not a new phenomenon. In fact, it emerged in the late 19th and early 20th centuries through "yellow journalism", which sensationalized news concerning crimes, disasters, and rumors [18]. While traditional forms of fake news relied on print media, the digital age has amplified its prevalence. The sheer volume of information constantly streaming online makes manual verification nearly impossible. This challenge has become particularly evident during critical events, such as the 2016 US election [19], the Syrian conflict [20], and the COVID-19 pandemic [1]. Fake news detection methods have been applied for languages other than Arabic. For example, a recent research study, published in [21], presented a lexicon-based approach for detecting Italian fake reviews focusing on the cultural heritage domain. In their methodology, the authors explored two types of lexicons including linguistic features and sentiment analyses for classifying deceptive reviews. The key findings proved the effectiveness of lexical modifiers, such intensifiers and downtowners, in the detection of Italian deceptive reviews. The quantitative and qualitative analysis showed a large impact of the sentiment lexicon on the deceptive text. Another study [22] explored fake news detection utilizing language-independent textual features across multiple languages. These authors targeted news content published in American English, Brazilian Portuguese, and Spanish texts by examining textual complexity and stylometric and psychological features. Four machine learning algorithms, including k-Nearest Neighbors (k-NNs), Support Vector Machines (SVMs), Random Forest (RF), and Extreme Gradient Boosting (XGB), were trained to classify the factuality of news texts. The results obtained show that the curated features successfully discriminate between the fake, satirical, and real news obtained using Random Forest, reporting a classification accuracy of 85.3%.

Research on FND can be organized into two lines of research: transformer approaches and shared tasks and public datasets.

2.1. Transformer Approaches

In the FND literature, there is a large body of research that employs transfer learning solutions and pre-trained-based models for identifying fake news using detection approaches.

The work in [23] proposes a two-step classification pipeline to predict the factual content of online news for the English language, acknowledging that some news may contain subjective opinions that cannot be definitively labeled as fake or real. In the first step, the authors filtered out opinion-based articles from the dataset to focus solely on factual news prediction. Subsequently, they employed attention-based transformer models, including BERT, DistilBERT, and DeBERTa, to classify the remaining data into "fake" and "real" categories. For training, they utilized two datasets: the ISOT Fake News Dataset and the Combined Corpus Dataset (CC), each containing approximately 45,000 and 80,000 news articles categorized as fake or real. Their experiments demonstrated that removing opinion-based news leads to more accurate predictions compared to including them in the training data. Notably, DeBERTa achieved the best performance, reaching an F1 score of 0.79 in the two-step classification when trained and tested on different datasets. However, despite the significant progress made by transformer-based approaches in NLP tasks like fake news classification, research suggests that a single model can become biased by its training data, potentially hindering its performance when fine-tuned on different datasets.

Another relevant study [24] constructed a stacking ensemble model comprising five layers of vectorization to effectively determine the truthfulness of texts. They experimented with various feature representations, including manually extracted features, n-grams, and transformer-based contextual features. For the latter, the authors employed embedding tokenizers from three transformers (DistilBERT, RoBERTa, and XLM) using the sentence transformers library. In the final phase, the predictions from all embedding methods were combined and fed into a final decision classifier to generate the classification output. The training data consisted of 10,700 social media posts labeled as fake or real news, provided in the COVID-19 fake news detection shared task. The evaluation results yielded an F1 score of 0.97, demonstrating the proposed stacking approach's effectiveness, as it emerged as the leader on the challenge leaderboard. Interestingly, the authors observed that individual transformer models like DistilBERT exhibited signs of overfitting on the training data and underperformed compared to the latent space representation achieved by the ensemble model.

In contrast to the aforementioned research, De and Desarkar [25] proposed a multi-context transformer approach called MiCNA for identifying COVID-19-related fake news. Their approach goes beyond typical single-context training by leveraging rich representations from three transformer models trained in various contexts. MiCNA harnesses the strengths of these models by utilizing representations learned from language contexts, Tweet semantics, and COVID-19 connotations. To address the high dimensionality of the combined representation, MiCNA applies average pooling to the outputs of the three transformers. This resulting average vector is then fed into a feed-forward layer and an activation function before reaching the classification layer for label predictions. The authors evaluated MiCNA on a dataset of 10,700 tweets labeled as fake or real news, which were specifically collected during the COVID-19 pandemic. To demonstrate the model's effectiveness, they employed an ablation study. This involved removing specific transformer models from MiCNA and evaluating the performance with different combinations. Their findings show that MiCNA achieved the highest accuracy (98.69) and weighted average F1 score (98.64) compared to all combinations of individual or paired transformers.

Another important research direction explores multilingual systems to address fake news detection in low-resource languages. De et al. [26] investigated the performance of transformer-based models for classifying misleading information across multiple domains and languages. Their system aims to determine whether models can effectively transfer domains and language-agnostic features for the task of fake news classification. These authors conducted several experiments in language-specific, domain-specific, domain-independent, and language-independent settings using a translated Asian language dataset. This dataset was created by translating two English-language datasets, namely, Fake News AMT and Celebrity Fake News datasets, into four Asian languages (Hindi, Vietnamese, Indonesian, and Swahili) using Google Translate. The resulting dataset, encompassing 980 news items across multiple domains, provided a multilingual testbed. This study employed the BERT transformer for unimodal experiments and its multilingual variant (mBERT) for evaluating the multilingual dataset. The results reveal that mBERT achieved impressive zero-shot classification performance on unseen languages. It also significantly enhanced the results for low-resource languages, reaching a peak accuracy of 83%. However, this study has limitations. First, relying solely on Google Translate for language translation is not optimal for languages with complex morphology or dialects. Second, the dataset used in this study might be too small to fully train a language model like BERT, potentially leading to predictions with high variance.

The work in [27] is closely related to our approach, as it also examines an ensemble of fine-tuned transformer models for fake news detection, specifically focusing on the COVID-19 pandemic. Their methodology employed both hard- and soft-voting ensemble techniques to combine prediction vectors from multiple models, ultimately determining the final "fake" or "real" labels. Additionally, their experiment incorporated two heuristic features: username and URL link domain. The evaluation results demonstrate that soft voting outperformed hard voting, achieving a prediction accuracy of 0.98 (as measured by the F1 score). This result surpasses the performance of individual transformer models.

Recognizing the data limitations in Arabic fake news detection, the work presented in [28] presented a large-scale dataset called AraNews. Utilizing a novel method, they automatically generated fake news by manipulating genuine news articles. They then fine-tuned large pre-trained models (specifically, AraBERT) on the generated data, achieving an F1 score of 89.25, surpassing previous state-of-the-art results.

In the context of comparative analyses of detection approaches, a comparative analysis of Arabic fake news detection methods was conducted by [29]. The authors investigated the effectiveness of different neural network and transformer architectures alongside embedding methods for feature extraction. They evaluated their approach on various Arabic corpora, including ANS, COVID-19-Fakes, AraNews, and ArCOV19-rumors. This study revealed that transformers outperformed the best neural networks, with QARiB achieving the highest F1 score of 0.95, followed by GRU (0.83).

In the work of Harrag et al. [30], a BERT-based transformer model was developed to automatically detect deep fake texts in Arabic languages that were generated using the GPT2 transformer model. In their study, the authors utilized an existing Arabic dataset for human-generated text extracted from Twitter and then generated the fake data using a generative transformer, namely, GPT2. Using the GPT2 pre-trained model, they were able to collect 3512 auto-generated Arabic samples along with 1559 real texts obtained from a public Twitter dataset. Their system was trained to recognize whether a given Arabic text is human or a bot using the encoder–decoder transformer called BERT. In their experimental setting, they investigated the performance of four deep learning networks, including LSTM, GRU, Bi-LSTM, and BI-GRU models, as a baseline compared with the fine-tuned AraBERT Arabic pre-trained model. Their fine-tuned AraBERT transformer showed a competitive classification accuracy of 98.7%, exceeding the baseline line deep learning models in the detection of auto-generated texts. Different from the aforementioned study, we aimed to develop an Arabic transformer to classify genuine and fraudulent Arabic texts generated by humans, which is considered one of the more challenging tasks than detecting fake texts generated by machines.

2.2. Shared Tasks and Public Datasets

To encourage solutions for detecting COVID-19 misinformation on social media, several publicly shared tasks and datasets have been released. One example is NLP4IF2021, which provides a dataset and challenges participants to develop NLP-based solutions for identifying false information. In [31], the authors proposed a two-step pipeline utilizing the AraBERT transformer model to analyze misleading Arabic information on Twitter. They achieved an accuracy score exceeding 84%, using various experimental settings.

Another initiative towards combating the COVID-19 infodemic involved a large Arabic Twitter corpus presented in [32]. These authors collected and manually annotated 7 million tweets as "fake" or "genuine" using fact-checking websites. They then employed supervised learning with six machine learning classifiers, achieving the best F1 score of 93.4% with Logistic regression. This study concluded that additional pre-processing, like stemming or lemmatization, did not improve the results.

Similarly, Ref. [33] introduced the ARACOVID19-MFH dataset for Arabic COVID-19 fake news and hate speech detection. This dataset comprises 10,828 manually labeled tweets categorized into 10 classes. Baseline models based on pre-trained models (AraBERT, mBERT, and Distil-mBERT) were used to evaluate the annotation process and were fine-tuned for fake news detection. Further pre-training on a large Twitter dataset improved the performance compared to direct fine-tuning. AraBERT and mBERT showcased the best results, exceeding a 0.92 F1 score in various classification tasks.

In addition to the previous research, the work in [34] introduced a new naturally occurring claims dataset called AraFact for the Arabic language. They used five fact-checking websites to extract the data and normalized its labels into four categories: True, False, Partly False, and Sarcasm. AraFact consists of 6000 claims that were crawled along with metadata information. The constructed dataset covers diverse topics, including topics such as politics, Health, News, Science, social religion, Art and culture, and other topics. The annotation process was implemented using two of the authors, where each of them verified the veracity of the news separately and decided on the final labels in case of disagreements. In addition, a further analysis of the dataset was conducted to analyze the distribution of each feature as well as to demonstrate the use case scenarios to serve relevant research tasks such as claims. The authors presented a new dataset for the verification of Arabic claims. However, they did not evaluate the quality of the dataset for classifying claims automatically using machine learning models.

Similar to the work conducted by [32], Haouari et al. [35] presented an Arabic benchmark dataset, named ArCOVID19-Rumors, for misinformation detected on Twitter. ArCOVID19-Rumors was constructed using 138 verified claims scrapped from fact-checking websites and 9.4k tweets related to COVID-19 conversations annotated manually as True, False, and other. The proposed dataset was designed mainly to support the claims verification on Twitter, but it can support free text claims further. To confirm the annotation quality, they implemented several models that leveraged one of the features such as content-based attributes, user profiles, temporal features, and network-based features. The authors examined two Arabic pre-trained models, AraBERT and MARBERT, along with an ensemble of two deep learning architectures, RNN–CNN, and a graph convolution neural network to classify the text into either true or false. The evaluation result reported that MARBERT produced superior results compared to AraBERT, obtaining a 0.74 macro F1 score due to the matching domain of MARBERT, which was pre-trained on Twitter, compared with AraBERT, which was pre-trained on Wikipedia.

The research in [36] released a novel Arabic dataset called AraStance, which can be used for stance fact-checking tasks. In the AraStance dataset, a group of 4063 pairs of claims (false and true) were collected, where each article had one of the following stance labels: agree, disagree, discuss, and unrelated. The proposed dataset retrieved news from different Arab countries, including Saudi Arabia, the UAE, and Egypt, on different topics, such as politics, health, and sports. Basically, the constructed dataset was designed for stance detection as the main task, but it can also be used for fact-checking or claim veracity. Thus, the unbalanced issue is not a crucial factor for stance detection as for claims verification with two labels. To evaluate the dataset, they investigated the performance of different Arabic transformer models, which include Arabic BERT, MARBERT, ARBERT, and mBERT. The results show that ARBERT and MARBERT achieved better classification results, reaching a macro F1 score of 0.85 and 0.78 in stance detection, which outperforms the other two models. This could be explained by the importance of matching dataset types that the pre-trained models trained on before and the dataset the transformer fine-tuned on. The previous study experimented with the AraStance dataset only for stance detection. However, it is also possible to evaluate the dataset on the claim's veracity task.

The summary in Table 1 shows a comparative analysis of the related work in fake news detection across different languages. This review also highlights ongoing efforts to create benchmark datasets and shared tasks and to demonstrate the effectiveness of transformer-based models in addressing this complex issue.

Table 1. Comparative analyses of FND studies using transformers.

Reference	Language	Model(s)	Dataset	Best Results	
				Metric	F1 Result
(Blackledge and Abarghouei, 2021) [23]	English	BERT, DistilBERT, and DeBERTa	ISOT dataset and Combined 80k Corpus Dataset (CC)	Accuracy	0.80
(Koloski et al., 2021) [24]	English	Stacking ensemble transformers (DistilBERT, Roberta, and XLM) and ETMA	Twitter, Instagram, and Facebook	F1 score	0.97
(De and Desarkar, 2022) [25]	English	MiCNA approach (BERT Base, BERTweet, and COVID-19 Twitter-BERT)	Twitter	Accuracy F1 score	98.69 98.64
(De et al., 2021) [26]	Asian languages	Multi-lingual BERT	Multiple sources	Accuracy	0.83
(Das et al., 2021) [27]	English	A heuristic-driven transformer model (hard voting)	Twitter and fact-checking websites	F1 score	0.98
(Nagoudi et al., 2021) [28]	Arabic	AraBERT	News articles	F1 score	0.89
(Al-Yahya et al., 2021) [29]		GRU and QARiB			
(Harrag et al., 2021) [30]	Arabic	AraBERT		NLP4IF2021	AraBERT
Hussein et al., 2021 [31]	Arabic	AraBERT		10,828 real and fake	AraBERT
(Mahlous et al., 2021) [32]	Arabic	Logistic regression		3512 fake 1559 real	Logistic regression
(Ameur and Aliane, 2021) [33]	Arabic	MARBERT, AraBERT, and RNN–CNN		9.4k tweet	MARBERT
(Sheikh et al., 2021) [34]	Arabic	ARBERT, mBERT, MARBERT, and Arabic BERT		4063 article	AraBERT
(Haouari et al., 2021) [35]	Arabic	MARBERT, AraBERT, and RNN–CNN		ArCOV19-rumors	MARBERT
(Alhindi et al., 2021) [36]	Arabic	ARBERT and MARBERT		AraStance	ARBERT

3. Methodology

In this study our aim was to investigate to what extent an ensemble model of transformers can improve the performance of Arabic FND. The general approach we adopted is a general machine learning approach (fine-tuning PLM), as depicted in Figure 1. Here, the datasets were combined, cleaned, and pre-processed. Then, the PLMs were fine-tuned and evaluated to develop the final model. We approached this investigation by building an ensemble of transformer models using standard datasets (details of the datasets are shown in Table 2). Two of the datasets were collected from a single source written using

Modern standard Arabic (MSA). However, the third ArCOV19-rumors dataset is the only dataset that contains news from Twitter, which typically contains dialectal Arabic (DA). Research has shown that models trained on MSA datasets do not perfectly work in dialect datasets [37]. There is a growing interest in training models on large diverse datasets in order to achieve better results and reduce generalization errors. Therefore, in this study we used a combined dataset, which contains all three datasets, in an AMFND dataset to study its impact on the FND task.

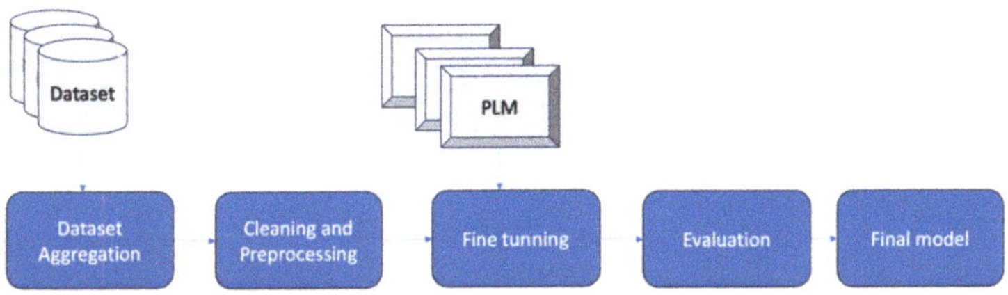

Figure 1. General approach to FND.

Table 2. Details of Arabic FND datasets used in this study.

Dataset	Source of News	Number of Instances	Labels	Topics	Benchmarked
AraNews	Fact-checking websites	108,194	True/Fake	Multiple topics	Yes
AraCOV19-Rumors	Twitter	9400	True/False	Health	Yes
AFND	Fact-checking websites	606,912	Credible/not credible/ undecided	Multiple topics	Yes

3.1. Arabic Multisource Fake News Dataset (AMFND)

We combine the three Arabic datasets, AraNews, AFND, and AraCOV19-Rumors, into one large dataset, AMFND. The combination of multiple datasets significantly enhances the overall size and diversity of data, which plays a crucial role in improving the generalization ability and enables machine learning models to capture a wide range of patterns and features for detecting fake news. To handle the diversity of labels, we first transformed the labels into one standard schema, in our case, to a binary classification (fake or real). For example, if the dataset contained multiple labels like the AFND dataset, which had the labels credible, not credible, and undecided, we first changed the labels into fake and real labels and removed items with the third label 'undecided', as the objective of our task was binary classification. After normalizing the labels, we removed the unnecessary columns element and kept only two columns, one for the text and one for the label. Finally, a unique ID was assigned for each news item. The three datasets were then merged sequentially to construct the final dataset. The resulted AMFND dataset consisted of the following attributes, *News_ID*, *News_Text*, and the *Label*, which is the normalized category of news.

The resulting AMFND dataset is composed of 56769 items classified as fake or real news. In the AMFND dataset, the labels were imbalanced (59% of the dataset was fake and 41% was real). An imbalanced dataset could lead to poor model performance biases against one label. To alleviate this problem, we considered using resampling strategies specifically under the sampling method, whereas the majority class was reduced until it became equal or balanced with the distribution of the other class.

3.2. Text Pre-Processing

Text pre-processing is a challenging task for data scientists and NLP researchers, especially when performed on datasets scrapped from social networks, which contain a lot of noise and unnecessary elements. The cleaning procedures were implemented using mathematical functions like regex and existing Python libraries called NLTK. We performed the following pipeline on all the three datasets before combing them.

Cleaning pipeline

1. Remove punctuation, diacritics, special characters, and non-Arabic text. Diacritics are vowel marks. As Arabic text does not provide information about pronunciation, the main purpose of diacritics is to provide a phonetic guide for correct pronunciation.
2. Remove duplicated sentences, missing or corrupted values, and handling missing values.
3. Normalize the Arabic text (transform the text to a unified form, removing elongation. Elongation is used to communicate a long vowel pronunciation) and remove stop words.
4. Remove hyperlinks, emojis, and Twitter handlers.

Pre-processing pipeline

1. Used text pre-segmentation requirements using the Farasa segmenter [38] from the official transformer documentation. Word segmentation involves breaking words into their constituent clitics.
2. Employ the transformer tokenizer. Tokenizers are essential tools in machine learning, especially in natural language processing (NLP). They break down a text into smaller units called tokens. These tokens can be words, sub-words, or characters. A tokenizer is in charge of preparing the inputs for a specific model.
3. Perform padding and truncations to handle sequence length inconsistencies. To avoid variable sequence lengths, we used padding and truncation strategies to handle the long input sequence and to ensure that all the sequences were in the same length that the model could accept, which typically adjusted to a maximum of 512 input tokens. The padding handled the short sequence by appending additional tokens or special tokens like [PAD] after the last tokens in the sentence so that all sentences had equal token lengths. The truncations worked differently by removing the end of long sequences in order to avoid mismatched sequence lengths and to reduce the overwhelming computational processing of long sequences.

Table 3 demonstrates the pre-processing steps applied on Arabic fake news using two examples prior to their input into a BERT-based model (e.g., AraBERT). Each text was tokenized into token IDs['CLS'] and segmented IDs['SEP'] using a BERT tokenizer. This table also shows how the text input was normalized, removing diacritics and standardizing certain characters. Additionally, it shows the text input after removing punctuations and non-alphabetic characters. For padding and truncation, Example 1 required both truncation and padding, whereas Example 2 required only padding. The input representation section shows how the text input was prepared for the model, including the token IDs and attention masks.

Table 3. Text-processing examples for the AMFND dataset.

Pre-Processing Step	Example 1	Example 2
News text	"الرئيس يعلن إلغاء جميع الديون الخارجية للدولة في خطوة غير مسبوقة."	"تراجع التضخم النصف سنوي الجزائر."
Translation	"The president announces the cancellation of all foreign debts of the state in an unprecedented move."	"Semi-annual inflation declines in Algeria."
Label	Fake	Real
Tokenization	[CLS] الرئيس [SEP] يعلن [SEP] إلغاء [SEP] جميع [SEP] الديون [SEP] الخارجية [SEP] للدولة [SEP] ... [SEP] [CLS]	[CLS] تراجع [SEP] التضخم [SEP] النصف [SEP] سنوي [SEP] الجزائر [SEP] [CLS]
Normalization	"الرَّئِيس" becomes "الرئيس" (removal of diacritics), normalization of "ى" to "ي"	"الجزائر" (removal of diacritics), normalization of "ى" to "ي"

Table 3. *Cont.*

Pre-Processing Step	Example 1	Example 2
Removing punctuations	"الرئيس يعلن إلغاء جميع الديون الخارجية للدولة في خطوة غير مسبوقة" (removal of non-alphabetic characters)	"تراجع التضخم النصف سنوي الجزائر" (removal of non-alphabetic characters)
Padding and truncation	Truncated: text length exceeded 128 tokens and was truncated. Padding: added padding to reach 128 tokens if necessary	Padded: text was shorter than 128 tokens and padded to the maximum length
Input representation	Token IDs: [101, 1479, 4800, . . ., 1000] Attention mask: [1, 1, 1, . . ., 0, 0]	Token IDs: [101, 85, 48, . . ., 1000] Attention mask: [1, 1, 1, . . ., 0, 0]

3.3. *Model Fine-Tuning and Ensemble*

Five transformer models were used in our study: AraBERT v1, AraGPT2, AraELECTRA, MARBERT, and ARBERT. Details of these models are presented in Table 4. They were fine-tunned for Arabic FND, using the three individual datasets, as well as the combined AMFND.

Table 4. Details of Arabic transformer models used in this study.

Model Name	Model Type	Size	Source	Data Type	No. of Params.
AraBERT	Encoder only	24 GB	Wikipedia + Abulkhair Corpus + OSIAN + news websites	MSA	136 M (base) 371 M (large)
AraGPT2	Decoder only	527 MB	Wikipedia + Abulkhair Corpus + OSIAN + As-safir News websites	MSA	135 M
AraELECTRA	Encoder only	516 MB	Wikipedia + Abulkhair Corpus+ OSIAN +As-safir News websites	MSA	135 M
MARBERT	Encoder only	128 GB	Twitter dataset	Dialectal Arabic (DA) and MSA	163 M
ARBERT	Encoder only	61 GB	6 sources	MSA	163 M

For model evaluation, we performed two resampling approaches to evaluate our system. The first evaluation approach was random sampling, in which we split the dataset into three sets, training–validation–test, with a size ratio equal to 80:10:10, respectively. Additionally, we used a k-fold cross validation (k = 5) to examine the model performance. Evaluating the model using a cross validation usually aids in achieving a more generalized machine learning classifier and avoids the overfitting problem during the training process [39,40]. We compared the results of each evaluation approach and selected the best results.

For ensemble methods, the voting ensemble is the most commonly used method in the literature, due to its superior performance achievements in classification and regression tasks [41]. Essentially, a voting ensemble involves calculating the prediction of each model for a specific class and predicting the label that has the majority vote. There are two policies of voting: hard voting and soft voting. A hard voting is computed by collecting the class voting generated by each model member. Soft voting, on the other hand, relies on predicting the largest probability of the classes obtained from each of the model members.

4. Experiments

For model fine-tuning, we used the transformer library from the huggingface repository to fine-tune the pre-trained models. Here, we ran the training process using the Pytorch library [42], which supports hardware accelerators such as GPUs and efficient code debugging. Then, we implemented segmentations using the Farasa library [38] on all models that required pre-processing in their official repo, such as AraBERT, AraELECTRA, and AraGPT2. For tokenization, we used the Auto Tokenizer library from the transformer which included all the models used for training. Using Trainer API from the huggingface library, we determined the training parameters and the model hyperparameters used to train a transformer model. For the training setting, we fine-tuned all the models for 3 to 5 epochs with a learning rate of 2×10^{-5} and with an Adam optimizer equal to 1×10^{-8}. The evaluation strategy was set according to the number of iterations, and the best model was loaded at the end of the training process. The models were evaluated using a macro F1 score, precision, recall, and accuracy in both the training and testing procedures. For the ensemble experiment, we loaded the model training weights and combined the predictions of the considered models on the test data using the ensemble methods.

We first developed a baseline using a zero-shot setting. Next, we conducted two major experiments, as shown in Figure 2.

1. Experiment 1: five Arabic transformers were fine-tuned on the combined dataset (AMFND).
2. Experiment 2: Each of the five Arabic transformer models were fine-tuned on the combined AMFND dataset. Then, an ensemble of five, three, and two transformers was created. We experimented with two kinds of ensemble strategies: the weighted-average ensemble and voting ensembles (hard and soft).

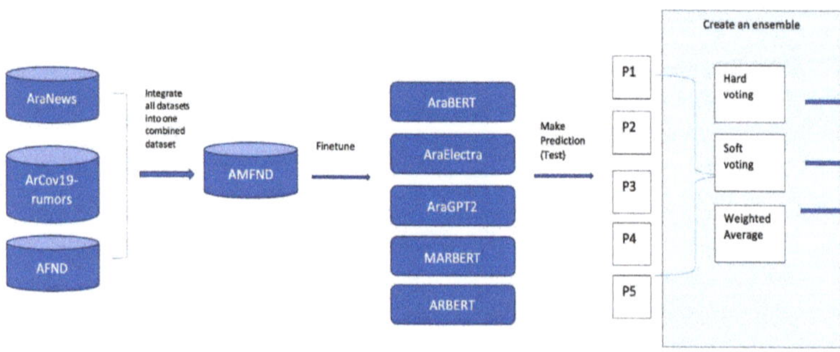

Figure 2. Fine-tuning each of the five Arabic transformer models on the combined AMFND dataset.

5. Results

The baseline results for all five models are shown in Table 5. Table 6 shows the performance results after fine-tuning on the combined AMFND dataset using a 5-fold cross validation. The results of experiment 2, fine-tuning each of the five Arabic transformer models on the combined AMFND dataset and then creating an ensemble, are shown in Table 7. Table 8 shows the performance results when the number of ensemble models was varied, depicting results using an ensemble of five, three, and two models.

Table 5. Performance of five baseline models (zero-shot)-highest value in bold.

Baseline	Accuracy	F1
AraBERT v2	0.71	0.70
MARBERT	0.76	0.75
AraELECTRA	0.76	**0.76**
AraGPT2	0.71	0.70
ARBERT	**0.77**	**0.76**

Table 6. Experiment 1—performance of models on AMFND dataset using a 5-fold cross validation-highest value in bold.

Baseline	Accuracy	F1
AraBERTv2	0.85	0.84
MARBERT	0.89	0.89
AraELECTRA	**0.93**	**0.92**
AraGPT2	0.90	0.90
ARBERT	0.77	0.76

Table 7. Experiment 2—performance of different ensemble methods using five transformer models on AMFND-highest value in bold.

Ensemble Method	Accuracy	F1 Score
Weighted Avg Ensemble	**0.94**	**0.94**
Hard voting	0.86	0.88
Soft voting	0.88	0.90

Table 8. Performance results of different ensemble numbers (5/3/2)-highest value in bold.

Ensemble Models	Result (F1 Score)		
	Hard Voting	Soft Voting	Weighted Avg
AraBERT + MarBERT + ARBERT + AraELECTRA + AraGPT2	**0.88**	**0.90**	**0.94**
AraBERT + MARBERT + AraELECTRA	0.87	0.88	**0.94**
AraELECTRA + MarBERT	0.85	0.88	0.91

6. Discussion

From the experiments, we observed that training a model using the common 80–20% ratio for training and testing produces lower performance for all models compared to a 5-fold cross validation. This can be explained by multiple reasons, such as the variance in the dataset; therefore, such a model is not able to capture a good representation from the training sample. The second reason for this is due to the sequential integration of the individual dataset into one large dataset, which might make the model biased to a specific dataset. Regarding experiment 1 (Table 5), among all models, AraELECTRA achieved the best F1 score using the stratified 5-fold cross validation, with a score of 0.92, followed by the AraGPT2 model, which reported 0.90% using the same training strategy. On the other hand, AraBERT recorded the lowest accuracy score of 0.84 under various settings compared to MarBERT and ARBERT. Our intuition for the cause of this result is that AraBERT has been trained on more structured and formal language corpora from Wikipedia, unlike our dataset, which contains a combination of MSA and dialectal texts.

With regards to experiment 2, we further conducted a comparative analysis of the ensemble model over state-of-the-art models reported in the literature, as shown in Table 9. We can observe that the ensemble model in this study is comparable to those of the literature. It outperformed some of the standalone models, reaching an F1 score of 94% using the weighted-average ensemble. The results show that composing predictions from multiple models yields the best overall performance, if we give the well-performing model the largest weights, which enable them to contribute more to the ensemble result and, therefore, to obtain a better prediction. On the other hand, a voting ensemble performs poorly, in general, with an F1 score equal to 88% and 90% for hard and soft voting, respectively. This is likely because it aggregates the class probabilities from each prediction to vote the final class, considering fair contributions for all ensemble members in the final ensemble prediction.

Table 9. Comparision results for SOTA methods against the ensemble.

Reference	Models	F1 Result
Nagoudi et al. [28]	AraBERT	0.89
Al-Yahya et al. [29]	AraBERT AraGPT2 QARiB MarBert ArBert ArElectra	0.81 0.90 0.95 0.93 0.89 0.93
Hussein et al. [31]	AraBERT	0.84
Mahlous and Al-Laith [32]	Logistic regression	0.93
Ameur and Aliane [33]	AraBERT mBERT	0.95 0.94
Haouari et al. [35]	AraBERT MARBERT	0.71 0.74
Harrag et al. [30]	ARBERT + GPT2	0.98
Ensemble model	Weighted-average ensemble Hard-voting ensemble Soft-voting ensemble	0.94 0.88 0.90

Our experiments show how the number of ensembled models (two, three, and five) affect the performance of Arabic fake news detection (Table 8). Our results suggest that there is no observed impact of the number of models in improving the accuracy of the ensemble model. Therefore, increasing the number of models in the ensemble may not be helpful, if multiple models produced similar accuracy results. For the first ensemble, we combined the prediction of five transformer models, including AraBERT + MarBERT + ARBERT + AraELECTRA + AraGPT2, using the three ensemble methods, namely, weighted-average ensemble, hard voting, and soft voting. The weighted-average ensemble achieved the best F1 score of 94%, whereas the results of hard and soft voting showed no improvement against the performance of individual models used in the ensemble, reporting similar F1 scores of 86.6% and 86.7%, against the best standalone F1 result of 0.92 achieved by the AraELECTRA model. This is expected, because the voting accuracy is determined by the majority vote of the class predicted by the ensemble members, unlike the weighted-average ensemble, which basically aggregated all the predictions from each model, multiplied by certain weights, according to their performance. For this reason, if three out of five models make incorrect predictions, the voting ensemble will probably result in a lower performance, since it considers all the models equally, meaning that each model in the ensemble will have the same contribution in the prediction.

Similarly, we found that an ensemble of three models, which consists of AraBERT + MARBERT + AraELECTRA, yielded successful improvements in terms of F1 results using all ensemble methods. It achieved similar performance to the five-ensemble model using the weighted-average ensemble. However, the hard-voting and soft-voting results show some improvements, F1 = 0.88 and F1 = 0.87, respectively. As for the last ensemble variant, which comprised two models, which were AraELECTRA and MarBERT, the weighted-average ensemble reached 0.91 in terms of the F1 score, whereas for voting, the highest F1 value was obtained by soft voting, with F1 = 0.88, surpassing the hard-voting result of F1 = 0.85.

Although a perfect comparison is impossible given the disparity of models and resources; however, to enrich the discussion, we considered FND for other languages. For example, the study by [21] on deceptive text classifications in the Italian Cultural Heritage Dataset showed an accuracy of 81% and a micro F1 of 85% using the Sentita and Sentix lexicons joined together. This result is comparable to our ensemble-model results, however, with a noticeable improvement in the latter. In addition, the reported accuracy for end-to-end transformer models in a comparative study [14] reached a score of 25% for the Liar dataset (multi-class), 100% for the ISOT dataset (binary), 94% for the COVID-19 dataset (binary), and 99% for the GM dataset (binary). These results are comparable to our work and other Arabic FND results reported in the literature.

7. Conclusions

In this work, we carried out multiple experiments aimed at enhancing Arabic FND by employing transformer-based ensemble models trained on a diverse dataset compiled by combining three publicly available sources. We developed a unified dataset, AMFND, by integrating multiple Arabic fake news datasets from diverse sources. This comprehensive dataset facilitates improved model generalizations across different forms of misinformation and various Arabic dialects. We further conducted a thorough evaluation of the proposed ensemble models against a baseline, showcasing substantial improvements in fake news detection performance across metrics such as accuracy, precision, recall, and F1 score, which were achieved through the use of the pre-trained model ensemble.

To the best of our knowledge, this is the first study to apply an ensemble of pre-trained language models specifically for Arabic FND. The performance of our ensemble models was assessed on the combined dataset, AMFND. Various ensemble methods, including different voting techniques, such as weighted averaging, hard voting, and soft voting, were implemented to aggregate predictions from several transformer models. Additionally, we investigated factors affecting ensemble performance and provided recommendations for the effective implementation of these techniques.

Our findings indicate that the best ensemble result was achieved by implementing the weighted-average ensemble. However, we do acknowledge that the performance of ensemble models can be influenced by factors related to the structure and implementation of an ensemble model. These factors include the performance of individual models in the ensemble and the number of ensemble models, in addition to the extent of diversity between the ensemble members. We observed that integrating an odd number of models can enhance the performance of an ensemble. Moreover, the ensemble strategy used to combine the prediction of individual models together can play an important role in the model performance.

Although constructing an ensemble from multiple transformer models showed improved performance, it is important to analyze the cost of combining more than one model compared to fine-tuning a single transformer model. The cost can be computed according to different factors, which include computational resources, memory usage, development costs, energy consumption, and performance and accuracy. Regarding computational resources, ensemble models require significantly more time to fine-tune multiple transformer models and a high memory consumption for every transformer model used in the ensemble. However, despite the cost, the ensemble can provide better performance compared to a single model. Therefore, in order to leverage the advantage of an ensemble model, considering the cost efficiency is indeed crucial against superior performance.

While the discussed limitations highlight the complexities of Arabic fake news detection, they also unveil exciting opportunities for future research and improvements. Exploring the adaptation of fake news detection models to specific Arabic dialects has potential and is important. This research direction can significantly improve social media detection accuracy by addressing the linguistic variations across different Arab regions. By accounting for dialectal differences, models can become more adept at identifying fake news content, leading to a more robust Arabic FND. Moreover, another avenue for future work is to address the challenge of data scarcity in Arabic languages, and investigating cross-lingual transfer-learning techniques emerges as a promising solution. This approach involves leveraging existing, well-trained fake news detection models from resource-rich languages like English and transferring their knowledge to Arabic models. This strategy has the potential to significantly improve the state of the art in Arabic FND research, particularly in settings with limited annotated data.

Author Contributions: Conceptualization, L.A.-Z. and M.A.-Y.; methodology, L.A.-Z. and M.A.-Y.; software, L.A.-Z.; validation, L.A.-Z.; investigation, L.A.-Z. and M.A.-Y.; writing—original draft preparation, L.A.-Z.; writing—review and editing, M.A.-Y.; supervision, M.A.-Y. All authors have read and agreed to the published version of the manuscript.

Funding: This research received no external funding.

Data Availability Statement: All data used in this study are publicly available.

Conflicts of Interest: The authors declare no conflicts of interest.

References

1. Balakrishnan, V.; Ng, W.Z.; Soo, M.C.; Han, G.J.; Lee, C.J. Infodemic and fake news—A comprehensive overview of its global magnitude during the COVID-19 pandemic in 2021: A scoping review. *Int. J. Disaster Risk Reduct.* **2022**, *78*, 103144. [CrossRef] [PubMed]
2. Verma, P.K.; Agrawal, P.; Amorim, I.; Prodan, R. WELFake: Word embedding over linguistic features for fake news detection. *IEEE Trans. Comput. Soc. Syst.* **2021**, *8*, 881–893. [CrossRef]
3. Ramos, J. Using tf-idf to determine word relevance in document queries. In Proceedings of the First Instructional Conference on Machine Learning, Citeseer, Los Angeles, CA, USA, 23–24 June 2003; pp. 29–48. Available online: https://citeseerx.ist.psu.edu/document?repid=rep1&type=pdf&doi=b3bf6373ff41a115197cb5b30e57830c16130c2c (accessed on 10 June 2024).
4. Khanam, Z.; Alwasel, B.N.; Sirafi, H.; Rashid, M. Fake news detection using machine learning approaches. In *IOP Conference Series: Materials Science and Engineering*; IOP Publishing: Bristol, UK, 2021; p. 012040. Available online: https://iopscience.iop.org/article/10.1088/1757-899X/1099/1/012040/meta (accessed on 17 February 2024).
5. Madani, M.; Motameni, H.; Roshani, R. Fake News Detection Using Feature Extraction, Natural Language Processing, Curriculum Learning, and Deep Learning. *Int. J. Inf. Technol. Decis. Mak.* **2023**, *23*, 1063–1098. [CrossRef]
6. Hamed, S.K.; Ab Aziz, M.J.; Yaakub, M.R. Fake News Detection Model on Social Media by Leveraging Sentiment Analysis of News Content and Emotion Analysis of Users' Comments. *Sensors* **2023**, *23*, 1748. [CrossRef]
7. Min, B.; Ross, H.; Sulem, E.; Ben Veyseh, A.P.; Nguyen, T.H.; Sainz, O.; Agirre, E.; Heintz, I.; Roth, D. Recent Advances in Natural Language Processing via Large Pre-Trained Language Models: A Survey. *arXiv* **2024**, arXiv:2111.01243. [CrossRef]
8. Wotaifi, T.A.; Dhannoon, B.N. Developed Models Based on Transfer Learning for Improving Fake News Predictions. *JUCS J. Univers. Comput. Sci.* **2023**, *29*, 491–507. [CrossRef]
9. Antoun, W.; Baly, F.; Hajj, H. AraBERT: Transformer-based Model for Arabic Language Understanding. *arXiv* **2020**, arXiv:2003.00104.
10. Antoun, W.; Baly, F.; Hajj, H. AraGPT2: Pre-Trained Transformer for Arabic Language Generation. In Proceedings of the Sixth Arabic Natural Language Processing Workshop, Kyiv, Ukraine, 19 April 2021; Association for Computational Linguistics: Stroudsburg, PA, USA, 2021; pp. 196–207. Available online: https://aclanthology.org/2021.wanlp-1.21 (accessed on 26 March 2022).
11. Antoun, W.; Baly, F.; Hajj, H. AraELECTRA: Pre-Training Text Discriminators for Arabic Language Understanding. In Proceedings of the Sixth Arabic Natural Language Processing Workshop, Kyiv, Ukraine, 19 April 2021; Association for Computational Linguistics: Stroudsburg, PA, USA, 2021; pp. 191–195. Available online: https://aclanthology.org/2021.wanlp-1.20 (accessed on 26 March 2022).
12. Abdul-Mageed, M.; Elmadany, A.; Nagoudi, E.M.B. ARBERT & MARBERT: Deep Bidirectional Transformers for Arabic. In Proceedings of the 59th Annual Meeting of the Association for Computational Linguistics and the 11th International Joint Conference on Natural Language Processing (Volume 1: Long Papers), Online, 1–6 August 2021; Association for Computational Linguistics: Stroudsburg, PA, USA, 2021; pp. 7088–7105. [CrossRef]
13. Wei, X.; Huang, J.; Zhao, R.; Yu, H.; Xu, Z. Multi-Label Text Classification Model Based on Multi-Level Constraint Augmentation and Label Association Attention. *ACM Trans. Asian Low-Resour. Lang. Inf. Process.* **2024**, *23*, 1–20. [CrossRef]
14. Farhangian, F.; Cruz, R.M.; Cavalcanti, G.D. Fake news detection: Taxonomy and comparative study. *Inf. Fusion* **2024**, *103*, 102140. [CrossRef]
15. Mohammed, A.; Kora, R. A comprehensive review on ensemble deep learning: Opportunities and challenges. *J. King Saud Univ. Comput. Inf. Sci.* **2023**, *35*, 757–774. [CrossRef]
16. Wang, H.; Li, J.; Wu, H.; Hovy, E.; Sun, Y. Pre-Trained Language Models and Their Applications. *Engineering* **2023**, *25*, 51–65. [CrossRef]
17. Mian, Z.; Deng, X.; Dong, X.; Tian, Y.; Cao, T.; Chen, K.; Al Jaber, T. A literature review of fault diagnosis based on ensemble learning. *Eng. Appl. Artif. Intell.* **2024**, *127*, 107357. [CrossRef]
18. de Beer, D.; Matthee, M. Approaches to Identify Fake News: A Systematic Literature Review. *Integr. Sci. Digit. Age* **2020**, *136*, 13–22. [CrossRef]

19. Bovet, A.; Makse, H.A. Influence of fake news in Twitter during the 2016 US presidential election. *Nat. Commun.* **2019**, *10*, 7. [CrossRef] [PubMed]
20. Abu Salem, F.K.; Al Feel, R.; Elbassuoni, S.; Ghannam, H.; Jaber, M.; Farah, M. Meta-learning for fake news detection surrounding the Syrian war. *Patterns* **2021**, *2*, 100369. [CrossRef]
21. Guarasci, R.; Catelli, R.; Esposito, M. Classifying deceptive reviews for the cultural heritage domain: A lexicon-based approach for the Italian language. *Expert Syst. Appl.* **2024**, *252*, 124131. [CrossRef]
22. Abonizio, H.Q.; de Morais, J.I.; Tavares, G.M.; Junior, S.B. Language-Independent Fake News Detection: English, Portuguese, and Spanish Mutual Features. *Future Internet* **2020**, *12*, 87. [CrossRef]
23. Blackledge, C.; Atapour-Abarghouei, A. Transforming Fake News: Robust Generalisable News Classification Using Transformers. *arXiv* **2021**, arXiv:2109.09796.
24. Koloski, B.; Stepišnik-Perdih, T.; Pollak, S.; Škrlj, B. Identification of COVID-19 Related Fake News via Neural Stacking. In *Communications in Computer and Information Science*; Chakraborty, T., Shu, K., Bernard, H.R., Liu, H., Akhtar, M.S., Eds.; Springer International Publishing: Cham, Germany, 2021; Volume 1402, pp. 177–188. [CrossRef]
25. De, A.; Desarkar, M.S. Multi-Context Based Neural Approach for COVID-19 Fake-News Detection. In *Companion Proceedings of the Web Conference 2022, Virtual Event*; ACML: Lyon, France, 2022; pp. 852–859. [CrossRef]
26. De, A.; Bandyopadhyay, D.; Gain, B.; Ekbal, A. A Transformer-Based Approach to Multilingual Fake News Detection in Low-Resource Languages. *ACM Trans. Asian Low-Resour. Lang. Inf. Process.* **2021**, *21*, 1–20. [CrossRef]
27. Das, S.D.; Basak, A.; Dutta, S. A Heuristic-driven Ensemble Framework for COVID-19 Fake News Detection. *arXiv* **2021**, arXiv:2101.03545.
28. Nagoudi, E.M.B.; Elmadany, A.; Abdul-Mageed, M.; Alhindi, T.; Cavusoglu, H. Machine Generation and Detection of Arabic Manipulated and Fake News. In Proceedings of the Fifth Arabic Natural Language Processing Workshop, Barcelona, Spain, 12 December 2020; Association for Computational Linguistics: Stroudsburg, PA, USA, 2020; pp. 69–84. Available online: https://aclanthology.org/2020.wanlp-1.7 (accessed on 5 April 2022).
29. Al-Yahya, M.; Al-Khalifa, H.; Al-Baity, H.; AlSaeed, D.; Essam, A. Arabic Fake News Detection: Comparative Study of Neural Networks and Transformer-Based Approaches. *Complexity* **2021**, *2021*, 5516945. [CrossRef]
30. Harrag, F.; Debbah, M.; Darwish, K.; Abdelali, A. Bert Transformer model for Detecting Arabic GPT2 Auto-Generated Tweets. In Proceedings of the Fifth Arabic Natural Language Processing Workshop, Barcelona, Spain, 12 December 2020; Association for Computational Linguistics: Stroudsburg, PA, USA, 2020; pp. 207–214. Available online: https://aclanthology.org/2020.wanlp-1.19 (accessed on 5 April 2022).
31. Hussein, A.; Ghneim, N.; Joukhadar, A. DamascusTeam at NLP4IF2021: Fighting the Arabic COVID-19 Infodemic on Twitter Using AraBERT. In Proceedings of the Fourth Workshop on NLP for Internet Freedom: Censorship, Disinformation, and Propaganda, Online, 6 June 2021; Association for Computational Linguistics: Stroudsburg, PA, USA, 2021; pp. 93–98. [CrossRef]
32. Mahlous, A.R.; Al-Laith, A. Fake News Detection in Arabic Tweets during the COVID-19 Pandemic. *Int. J. Adv. Comput. Sci. Appl. IJACSA* **2021**, *12*, 30. [CrossRef]
33. Ameur, M.S.H.; Aliane, H. AraCOVID19-MFH: Arabic COVID-19 Multi-label Fake News & Hate Speech Detection Dataset. *Procedia Comput. Sci.* **2021**, *189*, 232–241. [CrossRef]
34. Ali, Z.S.; Mansour, W.; Elsayed, T.; Al-Ali, A. AraFacts: The First Large Arabic Dataset of Naturally Occurring Claims. In Proceedings of the Sixth Arabic Natural Language Processing Workshop, Kyiv, Ukraine, 19 April 2021; Association for Computational Linguistics: Stroudsburg, PA, USA, 2021; pp. 231–236. Available online: https://aclanthology.org/2021.wanlp-1.26 (accessed on 29 March 2022).
35. Haouari, F.; Ali, Z.S.; Elsayed, T. bigIR at CLEF 2019: Automatic Verification of Arabic Claims over the Web. In Proceedings of the Conference and Labs of the Evaluation Forum, Lugano, Switzerland, 9–12 September 2019.
36. Alhindi, T.; Alabdulkarim, A.; Alshehri, A.; Abdul-Mageed, M.; Nakov, P. AraStance: A Multi-Country and Multi-Domain Dataset of Arabic Stance Detection for Fact Checking. In Proceedings of the Fourth Workshop on NLP for Internet Freedom: Censorship, Disinformation, and Propaganda, Online, 6 June 2021; Association for Computational Linguistics: Stroudsburg, PA, USA, 2021; pp. 57–65. [CrossRef]
37. Kamr, A.M.; Mohamed, E. akaBERT at SemEval-2022 Task 6: An Ensemble Transformer-based Model for Arabic Sarcasm Detection. In Proceedings of the 16th International Workshop on Semantic Evaluation (SemEval-2022), Online, 14–15 July 2022; Association for Computational Linguistics: Seattle, DC, USA, 2022; pp. 885–890. [CrossRef]
38. Abdelali, A.; Darwish, K.; Durrani, N.; Mubarak, H. Farasa: A Fast and Furious Segmenter for Arabic. In Proceedings of the 2016 Conference of the North American Chapter of the Association for Computational Linguistics: Demonstrations, San Diego, CA, USA, 12–17 June 2016; DeNero, J., Finlayson, M., Reddy, S., Eds.; Association for Computational Linguistics: San Diego, CA, USA, 2016; pp. 11–16. [CrossRef]
39. Li, X.; Xia, Y.; Long, X.; Li, Z.; Li, S. Exploring Text-transformers in AAAI 2021 Shared Task: COVID-19 Fake News Detection in English. *arXiv* **2021**, arXiv:2101.02359.
40. Vijjali, R.; Potluri, P.; Kumar, S.; Teki, S. Two Stage Transformer Model for COVID-19 Fake News Detection and Fact Checking. *arXiv* **2020**, arXiv:2011.13253.

41. Mienye, I.D.; Sun, Y. A Survey of Ensemble Learning: Concepts, Algorithms, Applications, and Prospects. *IEEE Access* **2022**, *10*, 99129–99149. [CrossRef]
42. Paszke, A.; Gross, S.; Massa, F.; Lerer, A.; Bradbury, J.; Chanan, G.; Chintala, S. PyTorch: An Imperative Style, High-Performance Deep Learning Library. *arXiv* **2019**, arXiv:1912.01703. [CrossRef]

mathematics

Article

Few-Shot Learning Sensitive Recognition Method Based on Prototypical Network

Guoquan Yuan [1], Xinjian Zhao [1], Liu Li [2,*], Song Zhang [1] and Shanming Wei [2]

[1] State Grid Jiangsu Electric Power Co., Ltd., Information & Telecommunication Branch, Nanjing 210024, China; guoquan_yuan@163.com (G.Y.); zhaoxin-jian_nj@163.com (X.Z.); m18362973161_1@163.com (S.Z.)
[2] Department of Computer Science and Engineering, Nanjing University of Science and Technology, Nanjing 210094, China; weishanming@njust.edu.cn
* Correspondence: li_liu@njust.edu.cn

Abstract: Traditional machine learning-based entity extraction methods rely heavily on feature engineering by experts, and the generalization ability of the model is poor. Prototype networks, on the other hand, can effectively use a small amount of labeled data to train models while using category prototypes to enhance the generalization ability of the models. Therefore, this paper proposes a prototype network-based named entity recognition (NER) method, namely the FSPN-NER model, to solve the problem of difficult recognition of sensitive data in data-sparse text. The model utilizes the positional coding model (PCM) to pre-train the data and perform feature extraction, then computes the prototype vectors to achieve entity matching, and finally introduces a boundary detection module to enhance the performance of the prototype network in the named entity recognition task. The model in this paper is compared with LSTM, BiLSTM, CRF, Transformer and their combination models, and the experimental results on the test dataset show that the model outperforms the comparative models with an accuracy of 84.8%, a recall of 85.8% and an F1 value of 0.853.

Keywords: sensitive data recognition; NER; BiLSTM; CRF; prototypical network

MSC: 62Q05

1. Introduction

With the introduction of more smart devices in organizations, the size of data is increasing dramatically, placing higher demands on efficient processing and privacy protection. Increased demand for big data analytics requires sophisticated analysis of historical and real-time data while ensuring privacy security [1]. Edge computing applications alleviate the reliance on cloud services but require enhanced privacy protection on edge devices. In AI applications, privacy protection needs to be considered at the algorithm design stage to find a balance between data utilization and privacy protection [2]. The development of digitalization and intelligent technologies brings new challenges to data management and privacy protection. Therefore, comprehensive technical and policy tools are needed to ensure the secure management of sensitive data and to maintain system security and user privacy [3].

Named entity recognition (NER) [4] represents a pivotal aspect of the field of Natural Language Processing (NLP). The objective of NER is to identify entities with particular meanings within a given text. These entities may include names of individuals, locations, organizations, and other entities with particular meanings, such as dates, times, currencies and so forth [5]. Currently, NER tasks are divided into three main categories of methods: rule-based and dictionary-based methods, statistical learning-based methods, and deep learning-based methods. In early NER tasks, rule-based and dictionary-based methods were commonly used. These methods rely on manually developed rules, dictionaries, orthographic features and ontologies based on entity characterisation without the need for annotation data. Rule templates depend on the establishment of knowledge bases and dictionaries, offering a straightforward and efficient approach to managing numerous entities within a text [6]. Rule-based and dictionary-based methods usually rely on specific languages, domains, and knowledge bases, which limits their applicability and is expensive to maintain [7].

The traditional Recurrent Neural Network (RNN) model is inherently suited to processing sequential data. It processes words one by one in the order in which they are found in the sentence, and therefore naturally captures information about the order of words without additional processing [8]. The Transformer model, on the other hand, does not contain a traditional RNN or CNN structure. It feeds the words of an entire sentence into the network for processing at the same time, and therefore there is no explicit information about the relative or absolute position of the words during processing [9]. In order for the model to understand the position of each word in the sequence, we introduce the technique of Positional Encoding. This technique contributes an additional encoding to each word to represent its specific position in the sequence, thus enabling the model to efficiently understand the relative order of the words in the sentence.

In recent years, supervised learning methods based on features have gradually become mainstream methods for NER tasks. These methods usually require a large amount of labeled data to train the models, but they have achieved quite good performance in some specific tasks and domains. Prototypical networks, on the other hand, are suitable for dealing with few-shot learning problems, which is especially important in named entity recognition, since very often we may have very little labeled data [10].

While the existing methods show their strengths, they still face many challenges. Traditional machine learning-based entity extraction methods rely heavily on feature engineering by experts, and the generalization ability of the model is poor [11]. For the few-shot method, the accuracy and stability of the prototype may suffer and fail to capture subtle differences between different entity types. Prototypical networks still need to address challenges such as how to handle long sequences and unclear entity boundaries.

Based on the above observations, we propose a few-shot learning sensitive recognition method based on a prototypical network (FSPN-NER) for blockchain applications. With the prototypical network, the model can be effectively trained with few-shot labeled data, while the category prototype is used to enhance the generalization ability of the model. In addition, we use BiLSTM to integrate contextual information so as to better capture the subtle differences between entities and solve the problem of unclear entity boundaries with the boundary detection module.

In this paper, Section 2 details the related work we conducted before embarking on our research, focusing on named entity recognition techniques based on prototypical networks. Section 3 provides a FSPN-NER model with a comprehensive overview, including its structure, principles and advantageous features. Section 4 fully validates the superior performance and advantages of our proposed model over existing models through comparative experiments and ablation studies, contributing new insights and approaches to the development of this research area.

The primary contributions of this paper are outlined below.

1. A FSPN-NER model based on named entity recognition is proposed for grid-sensitive data recognition.
2. In this paper, the positional coding model (PCM) is used instead of BERT in the pre-training of the feature extraction module, and full word masks and N-gram masks are applied to improve the performance of PCM.
3. In the entity matching module, the prototype vectors are computed based on the prototypical network, and the feature vectors of the text are matched with the prototype vectors to obtain the probability that each word belongs to a different entity.
4. After conducting numerous comparative experiments, the FSPN-NER model outperforms LSTM, BiLSTM, CRF, Transformer and their combination models.

2. Related Work

Blockchain technology, through its decentralized, encrypted and tamper-proof nature, can help ensure the secure storage and transmission of sensitive data. In particular, in the supply chain blockchain, the use of prototype networks to identify and categorize sensitive products or transactions can ensure product compliance and security and detect problems in a timely manner. Analyzing user behavior on the blockchain and identifying abnormal behavioral patterns by learning from fewer samples can enhance the detection of fraud and other malicious activities. By storing hashes of sensitive data on the blockchain, data tampering and leakage can be prevented. Blockchain can also be used to establish and manage smart contracts for data access control, ensuring that only authorized users can access specific sensitive data, thus improving data security. Currently, identification techniques for sensitive data are mainly realized through named entity identification.

Named entity recognition and classification (NERC) is a crucial task in natural language processing (NLP) for extracting information units, such as persons, dates and locations from unstructured text [12]. Over the years, NER has evolved from rule-based methods to models that leverage deep learning techniques and pre-trained language models.

Early NER tasks depended on lexical features extracted from extensive datasets and named entity libraries [13]. Rule-based approaches made use of pre-defined patterns that were constructed using features like keywords, syntactic-lexical patterns and statistical data to match strings. Kim [14] suggested the application of Brill's rule-based inference approach for speech input, wherein rules are automatically generated based on Brill's part-of-speech tagger. Quimbaya et al. [15] introduced a lexicon-driven methodology for named entity recognition (NER) within electronic health records. However, these methods were labor-intensive, costly and rigid.

To address the limitations of rule-based methods, researchers proposed treating NER as a sequence labeling challenge, which led to the development of various models, such as Hidden Markov Models (HMMs) [16], maximum-entropy Markov models (MEMMs) [17], support vector machines (SVMs) [18], and conditional random fields (CRFs) [19]. These models relied on manually crafted discrete features for sequence labeling. Stapelberg and Keara-Linn [20] introduced an automatic English speech recognition system combining the Hidden Markov Model and the conditional random field algorithm, aiming to improve the accuracy and stability of the recognition and discuss its application in the field of computers. Krishnan and Manning [21] introduced a dual-stage methodology utilizing two interconnected conditional random field (CRF) classifiers. The secondary CRF incorporates latent representations obtained from the output of the primary CRF.

The latest progress in deep learning has resulted in the utilization of neural networks for NER tasks. These models autonomously acquire characteristics from the input data, lessening the dependence on manually designed features. The use of unidirectional LSTMs, convolutional neural networks, bidirectional LSTMs with CRFs, and character-level CNNs has been explored in NER literature. The rise of pre-trained language models like BERT and ELMo has significantly enhanced the performance of NER through advanced feature extraction capabilities. L Luo et al. [22] introduced an attention-based bidirectional Long Short-Term Memory with a conditional random field layer (Att-BiLSTM-CRF) neural network approach for document-level chemical named entity recognition. Liu et al. [23] presented a novel approach using BERT, BiLSTM and CRF for named entity recognition in citrus pests and diseases, aiming to extract specific entities from unstructured text data to facilitate the construction of a knowledge map for accurate prevention and control methods in agriculture. Yuan et al. [24] suggested incorporating adversarial training into the model training process as a regularization technique to reduce the impact of noise on the model. In addition, they introduced self-attention to the BiLSTM-CRF model in order to capture significant features that affect entity classification and enhance the accuracy of entity classification. Liang et al. [4] proposed a Chinese named entity recognition (NER) method and a Relation Extraction (RE) method in the field of Chinese literature. Their approach is built upon the self-attention mechanism, the BiLSTM neural network and the

CRF model. Specifically, they introduced a BiLSTM-Self-Attention-CRF framework for NER and a BiLSTM-Multilevel-Attention framework for RE.

Recently, most of the research has been devoted to the study of combining prototypical networks and named entity recognition. The advantages of prototypical networks are their adaptability to few-shot learning and their strong generalization ability, properties that are useful for NER tasks characterized by scarce labeled data and strong entity context dependency. Bin Ji et al. [25] introduced an entity-level prototypical network (EP-Net) enhanced with decentralized distributed prototypes, where text spans are treated as candidate entities, eliminating the need for labeling dependencies. Ritesh Kumar et al. [26] introduced ProtoNER, an end-to-end KVP extraction model based on prototypical networks. This model enables the addition of new classes to a pre-existing model with minimal newly annotated training samples. Yucheng Huang et al. [27] introduced COPNER, which offers a unique prompt consisting of class-specific words to provide supervision signals, enabling contrastive learning to optimize token representations and metric referents for distance-metric inference on test samples.

Overall, NER research has made great progress in recent years, from lexical and rule-based approaches to more complex models utilizing deep learning techniques and pre-trained language models. Currently, there are problems of data scarcity and diversity in sensitive data recognition, while in this paper, prototype networks are applied to named entity recognition, which can not only effectively solve the problems of data scarcity and diversity but also combine the advantages of deep learning to provide fast and accurate recognition capabilities for named entities in various textual data. Therefore, this paper proposes a prototype network-based named entity recognition method combined with deep learning for sensitive data recognition.

3. Methodology

3.1. Overview

Our model is roughly divided into three parts, as shown in Figure 1, including the feature extraction module, the entity matching module and the boundary detection module. In the feature extraction module, we first pre-train the data by an improved location coding model based on BERT, and then realize the feature extraction of word vectors by BiLSTM, i.e., the pre-trained word vectors are encoded to transform the input sequence into a series of feature vectors. In the entity matching module, the prototype vectors are computed based on the feature vectors obtained from the feature extraction module, and the features in the query set are matched with the type-averaged features to obtain the type of each word and realize the recognition of sensitive data. In addition, in order to improve the performance of the prototypical network in the case of the few-shot model, we introduce the boundary detection module. This module computes the boundary labeling probability of each word by combining contextual features and type information, thus improving the performance of the prototypical network in the named entity recognition task.

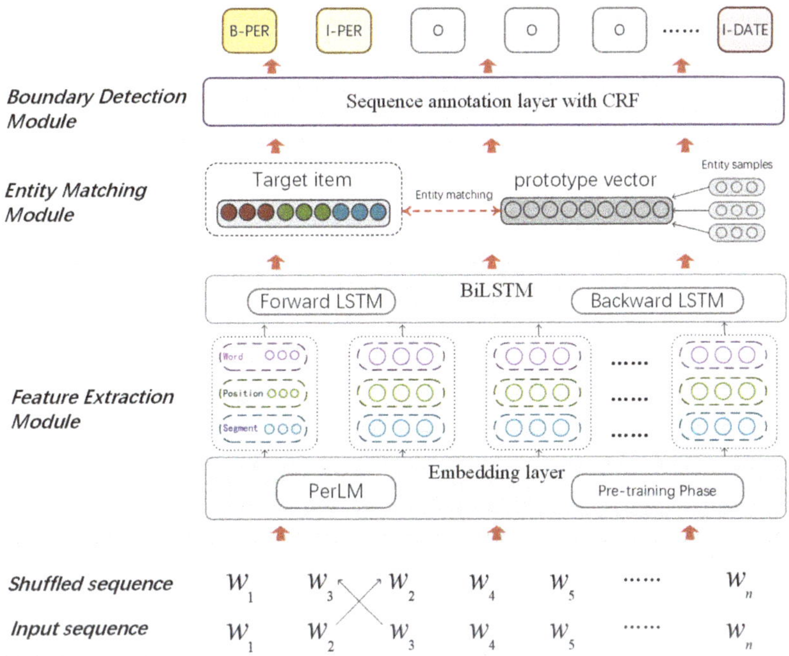

Figure 1. The overall architecture of the model.

3.2. Feature Extraction Module

3.2.1. Pre-Training

The PCM is an improvement on BERT. They have the same neural structure but differ slightly in the input and training goal. The PCM uses rewritten sentences as input, and the training goal is to predict the position of the original token. In this model, we use WordPiece for tokenization, directly employ vocabularies and replace the Masked Language Model (MLM) with PerL. The prediction space is based on the input sequence length instead of whole vocabularies (like MLM), and no artificial masking tokens [MASK] are used, while we use whole-word masking and N-gram masking to further improve performance. Among other things, MLM is a deep learning technique widely used in natural language processing (NLP) tasks. In MLM, a portion of the input text is "masked" or randomly replaced with special tokens (usually [MASK]), and the model is trained to predict the original tokens based on their surrounding context.

We use whole-word masking and N-gram masking strategies to select candidate tokens for masking, where the word-level unit word features to 4 g are 40%, 30%, 20% and 10%, respectively. We use 15% of the input word percentage for masking. Of these, we randomly select 90% of the tokens and permute their order. Note that the blending process is performed only for these 90% tokens and not for the entire input sequence. For the remaining 10% of tokens, we keep them unchanged and treat them as negative samples.

Formally, considering two sequences $A = \{ A_1, \ldots, A_n \}$ and $B = \{B_1, \ldots B_m \}$, we first create new pairs of input sequences $A' = \{ A'_1, \ldots, A'_n \}$ and $B' = \{B'_1, \ldots, B'_m \}$, where some of the word positions are swapped. The two sequences are combined together to create the input sequence X of PCM.

$$X = [CLS]A'_1 \ldots A'_n[SEP]B'_1 \ldots B'_m[SEP] \quad (1)$$

where $[CLS]$ is usually located at the beginning of the input sequence and is used to indicate the classification result of the sequence. $[SEP]$ is used to separate two sentences or paragraphs.

The PCM then transforms X into a contextual depiction $H \in R^{N \times d}$, where N is the longest sequence allowed and d is the size of the hidden layer, through the utilization of an embedding layer that includes word embeddings, positional embeddings, and token type (segment) embeddings, along with a series of L-layer converters.

$$H^{(0)} = Embedding(X) \tag{2}$$

$$H^{(i)} = Transformer(H^{(i-1)}), i \in \{1, \ldots, L\}, H = H^{(L)} \tag{3}$$

Like MLM and Mac (MacBERT target), we only need to predict the positions selected in PerLM. We gather a subset with respect to these spots to create a candidate representation $H_m \in R^{k \times d}$, where k is the quantity of selected tokens. Based on the definition of PerLM, we use a masking rate of 15%, which provides us with $k = [N \times 15\%]$.

We then use a feedforward dense layer (FFN) subsequent to a dropout layer and a normalization layer.

$$\widetilde{H^m} = LayerNorm(Dropout(FFN(H^m)))) \tag{4}$$

Calculating the position of the initial token, we simply make a dot product between "H_m" and "H". Then, we add a bias term $b \in R^L$ and use the softmax function to obtain the normalized probability.

$$p_i = softmax(\widetilde{H_i^m} H^T + b),\ p_i \in R^L \tag{5}$$

Finally, we employ the standard cross-entropy loss to optimize the pre-training task.

$$L = -\frac{1}{M} \sum_{i=1}^{M} y_i log p_i \tag{6}$$

3.2.2. Feature Extraction

This part mainly encodes the word vectors in the previous step by BiLSTM and transforms the input sequence into a series of feature vectors. The word vectors with n-dimensions, acquired in the preceding step, are employed as inputs at every time step of the BiLSTM. This process results in the generation of hidden state sequences from the bi-directional LSTM layer. After both the forward LSTM and the backward LSTM complete their respective processes, the hidden state sequences from each are combined based on their positions, producing the complete hidden state sequences represented as t = {1, 2, . . . , n}. Subsequently, the linear output layer converts these full hidden state sequences into "s", with "n" denoting the number of categories for labeling in the label set. Remembering the final captured sentence characteristics as the sequence post all mappings into a matrix, each dimension l_u, l_v of the matrix L corresponds to the fraction value of its word a_u corresponding to each category label b_v, where u = {1, 2, . . . , n}, v = {1, 2, . . . , n}. If at this time we opt to categorize the score value of each position separately and simply choose the highest score for each to obtain the output result directly, we fail to take into account the information between adjacent sentences. As a result, we are not able to achieve the global optimum, leading to less than ideal classification results. To address this issue, we introduce the final layer of the model.

The BiLSTM model is composed of an input layer, a forward LSTM layer, a backward LSTM layer, and an output layer. Each training sequence is trained with one forward LSTM and one backward LSTM. This bidirectional network architecture divides the outputs of the LSTM into forward and backward sequences, enabling the model to comprehensively grasp the contextual significance of every word.

3.3. Entity Matching Module

This module focuses on first calculating the average features of each type of entity in the support set and optimizing them with a joint loss function. Then, the features in the query set are matched with the average features of the types, the distance situation between each query point and each prototype representation of the classification is calculated, and the soft maximum probability result is calculated to generate the probability distribution of each classification. The probability of each word belonging to a different type can then be calculated, yielding the probability of what type each word belongs to in order to determine the sensitive data.

3.3.1. Computing the Prototype Vector

For each entity type k, the average of all sample features of the support set is computed to obtain the prototype vector c_k for that type:

$$c_k = \frac{1}{|S_k|} \sum_{(x_i, y_i) \in S_k} f_\theta(x_i) \tag{7}$$

where $f_\theta(x_i)$ denotes the features of each entity sample and S_k denotes the set of all samples of the kth class of entities.

Here, the model performance is optimized by designing a joint loss function that combines classification loss and prototype matching loss.

In this case, to calculate the classification loss, the prototype vector is used to classify the input samples, the distance between the samples and each prototype is calculated, and the prototype with the smallest distance is selected as the predicted category. The cross-entropy loss function is used to measure the difference between the predicted category and the real category.

For each input sample, the classification loss is calculated using the cross-entropy loss function based on the distance of its feature vector $f_\theta(x)$ from the prototype vector c_k of each type:

$$L_{classification} = -\sum_i logP(y_i|x_i) \tag{8}$$

The prototype matching loss is computed by ensuring that the feature representation of the input sample has the smallest distance from its true category prototype vector and a larger distance from the prototype vectors of other categories. This step is achieved by minimizing the Euclidean distance between the sample and its true category prototype:

$$L_{prototype} = \sum_i ||f_\theta(x_i) - c_{y_i}||^2 \tag{9}$$

Finally, the classification loss and the prototype matching loss are combined and optimized by means of a weighted sum in order to consider both classification accuracy and feature matching during the training process.

$$L_{total} = \lambda L_{classification} + (1 - \lambda) L_{prototype} \tag{10}$$

where λ is a weighting parameter to balance the effects of the two losses.

3.3.2. Entity Matching

For each sample in the query set x_q, extract its feature representation $f_\theta(x_q)$. Compute the Euclidean distance between each query point x_q and each classification prototype representation c_k:

$$d(x_q, c_k) = ||f_\theta(x_q) - c_k|| \tag{11}$$

Convert the distances to softmax probabilities to generate probability distributions for each classification:

$$P(y = k|x_q) = \frac{exp(-d(x_q, c_k))}{\sum_{k'} exp(-d(x_q, c_{k'}))} \tag{12}$$

where $P(y = k|x_q)$ denotes the probability that sample x_q belongs to type k.

Determine the most likely entity type for each query sample based on its probability distribution:

$$\hat{y_q} = arg \max_k P(y = k|x_q) \tag{13}$$

In this way, the probability of each word belonging to a different type is calculated to determine the type of entity belonging to the sensitive data.

3.4. Boundary Detection Module

The contextual feature representation $h = (h_1, h_2, \ldots, h_T)$ obtained in Section 3.2.2 is input into the CRF layer, which combines the type information (e.g., entity type labels) and contextual information to compute the boundary labeling probability of each word. CRF is able to capture the transfer probability between labels by modeling the dependencies between label sequences, thus improving the accuracy of the boundary labeling prediction. The CRF layer finds the globally optimal labeling when decoding sequences, making boundary detection more reliable.

Linear layer mapping: the feature representation h is mapped to the labeling space through a linear layer, generating the firing score matrix E. The mapping is performed by a linear layer:

$$E = Wh + b \tag{14}$$

where W is the weight matrix, b is the bias term, $E \in \mathbb{R}^{T \times K}$, and K is the number of labels.

The CRF layer does this by defining a transfer matrix $A \in \mathbb{R}^{K \times K}$, where B denotes the score for transferring from label i to label j. For a sequence of labels $y = (y_1, y_2, \ldots, y_T)$, the score is

$$score(x, y) = \sum_{t=1}^{T} E_{t,y_t} + \sum_{t=2}^{T} A_{y_t-1,y_t} \tag{15}$$

where E_{t,y_t} is the emission fraction and A_{y_t-1,y_t} is the transfer fraction.

Next, the total score of all possible label sequences is calculated as a normalization factor:

$$Z(x) = \sum_{y' \in y(x)} exp(score(x, y')) \tag{16}$$

where $y(x)$ is the set of all possible labeling sequences.

Given a sequence of labels y, we compute its conditional probability, i.e., the boundary labeling probability:

$$P(y|x) = \frac{exp(score(x, y))}{Z(x)} \tag{17}$$

We optimize the log-likelihood to maximize the model fit to the training data. The objective function is

$$L = logP(y|x) = score(x, y) - logZ(x) \tag{18}$$

In prediction, boundary detection is achieved by finding the optimal label sequence through the Viterbi algorithm. That is, the label sequence is found that makes the score maximum:

$$\hat{y} = arg \max_{y' \in y(x)} score(x, y') \tag{19}$$

4. Experimentation

In this section, we first focus on the dataset, second on the evaluation metrics, including the correctness (P), recall (R) and F1 value, and finally on the comparison and ablation experiments.

4.1. Data Sets

We collected grid traffic data which include common information such as name, time and address. We created a few-shot dataset of 48,821 sentences from these data. We partitioed the dataset according to specific criteria, setting aside the last 10% of the data for testing purposes. The remaining data were then split into training and validation sets at a ratio of 9:1, respectively. The specific division results are shown in Table 1.

Table 1. Data set splitting.

Dataset	Train	Validation	Test	Sum
samples	39,545	4394	4882	48,821

For the ablation study, we used the ChFinAnn dataset and the AdminPunish dataset. In the ChFinAnn dataset, we appropriately combined entities according to their actual meanings in order to simplify the problem to a certain extent. For instance, the terms "HighestTradingPrice" and "LowestTradingPrice" both denote prices; therefore, we consolidated them into a unified entity called "Price". This integration strategy resulted in a total of 10 categories of entities for the ChFinAnn dataset. The seven entities in the AdminPunish dataset remained unchanged. Table 2 presents the names of the entities and their respective proportions in the associated datasets.

Table 2. Names of entities and their corresponding scales for each dataset.

ChFinAnn		AdminPunish	
Entry Name	**Proportion (%)**	**Entry Name**	**Proportion (%)**
Price	3.43	Client	27.51
Shares	27.76	FileNumber	18.33
Institution	0.51	Punishing Authority	18.65
Company	8.49	Unified Social Credit Codes	7.82
StockAbbr	8.45	Legal Representative	11.38
StockCode	9.66	Id Card Number	3.41
Date	19.77	Address	12.90
Ratio	5.50		
EquityHolder	10.42		
Pledgee	6.00		

4.2. Data Process

Traditional preprocessing approaches usually involve mapping the character IDs in a sentence to a multi-dimensional space and then processing these multi-dimensional data using a word2vec model. To enable end-to-end model building, a new approach is to use an embedding layer instead of a word2vec model for the transformation of multi-dimensional features. In this approach, the preprocessing stage simply converts the characters in the sentence to IDs and converts the entities to the corresponding category IDs, thus providing more efficient and accurate input data for the subsequent model. This approach not only simplifies the whole processing flow, but also improves the performance and efficiency of the model.

4.3. Evaluation Indicators

In named entity recognition tasks, the evaluation criteria usually include precision, recall and F1 value. The F1 score is a widely used evaluation metric for assessing the effectiveness of classification models. For each category (e.g., address, book, company, etc.), the F1 score can be calculated. The F1 score combines accuracy and recall, and it provides a good measure of the model's combined performance in predicting positive and negative examples. Precision refers to the ratio of accurately predicted positive samples, while recall refers to the ratio of accurately predicted actual samples. F1 score represents the harmonized mean of precision and recall, allowing for a more comprehensive evaluation of the model's performance by incorporating both metrics.

4.4. Experimental Comparison

We used BiLSTM replacing FeedForward to optimize the Transformer structure. After conducting thorough comparative experiments, the study findings indicate that the enhanced Transformer–BiLSTM–CRF model outperforms the LSTM, BiLSTM, CRF, Transformer and their individual combination models in terms of performance [28]. Based on the data in Table 3, we trained nine different models and obtained their metrics such as precision, recall and F1 value for detailed comparison and analysis.

Table 3. Evaluation indicator results.

Model	Precision	Recall	F1-Score
DNN	48.9%	49.6%	49.3%
CRF [19]	70.8%	70.4%	70.6%
LSTM	70.9%	69.7%	70.3%
BiLSTM	70.8%	73.9%	72.4%
BiLSTM + CRF [24]	73.9%	76.1%	75.0%
Transformer	42.1%	46.2%	44.2%
Transfoemer + BiLSTM	83.5%	83.9%	83.7%
Transformer + BiLSTM + CRF [22]	83.2%	84.9%	84.1%
Our model	84.5%	85.5%	85.0%

Compared with simple neural networks, LSTM has obvious advantages in processing sequence data. LSTM is a unique type of recurrent neural network architecture designed to manage the flow of information using input gates, forget gates and output gates, enabling it to effectively capture long-term dependencies within sequential data [29]. Compared with traditional forward deep neural networks, LSTM can better capture long-term features in sequence data and is suitable for tasks that require memorizing long-distance information.

For tasks involving more intricate sequence data, the BiLSTM is better suited than a unidirectional LSTM. BiLSTM combines two directions of information flow, forward and backward from the current timestep, so it can better capture the features and patterns amidst the time sequential data, improving the ability of modeling the sequence data, which is suitable for tasks that need to consider contextual information [30].

Furthermore, the Transformer is a kind of neural network structure that utilizes a self-attention mechanism, comprising numerous layers of feed-forward neural networks. It is adept at dealing with dependencies between positions in an input sequence, better able to learn long-range dependencies and adept at extracting underlying features from data embedded in a high-dimensional space. However, Transformer does not perform well in tasks that require complex combinations of features because its self-attention mechanism is more suitable for capturing local rather than global information and cannot directly accomplish some tasks that require complex combinations of features.

Since machine learning heavily depends on artificial features and the selection of features, CRF itself does not show good performance. However, with the introduction of BiLSTM for feature extraction, CRF can improve its results by effectively combining features through its transition matrix. Superior results can be achieved by more intricate neural network structures. The newly proposed model integrates the strengths of multiple models and surpasses the performance of the other models under comparison. Also, the introduction of Transformer to extract the underlying features is an important improvement. The improved Transformer uses BiLSTM instead of the traditional feed-forward network and performs much better in extracting the underlying temporal features. BiLSTM assists in more effectively extracting and integrating features. Ultimately, the probability distribution of the output is refined by training the transition matrix using CRF.

In the test few-shot dataset, the new model achieves an accuracy of 84.5%, a recall of 85.5%, and an F1 value of 0.85, values which outperform the performance of other compared models. The results indicate that the suggested model has made substantial progress in this task, showcasing its effectiveness and superiority.

4.5. Ablation Experiment

4.5.1. Impact of the Size of the Training Sample

Additionally, the performance of the FSPN-NER model was evaluated with varying training sample sizes. As illustrated in Tables 4 and 5, it can be concluded that the F1 scores of the FSPN-NER models trained with distinct sample sizes on the test samples exhibited notable discrepancies. In comparison to the BiLSTM-CRF model, the F1 scores of the FSPN-NER model demonstrate a gradual improvement with an increase in the training sample size. However, the FSPN-NER model appears to perform more robustly, further substantiating its superiority. Figure 2 presents the F1 scores obtained from the ChFinAnn and AdminPunish datasets, respectively. A comparison of the two datasets reveals that the F1 scores from the AdminPunish dataset are generally higher than those from the ChFinAnn dataset. This is mainly due to the entity sparsity phenomenon observed in the ChFinAnn dataset.

(**a**) ChFinAnn (**b**) AdminPunish

Figure 2. Effect of training sample size on F1 scores.

Table 4. The impact of the training sample size on F1 scores for the ChFinAnn dataset.

Training	FSPN-NER	BiLSTM-CRF
6.25%	90.32%	82.67%
12.5%	91.63%	85.56%
25%	92.21%	85.98%
50%	92.65%	87.47%
100%	93.46%	87.47%

Table 5. Effect of training sample size on F1 scores for the AdminPunish dataset.

Training	FSPN-NER	BiLSTM-CRF
6.25%	95.71%	86.53%
12.5%	95.79%	90.52%
25%	95.84%	92.63%
50%	96.43%	93.82%
100%	97.35%	96.11%

4.5.2. Impact of Embedded Dimensions

In our study, we examined the effect of word vector dimensionality on model performance. We utilized four distinct dimensions of pre-trained word vectors, including 50, 100, 200 and 300. According to the data in Table 6, when the word vector dimension is 100, the correctness and recall are higher, and the F1-score reaches the highest value of 73.50. Hence, we opted to establish the dimension of the pre-trained word vectors as 100 in order to achieve optimal model performance. However, when the dimensionality of the word vectors is increased to 200 and 300, the F1-score starts to decrease, which indicates that the dimension of the word vectors is not as large as it should be.

According to Figure 3, this phenomenon can be explained by the fact that although increasing the dimensionality of the embedded word vectors may result in the acquisition of more information and features, it also adds to the complexity of the model and the use of computational resources, and may even lead to overfitting problems. Furthermore, increasing the dimensionality of embedded word vectors also increases the training and inference time of the model, which is an unwise decision especially when resources are limited. Therefore, in practical applications, we need to weigh the impact of word vector dimensionality on model performance and avoid blindly pursuing higher dimensionality while neglecting the balance between performance and efficiency.

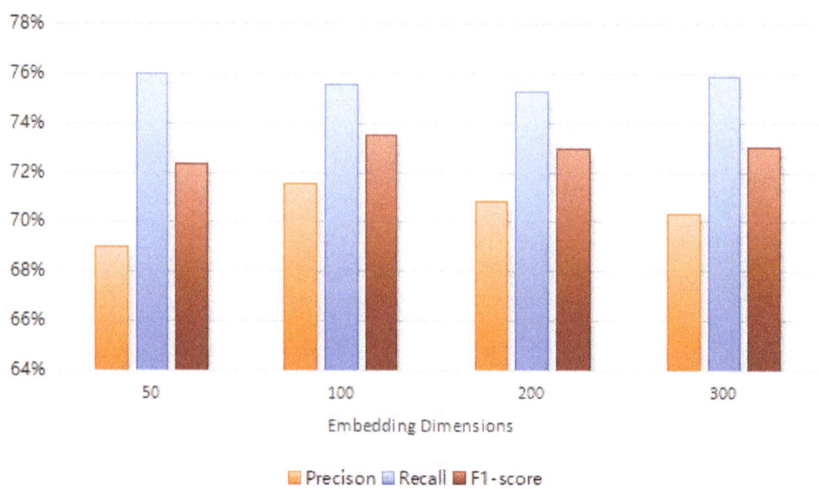

Figure 3. Comparing the performance of word vectors with different dimensions.

Table 6. Comparing the performance of word vectors with different dimensions.

Embedding Dimensions	Precison (%)	Recall (%)	F1-Score (%)
50	69.02	76.00	72.34
100	71.57	75.55	73.50
200	70.82	75.26	72.97
300	70.36	75.87	73.01

5. Discussion and Conclusions

The aim of this paper is to investigate the few-shot learning sensitive recognition method based on a prototypical network. The sensitive data recognition domain possesses a large amount of specialized knowledge texts in various formats, but the utilization of this information is relatively low. To extract sensitive data entities more efficiently, we propose a FSPN-NER model based on a prototypical network. We train and evaluate the model using a traffic few-shot dataset. The results show that the model outperforms the comparison model in terms of accuracy, recall and F1 value. Ablation experiments are used to verify the effect of training sample size and word vector embedding dimension on the model.

In our future research work, we aim to incorporate active learning techniques with the goal of allowing the model to identify and forward data that are highly uncertain to experts for annotation. This process will then enhance the performance of the model. The method will help to advance deep learning-based NER techniques to improve the efficiency and accuracy of extracting sensitive data entities.

Author Contributions: Methodology, X.Z. and L.L.; validation, X.Z. and G.Y.; formal analysis, X.Z. and S.Z.; investigation, X.Z., G.Y. and L.L.; writing—original draft, X.Z.; writing—review and editing, X.Z.; visualization, X.Z.; supervision, S.W.; funding acquisition, X.Z. All authors have read and agreed to the published version of the manuscript.

Funding: This work was supported by the Science and Technology Project of State Grid Jiangsu Electric Power Company Ltd., under Grant J2023179.

Data Availability Statement: The raw data supporting the conclusions of this article will be made available by the authors on request.

Conflicts of Interest: Authors Guoquan Yuan, Xinjian Zhao and Song Zhang were employed by the company State Grid Jiangsu Electric Power Co. The remaining authors declare that the research was conducted in the absence of any commercial or financial relationships that could be construed as a potential conflict of interest.

References

1. Dogan, A.; Birant, D. Machine learning and data mining in manufacturing. *Expert Syst. Appl.* **2021**, *166*, 114060. [CrossRef]
2. Mehrotra, S.; Sharma, S.; Ullman, J.D.; Ghosh, D.; Gupta, P.; Mishra, A. Panda: Partitioned data security on outsourced sensitive and non-sensitive data. *ACM Trans. Manag. Inf. Syst.* **2020**, *11*, 1–41. [CrossRef]
3. Wang, X.; Liu, J. A novel feature integration and entity boundary detection for named entity recognition in cybersecurity. *Knowl.-Based Syst.* **2023**, *260*, 110114. [CrossRef]
4. Liang, L.X.; Lin, L.; Lin, E.; Wen, W.S.; Huang, G.Y. A Joint Learning Model to Extract Entities and Relations for Chinese Literature Based on Self-Attention. *Mathematics* **2022**, *10*, 2216. [CrossRef]
5. Sun, J.; Liu, Y.; Cui, J.; He, H. Deep learning-based methods for natural hazard named entity recognition. *Sci. Rep.* **2022**, *12*, 4598. [CrossRef]
6. Cheng, J.; Liu, J.; Xu, X.; Xia, D.; Liu, L.; Sheng, V.S. A review of Chinese named entity recognition. *KSII Trans. Internet Inf. Syst.* **2021**, *15*, 2012–2030. [CrossRef]
7. Chen, X.; Ouyang, C.; Liu, Y.; Bu, Y. Improving the named entity recognition of Chinese electronic medical records by combining domain dictionary and rules. *Int. J. Environ. Res. Public Health* **2020**, *17*, 2687. [CrossRef]
8. Ali, S.; Masood, K.; Riaz, A.; Saud, A. Named entity recognition using deep learning: A review. In Proceedings of the 2022 IEEE International Conference on Business Analytics for Technology and Security (ICBATS), Dubai, United Arab Emirates, 16–17 February 2022; pp. 1–7.
9. Yan, H.; Deng, B.; Li, X.; Qiu, X. TENER: Adapting transformer encoder for named entity recognition. *arXiv* **2019**, arXiv:1911.04474.

10. de Lichy, C.; Glaude, H.; Campbell, W. Meta-learning for few-shot named entity recognition. In Proceedings of the 1st Workshop on Meta Learning and Its Applications to Natural Language Processing, Bangkok, Thailand, 5 August 2021; pp. 44–58.
11. Ji, Z.; Wang, X.; Cai, C.; Sun, H. Power entity recognition based on bidirectional long short-term memory and conditional random fields. *Glob. Energy Interconnect.* **2020**, *3*, 186–192. [CrossRef]
12. Li, Y.; Yu, Y.; Qian, T. Type-aware decomposed framework for few-shot named entity recognition. *arXiv* **2023**, arXiv:2302.06397.
13. Wang, Y.; Meng, X.; Zhu, L. Cell group recognition method based on adaptive mutation PSO-SVM. *Cells* **2018**, *7*, 135. [CrossRef]
14. Zhang, Y.; Sui, X.; Pan, F.; Yu, K.; Li, K.; Tian, S.; Erdengasileng, A.; Han, Q.; Wang, W.; Wang, J.; et al. BioKG: A comprehensive, large-scale biomedical knowledge graph for AI-powered, data-driven biomedical research. *bioRxiv* **2023**. [CrossRef]
15. Quimbaya, A.P.; Múnera, A.S.; Rivera, R.A.G.; Rodríguez, J.C.D.; Velandia, O.M.M.; Peña, A.A.G.; Labbé, C. Named entity recognition over electronic health records through a combined dictionary-based approach. *Procedia Comput. Sci.* **2016**, *100*, 55–61. [CrossRef]
16. Pan, W.; Li, H.; Zhou, X.; Jiao, J.; Zhu, C.; Zhang, Q. Research on pig sound recognition based on deep neural network and hidden Markov models. *Sensors* **2024**, *24*, 1269. [CrossRef]
17. Tillé, Y.; Panahbehagh, B. Maximum Entropy Design by a Markov Chain Process. *J. Surv. Stat. Methodol.* **2024**, *12*, 232–248. [CrossRef]
18. Li, J.; Li, Y.; Song, J.; Zhang, J.; Zhang, S. Quantum support vector machine for classifying noisy data. *IEEE Trans. Comput.* **2024**, *73*, 2233–2247. [CrossRef]
19. Pradhan, A.; Yajnik, A. Parts-of-speech tagging of Nepali texts with Bidirectional LSTM, Conditional Random Fields and HMM. *Multimed. Tools Appl.* **2024**, *83*, 9893–9909. [CrossRef]
20. Junling, Y. Online learning system for English speech automatic recognition based on hidden Markov model algorithm and conditional random field algorithm. *Entertain. Comput.* **2024**, *51*, 100729. [CrossRef]
21. Krishnan, V.; Manning, C.D. An effective two-stage model for exploiting non-local dependencies in named entity recognition. In Proceedings of the 21st International Conference on Computational Linguistics and 44th Annual Meeting of the Association for Computational Linguistics, Sydney, Australia, 17–21 July 2006; pp. 1121–1128.
22. Luo, L.; Yang, Z.; Yang, P.; Zhang, Y.; Wang, L.; Lin, H.; Wang, J. An attention-based BiLSTM-CRF approach to document-level chemical named entity recognition. *Bioinformatics* **2018**, *34*, 1381–1388. [CrossRef]
23. Liu, Y.; Wei, S.; Huang, H.; Lai, Q.; Li, M.; Guan, L. Naming entity recognition of citrus pests and diseases based on the BERT-BiLSTM-CRF model. *Expert Syst. Appl.* **2023**, *234*, 121103. [CrossRef]
24. Yuan, T.; Qin, X.; Wei, C. A Chinese named entity recognition method based on ERNIE-BiLSTM-CRF for food safety domain. *Appl. Sci.* **2023**, *13*, 2849. [CrossRef]
25. Ji, B.; Li, S.; Gan, S.; Yu, J.; Ma, J.; Liu, H. Few-shot named entity recognition with entity-level prototypical network enhanced by dispersedly distributed prototypes. *arXiv* **2022**, arXiv:2208.08023.
26. Kumar, R.; Goyal, S.; Verma, A.; Isahagian, V. ProtoNER: Few Shot Incremental Learning for Named Entity Recognition Using Prototypical Networks. In Proceedings of the International Conference on Business Process Management, Utrecht, The Netherlands, 11–15 September 2023; Springer: Berlin/Heidelberg, Germany, 2023; pp. 70–82.
27. Huang, Y.; He, K.; Wang, Y.; Zhang, X.; Gong, T.; Mao, R.; Li, C. Copner: Contrastive learning with prompt guiding for few-shot named entity recognition. In Proceedings of the 29th International Conference on Computational Linguistics, Gyeongju, Republic of Korea, 12–17 October 2022; pp. 2515–2527.
28. He, B.; Chen, J. Named entity recognition method in network security domain based on BERT-BiLSTM-CRF. In Proceedings of the 2021 IEEE 21st International Conference on Communication Technology (ICCT), Tianjin, China, 13–16 October 2021; pp. 508–512.
29. Yu, Y.; Si, X.; Hu, C.; Zhang, J. A review of recurrent neural networks: LSTM cells and network architectures. *Neural Comput.* **2019**, *31*, 1235–1270. [CrossRef]
30. Yang, M.; Wang, J. Adaptability of financial time series prediction based on BiLSTM. *Procedia Comput. Sci.* **2022**, *199*, 18–25. [CrossRef]

mathematics

Article

KCB-FLAT: Enhancing Chinese Named Entity Recognition with Syntactic Information and Boundary Smoothing Techniques

Zhenrong Deng [1,2], Zheng Huang [1], Shiwei Wei [3,*] and Jinglin Zhang [1]

1 Guangxi Key Laboratory of Images and Graphics Intelligent Processing, Guilin University of Electronic Technology, Guilin 541004, China; zhrdeng@guet.edu.cn (Z.D.); 22032303154@mails.guet.edu.cn (Z.H.); 22032303126@mails.guet.edu.cn (J.Z.)
2 Nanning Research Institute, Guilin University of Electronic Technology, Guilin 541004, China
3 School of Computer Science and Engineering, Guilin University of Aerospace Technology, Guilin 541004, China
* Correspondence: swwei@guat.edu.cn

Abstract: Named entity recognition (NER) is a fundamental task in Natural Language Processing (NLP). During the training process, NER models suffer from over-confidence, and especially for the Chinese NER task, it involves word segmentation and introduces erroneous entity boundary segmentation, exacerbating over-confidence and reducing the model's overall performance. These issues limit further enhancement of NER models. To tackle these problems, we proposes a new model named KCB-FLAT, designed to enhance Chinese NER performance by integrating enriched semantic information with the word-Boundary Smoothing technique. Particularly, we first extract various types of syntactic data and utilize a network named Key-Value Memory Network, based on syntactic information to functionalize this, integrating it through an attention mechanism to generate syntactic feature embeddings for Chinese characters. Subsequently, we employed an encoder named Cross-Transformer to thoroughly combine syntactic and lexical information to address the entity boundary segmentation errors caused by lexical information. Finally, we introduce a Boundary Smoothing module, combined with a regularity-conscious function, to capture the internal regularity of per entity, reducing the model's overconfidence in entity probabilities through smoothing. Experimental results demonstrate that the proposed model achieves exceptional performance on the MSRA, Resume, Weibo, and self-built ZJ datasets, as verified by the F1 score.

Keywords: named entity recognition; Chinese NER; syntactic information; word-boundary smoothing

MSC: 68T99

1. Introduction

Recently, the study of named entity recognition (NER) in Chinese has become a significant area of interest in natural language processing research. Due to the swift advancement of big data analytics and artificial intelligence technology, the precise recognition and categorization of named entities from vast amounts of textual information has gained significant importance. As smart mobile devices gain popularity, the Internet user base in developing nations is experiencing a surge. Recently, on 28 August 2023, the China Internet Network Information Centre unveiled its 52nd Statistical Report on China's Internet Development Status in Beijing. The report reveals that by June 2023, China boasted 1.079 billion Internet users, marking an escalation of 11.09 million since December 2022. Notably, the Internet penetration stood at 76.4%. The growing access to information, content searches, and online interactions has resulted in a massive accumulation of Chinese text data. In the realm of Chinese NLP, NER is a foundational and vital task, playing a pivotal role in diverse downstream applications including one-question-one-answer dialogue system [1], intelligent personalized recommendation [2], text generation [3], and content understanding [4,5]. An important task of Chinese NER is to identify all possible entities from a text and classify them based on their attributes, such as names, places, institutions, and other similar groups [6]. However, Chinese NER presents unique challenges compared with its English counterpart. First of all, Chinese NER has been developed relatively late, and there are fewer available corpora, which limits its development [7,8]. Secondly, Chinese does not have a corpus like English [9]. Furthermore, Chinese does not have obvious word spacing like English [10]. The fact that Chinese has no obvious word spacing like English makes word segmentation a necessary preprocessing step. Moreover, the flexible nature of Chinese word formation allows the same character sequences to be segmented differently depending on the context, adding to the complexity of NER.

To accomplish the objective of Chinese NER, the model undergoes learning by analyzing a substantial volume of annotated training data and fine-tunes its parameters through a likelihood function aimed at optimizing the fit to the training dataset. However, overconfidence is a potential problem in Chinese NER research. If there are specific patterns in the training data, the model may over-learn these patterns, resulting in over-confidence in these patterns when making predictions [11]. This situation may degrade the performance and calibration of the model, as the model may be too biased towards predicting specific entity classes while ignoring other situations. In other words, it is possible that the model does not really understand the concepts or syntax behind these patterns, which is akin to memorizing the answers rather than really understanding the meaning of the question. In addition, some studies have identified incorrect entity boundaries as one of the main reasons for incorrect entity identification [12]. Therefore, addressing the problem of over-confidence in NER models is crucial to improving their performance and usefulness.

Empirical evidence shows that positive samples (i.e., real entities) are sparsely distributed across the candidate ranges in a dataset. For example, in the Resume dataset, entities make up only 11% of the candidate ranges. To address this, assigning explicit probabilities to the adjacent ranges helps reduce overconfidence by blurring the boundaries, preventing the model from concentrating all its probability mass on areas with few or no positive samples. For example, in the Chinese context, "莲花清瘟胶囊" ("Lotus Clear Fever capsule") and "莲花清瘟" ("Lotus Clear Fever") are not fully distinguishable and refer to the same medicine. In previous NER work, the model may not recognize an example like "莲花清瘟"as an entity. With the introduction of the Boundary Smoothing (BS) module, the model will assign the probability of belonging to the "Lotus Clear Fever capsule" to the entity boundary, thus alleviating the problem of over-dependence on the probability of some entities in the model, allowing the model to recognize "Lotus Clear Fever "as an entity in the learning process. In response to this issue, inspired by Zhu et al. [13], this project proposes the KCB-FLAT model based on the complex semantic structure of the Chinese language and our previous work [14]. This model is built on the Flat-Lattice Transformer (FLAT) [15] architecture, chosen for its lightweight design and parallel computing capabilities. The KCB-FLAT model enhances this foundation by extracting three distinct types of syntactic data along with their contextual features. These features are encoded using a Key-Value Memory Network (KVMN) and are subsequently fused through an attention mechanism. The model then integrates lexical and syntactic information via a Cross-Transformer (CT). Additionally, the Boundary Smoothing module, operating in synergy with an internal regularity perception function, further boosts the model's capability to precisely detect named entities. This combination explores the internal consistency of each entity and applies smoothing to refine the entity boundaries.

In summary, incorporating Boundary Smoothing (BS) can assist NER models in tackling the issue of overconfidence. Through the redistribution of probabilities in the vicinity of labeled entities, BS enhances the model's prediction caution and diminishes excessive confidence on specific boundaries. This adjustment facilitates the model's adaptability to novel domains and evolving data distributions, ultimately elevating the precision and reliability of named entity recognition. Our specific contributions are outlined below:

1. This article proposes a method KCB-FLAT that achieves good results on four Chinese datasets: Weibo, MSRA, Resume, and a self-built dataset ZJ.
2. We combine the smoothing process with syntactic information extraction, which discretizes the entity probabilities to the entity boundaries, effectively alleviating the problem of over-confidence of the model in entity labelling.
3. We control the smoothing factor on the Boundary Smoothing method to control the degree to which the model differentiates the probability of entities and analyze how these adjustments impact overall model performance.
4. We conducted experiments on our self-built dataset, ZJ, by integrating it, and the results show that our model is well-suited for Chinese named entity recognition tasks within the judicial domain.

Through experiments with the KCB-FLAT model, it was observed that the model significantly boosts performance in complex and fuzzy boundary cases. This integration method not only improves the model's ability to process Chinese text, but also enhances its ability to respond to specific problems.

2. Related Work

2.1. *Current Status of Named Entity Identification*

Named entity recognition (NER) has been a long-standing and elemental research topic within the realm of natural language processing. Traditional methods can generally be divided into two main categories: token-based and span-based approaches. Token-based methods (e.g., Tourani et al., 2024 [16]; Wang et al., 2020 [17]) typically perform sequence labelling at the token level, which is then converted into span-level predictions. Meanwhile, span-based methods (e.g., Sohrab and Miwa 2018, [18]; Eberts and Ulges, 2020 [19]; Shen et al., 2021 [20]; Li et al., 2022 [21]) directly perform entity classification of potential spans for prediction. In addition to this, some approaches attempt to formalize NER as a sequence to set (Tan et al., 2021 [22]; Ma et al., 2016 [23]), and even more methods attempt reading comprehension (Li et al., 2019 [24]; Yu et al., 2020 [25]; Yu et al., 2019 [26]) tasks for prediction. In addition, some have used autoregressive generative NER methods (e.g., Yang et al., 2019 [27]; Athiwaratkun et al., 2020 [28]), i.e., relying on sequence-to-sequence language models (e.g., BART [29], Sentence-T5 [30] etc.) that linearize structured named entities into sequences to decode entities. Recent breakthroughs in the realm of text classification, exemplified by the refinement of feature selection via an improved Discrete Egg Laying Chicken Algorithm (DELCA) [31] have yielded substantial improvements not only in classification efficacy but also in the domain of named entity recognition (NER). Enhanced precision in feature extraction has been instrumental in bolstering the accuracy of NER systems' recognition and categorization capabilities. These works have designed various translation models to unify NER to text generation tasks and have achieved good performance and generalization.

2.2. *Current Status of Syntactic Information Extraction in NLP*

Syntactic information extraction work usually includes several categories such as dependent syntactic analysis, phrase structure syntactic analysis, and syntactic information extraction and semantic annotation. The focus of dependency syntactic analysis lies in determining the dependency relationships among words within a sentence, and resolving these relationships aids in comprehending the sentence's structure and meaning, as exemplified in Liang et al., 2020. [32], which utilizes the idea of graph-based dependency syntactic analysis by introducing a bi-affine model that provides the model with a global view of the inputs, thus enabling accurate prediction of named entities. Phrase structure syntactic analysis strives to ascertain the structure and arrangement of phrases within a sentence, enabling a deeper comprehension of the sentence's syntactic makeup and semantic significance. Lou et al.'s study, 2022 [33], explored the problem of nested named entity recognition and proposed a span-based syntactic analyzer to deal with nested NERs, while exploiting the lexicalized organizational tree structure of headword annotation and a new training strategy. Syntactic information extraction and semantic annotation entail assigning labels to each predicate in a sentence, indicating its corresponding semantic role, thereby facilitating a more precise comprehension of the sentence meaning and enabling inference of semantic information (e.g., Ma et al., 2022 [34]; Nie et al., 2020 [35]). By utilizing these syntactic information extraction methods, the performance and efficacy of the NLP models in different tasks can be enhanced, making them more suitable for practical application in real-world scenarios.

2.3. Application of Smoothing Techniques in Model Performance Enhancement

Boundary smoothing technology plays an important role in NLP tasks, machine learning, and deep learning. It helps to handle zero probability problems, improve model generalization ability, optimize the training process, enhance model robustness, and promote model interpretability. In sequence annotation tasks such as NER, the use of smoothing techniques has significantly improved model performance. These techniques typically reduce over-confidence in individual labels by adjusting the probability distribution of the model's output, thereby bolstering the capacity to manage boundary ambiguity and uncertainty.

Label smoothing [36], for instance, is a widely used technique in deep learning that modifies the probability distribution by assigning weights to both the true labels and a uniform distribution. It has been demonstrated that this approach enhances the generalization performance of models in tasks like image recognition and text classification [37–41]. In the context of the NER task, label smoothing proves effective in mitigating the issue of category imbalance, particularly in datasets where coronal and modifier descriptors of entities are highly frequent.

Additionally, the probabilistic output of the model can be refined through the introduction of a context-driven smoothing approach. As an illustration, the Conditional Random Field (CRF) layer [42], often employed in NER tasks, considers inter-label dependencies. By establishing a globally normalized probability distribution, the CRF layer aids the model in making more precise predictions across the entire sequence. Nevertheless, it is important to note that the CRF does not directly address the smoothing of the initial probability distribution, a distinctive feature offered by the Boundary Smoothing module.

Hence, we propose the Boundary Smoothing module to assess its efficacy and practicality. This module enhances the model's resilience and precision when handling boundary vagueness and contextual intricacies by refining the model's output probabilities. We anticipate that incorporating the smoothed boundary module into the Baseline model will lead to substantial performance improvements in NER tasks, particularly in pinpointing and categorizing entity boundaries.

3. Methodology

3.1. The Overview of the KCB-FLAT

The KCB-FLAT consists of three modules: (1) Key-Value Memory Network (KVMN), which is used to encode syntactic information and contextual features; (2) Cross-Transformer module encoding two different types of information, including lexical information and syntactic information; (3) Boundary smoothing module to study internal regularities. The following chart provides a visual illustration of this structure (Figure 1).

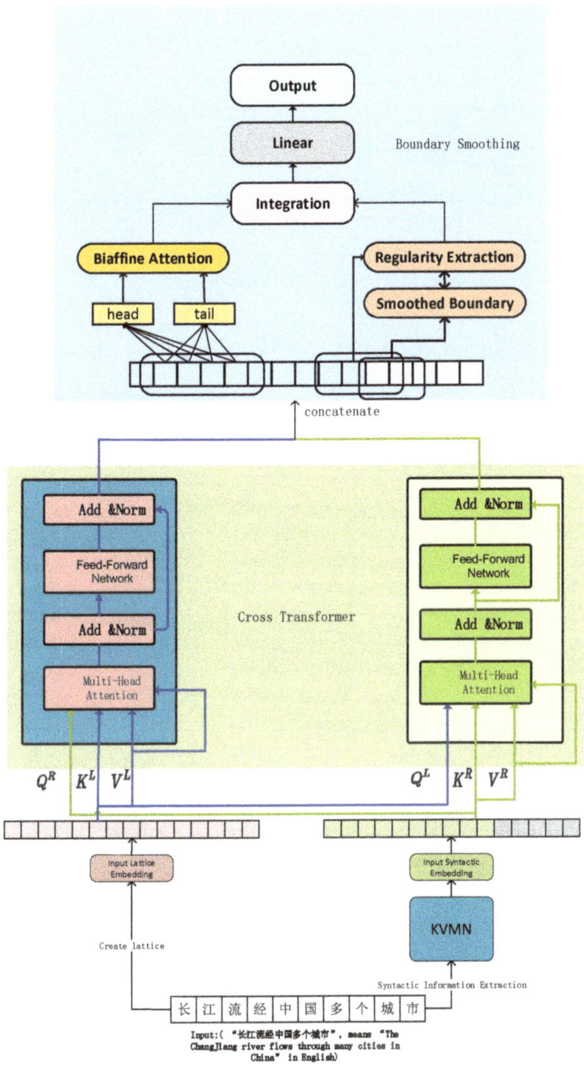

Figure 1. The general structure of KCB-FLAT.

3.2. *KVMN for Syntactic Embedding*

In the Chinese NER task, accurately identifying entity boundaries is challenging due to the varied meanings Chinese characters can have in different contexts and the lack of clear separation between them. To overcome this challenge, we utilize a character-level NER approach and integrate lexical information as supplementary data, aiming to enrich the input and improve the accuracy of entity boundary recognition. For instance, in the sentence "长江流经中国多个城市" (The Changjiang River flows through multiple cities in China), the ambiguity associated with the character "江" can be resolved through syntactic analysis. By distinguishing between "江流" (flow) and "长江" (The Changjiang River), we can more accurately identify entities such as "长江" (The Changjiang River) and "城市" (city). In this paper, we introduce syntactic information to clarify ambiguities by encoding diverse contextual features along with their corresponding syntactic data, such as POS tags, syntactic constituents, and dependencies. To enhance the model's accuracy in recognizing named entities within various contexts, we incorporated KVMN. Figure 2 depicts the process of extracting syntactic information.

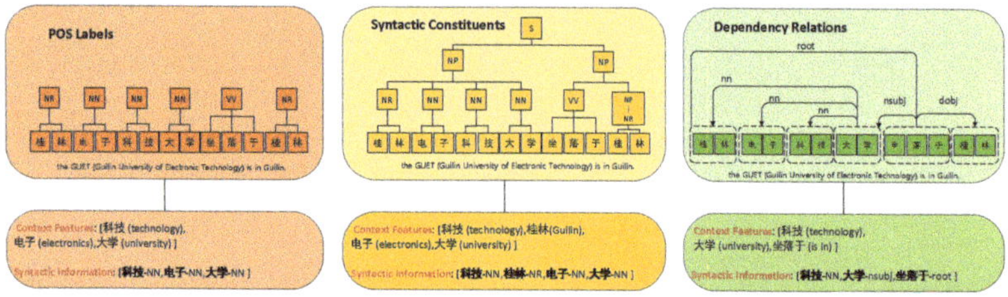

Figure 2. The process of extracting syntactic information: POS Labels, syntactic constituents, and 211 dependencies of "科" (science) in the lexical labels.

In this study, we used Key-Value Pair Storage Network (KVMN) to encode different syntactic information and introduced attention mechanisms into the sentence level vector expression of Chinese characters. By encoding syntactic information with the KVMN and extracting useful features, we then applied an attention mechanism to obtain syntactic-level feature embeddings for Chinese characters. We integrated an attention mechanism to automatically assign weights to different syntactic information. This allowed our model to dynamically adjust and focus on various syntactic data during both the encoding and decoding stages, effectively highlighting essential information while downplaying less critical details. This approach does not necessitate pre-determined weights, as it allows the model to autonomously learn weight allocation strategies during the training process.

Figure 3 illustrates this process, using the example sentence "桂林电子科技大学坐落于桂林", which means the GUET (Guilin University of Electronic Technology) is in Guilin.

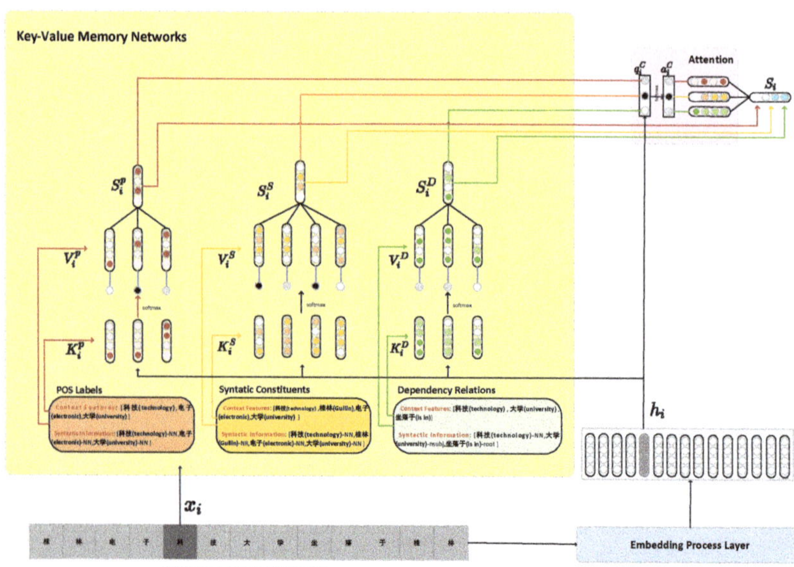

Figure 3. Encoding Syntactic Information with KVMN.

While parsing the input sequence X, every character x_i within X belongs to a word that serves as the focal point for mapping contextual features and relevant information with syntax into the collection of keys and values. These are denoted as $K_i^c = [k_{i,1}^c, \ldots, k_{i,j}^c$

..., k^c_{i,m_i}] and V^c_i = [$v^c_{i,1}$,..., $v^c_{i,j}$..., v^c_{i,m_i}], where $c \in C = \{P, S, D\}$. Here, P, S, D represent three different syntactic types, respectively, and m_i denotes the count of text context features of information with syntax type c for x_i. The $k^c_{i,j}$ represents the jth contextual feature of syntactic type c, while $v^c_{i,j}$ is the syntactic information corresponding to $k^c_{i,j}$. These keys and values, k^c_i and v^c_i, are mapped into matrix forms, denoted as $e^{k_c}_{i,j}$ and $v^{k_c}_{i,j}$. The syntactic information is computed by the following formula:

$$p^c_{i,j} = \frac{exp\left(h_i \cdot e^{k_c}_{i,j}\right)}{\sum_{j=1}^{m_i} exp\left(h_i \cdot e^{k_c}_{i,j}\right)} \quad (1)$$

we use $p^c_{i,j}$ to express the weighting of syntactic information. Chinese, a pictographic script, differs from English in that the meaning of its grammatical words relies on individual characters. Moreover, within a given word, every character carries an equal weight of syntactic information. For instance, in the word "大学" (The University), both "大" and "学" are encoded by the same vector representing their shared syntactic information. To differentiate between the representations of various characters within the same word h_i is introduced, which is obtained by the following equation:

$$h_i = E(x_i) \quad (2)$$

The weights $p^c_{i,j}$ are applied to the corresponding syntactic data $v^{k_c}_{i,j}$, as calculated by the formula:

$$s^c_i = \sum_{j=1}^{m_i} p^c_{i,j} e^{v_c}_{i,j} \quad (3)$$

The output of the KVMN, denoted as s^c_i, encapsulates the weighted syntactic information of type c. This approach ensures that syntactic data are weighted and encoded in alignment with its contextual features, thereby optimizing the use of the most pertinent information.

Firstly, we perform syntactic analysis on the input to obtain a syntactic information vector s^c_i. Then, the three types of syntactic data are processed uniformly to give each syntactic information a unique weight. Attention mechanism helps with this integration. The weights of the q^c_i are calculated as follows:

$$q^c_i = \sigma\left(W^c_q \cdot (h_i \oplus s^c_i) + b^c_q\right) \quad (4)$$

In this equation, W represents the trainable weight vector, b^c_q represents the bias for implementing residual linking, $\oplus$ represents the concatenation, and σ is the sigmoid function. Next, we use the $softmax$ function to calculate the attention of the input syntactic information a^c_i. The attention score is calculated according to the following formula:

$$a^c_i = \frac{exp(q^c_i)}{\sum_{c \in C} exp(q^c_i)} \quad (5)$$

Here, a^c_i represents the attention for syntactic information of type c. Finally, the attention mechanism utilizes different features through calculated weights, effectively resolving the inherent contradictions between syntax and syntax. Different types of syntactic data are combined to form s_i:

$$s_i = \sum_{c \in C} a^c_i s^c_i \quad (6)$$

Rather than simply concatenating three types of syntactic information, then the attention mechanism selectively emphasizes the most relevant features, resolving conflicts among the different syntactic data types. As a result, the various syntactic data are selectively encoded and combined.

3.3. Cross Transformer for Semantic Fusion

Vocabulary information can more readily identify local details like word positions and boundaries because it concentrates on the vocabulary and the relationships among its constituent characters. This focus enhances the sensitivity of vocabulary information to the internal structures and characteristics of words, allowing for more precise determination of word boundaries and positions. In contrast, syntactic information emphasizes the overall structure of sentences, considering the combinations and relationships among words and their functions and roles within sentences. Consequently, syntactic information is more concerned with sentence-level features and constraints than with the internal characteristics of individual words. This gives syntactic information a distinct advantage in delineating sentence structures and relationships, rectifying segmentation errors introduced by vocabulary-based information, and offering a more comprehensive sentence comprehension. To fully capitalize on the benefits of syntactic information, the model employs syntactic constraints to rectify segmentation errors arising from vocabulary-based information. After acquiring the embedded representations of syntactic information, in this study we utilize a Cross-Transformer to synthesize lexical and syntactic data. The Cross-Transformer network effectively fuses syntactic and lexical information through a self-attention mechanism and feed-forward network, augmented by residual connections and normalization, as illustrated in Figure 4 for the specific structure of the Cross-Transformer.

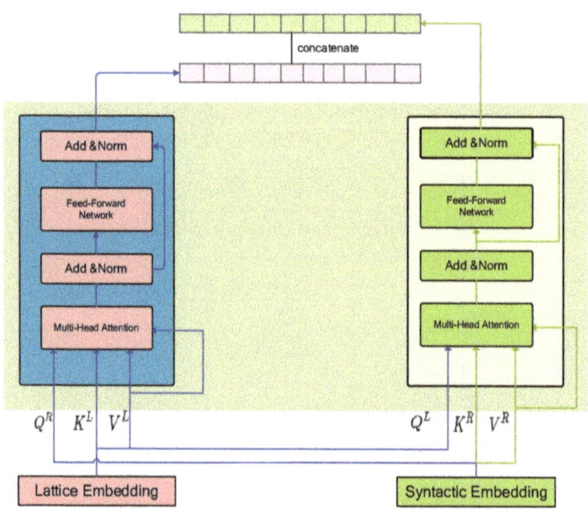

Figure 4. The Cross-Transformer module.

The left Transformer encoder receives an input denoted as (Q_x^L, K_x^L, V_x^L), which is derived from the lattice embedding containing lexical information via a linear transformation. The query (Q), key (K), and value (V) matrices are specifically computed as follows:

$$\left[Q_x^L, K_x^L, V_x^L\right] = E_x^L\left[W_Q^L, W_K^L, W_V^L\right] \tag{7}$$

Here, E_x^L signifies the lattice embedding of input, where $E_x^L \in \{x_1, \ldots.x_i, \ldots., x_N\}$, each x_i represents the lexical representation of input, to ensure that the length of input sequence X in the cross converter are consistent, we set the length of the sequence as N, and each

W^L is a parameter that can be autonomously learned. Similarly, for the right Transformer encoder, we have

$$\left[Q_S^R, K_S^R, V_S^R\right] = E_S^R\left[W_Q^R, W_K^R, W_V^R\right] \tag{8}$$

Among them, E_S^R represents the syntactic embedding, where $E_S^R \in \{s_1, \ldots, s_i, \ldots, s_N\}$, each s_i denotes a syntactic input. During this period, each W_Q^R value is a learnable parameter. The Cross-Transformer includes 2 encoders, each encoder includes a front network called feed-forward network (FFN), which is a special multi-level perceptron that can perform nonlinear transformations in semantic space and can process positional information, followed by two processes: residual connectivity and hierarchical normalization. The main function of self-attention is to extract semantic-level information from text. Calculate the attention according to following method:

$$Att(A, V) = softmax(A)V \tag{9}$$

$$A_{i,j} = \left(\frac{Q_i K_j^T}{\sqrt{d_k}}\right) \tag{10}$$

where d_k denotes the size of the lattice. Based on syntactic and lexical data obtained from Equations (7) and (8), use relative position encoding in FLAT mode to perform the following operations:

$$Att^L = softmax\left(A^R\right)V^L \tag{11}$$

$$Att^R = softmax\left(A^L\right)V^R \tag{12}$$

In these equations, A^R represents the score of syntax, while A^L denotes the score of lattice attention. The calculation for A^R is according to the following method:

$$A_{i,j}^R = \left(Q_i^R + u^R\right)^T K_j^R + \left(Q_i^R + v^R\right)^T \left(R_{i,j}^R W_r^R\right) \tag{13}$$

where u^R and v^R are attention biases, W_r^R is the learnable parameter $R_{i,j}^R$ is the relative position coding, calculated as the following method:

$$R_{i,j}^R = ReLU\left(W_r\left(p_{h_i - h_j} \oplus p_{t_i - h_j} \oplus p_{h_i - t_j} \oplus p_{t_i - t_j}\right)\right) \tag{14}$$

Relative Position Coding, $R_{i,j}^R$, mitigates directional loss caused by the internal dot product of vectors. Each p represents the relativistic distance. Similarly, the calculation of Att^L and Att^R is generally the same, the specific calculation of Att^R can also be derived.

3.4. Boundary Smoothing Module

In NER tasks, two classic approaches exist. NER is treated as a sequence annotation task by one approach, in which each input character is labeled by category. The other divides the input into multiple spans, each a potential named entity, for recognition and classification. This chapter adopts the span method for handling named entities and uses the pattern perception function to capture the intrinsic features of each span.

In Chinese lexical formation and linguistic structure, specific naming patterns are evident. For instance, terms like "XX Hotel" and "XX Court" typically denote place names, while "XX Mountain" indicates a location. For example, "桂林电子科技大学花江校区" (Huajiang Campus of the University of Electronic Science and Technology of Guilin) refers to the full name "桂林电子科技大学花江校区" rather than separating "桂林" (Guilin) and "电子科技大学" (University of Electronic Science and technology) and "花江校区" (Huajiang Campus). It signifies the Huajiang campus of GUET, not the UESTC's campus in Guilin city.

The inherent complexity of implementing Boundary Smoothing (BS) is primarily due to its elevated computational demands. To mitigate this and efficiently identify naming patterns, we introduce a synergistic application of the Boundary Smoothing function complemented by the Regularity-Aware (RA) function, pioneered by Huawei Cloud in 2022 [43]. This RA function is adept at uncovering inherent regularities within data, concentrating computational efforts on the most critical boundary points. This strategic focus significantly reduces unnecessary computations and enhances overall performance. Furthermore, the integration of state-of-the-art optimization techniques ensures that our model maintains computational tractability, which means that our approach can remain both effective and feasible within the realms of computational resources available.

To prevent overfitting from the model learning the intrinsic rules of named entities, we use the Boundary Smoothing function proposed by Zhu et al. [13] This smooths the entity probability of spans, helping the model maintain calibration during training and ensuring that generated confidence better represents prediction accuracy.

In Figure 5, the regularity representation of each span is derived by enhancing the interaction between the head and tail in the Biaffine layer and incorporating a linear attention mechanism to capture the intrinsic regularity features extracted by the Cross-Transformer. The specific calculation method is as follows:

$$h_{s_{i,j}}^{rec} = \sum_{t=i}^{j} \alpha_t \cdot h_t \tag{15}$$

where h_t is the cascaded output from the Cross-Converter, and $t \in \{i,\ i+1, ., j\}$ represents index of the span $s_{i,j}$. α_t, means the attention score, and is calculated according to the following method:

$$\alpha_t = \frac{exp(a_t)}{\sum_{k=i}^{j} exp(a_k)} \tag{16}$$

$$a_t = W_{reg}^T h_t + b_{reg} \tag{17}$$

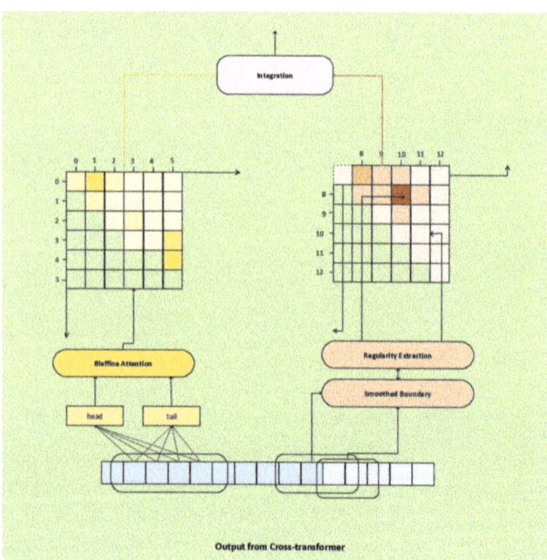

Figure 5. The Boundary Smoothing module.

Here, $W_{reg}^T \in R^{d \times 1}$ and $b_{reg} \in R^1$ represent the learnable weights and biases, respectively. To capture the interactions between head and tail features, this model utilizes a biaffine attention mechanism, thereby integrating regularities between entities into a span representation:

$$h_{s_{i,j}}^{(span)} = h_i^T u^{(1)h_j} + (h_i \oplus h_j)u^{(2)} + b_1 \tag{18}$$

Here, h_i represent the head of span $s_{i,j}$, h_j represent the tail, while $U^{(1)} \in R^{2d\times 2d\times 2d}$ and $U^{(2)} \in R^{4d\times 2d}$. The integration of regularity and span representations is performed through gate networks:

$$g_{s_{i,j}} = \sigma\left(u^{(3)}\left[h_{s_{i,j}}^{(span)}; h_{s_{i,j}}^{(reg)}\right] + b_2\right) \tag{19}$$

$$h_{s_{i,j}} = g_{s_{i,j}} \odot h_{s_{i,j}}^{(span)} + \left(1 - g_{s_{i,j}}\right) \odot h_{s_{i,j}}^{(reg)} \tag{20}$$

where b_2 is the deviation term, σ represents the sigmoid function, $U^{(3)} \in R^{4d\times 1}$ represents learnable weights, and $\odot$ refers to the multiplication of corresponding elements.

Next, we use a $softmax$ linear classifier to predict the entity classification for each span:

$$\tilde{y}_{s_{i,j}} = Softmax\left(W_{type}^T h_{s_{i,j}} + b_3\right) \tag{21}$$

where $W_{type}^T \in R^{2d\times c}$ represents a learnable weight through attention, b_3 is a bias. Then, the loss function we use is calculated by

$$L_{aware} = -\frac{1}{n}\sum_{n=1}^{N}\sum_{i=1}^{l}\sum_{j=1}^{l} y_{s_{i,j}}^{(n)} log\left(\tilde{y}_{s_{i,j}}^{(n)}\right), i \le j \tag{22}$$

where $\tilde{y}_{s_{i,j}}^{(n)}$ is the predicted value of span, $y_{s_{i,j}}^{(n)}$ is the true value of span, and N is the number of all spans.

To perform smoothing, we use the Manhattan distance d to measure the distance between the surrounding span (span) and the specified original span (Ground-truth span) and to specify the smoothing range (Smoothing size) D ($D \in \{1,2\}$). Where $d < D < N$, the distribution probability $\tilde{y}_{s_{i,j}}^{(n)'}$ is obtained by the following:

$$\tilde{y}_{s_{i,j}}^{(n)'} = (1 - \alpha) * \tilde{y}_{s_{i,j}}^{(n)} + \alpha / D \tag{23}$$

where α is the smoothing factor. We consider the other spans (spans) that are not assigned to probabilities as non-entity, and the final loss is still expressed in terms of cross-entropy.

The KCB-FLAT model, while enhancing named entity recognition (NER) performance, introduces additional computational demands primarily due to the integration of Key-Value Memory Network (KVMN) and Cross-Transformer module. The KVMN, which encodes syntactic information and contextual features, operates with a time complexity proportional to the number of syntactic features and the dimensionality of the embedding space, approximately $O(m \times d)$, where m is the number of syntactic features and d is the embedding dimension. The Cross-Transformer module, responsible for fusing lexical and syntactic information, involves matrix multiplications that scale with the input size, contributing a complexity of $O(n^2 \times d)$ per layer, where n represents the input length. Additionally, the Boundary Smoothing module, which refines entity boundaries, has a complexity tied to the number of entities and the smoothing factor applied. Despite these factors, the model is designed with parallel computing capabilities, particularly in the Cross-Transformer module, which mitigates the overall computational load, making it feasible for practical applications while balancing performance and efficiency.

4. Experimental Design

4.1. Datasets and Evaluation Indicators

In this section, we will evaluate KCB-FLAT using four Chinese corpus datasets. To comprehensively evaluate the performance of the model, we use the span method, F1 score (F1), precision (P), and recall (R) as evaluation criteria. On this basis, we will gain a more precise understanding of the performance of the KCB-FLAT on different samples.

To validate our model, we utilized four Chinese NER datasets: MSRA, Resume, Weibo, and our custom dataset, named ZJ, which we manually curated and refined. The MSRA dataset, which was sourced from the 3rd International Chinese Language Processing Contest, primarily consisted of news data and is widely recognized for NER tasks. The Resume dataset encompassed a vast array of personal, place, and company names. Meanwhile, the Weibo dataset covered various Weibo contexts, broadening the application scope of the NER model. Specifically, the Weibo dataset classified entities into person, organization, location, and government wide entry point. The Resume dataset identified eight types of entities: country, education, profession, race, and title, while the MSRA dataset focuses on three main entity types: organization, person, and location.

Our ZJ dataset comprised criminal verdicts issued by the China Judgement Network (CJN) spanning from 2013 to 2019. These comprehensive texts include critical case details in the factual description section, marked by a higher concentration of entities and concise wording, amounting to over 410,000 words. Table 1 outlines our dataset statistics, with a 70–10–20 split for training, validation, and testing. The legal documents in this corpus were manually annotated using the {B, I, O} system. The labeled entities encompassed crime location, place name, person name, organization name, accusation, verdict, laws, and regulations, utilizing a total of 15 distinct labels tailored for various tasks.

Table 1. The ZJ dataset composition.

Entity Type	Amount of Entity	Number of Tags
Crime Location	3356	28,976
Place Name	3360	23,076
Person Name	5047	13,487
Organization Name	1667	6353
Accusation	1846	5837
Laws and regulations	1517	6203
Judgement	2086	7456
Total	19,079	91,348

In this paper, the evaluation index employed is the weighted summed average F1, which is computed using the formula:

$$F1 = \frac{2 * P * R}{P + R} \tag{24}$$

Here, P represents the accuracy rate, and R represents the recall rate; P and R are determined using the following equations:

$$P = \frac{TP}{TP + FP} \tag{25}$$

$$R = \frac{TP}{TP + FN} \tag{26}$$

Here, TP represents the number of accurately detected individuals, FP represents the number of misidentified individuals, and $TP + FP$ represent the total number of predicted entities. FN represents the number of lost entities, and $TP + FN$ represents the total number of real entities.

4.2. Parameter Settings

Our experiments were conducted using PyTorch 1.8.2 and Python 3.6, running on a Windows 10 operating system. The hardware configuration included an Intel (R) Xeon (R) CPU E5-2698 v4 @ 2.20 GHz, equipped with 16 GB RAM, and an NVIDIA Tesla K80 GPU with 16 GB of RAM. The experimental parameters were as follows:

For the Weibo, Resume, ZJ datasets, the Cross-Transformer's FFN layer had 384 hidden layer nodes, a dropout parameter of 0.3, 8 heads in the multi-head attention layer with a dimensionality of 16 per head, resulting in a total of 128 nodes. Learning rate was fixed at 0.0018, and the training was run for 50 epochs.

For the MSRA dataset, the Cross-Transformer's FFN layer featured 480 hidden layer nodes, a dropout of 0.3, 8 heads in the multi-head attention with a dimensionality of 20 per head, totaling 160 nodes. Learning rate was set at 0.0014, and the model was trained for 100 epochs. Additionally, in our experiments, the smoothing factor α was adjusted to 0.1 and 0.2, respectively.

4.3. Results and Discussion

From Table 2, each method has a certain improvement on the performance of the FLAT model. Among them, the performance improvement of the model was the greatest after adding KVMN, with a 2-point increase on MSRA, Resume, and ZJ, respectively, and an improvement of about 6% on the Weibo dataset. This improvement can be attributed to the advanced technologies introduced by KVMN, such as knowledge enhancement and memory mechanisms. KVMN enabled the model to better understand contextual information in text, effectively capturing long-distance dependencies between entities and adapting to various types of text and datasets. The MSRA and Weibo datasets contain more diverse and complex text types, which the Cross-Transformer module can use to better utilize the cross-text information interaction ability in the module, thereby improving the recognition performance of our model. The Resume dataset may mainly consist of highly formatted text, such as personal information and work experience in resumes, which have relatively fixed structures and regular entity distributions. In this case, the Cross-Transformer module may not be able to fully leverage its advantages and may even experience a decrease in effectiveness due to the introduction of unnecessary complexity. This can explain why by adding the Cross-Transformer module, the model's performance on MSRA and Weibo datasets improved by 0.5% but decreased by 0.25% on the Resume dataset. The regularity-aware feature bumps the model's efficacy by an average of 2%. After incorporating the Boundary Smoothing module into the baseline, the model's performance demonstrated improvement across all four datasets, with an approximate increase of 2.57% on the MSRA dataset, 1.05% on the ZJ dataset, 0.79% on the Resume dataset, and 3.41% on the Weibo dataset. The KCB-FLAT outperforms the baseline FLAT model on the MSRA, ZJ, Resume, and Weibo datasets by margins of 3.28%, 2.61%, 2.09%, and 7.95%, respectively, in summary. By tempering the model's predictions and curbing overconfidence on specific boundaries, the introduction of the Boundary Smoothing module enhances the model's adaptability to new domains and changing data distributions, thereby improving the precision and stability of named entity recognition.

Table 2. The results of ablation experiments.

Model	KVMN	CT	RA	BS	MSRA	ZJ	Resume	Weibo
Baseline (FLAT)					93.45	94.27	94.93	63.42
+KVMN	√				95.98	96.04	96.23	69.27
+KVMN&CT	√	√			96.24	95.64	95.98	69.78
+RA			√		96.14	95.66	96.02	66.98
+BS				√	96.02	95.32	95.72	66.83
+BS&RA			√	√	96.30	95.97	96.09	67.15
Ours ($\mathrm{KCB-FLAT}.\alpha = 0.2$)	√	√	√	√	96.59	96.87	97.02	71.37

The improvements indicated in Table 2 are mathematically correlated with the optimization of boundary conditions, which are critical for reducing boundary recognition errors. The Boundary Smoothing technique allows for a more accurate determination of boundary values, which in turn significantly impacts the model's performance by minimizing boundary residuals. Additionally, the enhanced boundary conditions contribute to a more robust convergence, reflected in the decreased variance of our error metrics. These mathematical refinements are essential for enhancing the model's overall efficacy.

In this experiment, we selected NFLAT model [44], Li et al.'s model [21], Xiong et al.'s model [45], DiffusionNER [46], RICON and MECT [47], LSTM + Lexicon augmentation model [48], AESINER [35], Mao et al. [49], and SLK-NER [50]. Comparison experiments were conducted with our KCB-FLAT, and the experimental results are as follows (Table 3).

Table 3. The comparative test results.

Models	MSRA	ZJ	Resume	Weibo
NFLAT [44]	94.55	95.40	95.58	61.94
Li et al. (2022a) [21]	95.97	96.08	96.32	72.18
Xiong et al. (2023) [45]	95.40	95.51	95.97	68.14
DiffusionNER (2023) [46]	/	94.88	94.53	/
RICON [47]	96.12	96.01	95.98	66.82
MECT [47]	96.21	96.13	95.91	70.40
LSTM + Lexicon augment [48]	93.47	96.02	95.58	61.22
AESINER [35]	96.53	96.42	96.40	70.54
Mao et al. (2022) [49]	/	95.98	96.29	70.81
SLK-NER [50]	/	96.01	95.78	64.00
Ours (KCB-FLAT)	96.59	96.87	97.02	71.37

4.4. Analysis and Discussion

In comparison with recent Chinese NER models, the model presented in this study exhibits notable superiority on four datasets: MSRA, Resume, Weibo, and ZJ. When compared with MECT, our proposed model offers a marginal improvement on the MSRA and Resume datasets, and a substantial 0.97% enhancement on the Weibo dataset. This advancement is credited to the integration of syntactic information encoded within KNMN, coupled with the inclusion of the Smoothed Boundary module, thereby validating the augmented model's efficacy. The inclusion of syntactic details elevates the precision of Chinese named entity recognition within context-heavy texts. However, our model is slightly inferior to Li et al.'s model on the Weibo dataset, trailing by 0.81 percentage points. Li et al. [21] adeptly tackled the primary challenge of unified NER by framing it as a classification task for inter-word relationships, particularly those between adjacent entity words, yielding impressive outcomes on the Weibo dataset. Although regularity can sometimes hinder the recognition precision of named entities within diverse contexts, the introduction of Boundary Smoothing allows the generated confidence to more accurately mirror the predicted entities' correctness, bolstering generalizability. Specifically, the Boundary Smoothing module elevates named entity recognition precision in certain scenarios. As an illustration, on both the MSRA and Resume datasets, our model surpasses MECT, RICON, and Mao et al. 2022 [49].

4.5. In-Depth Analyses

To better understand how our ground model leads to improvements, we recorded the LOSS values when training the model on MSRA and Resume, respectively. Figures 6 and 7 visualize the loss on MSRA and Resume for models with smoothing of 0.1 and 0.2. We can conclude that when KCB-FLAT integrates the Boundary Smoothing module, we get lower LOSS values in the training of the model; at $\alpha = 0.2$, our model has a lower LOSS value compared with the case of $\alpha = 0.1$. CE means that without any Boundary Smoothing, we get smaller LOSS values overall. The lower LOSS value means that our improvement makes the model effective in reducing the bias between predicted and actual results during training, and makes our model better at completing the segmentation task first, thus obtaining better results in the named entity recognition.

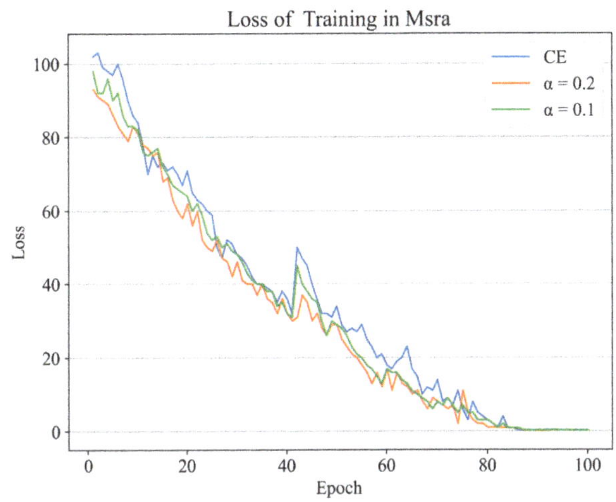

Figure 6. LOSS values of MSRA during training.

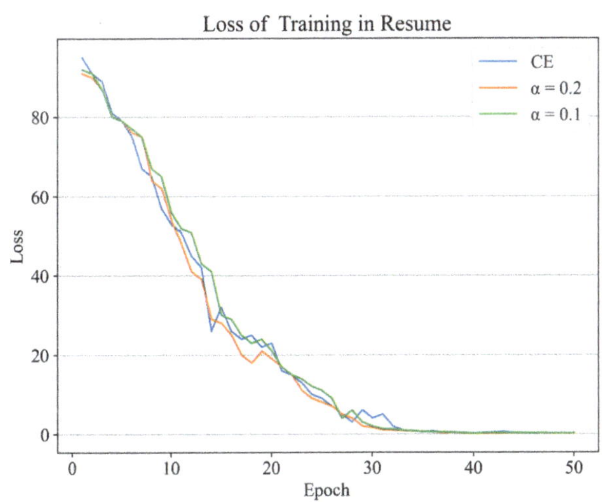

Figure 7. LOSS values of Resume during training.

In this section, we perform a case analysis and use examples from the ZJ and Weibo datasets for our case analysis. We compare the basic FLAT model with our designed KCB-FLAT model, presenting the entity recognition outcomes in a tabular format. In this context, B, I, and E represent the beginning, interior, and the end of an entity, respectively. While O signifies a character that means non-entity. Entity types are represented by ORG, LOC, NAM (unique noun), and NOM (common noun). For instance, B-ORG designates the commencement, category, and position of an organizational entity. The table reveals that our customized Chinese named entity recognition model, KCB-FLAT, enhances recognition precision and boundary detection compared with the baseline FLAT model.

Referring to Table 4, when identifying "Congtai Branch of Handan Public Security Bureau", FLAT only recognizes "Handan Public Security Bureau," omitting "Congtai Branch" as it is not perceived as a full entity. However, even though "Handan Public Security Bureau" is identified, it does not align with the contextual entity type. Syntactically, both "Handan Public Security Bureau" and "Congtai Branch" belong to the same syntactic category and should carry equal syntactic weight. KCB-FLAT more precisely identifies "Congtai Branch of Handan Public Security Bureau" as a unified, independent entity.

Table 4. Case analysis of Weibo dataset.

Weibo	**奥林匹克公园 (The Olympic Park)**					
Entity	AO	LIN	PI	KE	GONG	YUAN
Gold label	B-LOC.NAM	I-LOC.NAM	I-LOC.NAM	I-LOC.NAM	I-LOC.NAM	E-LOC.NAM
Baseline (FLAT)	B-LOC.NAM	I-LOC.NAM	I-LOC.NAM	E-LOC.NAM	B-LOC.NOM	E-LOC.NOM
KCB-FLAT(Ours)	B-LOC.NAM	I-LOC.NAM	I-LOC.NAM	I-LOC.NAM	I-LOC.NAM	E-LOC.NAM

In Table 5, FLAT's recognition splits "Olympics" and "park" into separate entities, failing to recognize them as a cohesive unit. Upon closer inspection, "Olympics" is categorized as a unique noun, whereas "park" is deemed a common noun. Conversely, KCB-FLAT accurately identifies the phrase as a singular address entity, indicating that our enhancements have bolstered the model's text recognition.

Table 5. Case Analysis of ZJ Dataset.

ZJ	**邯郸市公安局丛台分局 (Congtai Branch of Handan Public Security Bureau)**									
Entity	HAN	DAN	SHI	GONG	AN	JU	CONG	TAI	FEN	JU
Gold label	B-ORG	I-ORG	I-ORG	I-ORG	I-ORG	I-ORG	I-ORG	I-ORG	I-ORG	E-ORG
Baseline (FLAT)	B-ORG	I-ORG	I-ORG	I-ORG	I-ORG	E-ORG	O	O	O	O
KCB-FLAT(Ours)	B-ORG	I-ORG	I-ORG	I-ORG	I-ORG	I-ORG	I-ORG	I-ORG	I-ORG	E-ORG

5. Conclusions

In this study, we present KCB-FLAT, a Chinese NER model incorporating multiple innovations. It specifically employs a Key-Value Memory Network to encode syntactic data, fuses syntactic and lexical data through a Cross-Transformer module, and refines boundary recognition with a Boundary Smoothing module during the decoding stage. Through rigorous experimentation on four datasets, our model effectively mitigates over-confidence issues and significantly boosts Chinese NER performance. Detailed examinations underscore the superiority of our methodology in training efficacy, suggesting that the Boundary Smoothing mechanism significantly bolsters model performance and calibration. Our forthcoming research will endeavor to extend the KCB-FLAT model along several avenues, aiming to augment its generalizability and adaptability, and to integrate the model into practical scenarios. We envision future studies to probe the applicability of this model across diverse linguistic frameworks and to scrutinize the scalability of the Boundary Smoothing technique within expansive datasets. Enhancements in computational efficiency and the fine-tuning of boundary conditions could also be considered. Moreover, the methodologies introduced in this research are poised for adaptation to other languages, entailing the customization of the Boundary Smoothing algorithm to accommodate the distinct linguistic traits of each language. This endeavor may confront unique challenges, such as the adaptation to varied syntactic architectures and the intricacies of diverse phonological systems.

Author Contributions: Conceptualization, Z.D. and Z.H.; methodology, Z.D. and Z.H.; validation Z.D., Z.H. and J.Z.; formal analysis, Z.D., Z.H. and S.W.; investigation Z.D., Z.H., S.W. and J.Z.; writing original draft and visualization, Z.H. and S.W.; supervision S.W. and J.Z. All authors have read and agreed to the published version of the manuscript.

Funding: This work was partially supported by the Guangxi Science and Technology Project (nosAB22035052, AB20238013), the National Natural Science Foundation of China (No. 62362016), and Guangxi Key Laboratory of Image and Graphic Intelligent Processing Project (nos. GIP2211, GIP2308), and the Innovation Project of GUET Graduate Education (No. 2023YCXS062).

Data Availability Statement: There are no restrictions on the sharing of relevant data in this study.

Acknowledgments: The authors thank the Special Issue editors and anonymous reviewers for their valuable comments.

Conflicts of Interest: The authors declare no conflicts of interest.

References

1. Yin, D.; Cheng, S.; Pan, B.; Qiao, Y.; Zhao, W.; Wang, D. Chinese Named Entity Recognition Based on Knowledge Based Question Answering System. *Appl. Sci.* **2022**, *12*, 5373. [CrossRef]
2. Bose, P.; Srinivasan, S.; Sleeman, W.C., IV; Palta, J.; Kapoor, R.; Ghosh, P. A Survey on Recent Named Entity Recognition and Relationship Extraction Techniques on Clinical Texts. *Appl. Sci.* **2021**, *11*, 8319. [CrossRef]
3. Chen, S.; Pei, Y.; Ke, Z.; Silamu, W. Low-Resource Named Entity Recognition via the Pre-Training Model. *Symmetry* **2021**, *13*, 786. [CrossRef]
4. Ahmad, P.N.; Shah, A.M.; Lee, K. A Review on Electronic Health Record Text-Mining for Biomedical Name Entity Recognition in Healthcare Domain. *Healthcare* **2023**, *11*, 1268. [CrossRef] [PubMed]
5. Huang, C.; Wang, Y.; Yu, Y.; Hao, Y.; Liu, Y.; Zhao, X. Chinese Named Entity Recognition of Geological News Based on BERT Model. *Appl. Sci.* **2022**, *12*, 7708. [CrossRef]
6. Szczepanek, R. A Deep Learning Model of Spatial Distance and Named Entity Recognition (SD-NER) for Flood Mark Text Classification. *Water* **2023**, *15*, 1197. [CrossRef]
7. Yang, J.; Teng, Z.; Zhang, M.; Zhang, Y. Combining discrete and neural features for sequence labeling. In Proceedings of the Computational Linguistics and Intelligent Text Processing: 17th International Conference, CICLing 2016, Konya, Turkey, 3–9 April 2016; pp. 140–154. [CrossRef]
8. He, H.; Sun, X. F-score driven max margin neural network for named entity recognition in Chinese social media. In Proceedings of the 15th Conference of the European Chapter of the Association for Computational Linguistics, Part 3: 15th Conference of the European Chapter of the Association for Computational Linguistics (EACL 2015), Valencia, Spain, 3–7 April 2017; pp. 713–718. [CrossRef]
9. Yao, L.; Huang, H.; Wang, K.-W.; Chen, S.-H.; Xiong, Q. Fine-Grained Mechanical Chinese Named Entity Recognition Based on ALBERT-AttBiLSTM-CRF and Transfer Learning. *Symmetry* **2020**, *12*, 1986. [CrossRef]
10. Chiu, J.P.; Nichols, E. Named entity recognition with bidirectional LSTM-CNNs. *Trans. Assoc. Comput. Linguist.* **2016**, *4*, 357–370. [CrossRef]
11. Guo, C.; Pleiss, G.; Sun, Y.; Weinberger, K.Q. On calibration of modern neural networks. In Proceedings of the 34th International Conference on Machine Learning, ICML 2017, Sydney, Australia, 6–11 August 2017; Volume 3. [CrossRef]
12. Wang, Z.; Shang, J.; Liu, L.; Lu, L.; Liu, J.; Han, J. Crossweigh: Training named entity tagger from imperfect annotations. *arXiv* **2019**, arXiv:1909.01441.
13. Enwei, Z.; Jinpeng, L. Boundary Smoothing for Named Entity Recognition. In *Proceedings of the 60th Annual Meeting of the Association for Computational Linguistics, Dublin, Ireland, 22–27 May 2022*; Muresan, S., Nakov, P., Villavicencio, A., Eds.; Association for Computational Linguistics: Stroudsburg, PA, USA, 2022; Volume 1, pp. 7096–7108. [CrossRef]
14. Deng, Z.; Tao, Y.; Lan, R.; Yang, R.; Wang, X. Kcr-FLAT: A Chinese-Named Entity Recognition Model with Enhanced Semantic Information. *Sensors* **2023**, *23*, 1771. [CrossRef]
15. Li, X.; Yan, H.; Qiu, X.; Huang, X. FLAT: Chinese NER Using Flat-Lattice Transformer. *arXiv* **2020**, arXiv:2004.11795.
16. Tourani, A.; Bavle, H.; Avşar, D.I.; Sanchez-Lopez, J.L.; Munoz-Salinas, R.; Voos, H. Vision-Based Situational Graphs Exploiting Fiducial Markers for the Integration of Semantic Entities. *Robotics* **2024**, *13*, 106. [CrossRef]
17. Wang, N.; Ge, R.F.; Yuan, C.F.; Wong, K.F.; Li, W.J. Company name identification in Chinese financial domain. *J. Chin. Inf. Pro.* **2002**, *16*, 1–6.
18. Sohrab, M.G.; Miwa, M. Deep exhaustive model for nested named entity recognition. In Proceedings of the 2018 Conference on Empirical Methods in Natural Language Processing, Brussels, Belgium, 31 October–4 November 2018; pp. 2843–2849. [CrossRef]
19. Markus, E.; Kevin, P.; Adrian, U. ManyEnt—A Dataset for Few-shot Entity Typing. In Proceedings of the 28th International Conference on Computational Linguistics, Barcelona, Spain, Online, 8–13 December 2020; pp. 5553–5557. [CrossRef]
20. Shen, Y.; Ma, X.; Tan, Z.; Zhang, S.; Lu, W. Locate and label: A two-stage identifier for nested named entity recognition. *arXiv* **2021**, arXiv:2105.06804.
21. Li, J.; Fei, H.; Liu, J.; Wu, S.; Zhang, M.; Teng, C.; Ji, D.; Li, F. Unified named entity recognition as word-word relation classification. In Proceedings of the AAAI conference on artificial intelligence, Seattle, WA, USA, 28 June 2022; pp. 10965–10973. [CrossRef]

22. Tan, Z.; Shen, Y.; Zhang, S.; Lu, W.; Zhuang, Y. A sequence-to-set network for nested named entity recognition. *arXiv* **2021**, arXiv:2105.08901.
23. Ma, X.; Hovy, E. End-to-end sequence labeling via bi-directional lstm-cnns-crf. *arXiv* **2016**, arXiv:1603.01354.
24. Li, X.; Feng, J.; Meng, Y.; Han, Q.; Wu, F.; Li, J. A unified MRC framework for named entity recognition. *arXiv* **2019**, arXiv:1910.11476.
25. Yu, J.; Bohnet, B.; Poesio, M. Named Entity Recognition as Dependency Parsing. *arXiv* **2020**, arXiv:2005.07150.
26. Yu, B.; Hang, Z.; Shu, X.; Liu, T.; Wang, Y.; Wang, B.; Li, S. Joint extraction of entities and relations based on a novel decomposition strategy. *arXiv* **2019**, arXiv:1909.04273.
27. Yang, Z.; Dai, Z.; Yang, Y.; Carbonell, J.; Salakhutdinov, R.R.; Le, Q.V. Xlnet: Generalized autoregressive pretraining for language understanding. *arXiv* **2019**, arXiv:1906.08237.
28. Athiwaratkun, B.; Santos, C.N.D.; Krone, J.; Xiang, B. Augmented natural language for generative sequence labeling. *arXiv* **2020**, arXiv:2009.13272.
29. Lewis, M.; Liu, Y.; Goyal, N.; Ghazvininejad, M.; Mohamed, A.; Levy, O.; Stoyanov, V.; Zettlemoyer, L. Bart: Denoising sequence-to-sequence pre-training for natural language generation, translation, and comprehension. *arXiv* **2019**, arXiv:1906.08237.
30. Ni, J.; Abrego, G.H.; Constant, N.; Ma, J.; Hall, K.B.; Cer, D.; Yang, Y. Sentence-t5: Scalable sentence encoders from pre-trained text-to-text models. *arXiv* **2021**, arXiv:2108.08877.
31. Daneshfar, F.; Aghajani, M.J. Enhanced text classification through an improved discrete laying chicken algorithm. *Expert Syst.* **2024**, *41*, e13553. [CrossRef]
32. Liang, L.-X.; Lin, L.; Lin, E.; Wen, W.-S.; Huang, G.-Y. A Joint Learning Model to Extract Entities and Relations for Chinese Literature Based on Self-Attention. *Mathematics* **2022**, *10*, 2216. [CrossRef]
33. Lou, C.; Yang, S.; Tu, K. Nested named entity recognition as latent lexicalized constituency parsing. *arXiv* **2022**, arXiv:2203.04665.
34. Ma, J.; Ballesteros, M.; Doss, S.; Anubhai, R.; Mallya, S.; Al-Onaizan, Y.; Roth, D. Label Semantics for Few Shot Named Entity Recognition. In Proceedings of the Findings of the Association for Computational Linguistics: ACL 2022, Dublin, Ireland, 22–27 May 2022; pp. 1956–1971.
35. Nie, Y.; Tian, Y.; Song, Y.; Ao, X.; Wan, X. Improving named entity recognition with attentive ensemble of syntactic information. *arXiv* **2020**, arXiv:2010.15466.
36. Petrovska, B.; Atanasova-Pacemska, T.; Corizzo, R.; Mignone, P.; Lameski, P.; Zdravevski, E. Aerial Scene Classification through Fine-Tuning with Adaptive Learning Rates and Label Smoothing. *Appl. Sci.* **2020**, *10*, 5792. [CrossRef]
37. Wu, P.; Cui, Z.; Gan, Z.; Liu, F. Three-Dimensional ResNeXt Network Using Feature Fusion and Label Smoothing for Hyperspectral Image Classification. *Sensors* **2020**, *20*, 1652. [CrossRef]
38. Mahayossanunt, Y.; Nupairoj, N.; Hemrungrojn, S.; Vateekul, P. Explainable Depression Detection Based on Facial Expression Using LSTM on Attentional Intermediate Feature Fusion with Label Smoothing. *Sensors* **2023**, *23*, 9402. [CrossRef]
39. Ashish, V.; Noam, S.; Niki, P.; Jakob, U.; Llion, J.; Aidan, N.G.; Lukasz, K.; Illia, P. Attention is all you need. *Adv. Neural Inf. Process. Syst.* **2017**, *30*, 5998–6008. [CrossRef]
40. Rafael, M.; Simon, K.; Geoffrey, H. When Does Label Smoothing Help? *Adv. Neural Inf. Process. Syst.* **2019**, *32*, 4696–4705. [CrossRef]
41. Lukasik, M.; Bhojanapalli, S.; Menon, A.; Kumar, S. Does label smoothing mitigate label noise? In Proceedings of the International Conference on Machine Learning, Virtual, 13–18 July 2020; pp. 6448–6458. [CrossRef]
42. Collobert, R.; Weston, J.; Bottou, L.; Karlen, M.; Kavukcuoglu, K.; Kuksa, P. Natural language processing (almost) from scratch. *JML* **2011**, *12*, 2493–2537. [CrossRef]
43. Gu, Y.; Qu, X.; Wang, Z.; Zheng, Y.; Huai, B.; Yuan, N.J. Delving deep into regularity: A simple but effective method for Chinese named entity recognition. *arXiv* **2022**, arXiv:2204.05544.
44. Wu, S.; Song, X.; Feng, Z.; Wu, X. NFLAT: Non-Flat-Lattice Transformer for Chinese Named Entity Recognition. *arXiv* **2022**, arXiv:2205.05832.
45. Xiong, L.; Zhou, J.; Zhu, Q.; Wang, X.; Wu, Y.; Zhang, Q.; Gui, T.; Huang, X.; Ma, J.; Shan, Y. A Confidence-based Partial Label Learning Model for Crowd-Annotated Named Entity Recognition. *arXiv* **2023**, arXiv:2305.12485.
46. Shen, Y.; Song, K.; Tan, X.; Li, D.; Lu, W.; Zhuang, Y. Diffusionner: Boundary diffusion for named entity recognition. *arXiv* **2023**, arXiv:2305.13298.
47. Wu, S.; Song, X.; Feng, Z. MECT: Multi-Metadata Embedding based Cross-Transformer for Chinese Named Entity Recognition. *arXiv* **2021**, arXiv:2107.05418.
48. Ma, R.; Peng, M.; Zhang, Q.; Huang, X. Simplify the usage of lexicon in Chinese NER. *arXiv* **2019**, arXiv:1908.05969.
49. Mao, Q.; Li, J.; Meng, K. Improving Chinese Named Entity Recognition by Search Engine Augmentation. *arXiv* **2022**, arXiv:2210.12662.
50. Hu, D.; Wei, L. SLK-NER: Exploiting second-order lexicon knowledge for chinese NER. *arXiv* **2020**, arXiv:2007.08416.

mathematics

MDPI

Article

Enhancing Knowledge-Concept Recommendations with Heterogeneous Graph-Contrastive Learning

Liting Wei [1,2], Yun Li [2,*], Weiwei Wang [2] and Yi Zhu [2]

[1] Jiangsu Provincial Key Constructive Laboratory for Big Data of Psychology and Cognitive Science, Yancheng Teachers University, Yancheng 224002, China; weilt@yctu.edu.cn
[2] School of Information Engineering, Yangzhou University, Yangzhou 225012, China; yangzhouwangweiwei@163.com (W.W.); zhuyi@yzu.edu.cn (Y.Z.)
* Correspondence: liyun@yzu.edu.cn; Tel.: +86-138-5278-5198

Abstract: With the implementation of conceptual labeling on online learning resources, knowledge-concept recommendations have been introduced to pinpoint concepts that learners may wish to delve into more deeply. As the core subject of learning, learners' preferences in knowledge concepts should be given greater attention. Research indicates that learners' preferences for knowledge concepts are influenced by the characteristics of their group structure. There is a high degree of homogeneity within a group, and notable distinctions exist between the internal and external configurations of a group. To strengthen the group-structure characteristics of learners' behaviors, a multi-task strategy for knowledge-concept recommendations is proposed; this strategy is called Knowledge-Concept Recommendations with Heterogeneous Graph-Contrastive Learning. Specifically, due to the difficulty of accessing authentic social networks, learners and their structural neighbors are considered positive contrastive pairs to construct self-supervision signals on the predefined meta-path from heterogeneous information networks as auxiliary tasks, which capture the higher-order neighbors of learners by presenting different perspectives. Then, the Information Noise-Contrastive Estimation loss is regarded as the main training objective to increase the differentiation of learners from different professional backgrounds. Extensive experiments are constructed on MOOCCube, and we find that our proposed method outperforms the other state-of-the-art concept-recommendation methods, achieving 6.66% with *HR*@5, 8.85% with *NDCG*@5, and 8.68% with *MRR*.

Keywords: knowledge-concept recommendation; group-structure feature of learner preferences; graph-contrastive learning

MSC: 68Txx

1. Introduction

Online learning platforms, including MOOCs (massive open online courses), have revolutionized the way people learn by offering a flexible and accessible mode of education. They have played a crucial role during the pandemic by providing an alternative mode of education that enables learners to continue their education without being physically present in a classroom [1,2]. XuetangX [3,4] is one of the largest MOOC platforms in China, and it has gained popularity among learners due to its effective and fine-grained course concepts that help students understand course material in a faster and more efficient way. Additionally, a large-scale data repository, MOOCCube [5], has been made available by XuetangX to facilitate natural language processing (NLP) and artificial intelligence (AI) research for educational applications.

Knowledge-concept recommendations are designed to predict concepts that learners might be interested in according to their historical learning behaviors. Previous research studies have demonstrated that [4,6] have indicated that learners from varying professional backgrounds tend to focus on distinct knowledge concepts even when taking the same courses with different teachers. Moreover, it has been found that clicking on relevant knowledge concepts can enhance learning progress and speed. By taking a more microscopic view of a learner's needs, knowledge-concept recommendations [7,8] can provide more fine-grained services and experiences compared to course recommendations, ultimately enhancing the overall online learning experience.

Collaborative filtering (CF) has been widely applied to recommendation tasks; it involves mapping users and items to a latent representation space and preserving the structural feature information of user–item interactions. It is also an effective method for solving the problem of concept recommendations. However, as the number of learners and concepts increases, the sparsity of interactions becomes a challenging issue. To alleviate the issue of data sparsity, most knowledge-concept recommendation methods have constructed a heterogeneous information network (HIN) on MOOC platforms. The approach helps enrich the representation of interaction entities and improve recommendation performance [4,9,10].

In real-world educational settings, learners' behaviors are influenced by the characteristics of group structures. As illustrated in Figure 1, the MOOCCube dataset includes 50 students selected from three different academic backgrounds: medicine, chemistry, and the dialectics of nature. Students with a background in medicine numbered 0–9, those in chemistry numbered 10–46, and those in the dialectics of nature numbered 47–49. The heatmap shows the probabilities representing the intersection and union ratios of the students' clicks on knowledge concepts. It is evident from the heatmap that students' preferences for knowledge concepts are highly similar within the same group structure, and there are noticeable differences between different group structures. Knowledge-concept recommendation methods based on heterogeneous graphs focus on similarities within group structures, and they extract features from learners in various dimensional neighborhoods to enrich learner representations.

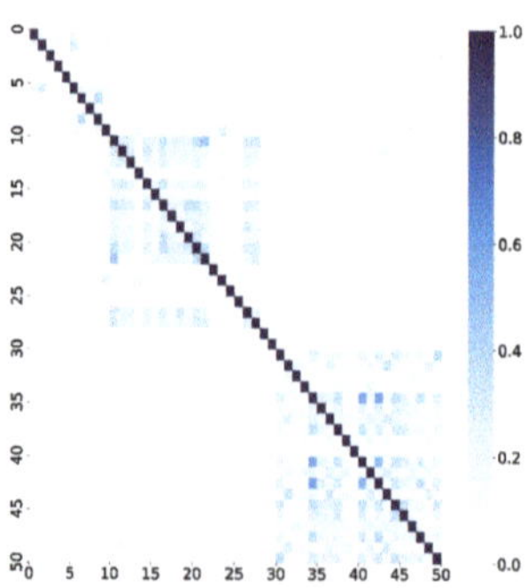

Figure 1. MOOCCube dataset behavior heatmap showing probability as the proportion of learners' clicks on the intersection and union of knowledge concepts.

However, two key limitations are hindering further development in concept recommendations: (1) Due to data sparsity, the similar relationships within group structures cannot be explicitly utilized to enrich graph information when using a graph convolution-based collaborative filtering method, resulting in the insufficient mining of learner characteristics. (2) Ignoring the differences between group structures undoubtedly affects the capture of learner preferences, leading to biased results in knowledge-concept recommendations.

To address the aforementioned challenges in knowledge concept-recommendation tasks, a novel multi-task method called Knowledge Concept Recommendation with Heterogeneous Graph-Contrastive Learning (KCRHGCL) is proposed in this paper. The goal of KCRHGCL is to enhance learner representations by extracting features of similarities and differences in group structures, thereby improving the effectiveness of knowledge-concept recommendations. "Birds of a feather flock together". Learners' neighbors can enhance their feature representations. Intuitively, Structural neighbors, by considering the local structure of learners in the graph, capture subtle differences and similarities in their features, thereby enriching the characteristic features of learners' preferences. Specifically, by using a structure-aware contrastive learning method on each predefined meta-path, the representations of learners are brought closer to the embedding of their structural neighbors, thereby enhancing the learners' representations. The structural neighbors of a learner are defined as the embeddings of the learner based on the output of the graph convolutional layer. These self-supervised tasks are treated as auxiliary tasks to improve the recommendation performance. In addition, negative sampling techniques are used to distinguish features of different group structures by selecting negative samples that are more likely to be confused with positive samples. By combining this with InfoNCE, our proposed method can effectively maximize the mutual information between similar learners and minimize it between dissimilar learners, thereby enhancing the overall recommendation performance.

In summary, this paper makes the following contributions:

(1) A new method called the Heterogeneous Graph-Contrastive Learning for Knowledge concept recommendation is proposed. It incorporates structure-aware contrastive learning to mine higher-order similarities within the learner-group structure while aggregating learner-neighbor features from different dimensions, more fully capturing the preferences of learners.
(2) Data analysis finds that, unlike commercial recommendations, learner behavior in knowledge-concept recommendations shows significant differences between group structures due to the influence of professional backgrounds. Negative sampling techniques better learn to distinguish features of different group structures by selecting negative samples that are more likely to be confused with the positive samples. InfoNCE loss enhances the differences between groups by maximizing the similarity of positive sample pairs and minimizing the similarity between positive and negative samples, thereby capturing the differences between different group structures.
(3) Comprehensive experiments are conducted on a MOOCCube dataset to validate the effectiveness of KCRHGCL. The results demonstrate that KCRHGCL outperforms other state-of-the-art methods.

2. Materials and Methods

2.1. Recommender Systems in MOOCs

MOOC platforms have seen a huge influx of learning resources, and the ever-increasing amount of material has left learners overwhelmed, unable to ensure the quality of online learning and leading to a loss of interest and persistently high dropout rates. Researchers have made numerous attempts, such as learner profiles and course recommendations. Currently, course recommendations [7,11,12] are one of the most widely applied tools. Collaborative filtering is one of the common techniques of course recommendation; it maps learners and courses to a latent space and captures learners' preferences. Some studies have shown that enhancing the characteristics of learners and courses can improve the effectiveness of course recommendations. For example, Jing et al. [13] introduced a course recommendation method that uses a collaborative filtering strategy incorporating user interests, demographic profiles, and course prerequisite relations. Zhang et al. [7] employed a hierarchical reinforcement learning algorithm to revise user profiles, and they combined it with the basic collaborative filtering model to improve the course recommendation task. Jung et al. [14] included a level-embedding module for students and courses in their course recommendation system, excluding the incorporation of a knowledge graph containing internal information about MOOCs and an external knowledge base. Knowledge concepts are smaller instructional units than courses, and they can be integrated according to different domains or topics. Using them as the target of recommendations allows for the tracking of learners' preferences from a more detailed perspective. As learning resources on online platforms are tagged with knowledge-concept labels, knowledge-concept recommendations have emerged. For example, Gong et al. [4] leverage an attention-based graph convolutional network to obtain representations of meta-paths that can capture the multivariate preferences of learners. Building upon this work, Piao et al. [9] made three improvements: using implicit feedback instead of ratings, exploring more advanced attention mechanisms, and estimating the preference score of a concept in the prediction layer. Gong et al. [10] took token-modeling of the dynamic interactions among learners and concepts into consideration by treating concept recommendations as the reinforcement learning problem. However, learners' preferences are influenced by their professional backgrounds, which naturally form group characteristics. There is a similarity within these group structures and significant differences between the groups.

2.2. Recommendations with Contrastive Learning

Self-supervised learning [15,16] extracts transferable knowledge directly from the data itself without the need for labeled data, providing a new learning paradigm for addressing the data sparsity issues of interaction-based collaborative filtering methods. Contrastive learning, due to its lightweight model and flexible design, has gradually become the leading method recommended for self-supervised learning. The idea of CL is to maximize the agreement between different views, and the agreement is usually measured via mutual information [17]. Recently, many CL paradigms have been developed for interaction-based recommendation systems to enhance recommendation performance. For example, Xie et al. [18] applied a CL framework that tries three approaches to data augmentation to extract user representations based only on users' interactions. Yang et al. [19] proposed a novel approach that involves using cross-view self-discrimination supervision signals, along with a knowledge-aware contrastive objective, to improve recommendation robustness and address issues related to data noise and sparsity. Cai et al. [20] proposed the graph-contrastive learning paradigm LightGCN, which uses singular value decomposition for contrastive augmentation, allowing for the unconstrained refinement of the structure of global collaborative relationships. Lin et al. [21] introduced graph structure and semantic neighbors as contrastive pairs to enrich the representation of a current node. The aforementioned contrastive learning-based recommendation methods are based on homogeneous graphs. However, heterogeneous information networks can accurately distinguish between different semantics in the network by analyzing various types of nodes and the links between them, and they can mine the potential value and more meaningful knowledge from these rich objects and connections, making them widely used in recommendation systems. The application of contrastive learning to heterogeneous graphs has attracted the attention of researchers. Chen et al. [22] proposed a method called Heterogeneous Graph-Contrastive Learning for Recommendations, which incorporates heterogeneous relational semantics into user–item interaction modeling and enhances the knowledge transfer across different views using contrastive learning, and it is further enhanced with meta-networks for personalized and adaptive contrastive augmentation. Zheng et al. [23] proposed a method called Heterogeneous Information Crossing on Graphs, which captures both current interests and long-term preferences by constructing heterogeneous graphs from various user behaviors, and it incorporates contrastive learning to improve item representation and recommendation performance by leveraging items' co-occurrence across sessions. Inspired by these works, we proposed multi-task, meta-path, heterogeneous graph-contrastive learning to enhance learners' representations from multiple perspectives for knowledge-concept recommendations.

3. Preliminaries

Problem statement. Knowledge-concept recommendations aim to automatically recommend relevant knowledge concepts that learners might want to click on based on their historical behavior. Firstly, $\mathcal{L} = \{L_1, L_2, \cdots, L_L\}$, $\mathcal{C} = \{C_1, C_2, \cdots, C_C\}$, $\mathcal{V} = \{V_1, V_2, \cdots, V_V\}$, $\mathcal{T} = \{T_1, T_2, \cdots, T_T\}$, and $\mathcal{K} = \{K_1, K_2, \cdots, K_K\}$ were defined to represent the set of learners, courses, videos, teachers, and knowledge concepts, respectively. **Input:** for the learners' $\mathcal{U}$ and knowledge concepts $\mathcal{K}$, their corresponding interactive data $\mathcal{R}$, which can reveal relations from different meta-paths, $\mathcal{MP} = \{mp_1, mp_2, \cdots, mp_M\}$, based on a heterogeneous information network, the details are described in the next section. **Output:** a predict function, f, generates N knowledge-concept recommendation list, S (e.g., "osteoarthrosis", "quantum theory", etc.), such that $f : l \rightarrow \{K_i \mid K_i \in \mathcal{K}, i < \mathcal{K}\}$.

Meta-paths based on the heterogeneous information network. On the MOOCs platform, interactive data, $\mathcal{R}$, can be organized as a heterogeneous information network (HIN), $\mathcal{G} = \{\mathcal{N}, \mathcal{E}\}$, where $\mathcal{N} = \{\mathcal{L} \cup \mathcal{C} \cup \mathcal{V} \cup \mathcal{T} \cup \mathcal{K}\}$ denotes the sets of objects, $\mathcal{E} = \{\{E_i\} | E_i \in \mathcal{O}\}$ denotes the set of links, $\mathcal{O} = \{\{Teach, Learn, Watch, Next, Include\}$, and $|\mathcal{N}| + |\mathcal{E}| > 2$. Meta-paths [24] are defined as paths in the form of a sequence of entity types, $\mathcal{V}$, connected by relationship types, $\mathcal{E}$, one of which is formally expressed as follows: $V_1 \xrightarrow{E_1} V_2 \xrightarrow{E_2} \cdots \xrightarrow{E_l} V_{l+1}$.

4. Proposed Methods

First, the representation learning of the learners is introduced in Section 4.1. The final outputs contain the structural relations between learners on different meta-paths, aggregating through the layer propagation of GCN. Figure 2 illustrates the method flow of the overall framework. We first introduce the representation learning of the learners in Section 4.1, whose final outputs contain the structural relations between learners on different meta-paths aggregating through the layer propagation of GCN. Then, the representation learning of the concepts is introduced in Section 4.2, which uses the heterogeneous graph attention network to capture the representations from meta-paths. Finally, we describe a multi-task learning strategy in Section 4.3.

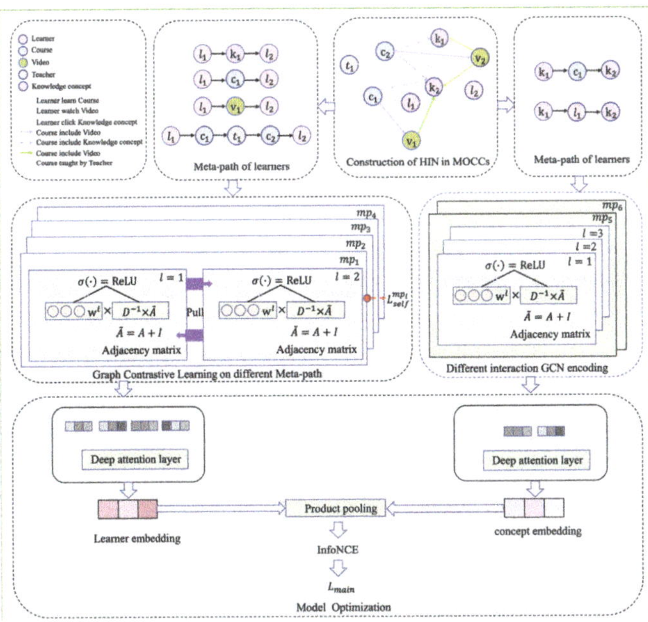

Figure 2. The method flow of the KCRHGCL framework, which consists of the following three main workflows: (i) the representation learning of the learners—in the constructed heterogeneous graph, appropriate meta-paths are selected, graph convolutional networks are used to extract features on these predefined meta-paths, and structural neighbors are introduced to enhance learner representations; (ii) the representation learning of the concepts—heterogeneous graph attention networks are used to capture the representations of concepts from different meta-paths; and (iii) the model optimization of the multi-task—negative sampling techniques and Information Noise Contrastive Estimation (InfoNCE) are utilized as the training objective loss to more effectively distinguish between differences in learners' preferences across group structures.

4.1. The Representation Learning of the Learners

Meta-paths for learners selected from HIN in MOOCs. Figure 2 (The construction of an HIN in MOOCs) illustrates the network schema for HINs in MOOCs. The schema comprises five distinct entities: course, knowledge concept, video, teacher, and learner. There are various relationships between these entities. For example, learners watch videos, and videos are linked to different knowledge concepts. Based on previous research [4,9], this study also selected the following four meta-paths to represent learners from different dimensions, which are detailed in Table 1.

- $mp_1(U_1 - K - U_2)$ means that two users could make a connection if they have learned the same concept.
- $mp_2(U_1 - C - U_2)$ denotes that users will be connected if they take the same courses.
- $mp_3(U_1 - V - U_2)$ denotes that users who have watched the same video will make a connection.
- $mp_4(U_1 - C_1 - T - C_2 - U_2)$ means that users are connected by taking a course with the same same teacher.

Table 1. Meta-paths selected based on HIN to extract learner–learner and concept–concept relationships.

Type	Meta-Math
Learners	$Learner \rightarrow Concept \xrightarrow{-1} Learner$ $Learner \rightarrow Course \xrightarrow{-1} Learner$ $Learner \rightarrow Video \xrightarrow{-1} Learner$ $Learner \rightarrow Course \rightarrow Teacher \xrightarrow{-1} Course \xrightarrow{-1} Learner.$
Concepts	$Concept \rightarrow Course \xrightarrow{-1} Concept$ $Concept \rightarrow Learner \xrightarrow{-1} Concept$

Enhancing learner representation with graph-contrastive learning. Recent studies have highlighted the efficacy of graph convolutional networks (GCNs) in representation learning for knowledge-concept recommendations [4,9,10]. To generalize learners' representations, h_{mp_i}, from an HIN along the each meta-path, GCNs are applied to aggregate the similarity information between learners on different meta-paths with the following layer-wise propagation rule:

$$h^{l+1}_{mp_i} = \sigma(Ph^{l}_{mp_i}W^{l}_{mp_i}) \tag{1}$$

where $\sigma()$ represents the non-linear activation function, specifically $ReLu$. Matrix P is defined as $D^{-1}\widetilde{A}$, with D being the degree matrix of A. $D^{-1}\widetilde{A}$ aims to get the average embedding of a node and its neighborhoods. Matrix $\widetilde{A}$ is defined as $\widetilde{A} = A + I$, where A is the adjacency matrix of the mate-path mp_i, and I is identity matrix. Matrix $W^{(l)}_{mp_i}$ is the trainable weight matrix of the mate-path mp_i at layer l. Here, the mate-path mp_i aggregate the relationships between learners.

As we mentioned before, the neighborhood information of learners has not been explored completely. It is difficult to identify a real neighborhood. We made use of graph-contrastive learning to explore higher-order neighborhood information. The first priority was constructing data augmentation. On each meta-path, the embedding of learners and the embedding of the output of the next layer of GCNs are treated as positive pairs; the propagation rules are shown in Equation (2):

$$h^{l'_{mp_i}} = P' h^{l}_{mp_i} \tag{2}$$

Unlike matrix P defined in Equation (1), weight matrix P' and the nonlinear activation operation are discarded. That is to say that the input only retains the average homogeneous neighborhood embedding.

$h^{l'_{mp_i}}$ contains the rich homogeneous graph structural information on the i-th meta-path. Based on the InfoNCE [25], the auxiliary task objectives for each meta-path are described in Equation (3):

$$\mathcal{L}_{self}^{mp_i} = \sum_{p \in P} -\log \frac{\exp((s(\mathbf{H}_p^{(l)}, \mathbf{H}_p^{(l)'})/\tau))}{\sum_{n \in \mathcal{N}_i} \exp((s(\mathbf{H}_p^{(l)}, \mathbf{H}_n^{(l)'})/\tau))} \tag{3}$$

where $\mathbf{H}^l$ and $\mathbf{H}^{l'}$ are the corresponding normalized embedding of the different layers of GCNs. τ is the temperature hyper-parameter of the softmax function. Function $s()$ denotes cosine similarity. $\mathcal{N}_i$ represents the negative sample set of the i-th mate-path, and P is a positive sample set. p can be searched according to hard negative samples. To generate our hard-negative-sample set, we selected samples with similarity values greater than 0 and ranked them from 100 to 200. Additionally, we extracted 10% of the hard negative sample set, while the remaining 90% was obtained through random sampling to serve as negative samples. Of these, 10% were extracted as hard negative samples, while the remaining 90% of the negative samples were obtained through random sampling.

In addition, graph-contrastive learning on different meta-paths has different objectives, which can be formulated as follows:

$$\mathcal{L}_{self} = \sum_{i \in |mp|} \lambda_i \mathcal{L}_{self}^{mp_i} \tag{4}$$

where $\mathcal{L}_{self}$ is the final contrastive loss function, and λ_i represents the different weights of the contrastive loss.

Intuitively, learners' embedding from different meta-paths should contribute different weights to the final results. The importance of meta-paths in learners' final embedding can be formulated as follows:

$$\alpha^{mp_i} = \frac{\exp\left(\mathbf{V}_e^T \sigma(\mathbf{W_e h}^{mp_i})\right)}{\sum_{j \in |mp_e|} \exp(\mathbf{V}_e^T \sigma(\mathbf{W_e e}^{mp_j}))} \tag{5}$$

The final representation of learners, $\mathbf{e}$, can be described as follows:

$$\mathbf{e} = \sum_{j \in |mp_e|} \alpha^{mp_j} \mathbf{e}^{mp_j} \tag{6}$$

where mp_e represents the selected meta-paths of learners.

4.2. The Representation Learning of the Concepts

The meta-paths of the concepts are listed in Table 1 as well. They are described as follows:

- $mp_5(K_1 - C - K_2)$ denotes the knowledge concepts that are connected and that have appeared in the same course.
- $mp_6(K_1 - L - K_2)$ indicates that the knowledge concepts were related if they were clicked on by one learner.

Knowledge concepts K embedding x can be learned through a graph heterogeneous attention network to aggregate the information along the selected meta-path. First, graph convolutional networks are utilized to represent the concept based on different meta-paths, which can be formulated as follows:

$$x_{mp_i}^{l+1} = \sigma(P x_{mp_i}^{l} W_{mp_i}^{l}) \tag{7}$$

where W^l represents the trainable weight matrix of the mate-path mp_i at layer l. Here, the mate-path mp_i aggregates the relationships between concepts.

Following [10], the representations with different meta-paths give different contributions to the final results. The importance of different meta-paths can be obtained via Equation (5):

$$\alpha^{mp_i} = \frac{\exp\left(\mathbf{V}^T\sigma(\mathbf{W_c}\mathbf{x}^{mp_i})\right)}{\sum_{j\in|mp_c|}\exp\left(\mathbf{V}^T\sigma(\mathbf{W_c}\mathbf{x}^{mp_j})\right)} \tag{8}$$

where $\mathbf{V}^T$ and $\mathbf{W_c}$ are the trainable weight matrixes. σ is the tanh function. The final representation of concepts can be described as follows:

$$\mathbf{z} = \sum_{j\in|mp_z|} \alpha^{mp_j}\mathbf{x}^{mp_j} \tag{9}$$

where mp_z represents the selected meta-paths of concepts. With the final representations, we make use of the inner product to predict how likely a learner, u, would be to click on the concept k:

$$\widehat{y}_{u,k} = e_u^T z_k \tag{10}$$

Here, e_u and z_k are normalized final representations of u and k that belong to e and z.

4.3. Multi-Task Training

A multi-task strategy is used to jointly optimize the main supervised task and the auxiliary graph-contrastive learning tasks. Specifically, the joint loss can be shown as follows:

$$\mathcal{L} = \mathcal{L}_{main} + \mu\mathcal{L}_{self} + \lambda\|\Theta\|^2 \tag{11}$$

where μ is the regularization strength of the contrastive learning tasks, and λ is the regularization strength of the L2 normalization.

Loss for the main task. A different main loss could be chosen according to the objectives. In knowledge-concept recommendations, we find that there exist two tendencies while learners are learning related concepts. First, learners from different professional backgrounds, aside from the knowledge concepts of specific general education courses, exhibit differences between groups divided by their professional backgrounds. Second, as they delve deeper into their studies, similar learners will become interested in the same concepts, showing high correlations within the group. To encourage the above properties, InfoNCE [26] loss is adopted, and it could maximize the mutual information of the positive-sample pair and minimize the mutual information of the negative-sample pair. The main loss function can be described as follows:

$$\mathcal{L}_{\text{main}} = \sum_{u,i\in UK} -\log\frac{\exp((s(CZ_u,\mathbf{X}_i)/\tau))}{\sum_{j\in N}\exp\left((s(\mathbf{Z}_u,\mathbf{X}_j)/\tau)\right)} \tag{12}$$

where Z_u is the user embedding, and u comes from learners via random sampling. X_i is the embedding of a concept. X_j is the concept embedding obtained via global uniform random sampling from the knowledge concept set. The algorithm of KCRHGCL is detailed in Algorithm 1.

Algorithm 1: KCRHGCL

Input: Given the meta-paths $\mathcal{MP}$, the interactive data matrix $\mathcal{R}$, the global epoch E, the batch size N, the number of negative samples in main tasks n_1, and the number of negative samples in auxiliary tasks n_2
Output: the list of predicted knowledge concepts *list*
Initialize learner embedding h_0 and concept embedding x_0;
foreach *mp in* $\mathcal{MP}$ **do**
  $P = D^{-1}(A + I)$
end
for *episodee* $= 1 \cdots E$ **do**
  foreach *mp in* $\mathcal{MP}_{\mathcal{L}}$ **do**
    Compute the representation on different meta-path of learners h_{mp}^{l+1} Compute the representation on different meta-path of learners via graph-contrastive learning $h_{mp}^{l+1'}$
  end
  foreach *mp in* $\mathcal{MP}_{\mathcal{K}}$ **do**
    Compute the representation on different meta-path of concepts x_{mp}^{l+1}
  end
  Recompute learner embedding e and concept embedding z via attention mechanisms Compute the prediction $\hat{Y} = e^T z$ Compute the loss $L = L_{main} + \mu L_{self} + \beta L_2$ Calculate gradient $\nabla_\theta L(f_\theta)$ Update θ with $\theta \leftarrow \theta - \eta \nabla_\theta L(f_\theta)$
end

5. Experiments

This section describes experiments that were conducted on a real-world dataset named MOOCCCube to evaluate the effectiveness of KCRHGCL for recommending knowledge concept tasks. To achieve this, the following research questions were addressed:

- RQ1: How effective is KCRHGCL in the concept recommendation compared with other baselines?
- RQ2: How does the performance of KCRHGCL vary with different meta-paths?
- RQ3: How do the different modules in KCRHGCL, such as using graph structure-aware contrastive learning on meta-paths to enhance the structural features of learner groups, or using InfoNCE as the main function to increase inter-group structural differences, contribute to the overall performance of the method?
- RQ4: How does the performance of KCRHGCL vary with different hyper-parameter settings, such as the embedding dimension size, the regularization weights, and the layer number of graph-based message propagation?
- RQ5: How does the convergence of the KCRHGCL method compare to the suboptimal method MOOCIR?

5.1. Experimental Settings

5.1.1. Datasets

Experiments were organized on the MOOCCube dataset [5] to validate the effectiveness of the method. MOOCCube is a large-scale, high-quality dataset designed for AI research in the field of education. Table 2 provides a detailed overview of the MOOCCube dataset used in our experiments, and it can be observed that the interactions between entities are sparse. The data preprocessing approach we adopted is consistent with that of [9]. Specifically, we extracted data from 1 January 2017 to 31 October 2019 for training and data from 1 November 2019 to 31 December 2019 for testing. Furthermore, we ensured that the data met two criteria: (i) learners were present in both the training and test datasets, and (ii) at least one new concept appeared in the test data.

Table 2. Details of the MOOCCube dataset.

Entities	Statistics	Relations	Statistics
Users	2005	User-concept	930,553
Concepts	21,037	user-course	13,696
Courses	600	Course-video	42,117
Videos	22,403	Teacher-course	1875
Schools	137	Video-concept	295,475
Teachers	138	Course-concept	150,811

5.1.2. Evaluation Metrics

Several evaluation metrics were selected in this paper, and they are commonly used in recommendation tasks. The hit ratio of the top K ($HR@K$) is a measure of recall that indicates the percentage of relevant concepts in the test set that appear in the top-K recommended concepts. It is a widely used measure of recall, and it assesses a system's ability to retrieve relevant concepts [27]. The normalized discounted cumulative gain of the top K ($NDCG@K$) is a ranking metric that takes into account the relevance of concepts in the top-K recommended items, as well as their positions in the ranking. It is a normalized measure of the cumulative graded relevance based on the top-K recommended concepts for all learners of recommendations [28]. The mean reciprocal rank (MRR) was used to evaluate the ranking of search results. It measures the effectiveness of the ranking by calculating the average reciprocal rank of relevant concepts in the ranking [29].

5.1.3. Compared Methods

To evaluate the validity of KCRHGCL, we compared KCRHGCL with the following state-of-the-art methods that utilized various deep-learning methods to improve the performance of recommendation tasks. The baseline details are described below.

- FISM [30] is an item-to-item collaborative-filtering recommendation method that predicts user preferences by aggregating the latent factors of the items the user has interacted with.
- NAIS [31] is another item-to-item collaborative filtering recommendation method that introduces an attention mechanism to weigh the importance of different historical interactions for a user. Therefore, NAIS focuses more on the interactions that are more relevant to predicting the user's preference for a specific item.
- Metapath2vec [32] is a representation learning method based on a heterogeneous information network. Random walk and skip-gram are two key components. By maximizing the co-occurrence probability of nodes and their neighboring nodes in random walk sequences, Metapath2vec learns high-quality node representations that capture the structural and semantic relationships within a network.
- ACKRec [4] is an end-to-end graph neural network-based method. It operates on heterogeneous graphs, defines predefined metapaths, uses graph convolution to extract entity representations from different metapaths, and employs an attention mechanism to aggregate the representations of different metapaths.
- MOOCIR [9] is another end-to-end graph neural network-based method for recommendations. Unlike ACKRec [4], MOOCIR uses implicit feedback instead of ratings and extends matrix factorization by incorporating learner and concept representations learned from different metapaths.
- HinCRec-RL [10] is a recommendation method that combines heterogeneous information networks and reinforcement learning for KCR to enhance performance.

5.1.4. Implementation Details

To ensure fairness, all of our methods were implemented using Python and run on a Linux server with two 2080ti GPUs and 64 GB of memory. The embedding initialization was obtained from the data provided by [9]. Our methods were optimized using the Adam optimizer [33], with an initial learning rate of 0.01. In addition, we used a single graph-based message propagation layer to avoid overfitting, and a dropout rate of 0.2 was applied. To reduce the impact of random numbers on the experimental results, we took the average of multiple operations. It is worth noting that the results of the compared methods were mostly from [9].

5.2. Performance Comparison

Table 3 shows the performance of different methods using the MOOCCube dataset. From the look of the results, the following conclusions can be drawn:

- It is evident that all the methods except for FISM and NAIS were based on an HIN. The methods based on HIN outperformed those that were not based on an HIN. For instance, metapath2vec outperformed FISM in terms of $HR@5$, $NDCG@5$, and MRR by over $9.9\%, 6.9\%, 5.3\%$, respectively. This indicates that constructing an HIN is an effective approach to alleviating sparsity in KCR tasks.
- KCRHGCL outperformed all other state-of-the-art recommendation methods with the MOOCCube dataset, with significant improvements in the HR@5, NDCG@5, and MRR metrics of $14.0\%, 12.5\%, 10.7\%$, respectively, when compared to ACKRec. This remarkable performance can be attributed to two key factors. Firstly, KCRHGCL incorporates self-supervised signals from different views to capture learners' interests by identifying structured similar neighbors. Secondly, the InfoNCE loss was utilized to adapt to the objective that conforms to the characteristics of learners' learning behavior.

Table 3. The performance of different methods with the MOOCCube dataset was compared, and the best-performing scores are marked in bold.

Methods	HR@5	HR@10	HR@20	NDCG@5	NDCG@10	NDCG@20	MRR
FISM	0.584	0.701	0.800	0.438	0.476	0.501	0.418
NAIS	0.568	0.691	0.811	0.420	0.461	0.491	0.403
metapath2vec	0.642	0.773	0.873	0.468	0.511	0.537	0.440
ACKRec	0.659	0.764	0.842	0.503	0.538	0.557	0.475
HinCRec-RL	0.662	0.815	0.887	0.462	0.513	0.532	0.428
MOOCIR	0.704	0.836	0.922	0.520	0.562	0.584	0.484
KCRHGCL	**0.751**	**0.866**	**0.934**	**0.566**	**0.603**	**0.621**	**0.526**

5.3. Effect of Different Meta-Paths

In this section, we explore the impact of different meta-paths and their combinations on the performance of our proposed method. We selected four meta-paths to represent the relationships between learners: $mp_1 : U_1 - K - U_2$, $mp_2 : U_1 - C - U_2$, $MP3 : U_1 - V - U_2$, and $MP4 : U_1 - C_1 - T - C_2 - T_2$. We present the results of different combinations of meta-paths in Table 3.

Interestingly, we found that selecting only a single meta-path, $MP2$, yielded the best performance, which contrasts with the findings of [4], where using more meta-paths led to better results. One possible explanation for this discrepancy is that, in MOOCs, knowledge concepts are structured around courses, and most learners acquire knowledge concepts centered around courses. Therefore, self-supervision signals that capture this feature more comprehensively may lead to better performance.

Furthermore, we observe that each individual meta-path produces different performance, with the order being $MP2 > MP4 > MP3 > MP1$. Additionally, the results of different combinations of meta-paths fall between the results of the individual meta-paths.

5.4. Ablation Study

This section proposes three variants of the KCRHGCL. Each variant focuses on a specific technique to improve the method's effectiveness. The three variants are as follows:

- $KCRHGCL_{nos}$ This method employs a single meta-path (mp_2) to learn node embedding, and it uses Bayesian personalized ranking (BPR) as the primary loss function. It does not utilize any additional structural neighbor information.
- $KCRHGCL_s$: This variant introduces structural neighbor information to explore the high-order similarity of learners on different meta-paths. BPR is still used as the main loss function.
- $KCRHGCL_i$: In this method, InfoNCE loss is used as the primary training objective. The approach aims to keep concepts that learners are not interested in away and bring concepts that learners are interested in closer.

The performance of three variants of KCRHGCL is shown in Table 4. The results in Table 5 indicate that utilizing the InfoNCE loss function leads to a significant improvement in performance for the HR@5, NDCG@5, and MRR metrics compared to using the BPR loss function. Comparing $KCRHGCL_{nos}$ to $KCRHGCL_s$ reveals that it improves $HR@5, NDCG@5, MRR$ over 22.8%, 31.5%, 30.9%. This suggests that InfoNCE loss is a more suitable training objective for KCR tasks than BPR, as it better distinguishes the interests and preferences of different professional learners, and it can better capture the similarity between learners with similar interests. When comparing $KCRHGCL$ to $KCRHGCL_i$, there is a small improvement in performance for the HR@5, NDCG@5, and MRR metrics of approximately 0.9%, 1.1%, 1.0%, respectively. This suggests that the enhanced structural neighbor achieved through graph-contrastive learning in the meta-path can contribute to the final performance of the model.

Table 4. Results of different combinations of meta-paths with the best-performing scores marked in bold.

Meta-Path	HR@5	HR@10	HR@20	NDCG@5	NDCG@10	NDCG@20	MRR
mp_1	0.713	0.840	0.918	0.533	0.574	0.594	0.498
mp_2	**0.751**	**0.866**	**0.934**	**0.566**	**0.603**	**0.621**	**0.526**
mp_3	0.718	0.840	0.919	0.536	0.576	0.596	0.500
mp_4	0.729	0.852	0.925	0.542	0.582	0.600	0.503
$mp_1\&mp_2$	0.726	0.845	0.920	0.543	0.582	0.595	0.506
$mp_1\&mp_3$	0.717	0.844	0.924	0.533	0.575	0.595	0.497
$mp_1\&mp_4$	0.718	0.844	0.924	0.534	0.575	0.596	0.498
$mp_2\&mp_4$	0.723	0.847	0.924	0.541	0.581	0.601	0.505
$mp_2\&mp_4$	0.738	0.854	0.926	0.555	0.593	0.611	0.517
$mp_3\&mp_4$	0.724	0.848	0.925	0.542	0.582	0.602	0.506
$mp_1\&mp_2\&mp_3$	0.720	0.843	0.921	0.538	0.579	0.598	0.502
$mp_1\&mp_2\&mp_4$	0.723	0.847	0.925	0.538	0.579	0.599	0.502
$mp_1\&mp_3\&mp_4$	0.718	0.841	0.920	0.536	0.577	0.597	0.501
$mp_2\&mp_3\&mp_4$	0.728	0.849	0.925	0.545	0.584	0.604	0.508
All	0.726	0.845	0.921	0.543	0.581	0.601	0.505

Table 5. Performance results of three variants of KCRHGCL with the best scores are marked in bold.

Methods	HR@5	HR@10	HR@20	NDCG@5	NDCG@10	NDCG@20	MRR
$KCRHGCL_{nos}$	0.584	0.742	0.854	0.394	0.446	0.474	0.365
$KCRHGCL_s$	0.606	0.755	0.859	0.426	0.475	0.501	0.398
$KCRHGCL_i$	0.744	0.860	0.930	0.560	0.597	0.615	0.521
$KCRHGCL$	0.751	0.866	0.934	0.566	0.603	0.621	0.526

5.5. Parameter Analysis

In this section, we present the results of further conducted experiments to show the effects of the three following hyper-parameters: (1) the embedding dimension size d; (2) the regularization weights μ in Equation (11); (3) the layer number of graph-based message propagation l. The experimental results are represented in Table 6 and Figures 3 and 4.

Table 6. The impact of the layer number of graph-based message propagation l, the best scores are marked in bold.

Layers	HR@5	HR@10	HR@20	NDCG@5	NDCG@10	NDCG@20
1	0.7514	0.8663	**0.9345**	**0.5658**	**0.6033**	**0.6207**
2	**0.7515**	**0.8676**	0.9337	0.5646	0.6025	0.6195
3	0.7511	0.8665	0.9326	0.5651	0.6028	0.6198

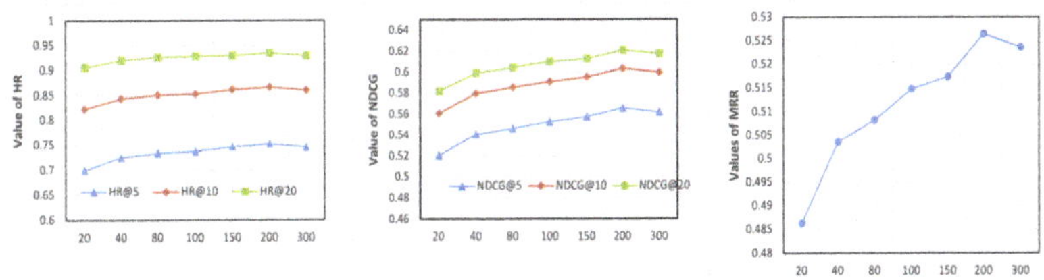

Figure 3. The results of the embedding dimension size d.

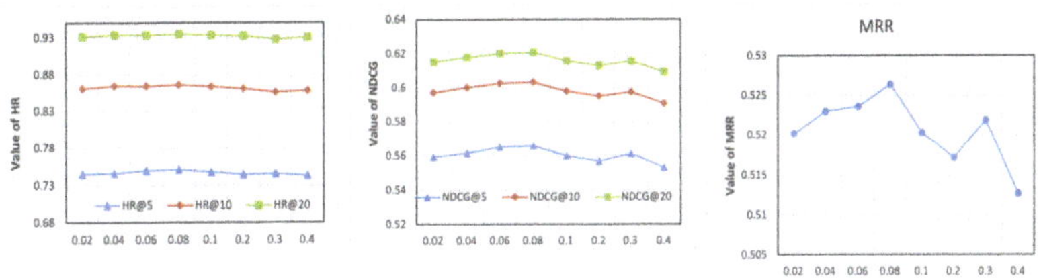

Figure 4. The results of the regularization weights μ.

The embedding dimension size d plays an important role in the method's performance. It is important to note that increasing the embedding dimension size d can also result in increased computational complexity and memory usage. Therefore, the choice of d should be balanced between performance and efficiency. It was observed that *HR*@5, *HR*@10, and *HR*@20 all improve as dimension d increases, but the rate of improvement gradually slows down. At lower dimensions (such as $d = 20$), HR increases quickly, whereas at higher dimensions (such as $d >= 200$), the improvement in HR tends to plateau or even show no change. This indicates that, beyond a certain dimension, increasing the dimension has a limited effect on improving HR, and it may even lead to model overfitting. *NDCG*@5, *NDCG*@10, *NDCG*@20, and *MRR* follow the same trend, indicating that lower dimensions may not fully capture the underlying structure of the data. Increasing the dimensions appropriately can improve the model performance, but excessively high dimensions may increase the model's complexity, leading to a slowdown in the performance improvement.

The regularization weights μ are introduced to balance the main and auxiliary losses, and we experimented with its value within the range of $[0.02, 0.04, 0.06, 0.08, 0.1, 0.2, 0.3, 0.4]$. The results are reported in Figure 3. Our findings show that an appropriate μ value can lead to better performance for KCRHGCL. Specifically, the best performance was achieved with $\mu = 0.08$.

The layer number of graph-based message propagation l was searched from 1 to 3 in GCNs. The results in Table 6 show that the methods achieve better performance with one or two layers for all the metrics. It is possible that lower layers can capture sufficient features, while more layers can lead to over-smoothing and introduce noise to the feature representation.

5.6. Convergence Analysis

The convergence rate analysis presented in Figure 5 demonstrates that the proposed method achieves a stable state after nine epochs of training. This suggests that the model has converged to a reliable solution within a relatively small number of epochs. In comparison, the MOOCIR model reaches a stable state after 15 epochs, indicating a slower convergence rate. Overall, the results suggest that the proposed method has a more robust convergence rate than the MOOCIR model.

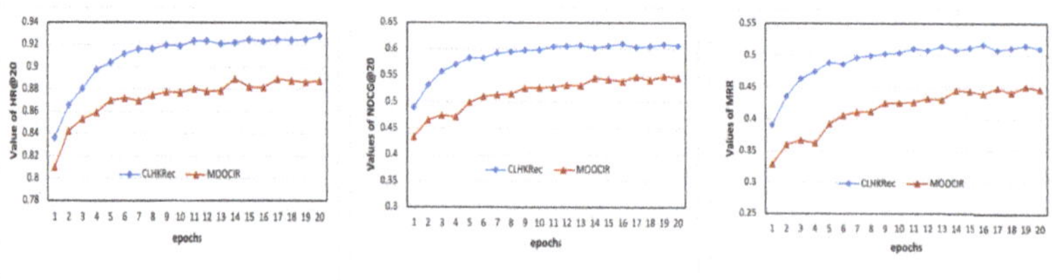

Figure 5. Convergence analysis for KCRHGCL.

5.7. Experimental Results

Extensive experiments were organized on MOOCCube to verify the effectiveness of the KCRHGCL method. Compared to other state-of-the-art methods, KCRHGCL showed improvements of 6.68%, 8.85%, and 8.68% in $HR@5$, $NDCG@5$, and MRR, respectively, over the suboptimal methods. The impact of different meta-path choices on performance was analyzed, revealing that, due to the course-centric organization of existing MOOCs, the $L_1 - C - L_2$ meta-path yielded better results. Ablation experiments validated the necessity of using heterogeneous graph-contrastive learning to enhance learner representations by exploring the similarity of structural neighbors in different dimensions, as well as the importance of negative sampling and contrastive loss functions in distinguishing structural differences. The study examined the impact of hyperparameters on KCRHGCL, identifying the optimal hyperparameters. A comparison and analysis of the convergence characteristics of KCRHGCL and MOOCIR showed that KCRHGCL converges faster.

6. Conclusions

In this paper, a muti-task knowledge-concept recommendation method called Contrastive Learning from Heterogeneous Information Networks has been proposed. The goal of KCRHGCL is to capture the group structural characteristics of learners' preferences as much as possible. On the one hand, the similarity within the structure of learner groups was further explored to enhance learner representations via heterogeneous graph-contrastive learning; on the other hand, hard negative sampling techniques and contrastive loss functions were used to guide the differentiation of learners between different group structures, thereby improving the recommendation effectiveness. Extensive experiments were organized on MOOCCube to verify the effectiveness of the KCRHGCL method. Compared to other state-of-the-art methods, KCRHGCL showed improvements of 6.68%, 8.85%, and 8.68% in HR@5, NDCG@5, and MRR, respectively. The performance of KCRHGCL is indeed impressive. However, it is worth noting that learners' study interests may change over time, whether in the short term or the long term. Therefore, it would be intriguing to explore methods that can capture such shifts in knowledge-concept recommendations in future research.

Author Contributions: Methodology, Y.L.; validation, W.W.; resources and Writing—original draft, L.W.; writing—review and editing, Y.Z. All authors have read and agreed to the published version of the manuscript.

Funding: This research was funded by the Pedagogy Program "The 13th Five Year Plan" of the National Social Science Foundation in 2019, grant No. BBA190021.

Data Availability Statement: The original contributions presented in the study are included in the article, further inquiries can be directed to the corresponding author.

Conflicts of Interest: The authors declare no conflicts of interest. The funders had no role in the design of the study, in the collection, analyses, or interpretation of data, in the writing of the manuscript, or in the decision to publish the results.

References

1. Adeniyi, I.S.; Al Hamad, N.M.; Adewusi, O.E.; Unachukwu, C.C.; Osawaru, B.; Chilson, O.U.; Omolawal, S.A.; Aliu, A.O.; David, I.O. Reviewing online learning effectiveness during the COVID-19 pandemic: A global perspective. *Int. J. Sci. Res. Arch.* **2024**, *11*, 1676–1685. [CrossRef]
2. Xia, D.; Zhang, Y.; Qiu, Y.; Zhang, S.; Tian, Y.; Zhao, X. Research on the Dynamic Evolution Law of Online Knowledge Sharing Under Trust. *Int. J. Chang. Educ.* **2024**, *1*, 32–40. [CrossRef]
3. Pan, L.; Wang, X.; Li, C.; Li, J.; Tang, J. Course concept extraction in moocs via embedding-based graph propagation. In Proceedings of the Eighth International Joint Conference on Natural Language Processing (Volume 1: Long Papers), Taipei, Taiwan, 27 November–1 December 2017; pp. 875–884.
4. Gong, J.; Wang, S.; Wang, J.; Feng, W.; Peng, H.; Tang, J.; Yu, P.S. Attentional graph convolutional networks for knowledge concept recommendation in moocs in a heterogeneous view. In Proceedings of the 43rd International ACM SIGIR Conference on Research and Development in Information Retrieval, Virtual, 25–30 July 2020; pp. 79–88.
5. Yu, J.; Luo, G.; Xiao, T.; Zhong, Q.; Wang, Y.; Feng, W.; Luo, J.; Wang, C.; Hou, L.; Li, J.; et al. MOOCCube: A large-scale data repository for NLP applications in MOOCs. In Proceedings of the 58th Annual Meeting of the Association for Computational Linguistics, Online, 5–10 July 2020; pp. 3135–3142.
6. Tang, C.L.; Liao, J.; Wang, H.C.; Sung, C.Y.; Lin, W.C. Conceptguide: Supporting online video learning with concept map-based recommendation of learning path. *Proc. Web Conf.* **2021**, *2021*, 2757–2768.
7. Zhang, J.; Hao, B.; Chen, B.; Li, C.; Chen, H.; Sun, J. Hierarchical reinforcement learning for course recommendation in MOOCs. In Proceedings of the AAAI Conference on Artificial Intelligence, Honolulu, HI, USA, 27 January–1 February 2019; Volume 33, pp. 435–442.
8. Al-Twijri, M.I.; Luna, J.M.; Herrera, F.; Ventura, S. Course Recommendation based on Sequences: An Evolutionary Search of Emerging Sequential Patterns. *Cogn. Comput.* **2022**, *14*, 1474–1495. [CrossRef]
9. Piao, G. Recommending Knowledge Concepts on MOOC Platforms with Meta-Path-Based Representation Learning. In *International Educational Data Mining Society, Proceedings of the International Conference on Educational Data Mining (EDM), Online, 29 June–2 July 2021*; International Educational Data Mining Society: Worcester MA, USA, 2021.
10. Gong, J.; Wan, Y.; Liu, Y.; Li, X.; Zhao, Y.; Wang, C.; Li, Q.; Feng, W.; Tang, J. Reinforced MOOCs Concept Recommendation in Heterogeneous Information Networks. *arXiv* **2022**, arXiv:2203.11011.
11. Lin, Y.; Lin, F.; Yang, L.; Zeng, W.; Liu, Y.; Wu, P. Context-aware reinforcement learning for course recommendation. *Appl. Soft Comput.* **2022**, *125*, 109189. [CrossRef]
12. Wang, X.; Ma, W.; Guo, L.; Jiang, H.; Liu, F.; Xu, C. HGNN: Hyperedge-based graph neural network for MOOC Course Recommendation. *Inf. Process. Manag.* **2022**, *59*, 102938. [CrossRef]
13. Jing, X.; Tang, J. Guess you like: Course recommendation in MOOCs. In Proceedings of the International Conference on Web Intelligence, Leipzig, Germany, 23–26 August 2017; pp. 783–789.
14. Jung, H.; Jang, Y.; Kim, S.; Kim, H. KPCR: Knowledge graph enhanced personalized course recommendation. In Proceedings of the AI 2021: Advances in Artificial Intelligence: 34th Australasian Joint Conference, AI 2021, Sydney, Australia, 2–4 February 2022; Springer: Berlin/Heidelberg, Germany, 2022; pp. 739–750.
15. Liu, X.; Zhang, F.; Hou, Z.; Mian, L.; Wang, Z.; Zhang, J.; Tang, J. Self-supervised learning: Generative or contrastive. *IEEE Trans. Knowl. Data Eng.* **2021**, *35*, 857–876. [CrossRef]
16. Wu, J.; Wang, X.; Feng, F.; He, X.; Chen, L.; Lian, J.; Xie, X. Self-supervised graph learning for recommendation. In Proceedings of the 44th International ACM SIGIR Conference on Research and Development in Information Retrieval, Virtual, 11–15 July 2021; pp. 726–735.
17. Jing, M.; Zhu, Y.; Zang, T.; Wang, K. Contrastive self-supervised learning in recommender systems: A survey. *ACM Trans. Inf. Syst.* **2023**, *42*, 1–39. [CrossRef]
18. Xie, X.; Sun, F.; Liu, Z.; Wu, S.; Gao, J.; Ding, B.; Cui, B. Contrastive learning for sequential recommendation. *arXiv* **2020**, arXiv:2010.14395.
19. Yang, Y.; Huang, C.; Xia, L.; Li, C. Knowledge graph contrastive learning for recommendation. In Proceedings of the 45th International ACM SIGIR Conference on Research and Development in Information Retrieval, Madrid, Spain, 11–15 July 2022; pp. 1434–1443.
20. Cai, X.; Huang, C.; Xia, L.; Ren, X. LightGCL: Simple yet effective graph contrastive learning for recommendation. *arXiv* **2023**, arXiv:2302.08191.
21. Lin, Z.; Tian, C.; Hou, Y.; Zhao, W.X. Improving Graph Collaborative Filtering with Neighborhood-enriched Contrastive Learning. In Proceedings of the ACM Web Conference 2022, Lyon, France, 25–29 April 2022; pp. 2320–2329.

22. Chen, M.; Huang, C.; Xia, L.; Wei, W.; Xu, Y.; Luo, R. Heterogeneous graph contrastive learning for recommendation. In Proceedings of the Sixteenth ACM International Conference on Web Search and Data Mining, Singapore, 27 February–3 March 2023; pp. 544–552.
23. Zheng, X.; Wu, R.; Han, Z.; Chen, C.; Chen, L.; Han, B. Heterogeneous information crossing on graphs for session-based recommender systems. *ACM Trans. Web* **2024**, *18*, 1–24. [CrossRef]
24. Sun, Y.; Han, J.; Yan, X.; Yu, P.S.; Wu, T. Pathsim: Meta path-based top-k similarity search in heterogeneous information networks. *Proc. VLDB Endow.* **2011**, *4*, 992–1003. [CrossRef]
25. Wu, C.; Wu, F.; Huang, Y. Rethinking infonce: How many negative samples do you need? *arXiv* **2021**, arXiv:2105.13003.
26. Oord, A.v.d.; Li, Y.; Vinyals, O. Representation learning with contrastive predictive coding. *arXiv* **2018**, arXiv:1807.03748.
27. Cremonesi, P.; Koren, Y.; Turrin, R. Performance of recommender algorithms on top-n recommendation tasks. In Proceedings of the Fourth ACM Conference on Recommender Systems, Barcelona, Spain, 26–30 September 2010; pp. 39–46.
28. Wang, Y.; Wang, L.; Li, Y.; He, D.; Chen, W.; Liu, T. A theoretical analysis of normalized discounted cumulative gain (NDCG) ranking measures. In Proceedings of the 26th Annual Conference on Learning Theory (COLT 2013), Princeton, NJ, USA, 12–14 June 2013; Citeseer: Camp Hill, PA, USA, 2023.
29. Lu, X.; Wu, J.; Yuan, J. Optimizing Reciprocal Rank with Bayesian Average for improved Next Item Recommendation. In Proceedings of the 46th International ACM SIGIR Conference on Research and Development in Information Retrieval, Taipei, Taiwan, 23–27 July 2023; pp. 2236–2240.
30. Kabbur, S.; Ning, X.; Karypis, G. Fism: Factored item similarity models for top-n recommender systems. In Proceedings of the 19th ACM SIGKDD International Conference on Knowledge Discovery and Data Mining, Chicago, IL, USA, 11–14 August 2013; pp. 659–667.
31. He, X.; He, Z.; Song, J.; Liu, Z.; Jiang, Y.G.; Chua, T.S. Nais: Neural attentive item similarity model for recommendation. *IEEE Trans. Knowl. Data Eng.* **2018**, *30*, 2354–2366. [CrossRef]
32. Dong, Y.; Chawla, N.V.; Swami, A. metapath2vec: Scalable representation learning for heterogeneous networks. In Proceedings of the 23rd ACM SIGKDD International Conference on Knowledge Discovery and Data Mining, Halifax, NS, Canada, 13–17 August 2017; pp. 135–144.
33. Kingma, D.P. A method for stochastic optimization. In Proceedings of the 3rd International Conference on Learning Representations, ICLR, San Diego, CA, USA, 7–9 May 2015.

mathematics

Article

DABC: A Named Entity Recognition Method Incorporating Attention Mechanisms

Fangling Leng, Fan Li *, Yubin Bao, Tiancheng Zhang and Ge Yu

School of Computer Science and Engineering, Northeastern University, Shenyang 110169, China; lengfangling@mail.neu.edu.cn (F.L.); baoyb@mail.neu.edu.cn (Y.B.); tczhang@mail.neu.edu.cn (T.Z.); yuge@mail.neu.edu.cn (G.Y.)
* Correspondence: 2301892@stu.neu.edu.cn

Abstract: Regarding the existing models for feature extraction of complex similar entities, there are problems in the utilization of relative position information and the ability of key feature extraction. The distinctiveness of Chinese named entity recognition compared to English lies in the absence of space delimiters, significant polysemy and homonymy of characters, diverse and common names, and a greater reliance on complex contextual and linguistic structures. An entity recognition method based on DeBERTa-Attention-BiLSTM-CRF (DABC) is proposed. Firstly, the feature extraction capability of the DeBERTa model is utilized to extract the data features; then, the attention mechanism is introduced to further enhance the extracted features; finally, BiLSTM is utilized to further capture the long-distance dependencies in the text and obtain the predicted sequences through the CRF layer, and then the entities in the text are identified. The proposed model is applied to the dataset for validation. The experiments show that the precision (P) of the proposed DABC model on the dataset reaches 88.167%, the recall (R) reaches 83.121% , and the F1 value reaches 85.024%. Compared with other models, the F1 value improves by 3∼5%, and the superiority of the model is verified. In the future, it can be extended and applied to recognize complex entities in more fields.

Keywords: DeBERTa; multi-attention mechanism; BiLSTM-CRF; named entity recognition

MSC: 68T50

1. Introduction

Named entity recognition (NER) is a basic task of natural language processing, and is also one of the sub-tasks of knowledge extraction. The main objective is to identify and extract specific categories of entities, such as people's names, places, aliases, etc., or domain-specific vocabulary from a large amount of text [1]. Chinese named entity recognition plays an important role in natural language processing technology as a component of information extraction, information retrieval, knowledge mapping, machine translation, and question answering systems [2].

In the development process of named entity recognition, people firstly mainly relied on lexicons and rule-based methods. These methods depended on hand-constructed rule templates by linguists, making them prone to errors and unable to be transplanted between different domains. Consequently, this approach could only handle simple text data but could not address complex unstructured data. Subsequently, with the advancement of machine learning, neural networks like word2vec [3] began to be applied in entity recognition. This model efficiently represents words into vector form based on a given corpus with an optimized training model, providing a new tool for applied research in natural language processing. For instance, Anil Sharma et al. [4] applied such methods for the ontology-based semantic retrieval of documents, enhancing the similarity index and accuracy of query results. With the advent of deep learning methods, pretrained models like BERT have been employed in named entity recognition. For instance, Zhao Xintong et al. [5] applied the BERT model in materials science named entity recognition, achieving promising results on the dataset. Gülsüm Kayabaşi Koru et al. [6] detected Turkish fake news from tweets using the BERT model, obtaining an precision (P) of 94% on the corpus set. However, BERT-based named entity recognition methods often neglect the relative positional information between text messages, exhibit insufficiently fine-grained feature extraction, and adopt a static masking strategy during masking. With the widespread application of the BERT model, the Facebook team led by Liu et al. [7] improved upon it by proposing the RoBERTa model. This model utilizes a larger training dataset compared to BERT and changes the masking strategy from static to dynamic, thereby enhancing performance. The RoBERTa model achieved an F1 value of 94.08% on the Chinese electronic medical record recognition domain dataset, surpassing previous models. Yin [8] et al. demonstrated that the NER model trained by their proposed method achieved an F1 value of 93.56% on actual winter sports textual news. Similarly, Li et al. [9] applied the RoBERTa model to predict nanoantibody paracrine sites, achieving excellent performance. Liang et al. [1] utilized the RoBERTa model for crop pest and disease name recognition, achieving precision, recall, and F1 values of 89.23%, 90.90%, and 90.04%, respectively. However, the RoBERTa model still underutilizes positional information of text data. Following this, He et al. [10] from the Microsoft team further improved BERT and introduced the DeBERTa model. Compared to BERT and RoBERTa, DeBERTa focuses on the impact of the relative position of text data on model performance. Yuna Jeong et al. [2] applied the DeBERTa model to information extraction from scientific and technical documents, demonstrating its superior performance in entity recognition tasks.

In previous work, Luo et al. [11] achieved better performance using the BiLSTM-CRF model, with F1 values of 91.14% and 92.57% for named entity recognition in the field of chemistry. Addressing the limitation of global probabilistic transfer modeling when using the BERT model alone for named entity recognition, Fábio Souza et al. [12] replaced the Softmax function with a CRF layer, resulting in a 1% to 4% improvement in the corpus of Portuguese named entity recognition. Building upon this, Dai et al. [13] utilized the BERT-BiLSTM-CRF model for named entity recognition of Chinese e-health records, achieving an F1 value of approximately 75%, which outperformed all other models during testing. Zhang et al. [14] further combined the RoBERTa-BiLSTM-CRF model for tourist attraction name extraction, outperforming other models on the dataset. Riyanto et al. [15] employed the BERT-BiLSTM-CRF model, achieving positive results on CLUENER2020. Arslan [16] utilized the BiLSTM-CRF model with FastText embeddings, achieving an F1 score value of 57.40%, a precision value of 55.78%, and a recall value of 59.12% in a Turkish e-commerce dataset. Chen et al. [17] applied the BERT-Bilstm-Selfatt-CRF model to public security department case records, holding significant implications for further utilization of this information. Jeong [18] utilized transfer learning to design an end-to-end information extraction framework based on BERT. Shibata et al. [19] evaluated the performance of named entity recognition (NER) and relation extraction (RE) using machine learning methods, revealing maximum micro-averaged F1 scores of 0.912 and 0.759 for NER and RE, respectively. Cai et al. [20] proposed a nested NER model based on span boundary perception, while Cai et al. [21] proposed an NER model that combines BERT, BiLSTM, and CRF based on adversarial training (ATBBC), achieving an F1 score of 85.39% on the test dataset. Cui et al. [22] designed a method based on prompt learning to reformulate the entity recognition task into a language inference-based task. Fan et al. [23] created a specialized training corpus and introduced a novel few-shot NER framework, yielding precision, recall, and F1 of 91.08%, 88.96%, and 90.00%, respectively. Farhan et al. [24] proposed a new NER solution by leveraging state-of-the-art NLP tools, while Goyal et al. [25] proposed a deep learning-based NER system using hybrid embedding, which is a combination of FastText and bidirectional LSTM-based character embedding. Mao et al. [26] proposed a simple yet effective span-level tagging scheme for discontinuous NER. Wang et al. [27] proposed a multi-modal feature fusing module based on the RoBERTa network, achieving state-of-the-art performance in recall and F1 score on three public datasets. Wu et al. [28] proposed an improved bidirectional gated recurrent unit neural network (BIGRU) method. Xu et al. [29] introduced a novel NER methodology tailored for the Chinese cybersecurity corpus, termed CSBERT-IDCNN-BiLSTM-CRF, surpassing existing Chinese NER frameworks with an F1 score of 87.30% and a precision rate of 85.89%. Cao et al. [30] introduced a new pretraining scheme that uses large-scale online question–answer pairs to enhance the model capacity on online biomedical text. Chu et al. [31] developed a named entity recognition model called Multi-Feature Fusion Transformer (MFT), which combines features such as words and radicals to enhance the semantic information of the sentences. Hu et al. [32] highlighted the potential of large language models, specifically GPT-3.5 and GPT-4, in processing complex clinical data and extracting meaningful information with minimal training data. Li et al. [33] proposed the Semantic Embedding with Chinese Character Structural Features (SECCSF) method to improve the accuracy of segmentation boundary detection and entity category determination in CNER. Mengliev [34] developed two algorithms that identify named entities in Uzbek language texts using a dictionary. Qiu et al. [35] established standards and principles governing engineering geology reports, achieving an impressive F1 value of 79.60% on the constructed datasets. Wang et al. [36] combined discourse topic and attention mechanism and proposed the Attention-based SoftLexicon with TF-IDF (ASLT) for agricultural diseases and pests entity recognition, achieving favorable recognition on CCNEDP, with the recognition accuracy, the recall rate, and the value of F1 of 93.57, 92.79, and 93.18%. Abdelghani Dahou et al. [37] proposed a framework that harnesses the potential of an MTL approach and a state-of-the-art pre-trained transformer-based model, enabling the extraction of comprehensive contextual features from Arabic social media posts. The framework attained an accuracy rate of 87% and 69% for binary and multi-classification, respectively. Nasir Ayub et al. [38] presented a novel approach called the Ensemble of DenseNet based on Aquila Optimizer (EDAO); the model achieved accuracy rates of 95%, 97%, and 96%, respectively, with DenseNet-AO. However, the above models do not address the problem of further refinement of features.

As mentioned above, this paper proposes a new named entity recognition model, DABC, with the aim of enhancing accuracy and robustness in Chinese entity recognition. Firstly, considering the ineffective utilization of text data location information in the BERT-BiLSTM-CRF model, the DeBERTa module is introduced to address this deficiency and improve the utilization of location information. Subsequently, to address the issue of insufficient refinement in key feature extraction within the DeBERTa-BiLSTM-CRF model, a multi-attention mechanism is incorporated to enhance key feature extraction refinement. The DABC model introduced in this paper exhibits enhanced entity recognition capabilities and improved model robustness.

However, existing models still face challenges in performing named entity recognition tasks:

1. The utilization of relative position information in text for feature extraction remains flawed.
2. Insufficient attention is given to key features during entity feature extraction.

Therefore, further improvements are necessary for the model.

2. The BERT-BiLSTM-CRF Model

Named entity recognition, as a fundamental task in natural language processing, has been the focus of this research. As a named entity recognition model that has been widely recognized, the BERT-BiLSTM-CRF model has been applied in named entity recognition work in several fields with good results. Its basic framework is shown in Figure 1.

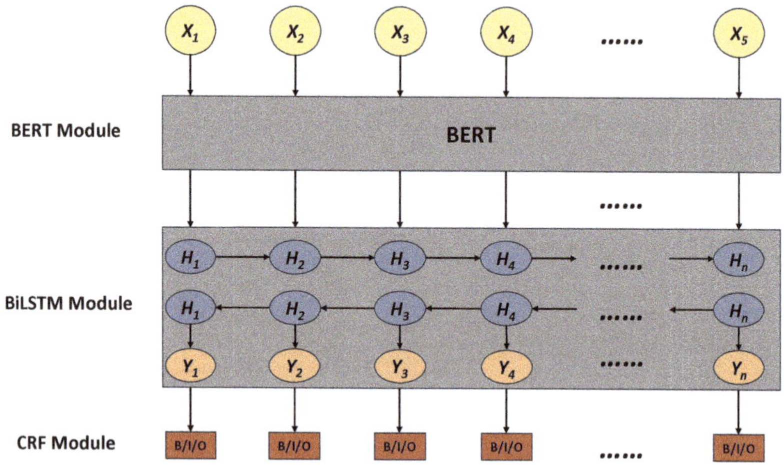

Figure 1. BERT-BiLSTM-CRF model framework.

Firstly, word vectors based on contextual information are generated through preprocessing with the BERT model. Secondly, the trained word vectors are fed into the BiLSTM-CRF model for further training [16]. BERT is a transformer-based pretrained language model that extracts contextual representations of text. It learns rich linguistic knowledge through unsupervised pretraining on large-scale corpora and can be fine-tuned for downstream tasks [13]. BiLSTM is a recurrent neural network with hidden states in both forward and backward directions, capturing sentence structure and dependencies in text. It effectively models contextual information and better understands the relationship between labels at the current location and the preceding and following text through bidirectional computation [11]. CRF is a conditional random field for labeling sequences, considering label interactions and using a global inference algorithm to optimize labeling results for entire sequences. The CRF model captures contextual constraints and transition patterns between labels in sequence labeling tasks [12].

The BERT-BiLSTM-CRF model is a mature and widely recognized named entity recognition model. It was selected because its advantage lies in eliminating the need for pretraining word vectors and inputting sequences directly into BERT, which automatically extracts rich features. However, the BERT-BiLSTM-CRF model still has certain shortcomings:

(1) The BERT model does not make further use of the location information of text data when extracting features.

(2) The features extracted by the BERT model are not prominent and refined enough.

3. DABC Model

In this paper, we propose a new entity recognition model called DABC, which aims to enhance the accuracy and robustness of Chinese entity recognition. The model is based on BERT-BiLSTM-CRF, with the introduction of the DeBERTa model. Addressing the issue of insufficient refinement in the BERT model's feature extraction process, a multi-attention mechanism is incorporated into the DeBERTa-BiLSTM-CRF model to enhance the model's focus on key information. The proposed model framework is depicted in Figure 2.

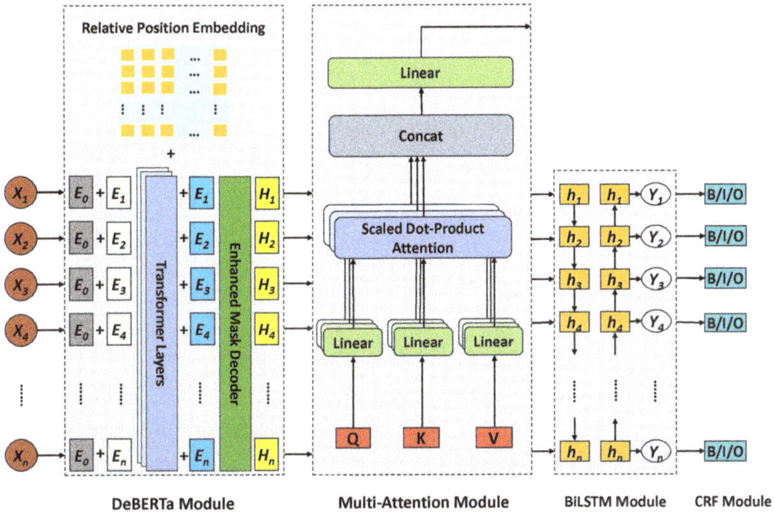

Figure 2. DABC model framework.

Firstly, the feature extraction capability of the DeBERTa model is utilized to extract the data features. Then, the attention mechanism is introduced to further enhance the extracted features. Finally, BiLSTM is employed to capture the long-distance dependencies in the text and obtain the predicted sequences through the CRF layer, thus identifying the entities in the text.

3.1. DeBERTa Module

As a further improvement of the BERT model by the Microsoft team led by He et al. [10], the DeBERTa model enhances the model's ability to focus on the relative position of text data as information during feature extraction by introducing a decoupled attention mechanism. Unlike BERT, where each word in the input layer is represented by the sum of its word (content) embedding and positional embedding, each word in DeBERTa is represented by two vectors encoding its content and position, respectively. The attention weights between words are computed using matrices based on their content and relative position. This is because attention between words depends not only on their textual content but also on their relative positions. The attention calculation is represented as in Equation (1):

$$\begin{aligned} A_{ij} &= \left\{H_i, P_{i|j}\right\} \times \left\{H_j, P_{j|i}\right\}^T \\ &= H_i H_j^T + H_i P_{j|i}^T + P_{i|j} H_j^T + P_{i|j} P_{j|i}^T \end{aligned} \tag{1}$$

where $A_{i,j}$ represents the calculated weights, and H and P represent the content information and position information, respectively. In the equation, i and j are tokens, and H_i and $P_{i|j}$ represent content and position. The whole formula can be divided into four parts: content–content (content-to-content), content–position (content-to-position), position–content (position-to-content), and position–position (position-to-position). Taking a single header as an example, the standard self-attention is given in Equations (2)–(6) below:

$$Q = HW_q \tag{2}$$

$$K = HW_k \tag{3}$$

$$V = HW_v \tag{4}$$

$$A = \frac{QK^T}{\sqrt{d}} \tag{5}$$

$$H_o = softmax(A)V \tag{6}$$

where $H \in R^{N \times d}$ denotes the input hidden vector, $H_o \in R^{N \times d}$ denotes the output of self-attention, $W_q, W_k, W_v \in R^{d \times d}$ denotes the corresponding projection matrix, $A \in R^{N \times N}$ is the attention matrix, N is the length of the input sequence, and d is the dimensionality of the hidden state. The decoupled attention formulation with the addition of relative position information becomes the following Equations (7)–(13):

$$Q_c = HW_{q.c} \tag{7}$$

$$K_c = HW_{k,c} \tag{8}$$

$$V_c = HW_{v,c} \tag{9}$$

$$Q_r = PW_{q,r} \tag{10}$$

$$K_r = PW_{k,r} \tag{11}$$

$$\tilde{A}_{i,j} = Q_i^c K_j^{cT} + Q_i^c {K_{\delta(j,i)}^r}^T + K_j^c {Q_{\delta(j,i)}^r}^T \tag{12}$$

$$Ho = softmax(\frac{\tilde{A}}{\sqrt{3d}})V_c \tag{13}$$

where Q_c, K_c, and V_c are the projected content vectors generated using the projection matrices $W_{q,c}$, $W_{k,c}$, and $W_{v,c} \in R^{d \times d}$, respectively; $P \in R^{2k \times d}$ denotes the relative positional embedding vector shared across all layers (i.e., it remains unchanged during forward propagation); and Q_r and K_r are the projected relative position vectors generated using the projection matrices $W_{q,r}$, and $W_{k,r} \in R^{d \times d}$, respectively. $\tilde{A}_{i,j}$ are elements in the attention matrix $\tilde{A}$ denoting the attention between token i to token j, Q_i^c denotes the ith row of Q_c, K_c^j denotes the j_{th} row of K_c, $K_{\delta(i,j)}^r$ denotes the $\delta(i,j)^{th}$ row of K_r, and $Q_{\delta(j,i)}^r$ denotes the $\delta(j,i)^{th}$ row. It should be noted that $\delta(j,i)$ is used here instead of $\delta(i,j)$; this is because given the position, the position–content calculates the attention weight of the content at position j in the key with respect to position i in the query, and thus the relative distance is $\delta(j,i)$. The position–content term is computed as $K_j^c Q_{\delta(j,i)}^r$. The content–position term is computed similarly. $\tilde{A}$ is divided by a scaling factor to stabilize the training process of the model.

3.2. Multi-Attention Mechanisms

The concept of attention was first introduced by Dzmitry Bahdanau et al. [39]. Subsequently, the paper "Attention Is All You Need" by Ashish Vaswani et al. [40] elevated the attention mechanism to a new level. In the standard attention mechanism, a weighted context vector is computed to represent the information in the input sequence. In contrast, in multi-head attention, multiple sets of attention weights are used, each of which learns different information and produces a context vector. Finally, these context vectors are concatenated together, followed by a linear transformation to obtain the final output. The framework is illustrated in Figure 3.

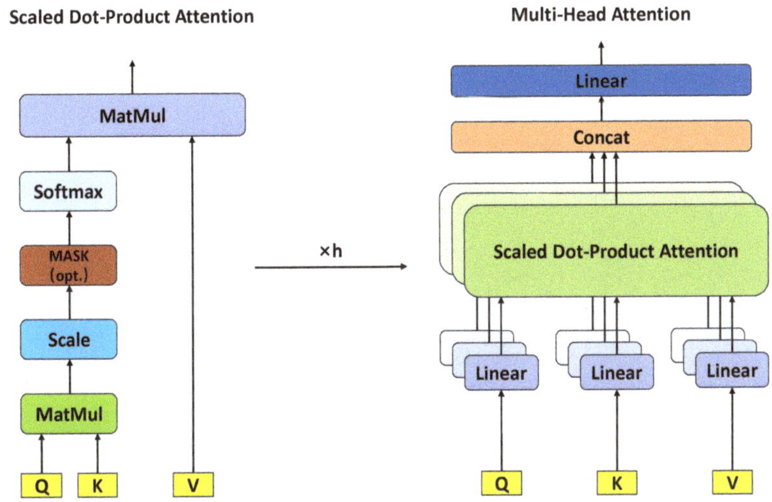

Figure 3. Multi-attention framework.

Attention need linear transformation.The attention calculation process for the input matrix X (which includes the query Q, key K, and value V) is as Equations (14)–(16):

$$Q = XW_Q \tag{14}$$

$$K = XW_K \tag{15}$$

$$V = XW_V \tag{16}$$

where W_Q, W_K, and W_V are the learnable parameter matrices.

The advantages of the multi-attention mechanism are as follows:

1. The features of input data can be learned from multiple dimensions, which improves the model's ability to capture information.

2. Each head can perform computation independently, which is suitable for parallel processing and improves computational efficiency.

3. The complexity and performance of the model can be flexibly controlled by adjusting the number and dimension of the heads. The mathematical formula is given in Equation (17) below:

$$\begin{gathered} MultiHead(Q,K,V) = Concat(head_1, ..., head_k)W^o \\ head_i = Attention(QW_i^Q, KW_i^K, VW_i^V) = softmax(\frac{QW_{Q_i}(KW_{K_i})^T}{\sqrt{d_k}})VW_{V_i} \end{gathered} \tag{17}$$

Multi-head attention takes the process of Scaled Dot-Product Attention and performs it h times, outputting its sum.

4. Experimentation and Analysis

4.1. Experimental Datasets and Evaluation Methods

The datasets used in this experiment are the Liaoning island dataset and Resume dataset. The Liaoning island dataset is mainly derived from the "China Island Journal (Liaoning Volume)". In order to make the dataset larger in order of magnitude, this paper uses the network to crawl public information and a small amount of the People's Daily dataset for a supplement and expansion. This is so that the information in it is more complex and varied, so as to construct a large dataset. Using the "BIO" labeling method,

"LOC" presents location, "DOM" presents topography and landscapes, and "TOZ" presents soil and tree. For example, "厦 B-LOC" and "门 I-LOC" represent the cities of China and "岩 B-DOM", "壁 I-DOM", "陡 I-DOM", and "峭 I-DOM" represent topography and landscapes. A total of seven tags are set up as follows: "B-LOC", "I-LOC", "B-DOM", and "I-DOM", "B-TOZ", "I-TOZ", and "O", where the number of LOC entity tags is 3143, there are 3129 DOM tags, and 2410 TOZ entity tags, as shown in Table 1.

Table 1. Labels dstribution of the Liaoning island dataset.

Labels	Count
LOC	3143
DOM	3129
TOZ	2410

The Liaoning island dataset training set, validation set, and test set are divided according to an 8:1:1 ratio. The dataset we used has 9517 sentences in which the training set is 7566 sentences, validation set is 856 sentences, and test set is 1095 sentences, as shown in Table 2.

Table 2. Dataset distribution of the Liaoning island dataset.

Labels	Count
Train	7566
Dev	856
Test	1095

Another dataset used is the Resume dataset, which is published by the Alibaba Tianchi Competition, and it uses the "BIO" labeling method. This dataset has 8 types of entity, including "CONT" representing nation, "EDU" representing education, "LOC" representing location, "NAME" representing name, "ORG" representing organization, "PRO" representing, "RACE" representing race, and "TITLE" representing title. For example, "汉 B-RACE" and "族 I-RACE" represent the race of interviewee and "本 B-EDU", "科 I-EDU", "学 I-EDU", and "历 I-EDU" represent whether this interviewee is holding a bachelor's degree. A total of seven tags are set up as follows: "B-CONT", "I-CONT", "B-EDU", "I-EDU", "B-LOC", "I-LOC", "B-ORG", "I-ORG", "B-NAME", "I-NAME","B-PRO", "I-PRO", "B-RACE", "I-RACE", "B-TITLE", "I-TITLE", and "O".

Additionally, the Resume dataset training set, validation set, and test set are divided according to a 8:1:1 ratio. The dataset we uses has 4761 sentences in which the training set is 3821 sentences, validation set is 463 sentences, and test set is 477 sentences, as shown in Table 3.

Table 3. Dataset distribution of the Resume dataset.

Labels	Count
Train	3821
Dev	463
Test	477

In measuring the effectiveness, this paper uses three metrics, precision (P), recall (R) and $F1$ value, which are calculated in the following Equations (18)–(20):

$$P = \frac{TP}{TP + FP} \times 100\% \tag{18}$$

$$R = \frac{TP}{TP + FN} \times 100\% \tag{19}$$

$$F1 = 2 \times \frac{P \times R}{P + R} \times 100\% \tag{20}$$

where TP represents the number of True Positives, FP represents the number of False Positives, and FN represents the number of False Negatives.

4.2. Experimental Environment

4.2.1. Environmental Setup

This experiment is built based on the Pytorch platform, and the specific training environment configuration is shown in Table 4.

Table 4. Experimental environment.

Name	Configuration
Operating System	Windows 11
CPU	Intel(R) Core(TM) i9-13900HX
GPU	NVIDIA GeForce RTX 4060
Python	3.9
Pytorch	1.13.0

4.2.2. Parameterization

In the process of performing model training, this paper chooses Adam in terms of optimizer; the learning rate is set to 1×10^{-5} , the length is set to 128, the dropout is set to 0.5 to prevent the model from overfitting, and the number of heads of the multi-head attention mechanism is set to 8. The specific parameter settings are shown in Table 5.

Table 5. Parameter configuration.

Parameter	Values
last state dim	768
batch size	16
learning rate	1×10^{-5}
dropout	0.5
num heads	8
attention dropout	0.3
num layers	3
epochs	5

4.3. Model Validation

When the model is trained, it can be observed that the training loss curve converges from high to low eventually and is close to 0, which proves the correctness of the model's training process; the loss curve is shown in Figure 4.

From the descending process of the loss curve, it can be seen that the model in this paper converges from about 1.4 to near 0.1 after iteration, which proves that the model has stability after many rounds of iteration, and the performance of the model in the training and validation sets is more stable compared to the time when the training was first started. The underperforming model is improved by constantly updating the model, so that we can finally obtain the model that is stable and has excellent performance.

It can be seen that the model proposed in this paper has strong robustness after many rounds of iterations. The variation of its scores is shown in Figure 5.

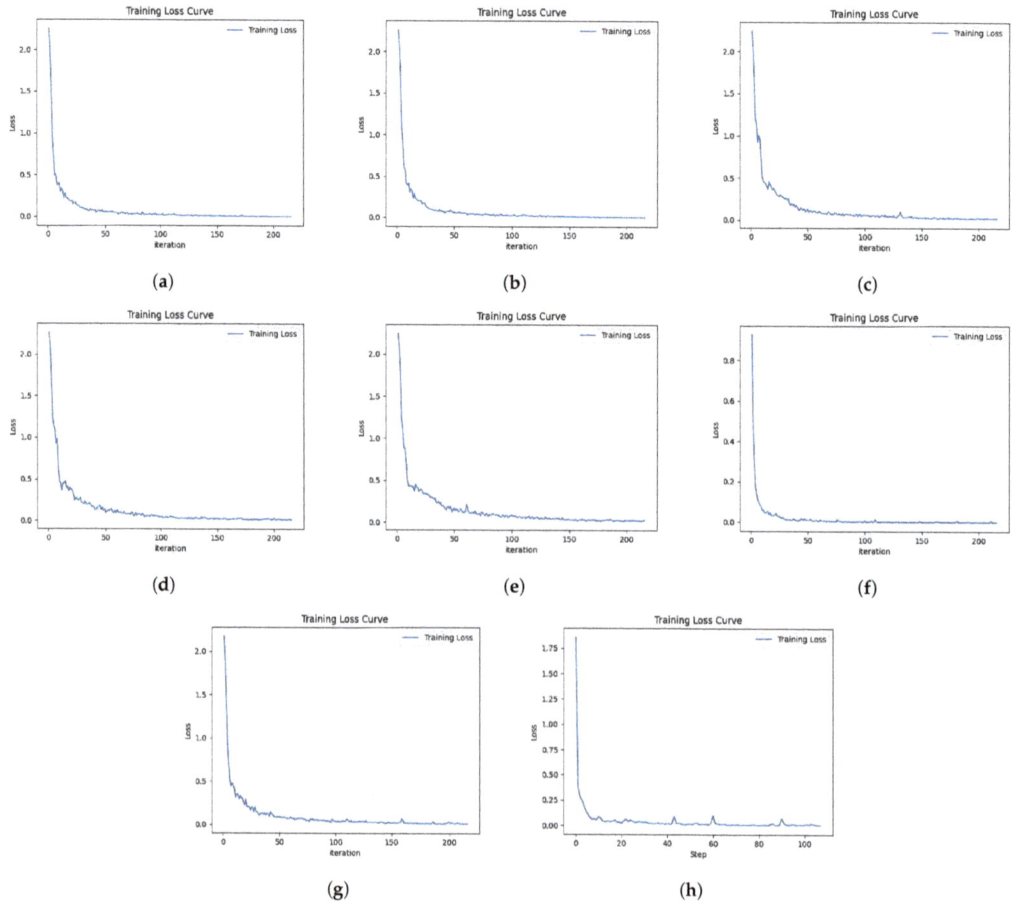

Figure 4. Training loss curves; (**a**) BERT-BiLSTM-CRF training loss curve; (**b**) DeBERTa-BiLSTM-CRF training loss curve; (**c**) BERT-Attention-BiLSTM-CRF training loss curve; (**d**) DeBERTa-BiLSTM-Attention-CRF training loss curve; (**e**) DebERTa-Self Attention-BiLSTM-CRF training loss curve; (**f**) DABC training loss curve; (**g**) RoBERTa-BiLSTM-CRF training loss curve; (**h**) XLNET training loss curve.

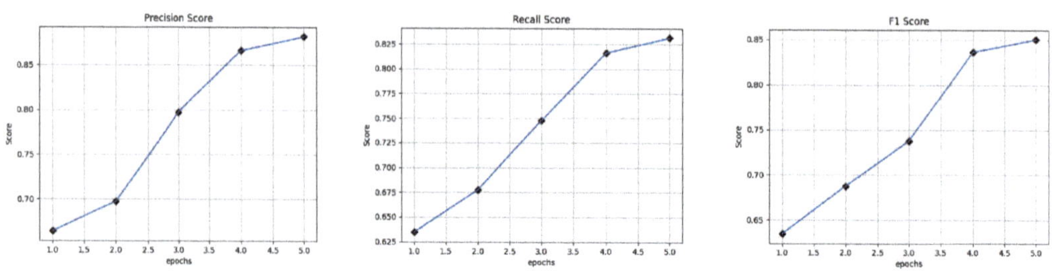

Figure 5. Variation in scores. (**a**) Variation in precision scores. (**b**) Variation in recall scores. (**c**) Variation in F1 scores.

From the data, it is proved that the difference between the performance of the model proposed in this paper on the training set and the test set is within the acceptable range, thus the effectiveness of the model proposed in this paper is verified.

From the figure, it can be seen that as the number of training rounds grows, the F1 value of the model on the validation set also grows, which indicates that the performance of the model becomes better with the increase in the number of rounds, which proves the error-free training of the model.

At the time of model validation, the performance on the training set and test set is shown in Table 5.

The data in Table 6 show the performance of the model on the training and test sets. In terms of precision (P), the model has a value of 88.055% on the training set and 88.167% on the test set, with a difference in value of 0.112%. In terms of recall (R), the model has a value of 83.110% on the training set and 83.121% on the test set, with a difference in value of 0.010%. In terms of F1 value, the model has a value of 85.013% on the training set and 85.024% on the test set with a difference of 0.011%.

Table 6. Model performance.

Dataset	P	R	F1
Train	88.055%	83.110%	85.013%
Test	88.167%	83.121%	85.024%

The experiments show that the DABC model sometimes treats island names and place names as similar. Such as "大三山岛 (Da Sanshan island)" and "大连 (Dalian city)"; that is why the DABC model can still be improved. In "TOZ" tags, the model sometimes treats soil and empty lots as similar, such as "苔藓 (moss)" and "无土壤和植被 (no soil and vegetation)". And in "DOM" tags, the model sometimes treats stone and landscapes as similar, such as "基岩 (bedrock)" and "岩壁陡峭 (cliff)".

In the Resume dataset, the model also mixes up similar entities. Because these category words in Chinese have a high similarity, the performance of model is influenced by this factor.

Due to the unpredictability and randomness of random errors, they cannot be completely eliminated. However, through repeated experiments, we have managed to control them within a reasonable range, thereby improving the accuracy of the results. The precision (P), recall (R), and F1 of every tag are shown in Tables 7 and 8.

Table 7. Model performance in Liaoning island dataset.

Labels	P	R	F1
LOC	88.055%	83.110%	85.013%
TOZ	88.167%	83.121%	85.024%
DOM	87.963%	82.982%	85.007%

Table 8. Model performance in Resume dataset.

Labels	P	R	F1
CONT	89.065%	88.110%	88.584%
LOC	90.307%	87.810%	89.040%
EDU	89.863%	86.992%	88.404%
NAME	91.322%	89.481%	90.392%
ORG	90.600%	88.162%	89.364%
PRO	91.052%	87.150%	89.058%
RACE	90.771%	88.283%	89.509%
TITLE	90.100%	88.611%	89.349%

4.4. Ablation Experiments

When module substitution and introduction are performed, the paper validates their effects respectively, and the results are shown in Table 9.

The results of the ablation experiments show that, compared with the baseline model, the introduction of the DeBERTa module improves the precision (P) from 80.919% to 85.016%, with an improvement of 4.097%; the recall (R) from 75.299% to 80.210%, with an improvement of 4.911%; and the F1 value from 77.102% to 81.854%, with an improvement of 4.752%. The model has a significant improvement in performance, thus proving the effectiveness of replacing the BERT module with the DeBERTa module in this paper.

After the introduction of the attention mechanism compared to the baseline model, the precision (P) decreases from 80.919% to 76.050%; the F1 value decreases from 77.102% to 76.449%; and the model performance decreases. After replacing the BERT module with the DeBERTa module, compared to the baseline model the precision (P) improves from 80.919% to 86.402%, with a 5.483% improvement; recall (R) from 75.299% to 80.300%, with a 5.001% improvement; and F1 value from 77.102% to 82.490%, with a 5.388% improvement. Compared with the baseline model, there is an increase in performance, and it can be concluded that the integration between the BERT module and the attention module is not as good as that between the DeBERTa module and the attention module in the Liaoning sea island dataset. It can be concluded that the fusion between the BERT module and the attention module in the Liaoning island dataset is not as effective as the fusion between the DeBERTa module and the attention module.

By changing the location of the attention module, precision (P) improves from 82.983% to 86.402%, recall (R) from 77.507% to 80.300%, and F1 value from 79.130 to 82.490%. It can be determined that the attention module is more suitable to be located between the DeBERTa module and BiLSTM module for the Liaoning sea island dataset. Finally, replacing the self attention module with multi-head attention module improves the precision (P) from 80.919% to 88.167% with 7.248%, recall (R) from 75.299% to 83.121% with 7.822%, and F1 value from 77.102% to 83.121% with a 7.822% improvement. The F1 value increases from 77.102% to 85.024% with a 7.922% improvement, and the model achieves the best results compared with other models on the Liaoning sea island dataset. The experiment illustrates the effectiveness and superiority of the DABC model proposed in this paper.

Table 9. Ablation experiments.

Models	P	R	F1
BERT-BiLSTM-CRF (baseline)	80.919%	75.299%	77.102%
DeBERTa-BiLSTM-CRF	85.016%	80.210%	81.854%
BERT-Attention-BiLSTM-CRF	76.050%	77.193%	76.449%
DeBERTa-BiLSTM-Attention-CRF	82.983%	77.507%	79.130%
DeBERTa-selfAttention-BiLSTM-CRF	86.402%	80.300%	82.490%
DABC	88.167%	83.121%	85.024%

4.5. Comparative Experiments

In order to make an objective evaluation of the proposed model in this paper, the performance of the XLNet, RoBERTa-wwm-BiLSTM-CRF, and DeBERTa-BiLSTM-CRF models on the Liaoning island dataset of this paper are selected to compare with the model of this paper to validate the performance level of the model.

The results are shown in Tables 10 and 11.

On the Liaoning sea island dataset used in this paper, the proposed DABC model is compared with the BERT-BiLSTM-CRF model. It showed improvement in terms of precision (P) from 80.919% to 88.167%, with a 7.248% improvement; recall (R) increased from 75.299% to 83.121%, with a 7.822% improvement; and in terms of F1 value, it rose from 77.102% to 85.024%, with a 7.922% increase.

Table 10. Comparative experiments On the Liaoning sea island dataset.

Models	P	R	F1
BERT-BiLSTM-CRF (baseline)	80.919%	75.299%	77.102%
DeBERTa-BiLSTM-CRF	85.016%	80.210%	81.854%
XLNet	85.564%	82.279%	83.889%
RoBERTa-BiLSTM-CRF	83.703%	78.651%	80.169%
DABC	88.167%	83.121%	85.024%

Compared with the XLNET model there is a 2.603% improvement in the precision (P) from 85.564% to 88.167%, a 0.842% improvement in the recall (R) from 82.279% to 83.121%, and a 1.141% improvement in the F1 value from 83.889% to 85.024%.

Compared with the RoBERTa-wwm-BiLSTM-CRF model, it improves from 83.703% to 88.167% in terms of precision (P), with an improvement of 4.464%; from 78.651% to 83.121% in terms of recall (R), with an improvement of 4.47%; and from 80.169% to 85.024% in terms of F1 values. The F1 value increased from 80.169% to 85.024%, with an improvement of 4.855%.

Compared with DeBERTa-BiLSTM-CRF model, in terms of precision (P), it increased from 85.016% to 88.167%, so there is a 3.151% improvement; in terms of recall (R) from 80.201% to 83.121%, so there is a 2.920% improvement; and in terms of F1 value from 81.854% to 85.024%, so there is a 3.17% improvement in F1 value.

On the Resume dataset used in this paper, the proposed DABC model is compared with the BERT-BiLSTM-CRF model. In terms of precision (P), it increased from 80.937% to 90.130%, with a 9.193% improvement; recall (R) went from 80.836% to 88.599%, with a 7.763% improvement; and in terms of F1 value, it rose from 80.732% to 88.918%, with a 8.186% increase.

Table 11. Comparative experiments on Resume dataset.

Models	P	R	F1
BERT-BiLSTM-CRF (baseline)	80.937%	80.836%	80.732%
DeBERTa-BiLSTM-CRF	88.505%	86.162%	86.287%
XLNet	86.668%	84.455%	85.547%
RoBERTa-BiLSTM-CRF	90.013%	85.668%	87.081%
DABC	90.130%	88.599%	88.918%

Compared with the XLNET model, there is a 3.462% improvement in the precision (P) from 86.668% to 90.130%, a 4.144% improvement in the recall (R) from 84.455% to 88.599%, and a 3.371% improvement in the F1 value from 85.547% to 88.599%.

Compared with the RoBERTa-wwm-BiLSTM-CRF model, it improves from 90.013% to 90.130% in terms of precision (P), with an improvement of 0.117%; from 85.668% to 88.599% in terms of recall (R), with an improvement of 2.931%; and from 87.081% to 88.918% in terms of F1 values with an improvement of 1.837%.

Compared with DeBERTa-BiLSTM-CRF model, in terms of precision (P) it increased from 88.505% to 90.130%, so there is a 1.625% improvement; in terms of recall (R) from 86.162% to 88.599%, so there is a 2.437% improvement; and in terms of F1 value from 86.287% to 88.918%, so there is a 2.631% improvement in F1 value. These comparative experiments verify the superiority of the proposed model in this paper.

5. Conclusions

To address the issue of underutilized relative position information in text data and insufficient attention to key features during feature extraction, this paper proposes a new entity recognition model called DABC. The aim is to enhance the accuracy and robustness of recognizing Chinese entities. Building upon the BERT-BiLSTM-CRF model, the DeBERTa model is introduced to rectify the deficiency in BERT's utilization of relative position information in text data and improve overall model performance. Additionally, to address the issue of insufficient attention to key features in the DeBERTa-BiLSTM-CRF model, a multi-attention mechanism is incorporated to enhance the model's ability to focus on key features. The proposed model is validated and analyzed using the Liaoning sea island dataset. Experimental results show that the DABC model has an improvement in F1 values compared to the other models. This validates the effectiveness of the proposed model. Compared to other models, the DABC model shows an improvement in the F1 value ranging from 2% to 5%, further confirming its superiority. The results indicate that the DABC model proposed in this paper effectively utilizes the location information of text data and focuses on key information. The model we proposed still has efficiency shortcomings compared to previous models. Further research is needed in the future; future work will explore additional domains in named entity recognition to uncover further opportunities for improvement.

Author Contributions: Conceptualization, F.L. (Fan Li); Methodology, F.L. (Fangling Leng); Software, F.L. (Fan Li); Validation, F.L. (Fan Li); Investigation, T.Z.; Data curation, F.L. (Fan Li); Writing—original draft, F.L. (Fangling Leng); Writing—review and editing, G.Y.; Supervision, Y.B. All authors have read and agreed to the published version of the manuscript.

Funding: This research was funded by the National Natural Science Foundation of China (grant numbers 62137001 and 62272093).

Data Availability Statement: Data are contained within the article.

Conflicts of Interest: The authors declare no conflicts of interest. The funders had no role in the design of the study; in the collection, analyses, or interpretation of data; in the writing of the manuscript; or in the decision to publish the results.

References

1. Liang, J.; Li, D.; Lin, Y.; Wu, S.; Huang, Z. Named entity recognition of Chinese crop diseases and pests based on RoBERTa-wwm with adversarial training. *Agronomy* **2023**, *13*, 941. [CrossRef]
2. Jeong, Y.; Kim, E. Scideberta: Learning deberta for science technology documents and fine-tuning information extraction tasks. *IEEE Access* **2022**, *10*, 60805–60813. [CrossRef]
3. Mikolov, T.; Sutskever, I.; Chen, K.; Corrado, G.S.; Dean, J. Distributed representations of words and phrases and their compositionality. *Adv. Neural Inf. Process. Syst.* **2013**, *26*, 3111–3119.
4. Sharma, A.; Kumar, S. Ontology-based semantic retrieval of documents using Word2vec model. *Data Knowl. Eng.* **2023**, *144*, 102110. [CrossRef]
5. Zhao, X.; Greenberg, J.; An, Y.; Hu, X.T. Fine-tuning BERT model for materials named entity recognition. In Proceedings of the 2021 IEEE International Conference on Big Data (Big Data), Orlando, FL, USA, 15–18 December 2021; pp. 3717–3720.
6. Koru, G.K.; Uluyol, Ç. Detection of Turkish Fake News from Tweets with BERT Models. *IEEE Access* **2024**, *12*, 14918–14931. [CrossRef]
7. Liu, Y.; Ott, M.; Goyal, N.; Du, J.; Joshi, M.; Chen, D.; Levy, O.; Lewis, M.; Zettlemoyer, L.; Stoyanov, V. Roberta: A robustly optimized bert pretraining approach. *arXiv* **2019**, arXiv:1907.11692.
8. Yin, X.; Zheng, S.; Wang, Q. Fine-grained chinese named entity recognition based on roberta-wwm-bilstm-crf model. In Proceedings of the 2021 6th International Conference on Image, Vision and Computing (ICIVC), Qingdao, China, 23–25 July 2021; pp. 408–413.
9. Li, S.; Meng, X.; Li, R.; Huang, B.; Wang, X. NanoBERTa-ASP: Predicting nanobody paratope based on a pretrained RoBERTa model. *BMC Bioinform.* **2024**, *25*, 122.
10. He, P.; Liu, X.; Gao, J.; Chen, W. DeBERTa: Decoding-enhanced BERT with Disentangled Attention. *arXiv* **2020**, arXiv:2006.03654. [CrossRef].
11. Luo, L.; Yang, Z.; Yang, P.; Zhang, Y.; Wang, L.; Lin, H.; Wang, J. An attention-based BiLSTM-CRF approach to document-level chemical named entity recognition. *Bioinformatics* **2018**, *34*, 1381–1388. [CrossRef]
12. Souza, F.; Nogueira, R.; Lotufo, R. Portuguese named entity recognition using BERT-CRF. *arXiv* **2019**, arXiv:1909.10649.
13. Dai, Z.; Wang, X.; Ni, P.; Li, Y.; Li, G.; Bai, X. Named entity recognition using BERT BiLSTM CRF for Chinese electronic health records. In Proceedings of the 2019 12th International Congress on Image and Signal Processing, Biomedical Engineering and Informatics (CISP-BMEI), Suzhou, China, 19–21 October 2019; pp. 1–5.
14. Zhang, C.; Zhang, Y.; Zhang, J.; Yao, J.; Liu, H.; He, T.; Zheng, X.; Xue, X.; Xu, L.; Yang, J.; et al. A Deep Transfer Learning Toponym Extraction and Geospatial Clustering Framework for Investigating Scenic Spots as Cognitive Regions. *ISPRS Int. J. Geo-Inf.* **2023**, *12*, 196. [CrossRef]

15. Riyanto, S.; Sitanggang, I.S.; Djatna, T.; Atikah, T.D. Plant-Disease Relation Model through BERT-BiLSTM-CRF Approach. *Indones. J. Electr. Eng. Inform. (IJEEI)* **2024**, *12*, 113–124. [CrossRef]
16. Arslan, S. Application of BiLSTM-CRF model with different embeddings for product name extraction in unstructured Turkish text. *Neural Comput. Appl.* **2024**, *36*, 8371–8382. [CrossRef]
17. Chen, X.; Tong, X.; Lin, H.; Xing, Y. Entity Recognition Method for Key Information of Police Records Based on Bert-Bilstm-Selfatt-Crf. *Acad. J. Comput. Inf. Sci.* **2024**, *7*, 78–85.
18. Jeong, H. A Transfer Learning-Based Pairwise Information Extraction Framework Using BERT and Korean-Language Modification Relationships. *Symmetry* **2024**, *16*, 136. [CrossRef]
19. Shibata, D.; Shinohara, E.; Shimamoto, K.; Kawazoe, Y. Towards Structuring Clinical Texts: Joint Entity and Relation Extraction from Japanese Case Report Corpus. In *MEDINFO 2023—The Future Is Accessible*; IOS Press: Amsterdam, The Netherlands, 2024; pp. 559–563.
20. Cai, Y.; Luo, D.; Gan, Y.; Hou, R.; Liu, X.; Liu, Q.; Shi, X. Nested Named Entity Recognition Based on Span Boundary Perception. *J. Softw.* **2024**, 1–14. [CrossRef]
21. Cai, B.; Tian, S.; Yu, L.; Long, J.; Zhou, T.; Wang, B. ATBBC: Named entity recognition in emergency domains based on joint BERT-BILSTM-CRF adversarial training. *J. Intell. Fuzzy Syst.* **2024**, *46*, 4063–4076. [CrossRef]
22. Cui, Z.; Yu, K.; Yuan, Z.; Dong, X.; Luo, W. Language inference-based learning for Low-Resource Chinese clinical named entity recognition using language model. *J. Biomed. Inform.* **2024**, *149*, 104559. [CrossRef]
23. Fan, Y.; Xiao, H.; Wang, M.; Wang, J.; Jiang, W.; Zhu, C. Few-shot named entity recognition framework for forestry science metadata extraction. *J. Ambient. Intell. Humaniz. Comput.* **2024**, *15*, 2105–2118. [CrossRef]
24. Farhan, N.; Sarker Joy, S.; Binte Mannan, T.; Sadeque, F. Gazetteer-Enhanced Bangla Named Entity Recognition with BanglaBERT Semantic Embeddings K-Means-Infused CRF Model. *arXiv* **2024**, arXiv:2401.17206. [CrossRef].
25. Goyal, A.; Gupta, V.; Kumar, M. Deep learning-based named entity recognition system using hybrid embedding. *Cybern. Syst.* **2024**, *55*, 279–301. [CrossRef]
26. Mao, T.; Xu, Y.; Liu, W.; Peng, J.; Chen, L.; Zhou, M. A simple but effective span-level tagging method for discontinuous named entity recognition. *Neural Comput. Appl.* **2024**, *36*, 7187–7201. [CrossRef]
27. Wang, M.; Chen, H.; Shen, D.; Li, B.; Hu, S. RSRNeT: A novel multi-modal network framework for named entity recognition and relation extraction. *PeerJ Comput. Sci.* **2024**, *10*, e1856. [CrossRef]
28. Wu, K.; Xu, L.; Li, X.; Zhang, Y.; Yue, Z.; Gao, Y.; Chen, Y. Named entity recognition of rice genes and phenotypes based on BiGRU neural networks. *Comput. Biol. Chem.* **2024**, *108*, 107977. [CrossRef] [PubMed]
29. Xu, Y.; Tan, X.; Tong, X.; Zhang, W. A Robust Chinese Named Entity Recognition Method Based on Integrating Dual-Layer Features and CSBERT. *Appl. Sci.* **2024**, *14*, 1060. [CrossRef]
30. Cao, L.; Wu, C.; Luo, G.; Guo, C.; Zheng, A. Online biomedical named entities recognition by data and knowledge-driven model. *Artif. Intell. Med.* **2024**, *150*, 102813. [CrossRef] [PubMed]
31. Chu, J.; Liu, Y.; Yue, Q.; Zheng, Z.; Han, X. Named entity recognition in aerospace based on multi-feature fusion transformer. *Sci. Rep.* **2024**, *14*, 827. [CrossRef] [PubMed]
32. Hu, Y.; Chen, Q.; Du, J.; Peng, X.; Keloth, V.K.; Zuo, X.; Zhou, Y.; Li, Z.; Jiang, X.; Lu, Z.; et al. Improving large language models for clinical named entity recognition via prompt engineering. *J. Am. Med. Inform. Assoc.* **2024**, ocad259. [CrossRef]
33. Li, P.; Zhou, G.; Guo, Y.; Zhang, S.; Jiang, Y.; Tang, Y. EPIC: An epidemiological investigation of COVID-19 dataset for Chinese named entity recognition. *Inf. Process. Manag.* **2024**, *61*, 103541. [CrossRef]
34. Mengliev, D.; Barakhnin, V.; Abdurakhmonova, N.; Eshkulov, M. Developing named entity recognition algorithms for Uzbek: Dataset Insights and Implementation. *Data Brief* **2024**, *54*, 110413. [CrossRef]
35. Qiu, Q.; Tian, M.; Huang, Z.; Xie, Z.; Ma, K.; Tao, L.; Xu, D. Chinese engineering geological named entity recognition by fusing multi-features and data enhancement using deep learning. *Expert Syst. Appl.* **2024**, *238*, 121925. [CrossRef]
36. Wang, C.; Gao, J.; Rao, H.; Chen, A.; He, J.; Jiao, J.; Zou, N.; Gu, L. Named entity recognition (NER) for Chinese agricultural diseases and pests based on discourse topic and attention mechanism. *Evol. Intell.* **2024**, *17*, 457–466. [CrossRef]
37. Dahou, A.; Ewees, A.A.; Hashim, F.A.; Al-qaness, M.A.; Orabi, D.A.; Soliman, E.M.; Tag-eldin, E.M.; Aseeri, A.O.; Abd Elaziz, M. Optimizing fake news detection for Arabic context: A multitask learning approach with transformers and an enhanced Nutcracker Optimization Algorithm. *Knowl.-Based Syst.* **2023**, *280*, 111023. [CrossRef]
38. Ayub, N.; Tayyaba; Hussain, S.; Ullah, S.S.; Iqbal, J. An Efficient Optimized DenseNet Model for Aspect-Based Multi-Label Classification. *Algorithms* **2023**, *16*, 548. [CrossRef]
39. Bahdanau, D.; Cho, K.; Bengio, Y. Neural machine translation by jointly learning to align and translate. *arXiv* **2014**, arXiv:1409.0473.
40. Vaswani, A.; Shazeer, N.; Parmar, N.; Uszkoreit, J.; Jones, L.; Gomez, A.N.; Kaiser, Ł.; Polosukhin, I. Attention is all you need. *Adv. Neural Inf. Process. Syst.* **2017**, *30*, 5998–6008.

mathematics MDPI

Article

A Novel Online Hydrological Data Quality Control Approach Based on Adaptive Differential Evolution

Qun Zhao [1], Shicheng Cui [1,*], Yuelong Zhu [2], Rui Li [1] and Xudong Zhou [3,4]

[1] School of Computer Engineering, Nanjing Institute of Technology, Nanjing 211167, China; qunzhao@njit.edu.cn (Q.Z.); lirui_92@njit.edu.cn (R.L.)
[2] College of Computer and Information, Hohai University, Nanjing 211100, China; ylzhu@hhu.edu.cn
[3] Institute of Hydraulics and Ocean Engineering, Ningbo University, Ningbo 315211, China; zhouxudong@nbu.edu.cn
[4] School of Civil and Environmental Engineering, Ningbo University, Ningbo 315211, China
* Correspondence: shicheng.cui@njit.edu.cn; Tel.: +86-13851822286

Abstract: The quality of hydrological data has a significant impact on hydrological models, where stable and anomaly-free hydrological time series typically yield more valuable patterns. In this paper, we conduct data analysis and propose an online hydrological data quality control method based on an adaptive differential evolution algorithm according to the characteristics of hydrological data. Taking into account the characteristics of continuity, periodicity, and seasonality, we develop a Periodic Temporal Long Short-Term Memory (PT-LSTM) predictive control model. Building upon the real-time nature of the data, we apply the Adaptive Differential Evolution algorithm to optimize PT-LSTM, creating an Online Composite Predictive Control Model (OCPT-LSTM) that provides confidence intervals and recommended values for control and replacement. The experimental results demonstrate that the proposed data quality control method effectively manages data quality; detects data anomalies; provides suggested values; reduces reliance on manual intervention; provides a solid data foundation for hydrological data analysis work; and helps hydrological personnel in water resource scheduling, flood control, and other related tasks. Meanwhile, the proposed method can also be applied to the analysis of time series data in other industries.

Keywords: hydrological data quality; data analysis; predictive control model; differential evolution algorithm; online optimization

MSC: 68T09

1. Introduction

The continuous development of the Information Age has led to the establishment and improvement of an increasing number of intelligent hydrological monitoring stations. The coverage of hydrological data has become more comprehensive, with massive numbers of historical and real-time hydrological data being collected and stored in databases. These hydrological data have a large quantity and diverse types. Extracting potential patterns from massive hydrological data and conducting data analysis of hydrological phenomena holds significant importance for hydrological work.

Hydrological data mining models have certain requirements for data quality. Only high-quality data can provide valuable information and knowledge, and a good dataset can reduce the instability of the models [1]. The quality of hydrological data significantly impacts hydrological data mining models, with stable and anomaly-free hydrological time series typically yielding more valuable patterns [2]. When mining hydrological data, addressing data quality issues such as missing values and anomalies within a controllable range is crucial to ensure the accuracy and credibility of experiments and applications. Factors such as inaccuracies in the installation, upgrading, and sensor interference of monitoring systems at hydrological stations, as well as abnormal jumps or failures of instruments caused by extreme weather conditions, may lead to anomalies, errors, and other phenomena in hydrological data. Such errors and anomalies in data records can sometimes mislead disaster management assessments, leading to serious consequences. However, there are still challenges in the current hydrological data quality control:

1. A strong reliance on manual intervention and high manual cleaning costs. In China, most hydrological data quality control methods are still in the theoretical research and modeling stage. The control of data quality often requires manual intervention [3], lacking intelligent data quality control algorithms and models.
2. Low credibility of short-term missing data imputation. For hydrological data with short-term missing values due to machine failures, commonly used interpolation methods such as the average method, weighted method, or simple spatial interpolation method [4,5] are employed. The effectiveness of linear interpolation methods [6,7] varies based on data collection density, rendering the credibility of imputed data difficult to assess.
3. Lack of reliable replacement values for anomalous data. Currently, many methods [8–13] detect anomalous data through basic checks and standard settings but fail to provide reliable replacement values for substituting anomalous data.

To address the aforementioned issues, this study investigates how to establish an intelligent hydrological data control method based on the continuity, periodicity, seasonality, and real-time characteristics of hydrological data. The aim is to reduce reliance on manual intervention, optimize hydrological data quality, and consequently enhance the stability and precision of data mining models.

2. Related Works

Data quality [14] is a measure of the accuracy, completeness, and consistency of data [15], forming the foundation for data applications. The advent of the big data era has brought challenges to data management and information extraction while ensuring data quality is a prerequisite for effective data analysis [16]. Data quality control involves taking specific measures to ensure that data collected, stored, and transmitted meet certain requirements. Implementing quality control measures on hydrological data can effectively detect missing and suspicious data, maintaining data quality within a controllable range. This lays the groundwork for hydrological predictions, flood forecasts, and other applications. Therefore, controlling the quality of hydrological data is essential to ensure the reliability of hydrological data.

Numerous scholars in the field of hydrology have proposed various schemes for the control, management, and assessment of hydrological data quality. Sciuto et al. [8] conducted control on temperature data by setting a sliding window for data consistency. They checked whether observed data fell within confidence intervals of two different fixed probabilities, aiming to identify anomalies in temperature data. Steinacker et al. [9] analyzed types of data errors and proposed an approach based on the spatial location of monitoring stations to establish a topological structure for determining weights between stations and guiding artificial assistance in control directions. Sciuto [10] and Abbot [11] used climate indices, atmospheric temperatures, and historical data from surrounding stations to forecast rainfall data at monitoring stations and set detection intervals, identifying data outside the intervals as anomalies. Fu Fangjing and Luo Xi [12] independently conducted a thorough examination and detection of hydrological data entering the database, focusing on overall rationality, completeness, and consistency, in order to identify anomalous data. Yu Yufeng [13] employed Benford's Law to detect the distribution pattern and overall rationality of hydrological data, proposing a semi-automatic cleaning approach to improve hydrological data quality [17], offering innovative insights for hydrological data quality control. Tang Dandan et al. [18], addressing the issue of detecting anomalies in continuous hydrological data, proposed two combination models. They used the confidence intervals provided by the models and statistical methods to determine data anomalies. Zhao et al. [19]

presented two control methods for different types of hydrological data, setting suspicious levels and recommended values for data reference by hydrological personnel. Li et al. [20] use the TOPographic Kinematic Approximation and Integration (TOPKAPI) distributed model for deterministic forecasts with low-quality input data and then use the Hydrologic Uncertainty Processor (HUP) to provide the probabilistic forecast results for operational practices. Yu et al. [21] detected abnormal patterns in hydrological time series based on weighted probability suffix trees, effectively identifying anomalies by combining trend characteristic symbols and clustering approximate patterns. Lattawit et al. [22] developed a median-based statistical outlier detection approach using a sliding window technique. The results show that the Spline interpolation method yielded a superior performance on non-cyclical data while the LSTM outperformed other interpolation methods on a distinct tidal data pattern. Hyojoong K and Heeyoung K proposed a method for contextual anomaly detection, particularly in the case where the response and contextual variables are both high-dimensional and complex [23], and a contextual anomaly detection method for multivariate time series data [24]. The experiments showed that the proposed methods all perform well.

However, there are still numerous challenges in the current hydrological data quality control. For instance, the current hydrological data quality control methods in China are mostly in the theoretical research and modeling stage. There is strong dependence on manual cleaning, and there is a lack of intelligent data quality control algorithms and models for real-time intelligent control of hydrological data.

3. Proposed Method

Hydrological time series data, such as water level and discharge, exhibit characteristics such as continuity, periodicity, seasonality, and real-time properties. These features make hydrological data subject to temporal variations. Moreover, the changes in hydrological data over a period of time exhibit spatial proximity on the time scale, displaying a certain similarity in the variations of samples with close temporal distances and data with the same spatial positions in different periods.

For historical hydrological data that have not undergone reorganization, we use deep learning methods [25,26] to establish a predictive control model. The model, based on the temporal continuity, periodicity, seasonality, and spatial positions on the time scale of hydrological data, establishes a Periodic Temporal LSTM Predictive Control Model (PT-LSTM). The model provides a prediction line, constructs confidence intervals to detect anomalous data, and offers recommended values. Additionally, considering the real-time nature of hydrological data, an improved version of the PT-LSTM model is proposed, termed the Online Optimized Combination Predictive Control Model (OCPT-LSTM). This model incorporates real-time data for real-time model correction, providing confidence intervals to detect data quality and recommending values for replacement.

On the foundation of basic quality controls (such as missing data and format checks, and extreme value checks), this study constructs a PT-LSTM Model and an OCPT-LSTM Model based on the characteristics of hydrological data, for predictive control. The models provide confidence intervals for detected data, and any data outside these intervals is considered suspicious and requires manual judgment on whether to replace it with the recommended values provided by the models. The process is illustrated in Figure 1.

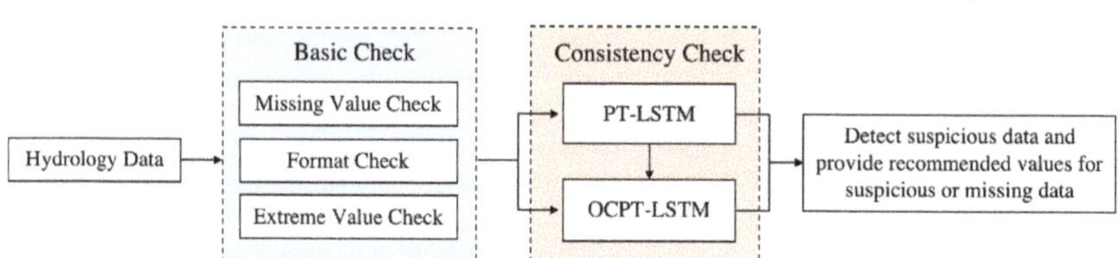

Figure 1. Quality control method of hydrological data.

3.1. Periodic Temporal Predictive Control Model

Hydrological data exhibit continuity and periodicity within a certain timeframe. Addressing their continuity, predictions for the data at time $n+1$ can be made using historical data from the previous n time steps. Regarding their periodicity, where data transformations at the same time on adjacent days fall within a certain range, predicting future hydrological conditions at the same time using historical data at the corresponding time is feasible.

3.1.1. Dataset Construction

The continuity of hydrological data ensures that data changes within the same period will fall within a certain range. Periodicity guarantees that data follow similar patterns across different cycles. Seasonality ensures that the magnitude of hydrological data changes is related within the same season. Constructing datasets based on the temporal characteristics and spatial positions on the time scale of hydrological data allows for the exploration of more patterns within the data and enables better analysis.

In addressing the continuity of hydrological data, predictions for the data at time $t+1$ are made based on the real-time data at historical times up to t. The historical hydrological data are divided into M groups continuously, each containing N^T data points. The input vector is represented as $[x_1, x_2, x_3, \ldots, x_{MN^T}]$. These are arranged into an $M \times N^T$ matrix X, where the matrix has a periodicity of N^T, and it is structured as follows:

$$X = \begin{bmatrix} x_1 & x_2 & \cdots & x_{N^T} \\ x_{N^T+1.} & x_{N^T+2} & & x_{2N^T} \\ & \vdots & \ddots & \vdots \\ x_{(M-1)N^T+1} & x_{(M-1)N^T+2} & \cdots & x_{MN^T} \end{bmatrix} \tag{1}$$

The above matrix is constructed from m subsequences with a periodicity of N^T, where x_{N^T+2} is one element. Apart from the adjacent x_{N^T+1} and x_{N^T+3} in both directions, which are in spatial proximity to x_{N^T+2}, there are also data points from the same time in the previous and subsequent cycles, such as x_2 and x_{2N^T+2} for the same time within the same day. Regarding the periodicity of hydrological data, the data at the same time (reference time) for the previous m days exhibit a similar trend to the data at the same time for the $m+1$ day. A day consists of 24 time points, and here N^T can be taken as 24 for a daily cycle.

In response to the seasonality of hydrological data, it is observed that different seasons exhibit distinct hydrological conditions. Specifically, summers are often characterized by flood seasons with heavy rainfall, leading to significant fluctuations in flow. Autumns experience continuous drizzle, causing a delayed end to the flood season and maintaining a high flow rate. Springs and winters are mostly dry seasons with less rainfall, resulting in relatively stable flow changes. Figure 2 depicts the daily flow rates for the WaiZhou station in 2007 and the AoXiaping station in 2008. The WaiZhou Station is located on the Ganjiang River in Poyang Lake, Jiangxi Province, at 115.83 east longitude and 28.63 north latitude. The AoXiaping Station is located on the Heyuan River in Poyang Lake, Jiangxi Province, at 114.43 east longitude and 26.18 north latitude. The AoXiaping Station is located in the southwest direction of the WaiZhou Station, with a relatively long latitude interval, which is of reference significance for comparison.

Despite the considerable difference in flow rates between the two stations, there are similarities in their trend patterns. For the WaiZhou station, significant flow variations occur from April to September, followed by a relatively steady period after September. Similarly, the AoXiaping station exhibits pronounced flow changes from May to November, particularly during the period from June to August, when flow fluctuations are significant. In summary, summers and autumns are often characterized by high flow periods, while springs and winters are generally dry seasons.

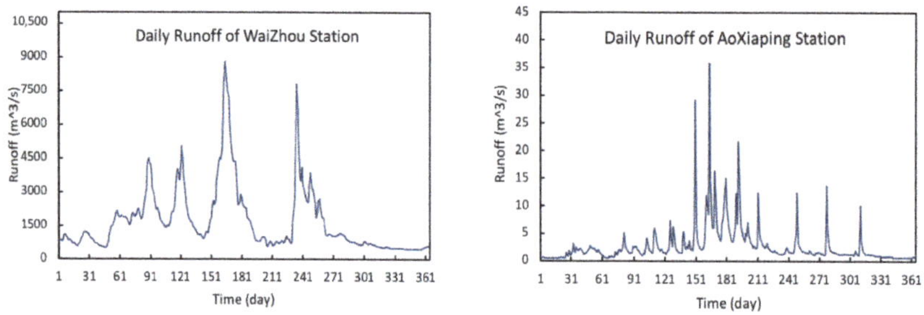

Figure 2. Daily discharge of WaiZhou station and AoXiaping station.

Given the significant differences in hydrological conditions across seasons, the dataset can be divided into two categories based on seasons: spring and winter (dry season) as one category, and summer and autumn (wet season) as another category. This allows for separate training based on distinct seasonal patterns.

3.1.2. PT-LSTM Model Construction

The LSTM neural network can retain long-term information and effectively capture hydrological patterns, providing certain advantages in modeling hydrological sequences. In this paper, considering the specific temporal characteristics of hydrological data, we propose the PT-LSTM model. The model based on the continuity, periodicity, and seasonality of time series, and their spatial proximity in the time scale, divides the time series into multiple sub-sequences according to periods. These subsequences are then arranged in matrices to facilitate spatial exploration. Next, the model linearly maps these sub-sequences by multiplying them with a weight matrix to obtain data with continuous and periodic characteristics. Subsequently, the data are fed into a recursive layer for exploration to obtain the prediction results. The network structure of the PT-LSTM model is illustrated in Figure 3. The PT-LSTM model not only considers the temporal characteristics of time series data and the spatial position in the time scale, reducing training complexity, but also minimizes the reduction in the neural network time step, thereby preserving the original data information to the maximum extent.

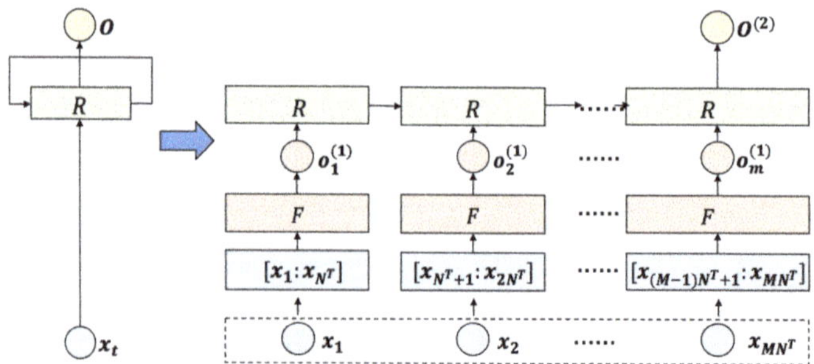

Figure 3. Network structure of PT-LSTM.

Where x_t, x_1, x_2, x_{MN^T} represent input data; $[x_1 : x_{N^T}], [x_{N^T+1} : x_{2N^T}], [x_{(M-1)N^T+1} : x_{NM^T}]$ are sub-sequences of the processed periodic matrix; F is the fully connected layer in PT-LSTM for linear mapping of the periodic matrix; $o_1^{(1)}, o_2^{(1)}, o_m^{(1)}$ are the outputs after linear processing; R is the recursive layer in PT-LSTM; and $O, O^{(2)}$ is the output after the recursive layer.

The following provides a detailed explanation of the PT-LSTM model:

(1) Data Preprocessing and Parameter Setting

Choose the data. First, divide the data into two categories based on the wet season and dry season. Process each category of data separately. Divide the historical hydrological data into M groups, each with N^T data points. The input vector is $[x_1, x_2, x_3, \ldots, x_{MN^T}]$. Arrange it into an $M \times N^T$ matrix with a period of N^T according to Equation (1). Normalize the data to be within the range of $[-1, 1]$. Shuffle the order randomly and select 60% of the data as the training set, 20% as the validation set, and 20% as the test set.

Initialize the network weights. Specify the activation functions as the sigmoid function and tanh function. Use the mean squared error function as the loss function, calculated as follows:

$$MSE = \frac{1}{n}\sum_{i=1}^{n}(y_i - Y_i)^2 \tag{2}$$

where y_i is the predicted value at time step i, Y_i is the true value at time step i, and n is the number of samples input into the model.

(2) Linear Mapping Processing

Perform linear mapping on the above M sets of subsequences, and input the dataset into the fully connected layer according to the pre-divided groups. The number of input nodes in this layer is N^T, and the number of output nodes is 1. The mathematical expression is as follows:

$$O^{(1)} = XW^{(1)} = \begin{bmatrix} x_1 & x_2 & \cdots & x_{N^T} \\ x_{N^T+1.} & x_{N^T+2} & & x_{2N^T} \\ & \vdots & \ddots & \vdots \\ x_{(M-1)N^T+1} & x_{(M-1)N^T+2} & \cdots & x_{MN^T} \end{bmatrix} \begin{bmatrix} w_{1,1}^{(1)} \\ \cdots \\ \cdots \\ w_{N^T,1}^{(1)} \end{bmatrix} \tag{3}$$

$$O^{(1)} = \begin{bmatrix} w_{1,1}^{(1)}x_1 & w_{2,1}^{(1)}x_2 & \cdots & w_{N^T,1}^{(1)}x_{N^T} \\ w_{1,1}^{(1)}x_{N^T+1.} & w_{2,1}^{(1)}x_{N^T+2} & & w_{N^T,1}^{(1)}x_{2N^T} \\ & \vdots & \ddots & \vdots \\ w_{1,1}^{(1)}x_{(M-1)N^T+1} & w_{2,1}^{(1)}x_{(M-1)N^T+2} & \cdots & w_{N^T,1}^{(1)}x_{MN^T} \end{bmatrix} = \begin{bmatrix} o_{1,1}^{(1)} \\ o_{2,1}^{(1)} \\ \cdots \\ o_{M,1}^{(1)} \end{bmatrix} \tag{4}$$

where $W^{(1)}$ is the weight matrix of this layer and X is the input matrix of $M \times N^T$. $O^{(1)}$ is used as the input to the recursive layer. In the sequence input, each element represents one time step, and the total number of steps in the network is M. For each time step, the output of the previous layer is used as the input for the current layer. $o_t^{(1)} = o_{t,1}^{(1)}, t = 1, 2, 3, \ldots, M$. The output of the second hidden layer at time step t is given by:

$$o_t^{(2)} = \sigma\left(o_{t-1}^{(2)}, o_t^{(1)}\right) \tag{5}$$

The output of the second hidden layer is denoted as $O^{(2)} = \left[o_1^{(2)}, o_2^{(2)}, \ldots, o_M^{(2)}\right]$, where $\sigma(\cdot)$ represents the activation function. The output at time step t for the n-th hidden layer is given by $o_t^{(n)} = \sigma\left(o_{t-1}^{(n)}, o_t^{(n-1)}\right)$, and the output of the n-th hidden layer is $O^{(n)} = \left[o_1^{(n)}, o_2^{(n)}, \ldots, o_M^{(n)}\right]$. Compared to traditional neural networks, this construction reduces the time step from MN^T to M, reducing the time step and lowering training complexity. It effectively addresses the vanishing gradient problem of LSTM while modeling long sequences as short sequences. This overcomes LSTM's limitations on the time step and retains a significant amount of original sequence information.

(3) Model Training

Take the output $O^{(1)}$ of the fully connected layer as input and perform forward calculation for each unit in the hidden layer using the following formula:

$$\text{Forget Gate: } F_t = \sigma\left(W_f \times \left[h_{t-1}, o_t^{(1)}\right] + b_f\right)$$

$$\text{Input Gate: } I_t = \sigma\left(W_i \times \left[h_{t-1}, o_t^{(1)}\right] + b_i\right)$$

$$\text{Output Gate: } O_t = \sigma\left(W_o \times \left[h_{t-1}, o_t^{(1)}\right] + b_o\right)$$

$$\text{Cell State: } c_t^{\sim} = \tanh\left(W_c \times \left[h_{t-1}, o_t^{(1)}\right] + b_c\right), c_t = F_t \odot c_{t-1} + i_t \odot c_t^{\sim}$$

$$\text{Hidden State: } h_t = O_t \odot tanh(c_t)$$

Calculate the prediction error of the model, then backpropagate the prediction error through each neuron, update the network weights, and iterate through the training process. When the mean squared error no longer decreases or meets certain criteria, the iteration concludes, and the network training is completed.

After obtaining the prediction reference line, confidence intervals can be constructed. The confidence interval is determined based on the estimated value to identify the range within which the true value may exist. With the predicted value y and mean squared error MSE, the confidence interval is formed as follows: $Z = [y - \delta \cdot MSE, y + \delta \cdot MSE]$. Here, δ is a weighted value with $\delta \in [2, 5]$, adjusted according to seasonal variations [27]. If $y - \delta \cdot MSE < 0$, then the confidence interval becomes $Z = [0, y + \delta \cdot MSE]$.

After obtaining the confidence interval, data control is performed using the confidence interval. Data outside the confidence interval are considered suspicious, and the predicted values from the model serve as suggested values for hydrological staff to decide whether to replace them.

3.2. *Online Optimization Combination Control Model*

The hydrological station needs to upload a large number of data every day, and these data have real-time characteristics. When detecting hydrological data, ordinary prediction control models may introduce errors gradually due to the lack of timely updates in the dataset, leading to biases in data prediction control and weak model timeliness. Building an online, real-time optimization model can provide timely and effective control of the data.

3.2.1. OCPT-LSTM Model Concept

This section combines the PT-LSTM model with the adaptive differential evolution algorithm to establish the OCPT-LSTM model. Drawing on the idea of preserving excellent individuals and their fitness values in a temporary array within the population, this approach involves selecting the top m excellent parameters as the initial parameters for the model. The goal is to establish a weighted combination prediction and control model, thereby enhancing the robustness of prediction and control.

The Online Optimization Combination Control Model employs the OCPT-LSTM model as the prediction model and the PT-LSTM model as the base model. After a certain period, a temporary base model group is constructed, using the $m + 1$ to $m + k$ excellent parameters from the temporary array to establish k temporary models. These models are trained using historical real-time data from the same period as the dataset. By comparing the temporary base models with the base models in the combination model, if the best model in the temporary models performs better than the worst model in the combination control model in terms of prediction, timely replacement occurs. Finally, the combination prediction and control model is reweighted based on prediction errors. The OCPT-LSTM model dynamically replaces the worst-performing excellent model with an outstanding temporary model. This process ensures the stability of the combination model with minimal changes, continually adjusting the timeliness of the control model. The model framework is illustrated in Figure 4.

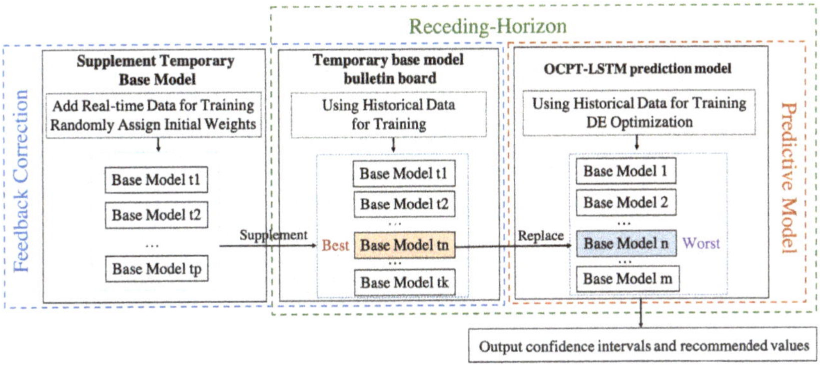

Figure 4. Framework of online optimal combined predictive control method.

3.2.2. OCPT-LSTM Model Construction

The Differential Evolution (DE) algorithm is an optimization algorithm based on human theories. It simulates the process of cooperation and competition among individuals in a population, guiding the group towards optimal solutions through the selection of cooperative and competitive interactions. Compared to other optimization algorithms, the DE algorithm demonstrates superior performance in local search for complex optimization problems.

The convergence performance of the DE algorithm is largely influenced by the selection value of mutation factors. The Adaptive Differential Evolution (ADE) algorithm adds an adaptive scaling factor on the basis of the DE algorithm. We use adaptive mutation factors to enhance the convergence performance of the model. In the early iterations, the mutation factor is large, helping to maintain the diversity of the population. As the number of iterations increases, the mutation factor decreases, preserving excellent population information and avoiding disruption to the optimal solution. The Adaptive Mutation Factor is as follows:

$$F = F_{max} - \frac{t(F_{max} - F_{min})}{T} \quad (6)$$

where F is the mutation factor, t is the iteration count, T is the maximum iteration count, F_{max} is the maximum value of the mutation factor, and F_{min} is the minimum value of the mutation factor.

Due to the need for real-time updates in the online predictive control model, the periodic time perspective may not effectively control data generated by sudden extreme weather events. Therefore, this paper adopts a continuous real-time time perspective for predictive control, predicting future conditions based on the preceding n time steps, such as the hydrological condition at the $n + 1$ time step. In this section, a single predictive control model is constructed based on the idea of an adaptive differential optimization algorithm, and an online optimized combination control model is developed, as illustrated in Figure 5.

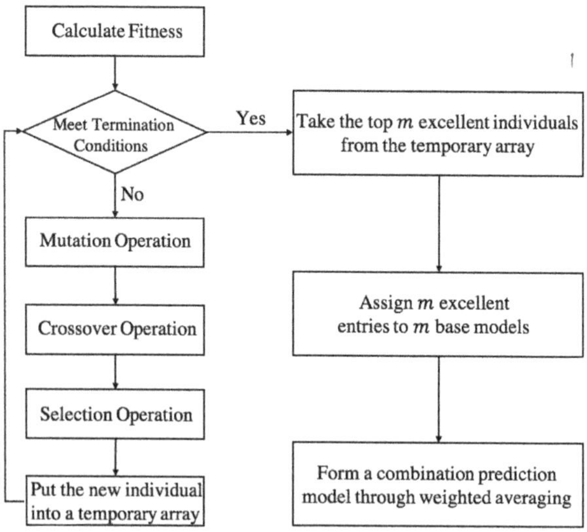

Figure 5. Online optimal combined prediction model process.

The specific steps of the online optimized combination control model are as follows:

(1) Training set construction. Select the dataset, apply the periodic matrix processing as described in Section 3.1.1, and normalize the data. Shuffle the order randomly and choose 60% of the data as the training set, 20% as the validation set, and 20% as the test set.

(2) Encoding. Uniformly encode the parameters of PT-LSTM into individuals.

(3) Initialization operation.

$$X_j^i(0) = x_j^{il} + rand(0,1)(x_j^{iu} - x_j^{il}) \tag{7}$$

where $x_j^i(0)$ is the ith individual in the jth dimension, x_j^{il} is the lower bound of the jth dimension, x_j^{iu} is the upper bound of the jth dimension, and $rand(0,1)$ represents a random number on [0, 1].

(4) Population Generation. Randomly generate the initial population in step 3 with a size of np and initialize mutation factor F, individual gene dimension D, maximum number of iterations T, and crossover probability CR.

(5) Fitness Calculation. Calculate the fitness of each individual using mean squared error as the fitness criterion.

(6) Mutation Operation. Randomly select two individuals from the population and perform adaptive mutation on the individuals, generating mutated individuals.

$$V_i(t) = x_j^{r1}(t) + F(x_j^{r2}(t) - x_j^{r3}(t)) \tag{8}$$

where $r1$, $r2$, and $r3$ are randomly generated integers, and $r \in 1, 2, \ldots, NP$, $x_j^{r1}(t)$, $x_j^{r2}(t)$, $x_j^{r3}(t)$ are the jth dimensional components of the three individuals, respectively. F is the variation factor corresponding to Formula (6).

(7) Crossover Operation. Perform a crossover operation on the mutated individuals to obtain new individuals. When $rand(0,1) \geq CR$, $u_j(t) = v_j(t)$, otherwise $u_j(t) = x_j(t)$. Generally speaking, the larger the CR, the faster the convergence speed, which is beneficial for local search. However, excessive crossover probability can lead to premature convergence and the poor robustness of the algorithm. The smaller the CR, the better the population diversity, which is beneficial for global search. After crossing, the new individual $U_i(t) = (u_1(t), u_2(t), \ldots, u_2(t))$.

(8) Selection Operation. Employ a greedy algorithm to select individuals from both the original population and the newly generated individuals. Individuals with lower fitness values are chosen to replace the corresponding individuals in the original population. The fitness values of the selected excellent individuals are saved in a temporary array.

(9) Selecting Excellent Individuals. Iteratively execute the mutation, crossover, and selection operations on the population until the iteration limit is reached or the position of the best individual is determined. Sort the temporary array in ascending order of fitness values, and use the top m individuals to construct the model.

(10) Establishing Base Models. Decode the m excellent individuals generated in (9) and build m base models. Assign differential initial weights to these base models and train them to construct m PT-LSTM models.

(11) Combination Model. Weightedly combine the PT-LSTM base models to establish the OCPT-LSTM model.

Once the model is established, every certain period, the m excellent individuals in the temporary array, along with k randomly generated individuals, form the initial population with a size of $n(m+k)$. The steps (5) to (10) are then executed. The individual with the minimum fitness among them is selected for decoding, and the optimal initial threshold is assigned for training. If the error of this new network is less than that of the network in the ensemble model, replace the base model with the maximum error in the ensemble model and re-establish the model; otherwise, keep the original ensemble model unchanged.

After obtaining the predicted values, a confidence interval is established for the detection of data. First, use the predicted data at different time points to draw a time series prediction reference line. For each time point on the prediction reference line, add the positive and negative error values of the 95% confidence interval of the model's prediction error as the upper and lower bounds. Finally, use wavelet transform to smooth the control boundaries, taking the part between the two smooth curves as the confidence interval.

This paper builds two models, PT-LSTM and OCPT-LSTM, for predictive control on the foundation of basic quality control. The models construct confidence intervals based on the prediction results to detect anomalous data. The detection interval is dynamically adjusted according to the data variations. Data outside the interval are considered suspicious and require manual judgment on whether to replace it with the suggested values provided by the model. Both models can effectively provide confidence intervals and advisory values. The choice between the models depends on the specific requirements of the control situation. When only detecting suspicious data or pursuing efficiency, the PT-LSTM model can be chosen. When accuracy is crucial and replacement values need to be provided, the OCPT-LSTM model is a suitable choice. Both models can also construct confidence intervals separately, and a comprehensive confidence interval can be created for data control. Additionally, the two models can cross-validate each other. Data corrected by the PT-LSTM model, which are based on cyclical temporal prediction control, can undergo a secondary quality confirmation through the OCPT-LSTM ensemble model in the online prediction control approach.

4. Experiment and Analysis

4.1. Evaluation Metrics

This section employs four evaluation metrics as performance indicators: Coefficient of Determination (R^2), Root Mean Squared Error ($RMSE$), Absolute Error (AE), and Maximum Error (ME).

Coefficient of Determination(R^2) represents the degree of agreement between predicted and observed values, with a range of [0, 1]. A higher R^2 value indicates higher prediction accuracy. The formula for calculation is:

$$R^2 = 1 - \frac{\sum_{i=1}^{n}\left(Y_i - \hat{Y}_i\right)^2}{\sum_{i=1}^{n}\left(Y_i - \bar{Y}\right)^2} \tag{9}$$

where Y_i is the observed value, $\hat{Y}_i$ is the predicted value, and $\bar{Y}$ is the mean of the observed values.

Root Mean Square Error ($RMSE$) calculates the mean of the squared differences between predicted and actual data errors, and a smaller value indicates better performance. The formula for calculation is:

$$RMSE = \sqrt{\frac{1}{n}\sum_{i=1}^{n}(Y_i - \hat{Y}_i)^2} \quad (10)$$

Absolute Error (AE) is the absolute difference between predicted and actual monitored values, while Maximum Error (ME) is the maximum absolute difference between predicted and actual values.

4.2. Experimental Dataset

Jiangxi Province is surrounded by mountains on three sides, with higher terrain in the central and southern parts, mostly consisting of hilly plateaus. The northern part is surrounded by mountains with lower terrain. The water flows from high to low areas, and the unique topography of Jiangxi Province makes it prone to water accumulation in low-lying areas. Excessive water accumulation, coupled with untimely reservoir scheduling, can easily lead to flooding disasters. Poyang Lake, located in the central-southern part of Jiangxi Province, is the largest freshwater lake in China and a frequent and severely affected area by flooding in the middle and lower reaches of the Yangtze River.

For the experiment, the hydrological stations selected are WaiZhou (Station code: 62302250, longitude 115.83, and latitude 28.63) and ShiShang (Station code: 62312050, longitude 116.2, and latitude 26.53) in the Gan River basin of Poyang Lake, Jiangxi Province. WaiZhou Station is located in WaiZhou Village, Taohua Township, Nanchang City, while ShiShang Station is located in ShiShang Town, Ningdu County, under Ganzhou City. Both stations belong to the Ganjiang River, experiencing large fluctuations in flow, high peak flows, and are prone to anomalous data. The experiment considered these two hydrological stations with relatively large flow rates as the experimental points and involved selecting a portion of the hourly flow rate data from the WaiZhou hydrological station for the period 2004 to 2008 after data reorganization, totaling 23,136 records. Sixty percent of the reorganized data was used for training, 20% for validation, and 20% for testing and adjusting confidence intervals. Similarly, the Stone Shang station's hourly data were selected for partial periods from 2004 to 2008 for experimentation. Among these, 60% of the reorganized data was used for training and 20% for validation, and 20% of the non-reorganized data was used for testing, totaling 17,520 records.

Before conducting the experiments, preprocessing was carried out on the experimental dataset. Hourly flow data that has not been controlled may contain missing values. For such data, linear interpolation was used for missing value imputation. Linear interpolation involves calculating the value of an unknown variable by connecting two known values with a straight line. The formula for linear interpolation is as follows:

$$y = y_b + \frac{y_a - y_b}{x_a - x_b}(x - x_b) \quad (11)$$

where (x_a, y_a) and (x_b, y_b) represent the coordinates of the known points, and y denotes the value of the unknown variable at a position x within the interval $[x_a, x_b]$ along the straight line.

Next, the data will undergo a normalization process. Data normalization is a procedure to scale the data to a specific range, aiming to shorten the convergence time during training. Max–Min normalization and mean normalization are two commonly used normalization methods. However, Max–Min normalization scales the data to the range $[0,1]$, while the size of the data after mean normalization cannot be fixed within a specific interval. To improve the training speed of the network, this study adopts the Max–Min normalization method to normalize the data, as shown in the following formula:

$$X_i^o = \frac{X_i - X_{min}}{X_{max} - X_{min}} \quad (12)$$

In the time series data X, where X_{max} is the maximum value and X_{min} is the minimum value.

4.3. Model and Parameter Settings Comparison

In the experiment, the comparative models include Support Vector Machine Regression (SVR), Long Short-Term Memory Network (LSTM), PT-LSTM, and OCPT-LSTM.

The Support Vector Machine (SVM) [28,29] analyzes the model structure to find the minimum risk and optimal structure, constructing the optimal classification hyperplane. This hyperplane maximizes the distance between the hyperplane and different types of sample sets while ensuring classification accuracy. SVR is a variant of SVM designed for regression tasks and prediction calculations. SVR characterizes the non-linear relationship between the vectors to be predicted and support vectors in the training set to predict the vectors to be predicted in the test set. LSTM has been described in detail in Section 2. PT-LSTM and OCPT-LSTM are the proposed models in this chapter, which have been detailed earlier.

Experimental Environment: Operating System Windows 10, Processor Intel i7-9700, 2.4 GHz, Memory 32 GB, and GPU GTX 1050Ti.

Training parameters based on experimental tuning, the optimal hyperparameter configurations are as follows: the penalty coefficient of SVM is 0.3, the kernel function is the radial basis kernel function, and the parameter g is 0.05. The number of neuron layers of $LSTM$ is 2, the number of hidden nodes is 50, the value of the learning factor lr is 0.004, the batchsize size is 64, and the number of iterations t is 50. The PT_LSTM in the period is 24, the number of neuron layers is 2, the number of hidden nodes is 150, the learning rate lr is 0.001, the batchsize is 64, and the number of iterations t is 50. In $OCPT - LSTM$, the range of the number of nodes in the hidden layer of the base model is 150, the learning factor lr is 0.005, the batchsize is 64, the model population size NP is set to 20, the dimensionality D is set to 30, the maximum variance factor F_{max} is 0.6, the minimum variance factor F_{min} is 0.2, the crossover probability CR is 0.5, and the maximum number of iterations T is 30.

4.4. Experimental Comparison and Result Analysis

This experiment conducts quality control on the data from the WaiZhou Station and ShiShang Station separately. The training data consist of cleaned hydrological data, and for the WaiZhou Station, the test data remain the cleaned data. The purpose of the WaiZhou Station experiment is to assess model accuracy and compare the prediction results of various models. Additionally, this experiment examines the usability of the prediction control model's confidence interval to observe whether the measured real data fall within the prediction control model's confidence interval and whether the interval effectively contains the measured real data. For the ShiShang Station, the training data comprise cleaned hydrological data, while the test data consist of raw hydrological data. This setup aims to assess whether the prediction control model can effectively detect abnormal data.

Firstly, the experiment predicts the flow at the WaiZhou Station, and the results are shown in Figure 6. It can be observed that the SVM model has significant fluctuations and intense shaking. The LSTM model, compared to the SVM model, shows considerable improvement, but there is still an issue with the peak values not reaching high points, and the prediction line is not sufficiently fitted. PT-LSTM improves upon the performance of LSTM, with most of the fitted parts of the peak values achieving a reasonably good effect. Constructing a confidence interval using such prediction results can completely envelop the true values. The OCPT-LSTM model, built on the basis of PT-LSTM, undergoes combined parameter optimization, resulting in more accurate predictions, especially fitting well during peak rise and fall. The specific evaluation metrics for the prediction results are shown in Table 1.

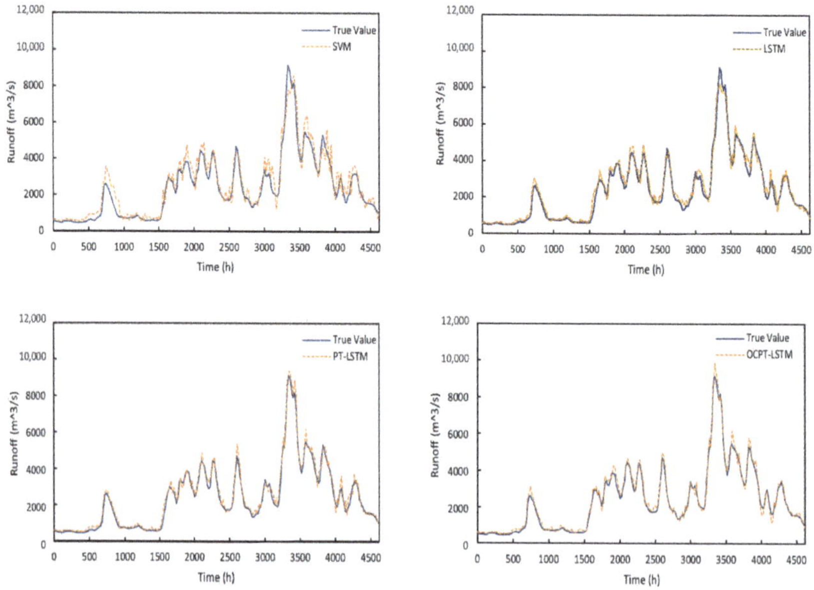

Figure 6. Comparison of flow prediction results of WaiZhou station in different models.

Table 1 presents a comparative evaluation of prediction results for different models. It can be observed that the SVM model performs the worst, with a low coefficient of determination, high root mean square error, and significantly larger maximum error for peak values compared to other models. The LSTM model, as an improved recurrent neural network model, shows much higher accuracy than the SVM model, with reduced root mean square error and maximum error. Both the PT-LSTM and OCPT-LSTM models are iteratively improved based on the basic LSTM model, resulting in better performance than the LSTM model. Among them, the OCPT-LSTM model exhibits the best performance with the fewest errors and more accurate predictions. As the OCPT-LSTM model combines and optimizes the PT-LSTM model, although it increases complexity, it also simultaneously improves accuracy. Both models, compared to other models, effectively enhance prediction performance.

Table 1. Comparison of WaiZhou station prediction results with different models.

Evaluation Index / Comparison Model	Coefficient of Certainty (R^2)	Root Mean Square Error ($RMSE$)/m^3	Maximum Error (ME)/m^3
SVM	0.940	213.12	1370
LSTM	0.974	106.85	1000
PT-LSTM	0.981	98.23	771
OCPT-LSTM	0.989	87.11	675

The construction results of the confidence intervals for the predictive control models are presented below. Figure 7 illustrates the confidence interval for PT-LSTM, while Figure 8 displays the confidence interval for OCPT-LSTM.

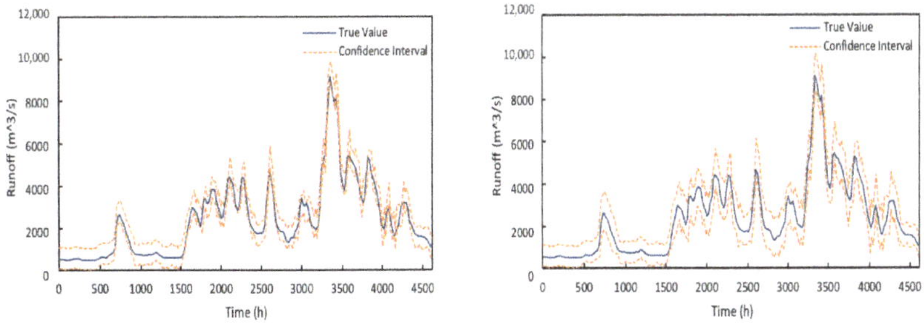

Figure 7. Confidence interval of PT-LSTM model before and after adjustment.

The first graph represents the conventional confidence interval for PT-LSTM, where the confidence interval coefficients are consistent. It can be observed that in situations where the flow rate experiences rapid increases and decreases, the measured values are prone to fall outside the confidence interval, leading to potential deviations in confidence interval control. Therefore, for parts of the flow with significant variations, the confidence interval is dynamically adjusted, as shown in the second graph. The adjusted confidence interval in the graph can easily envelop the measured values. Data falling between these adjusted confidence intervals are considered suspicious and require inspection for potential replacement.

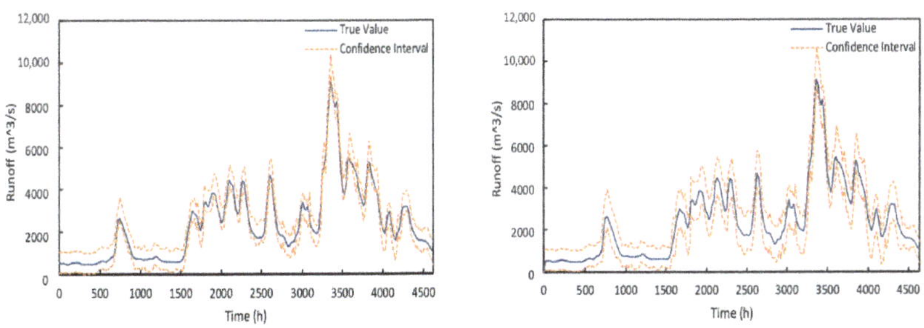

Figure 8. Confidence interval of OCPT-LSTM model before and after adjustment.

Similar to Figure 7, the two graphs in Figure 8 depict one with a conventional confidence interval and the other with an adjusted confidence interval. The first graph represents the conventional confidence interval for OCPT-LSTM. It can be observed that, similarly to the situation in the PT-LSTM case, in instances of large variations in flow rates, measured values tend to fall outside the confidence interval, leading to potential deviations in confidence interval control. Therefore, the confidence interval is adjusted for this portion, as shown in the second graph. In this graph, all measured values fall within the adjusted confidence interval. Data between these adjusted confidence intervals are considered suspicious and require inspection for potential replacement. After the establishment of the OCPT-LSTM model, it needs to be updated periodically, and the worst-performing base model should be replaced to ensure the timeliness of the model.

From the Table 2, it can be observed that the training time of the PT-LSTM model is approximately halved compared to LSTM, while the OCPT-LSTM model is the most complex and requires the longest training time. PT-LSTM simplifies the input based on LSTM, improving model efficiency and reducing training time. The OCPT-LSTM model involves the combination and continuous optimization replacement of PT-LSTM, resulting in longer training times and higher complexity. Therefore, when only detecting suspicious data or pursuing efficiency, the PT-LSTM model can be chosen. When accuracy and the provision of replacement values are crucial, the OCPT-LSTM model is more suitable. Both models can independently construct confidence intervals and, in the end, build a comprehensive confidence interval for data control. Additionally, the two models can validate each other, with data corrected by the Periodic Temporal LSTM (PT-LSTM) model being confirmed through the secondary quality assurance provided by the OCPT-LSTM combined model in online predictive control methods.

Table 2. Comparison of PT-LSTM and OCPT-LSTM training time.

Model	LSTM	PT-LSTM	OCPT-LSTM
Training time (s)	543	180	1298

Next, the experiment conducts quality control on the data from the ShiShang station. Confidence intervals are constructed separately for the two models, and then the two confidence intervals are combined as follows: $Z = [(y_1 - \delta_1 \cdot mse_1) + (y_2 - \delta_2 \cdot mse_2), (y_1 + \delta_1 \cdot mse_1) + (y_2 + \delta_2 \cdot mse_2)]/2$. This allows for the simultaneous evaluation of the usability of the two confidence intervals. After obtaining the confidence intervals, adjustments are made to the intervals in areas with significant changes in flow. Finally, using the confidence intervals, data are controlled, and values outside the intervals are identified as suspicious. The predicted values obtained from the models are suggested values; hydrological personnel decide whether or not to replace them. The results of the confidence interval construction are shown in Figure 9. It is evident that some data points fall outside the confidence intervals. These data points are marked with red asterisks.

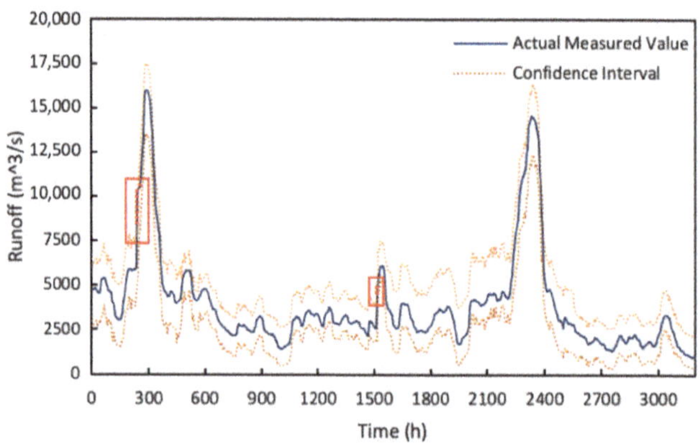

Figure 9. Abnormal data detected by combined confidence interval.

The data points in the red box in the figure represents the detected abnormal data. For the data points marked as anomalies, a search was conducted in the corresponding datasets. The identified time periods are from 2:00 a.m. to 10:00 p.m. on 8 March 2008, and from 6:00 p.m. to 10:00 p.m. on 12 May 2008. A comparison between the unprocessed data and processed data for these time periods is presented in Table 3. It also includes the interpolation effect of the Linear Interpolation method for comparison.

From the above table, it can be observed that the data detected by the confidence interval indeed exhibits some deviation from the cleaned data. Moreover, the predicted values are generally closer to the values of the clean data compared to the unprocessed data, resulting in overall smaller differences. Table 4 compares several sets of Absolute Error, which can more intuitively show that the suggested values provided by OCPT-LSTM are closer to clean data.

Table 3. Comparison of detected abnormal runoff data.

Date	Processed Data/m^3	Unprocessed Data/m^3	Estimated Value of OCPT-LSTM/m^3	Estimated Value of Linear Interpolation/m^3
8/3/2008 2:00	7050	10,200	6802	6236
8/3/2008 3:00	7103	10,209	6879	6442
8/3/2008 4:00	7159	10,227	6970	6648
8/3/2008 5:00	7213	10,248	7026	6735
8/3/2008 6:00	7288	10,263	7110	6964
8/3/2008 7:00	7322	10,280	7186	7147
8/3/2008 8:00	7386	10,296	7263	7249
8/3/2008 9:00	7442	10,312	7339	7556
8/3/2008 10:00	7498	10,328	7415	7693
8/3/2008 11:00	7554	10,345	7492	7875
8/3/2008 12:00	7611	10,361	7568	8058
8/3/2008 13:00	7649	10,378	7644	8240
8/3/2008 14:00	7790	10,400	7705	8422
8/3/2008 15:00	7970	10,411	7812	8604
8/3/2008 16:00	8150	10,419	7934	8786
8/3/2008 17:00	8354	10,429	8197	8969
8/3/2008 18:00	8542	10,439	8356	9151
8/3/2008 19:00	8734	10,448	8507	9333
8/3/2008 20:00	8926	10,450	8676	9515
8/3/2008 21:00	9118	10,461	8844	9697
8/3/2008 22:00	9310	10,469	9013	9880
12/5/2008 18:00	2583	3600	2733	2894
12/5/2008 19:00	2578	3850	2697	3188
12/5/2008 20:00	2570	4380	2592	3482
12/5/2008 21:00	2650	4670	2980	3776
12/5/2008 22:00	2770	4960	3200	4070

Table 4. Comparison of Absolute Error in detected abnormal runoff data.

Date	Processed Data/m^3	Absolute Error of Unprocessed Data/m^3	Absolute Error of OCPT-LSTM/m^3	Absolute Error of Linear Interpolation/m^3
8/3/2008 2:00	7050	3150	248	814
8/3/2008 3:00	7103	3106	224	661
8/3/2008 4:00	7159	3068	189	511
8/3/2008 5:00	7213	3035	187	478
8/3/2008 6:00	7288	2975	178	324
8/3/2008 7:00	7322	2958	136	175
8/3/2008 8:00	7386	2910	123	137
8/3/2008 9:00	7442	2870	103	114
8/3/2008 10:00	7498	2830	83	195
8/3/2008 11:00	7554	2791	63	321
8/3/2008 12:00	7611	2750	43	447
8/3/2008 13:00	7649	2729	5	591
8/3/2008 14:00	7790	2610	85	632
8/3/2008 15:00	7970	2441	158	634
8/3/2008 16:00	8150	2269	216	636
8/3/2008 17:00	8354	2075	157	615
8/3/2008 18:00	8542	1897	186	609
8/3/2008 19:00	8734	1714	227	599
8/3/2008 20:00	8926	1524	250	589
8/3/2008 21:00	9118	1343	274	579
8/3/2008 22:00	9310	1159	297	570

Table 4. *Cont.*

Date	Processed Data/m^3	Absolute Error of Unprocessed Data/m^3	Absolute Error of OCPT-LSTM/m^3	Absolute Error of Linear Interpolation/m^3
12/5/2008 18:00	2583	1017	150	311
12/5/2008 19:00	2578	1272	119	610
12/5/2008 20:00	2570	1810	22	912
12/5/2008 21:00	2650	2020	330	1126
12/5/2008 22:00	2770	2190	430	1300

5. Conclusions

This paper presents a method for online hydrological data quality control based on the characteristics of hydrological data and an adaptive differential evolution algorithm. Combining the principles of predictive control, a single predictive control model, PT-LSTM, is constructed by considering temporal features and spatial proximity at different time scales. Building upon PT-LSTM, an online optimization combination control model, OCPT-LSTM, is proposed to perform real-time rolling optimization and feedback correction. The introduced data quality control method reduces reliance on manual intervention, provides imputed values for missing data, effectively detects suspicious data, and offers suggested values. This approach contributes to enhancing the reliability of hydrological data analysis. In this study, it was observed that, besides anomaly detection, imputing missing data is another noteworthy issue. Currently, commonly used methods for missing data imputation include linear interpolation and mean imputation. However, these methods have accuracy limitations, prompting the consideration of further research into missing value imputation in future work.

Author Contributions: Conceptualization, Q.Z.; data curation, Y.Z.; formal analysis, X.Z. and S.C.; funding acquisition, Q.Z. and S.C.; investigation, Q.Z. and R.L.; methodology, Q.Z.; project administration, Y.Z. and R.L.; resources, Y.Z.; software, Q.Z.; supervision, Y.Z., X.Z. and S.C.; validation, Q.Z.; visualization, Q.Z. and X.Z.; writing—original draft, Q.Z.; and writing—review and editing, X.Z. and S.C. All authors have read and agreed to the published version of the manuscript.

Funding: This work has been partially supported by the Talent Startup project of Nanjing Institute of Technology (No. YKJ202117), the Jiangsu Provincial Department of Education's University Philosophy and Social Science Research Project (No. 2023SJYB0434), and the Talent Startup project of Nanjing Institute of Technology (No. YKJ202316).

Data Availability Statement: The datasets presented in this article are not available due to the confidentiality of the data provided by the relevant hydrological department.

Conflicts of Interest: The authors declare no conflicts of interest.

References

1. Soni, S.; Singh, A. Improving Data Quality using Big Data Framework: A Proposed Approach. *IOP Conf. Ser. Mater. Sci. Eng.* **2021**, *12*, 012092. [CrossRef]
2. Shanmugam, D.B.; Dhilipan, J.; Vignesh, A.; Prabhu, T. Challenges in Data Quality and Complexity of Managing Data Quality Assessment in Big Data. *Int. J. Recent Technol. Eng. (IJRTE)* **2020**, *9*, 589–593. [CrossRef]
3. Gou, J.; Miao, C.; Samaniego, L.; Xiao, M.; Wu, J.; Guo, X. CNRD v1.0: A High-Quality Natural Runoff Dataset for Hydrological and Climate Studies in China. *Bull. Am. Meteorol. Soc.* **2021**, *102*, 929–947. [CrossRef]
4. Veeraswamy, G.; Nagaraju, A.; Balaji, E.; Sreedhar, Y.; Narasimhlu, K.; Harish, P. Data sets on spatial analysis of hydro geochemistry of Gudur area, SPSR Nellore district by using inverse distance weighted method in Arc GIS 10.1. *Data Brief* **2019**, *22*, 1003–1011.
5. Yang, H. Random distributional response model based on spline method. *J. Stat. Plan. Inference* **2020**, *207*, 27–44. [CrossRef]
6. Mousa, M.; Kkhrajan, M.; Merzah, H.Y. Construct Polynomial of Degree n by Using Repeated Linear Interpolation. *IOP Conf. Ser. Mater. Sci. Eng.* **2020**, *928*, 042009.
7. Huang, G. Missing data filling method based on linear interpolation and lightgbm. *J. Phys. Conf. Ser.* **2021**, *1754*, 012187. [CrossRef]

8. Sciuto, G.; Bonaccorso, B.; Cancelliere, A.; Rossi, G. Probabilistic quality control of daily temperature data. *Int. J. Climatol.* **2013**, *33*, 1211–1227. [CrossRef]
9. Steinacker, R.; Mayer, D.; Steiner, A. Data Quality Control Based on Self-Consistency. *Mon. Weather Rev.* **2011**, *139*, 3974–3991. [CrossRef]
10. Sciuto, G.; Bonaccorso, B.; Cancelliere, A.; Rossi, G. Quality control of daily rainfall data with neural networks. *J. Hydrol.* **2008**, *364*, 13–22. [CrossRef]
11. Abbot, J.; Marohasy, J. Application of artificial neural networks to rainfall forecasting in Queensland, Australia. *Adv. Atmos. Sci.* **2012**, *29*, 717–730. [CrossRef]
12. Fu, F.; Luo, X. Study on Quality Control Method of Hydrological Data. *Water Resour. Informatiz.* **2012**, *5*, 12–15+19.
13. Yu, Y.; Wang, D. An Application Research of Benford's Law in Hydrological Data Quality Mining. *Microelectron. Comput.* **2011**, *8*, 180–183+186.
14. Ding, X.; Wang, H.; Zhang, X.; Li, J.; Gao, H. Association relationships study of multi-dimensional data quality. *J. Softw.* **2016**, *27*, 1626–1644.
15. Juliusz, L.; Kulikowski. Data Quality Assessment: Problems and Methods. *Int. J. Organ. Collect. Intell. (IJOCI)* **2014**, *4*, 24–36.
16. Reynolds, M.; Bourke, A.; Dreyer, N. Considerations when evaluating real-world data quality in the context of fitness for purpose. *Pharmacoepidemiol. Drug Saf.* **2020**, *29*, 1316–1318. [CrossRef]
17. Yu, Y.; Zhang, J.; Zhu, Y.; Wang, D. Data Quality Control and Management for Hydrological Database. *J. China Hydrol.* **2013**, *3*, 65–68.
18. Tang, D.; Cheng, X.; Wang, D.; Zhu, Y. Research and Application of Continuous Hydrologic Data Quality Control. *Inf. Technol.* **2017**, *4*, 8–12+16.
19. Zhao, Q.; Zhu, Y.; Wan, D.; Yu, Y.; Cheng, X. Research on the Data-Driven quality control method of hydrological time series data. *Water* **2018**, *10*, 1712. [CrossRef]
20. Binquan, L.; Zhongmin, L.; Qingrui, C.; Wei, Z.; Huan, W.; Jun, W.; Yiming, H. On the Operational Flood Forecasting Practices Using Low-Quality Data Input of a Distributed Hydrological Model. *Sustainability* **2020**, *12*, 8268. [CrossRef]
21. Yu, Y.; Wan, D.; Zhao, Q.; Liu, H. Detecting Pattern Anomalies in Hydrological Time Series with Weighted Probabilistic Suffix Trees. *Water* **2020**, *12*, 1464. [CrossRef]
22. Lattawit, K.; Chantana, C.; Montri, M.; Wongchaisuwat, P.; Wimala, S.; Sarinnapakorn, K.; Boonya-aroonnet, S. Anomaly Detection Using a Sliding Window Technique and Data Imputation with Machine Learning for Hydrological Time Series. *Water* **2021**, *13*, 1862. [CrossRef]
23. Hyojoong, K.; Heeyoung, K. Contextual anomaly detection for high-dimensional data using Dirichlet process variational autoencoder. *IISE Trans.* **2023**, *55*, 433–444.
24. Hyojoong, K.; Heeyoung, K. Contextual anomaly detection for multivariate time series data. *Qual. Eng.* **2023**, *35*, 686–695.
25. Li, D.; Cui, S.; Li, Y.; Xu, J.; Xiao, F.; Xu, S. Pad: Towards principled adversarial malware detection against evasion attacks. *IEEE Trans. Dependable Secur. Comput.* **2023**, *21*, 920–936. [CrossRef]
26. Cui, S.; Li, T.; Chen, S.C.; Shyu, M.L.; Li, Q.; Zhang, H. DISL: deep isomorphic substructure learning for network representations. *Knowl. Based Syst.* **2020**, *189*, 105086. [CrossRef]
27. Liu, X.; Ju, X.; Fan, S. A Research on the Applicability of Spatial Regression Test in Meteorological Datasets. *J. Appl. Meteor. Sci.* **2006**, *17*, 37–43.
28. Olivier, C.; Patrick, H.; Vladimir, V. Support vector machines for histogram-based image classification. *IEEE Trans. Neural Netw.* **1999**, *10*, 1055–1064.
29. Brown, M.; Steve, R.G.; Hugh, G. Support vector machines for optimal classification and spectral unmixing. *Ecol. Model.* **1999**, *20*, 167–179. [CrossRef]

mathematics

Article

Abnormal Traffic Detection System Based on Feature Fusion and Sparse Transformer

Xinjian Zhao [1], Weiwei Miao [1], Guoquan Yuan [1], Yu Jiang [2,*], Song Zhang [1] and Qianmu Li [2]

1 State Grid Jiangsu Electric Power Co., Ltd., Information & Telecommunication Branch, Nanjing 210024, China; zhaoxinjian_nj@163.com (X.Z.); miao_weiwei_sgcc@163.com (W.M.); guoquan_yuan@163.com (G.Y.); m18362973161_1@163.com (S.Z.)
2 School of Cyber Science and Engineering, Nanjing University of Science and Technology, Nanjing 210094, China; qianmu@njust.edu.cn
* Correspondence: jiangyu@njust.edu.cn

Abstract: This paper presents a feature fusion and sparse transformer-based anomalous traffic detection system (FSTDS). FSTDS utilizes a feature fusion network to encode the traffic data sequences and extracting features, fusing them into coding vectors through shallow and deep convolutional networks, followed by deep coding using a sparse transformer to capture the complex relationships between network flows; finally, a multilayer perceptron is used to classify the traffic and achieve anomaly traffic detection. The feature fusion network of FSTDS improves feature extraction from small sample data, the deep encoder enhances the understanding of complex traffic patterns, and the sparse transformer reduces the computational and storage overhead and improves the scalability of the model. Experiments demonstrate that the number of FSTDS parameters is reduced by up to nearly half compared to the baseline, and the success rate of anomalous flow detection is close to 100%.

Keywords: anomaly detection; feature fusion; convolutional neural network; sparse transformer; deep encoder

MSC: 68T07

1. Introduction

With society's increasing emphasis on renewable energy and the rapid development of distributed energy, distributed resource aggregation platforms play an increasingly critical role in the information interaction of power network enterprises. These platforms not only realize the monitoring, control, and optimal dispatch of distributed energy resources but also promote the intelligent and efficient operation of the network system. However, with the increasing scale of distributed energy access, the emergence of anomaly network traffic becomes a serious challenge [1]. Accurate evaluation of the collected network traffic data is necessary for researchers to spot objectionable behaviors in the traffic. Network traffic packets are typically separated into streams based on the source IP, destination IP, source port, destination port, protocol, and timestamp in order to improve the identification of anomalous network activity [2]. Accompanied by the rapid development of machine learning, the detection of anomaly traffic using network traffic classification has been one of the hotspots of common concern in academia, industry, and network regulators, the essence of which involves categorizing mixed traffic into distinct traffic categories depending on the features or attributes of various network applications or protocols. On the one hand, the network security field needs to identify the intrusion traffic; on the other hand, network management needs to analyze the traffic classification of different applications so as to reasonably control and allocate resources to ensure the network smoothness. With the massive increase of data volume and the variety of network traffic, traditional classification methods do not easily meet the requirements, and deep learning-based algorithms have become a research hotspot for network traffic anomaly detection [3].

Abnormal network traffic may be caused by a variety of factors such as malicious attacks, equipment failures, data communication anomalies, etc., which bring serious impacts upon the stable operation of the system and the quality of data interaction. Malicious attackers may utilize vulnerabilities or malicious codes to try to interfere with the normal operation of distributed resource aggregation platforms and network enterprise systems or even steal sensitive information. Meanwhile, device failures and misconfigurations may lead to the generation of anomaly data, which interferes with the operation of the network system. In addition, failures or congestion of data communication links may also lead to data transmission anomalies, which bring issues to network information interaction. In such a complex environment, it is particularly important to recognize and handle the anomaly traffic in a timely and accurate manner.

ChatGPT has experienced a significant increase in usage across academic, private, and professional sectors because of its capacity to respond to intricate cues and produce human-like texts of exceptional quality [4]. ChatGPT, similar to numerous other extensive language models, is built upon the transformer architecture. Transformer architectures are highly effective for natural language processing (NLP) activities due to their ability to capture distant dependencies and interactions among various elements of a sequence without requiring prior domain-specific knowledge or feature engineering. The transformer architecture, first intended for NLP, has demonstrated its versatility and potency in capturing intricate patterns and relationships in several forms of sequential data, encompassing images, graphics, and speech. Transformer-based models are well-suited for deep learning-based network traffic anomaly detection systems. These systems capture traffic data as sequences of packets or streams and require the ability to identify intricate patterns in order to perform effectively [5].

While many deep learning-based anomaly traffic detection systems have reached satisfactory detection performance, there remain three notable issues that have not yet been resolved:

1. Most traffic datasets are unbalanced datasets. In reality, often, the majority of the collected traffic is normal traffic, and the anomaly attack traffic is extremely unbalanced in comparison. Under-sampling and over-sampling are commonly employed techniques to address data imbalance. However, under-sampling results in the removal of data, leading to the loss of certain features. On the other hand, over-sampling introduces additional data, which alters the original data distribution. Both of these approaches have an impact on the accuracy of the experiment;
2. Acquiring previous information from concealed aspects of past traffic in conventional detection methods is challenging. Although network communications follow a sequential pattern, current ML (machine learning)-based anomaly traffic detection research often ignores sequential data and instead focuses on isolating and classifying individual network flow records;
3. Transformer models tend to have very large parameters and high training costs. For example, the GPT model parameter size is 110 M, the BERT model parameter size is 340 M, and the T5 model parameter size is as high as 11.7 B. This not only puts forward higher requirements for the hardware but also greatly increases the training time.

This paper proposes a feature fusion and sparse transformer-based anomalous traffic detection system (FSTDS). This system involves a feature fusion network when inputting the encoded traffic data sequence. The two-layer parallel convolutional network extracts shallow and deep features from the preprocessed flow data and fuses the extracted features to obtain the encoded flow data vector; then, a deep encoder based on sparse transformer is used to capture different network flows. Finally, a multi-layer perceptron is used to classify the traffic to detect abnormal traffic. The main contributions are as follows:

1. By introducing the feature fusion network in the encoding stage, the feature extraction effect of small sample data is improved;
2. Combination with deep encoders enhances the acquisition of remote information in complex network traffic patterns;
3. Through sparse transformer, computing and storage overhead are reduced, and the scalability of the model is increased.

2. Related Work

2.1. NetFlow

Monitoring network traffic is a crucial component of network security and management. There are two primary techniques employed for this objective: packet-based monitoring and flow-based monitoring. Packet-based monitoring entails capturing the headers and payloads of packets as they travel over the network, while flow-based monitoring gathers summarized information based on the sequence of packets between two endpoints [6]. However, packet-based continuous monitoring is difficult to implement in large-scale networks due to its resource-intensive nature. Moreover, packet capture gives rise to privacy problems, as it has the potential to gather sensitive information. On the other hand, flow-based monitoring offers a significantly condensed overview of network traffic, which makes it a more efficient and adaptable option. Flow-based traffic export and collection are extensively utilized in expansive networks, with a plethora of technologies readily accessible for this purpose.

NetFlow is a popular protocol developed by Cisco for collecting and monitoring flow-based network traffic statistics. The operation involves combining a sequence of packets in a transmission, which can be either one-way or two-way, that share common attributes such as the same source and destination IP, source and destination port, and transfer protocol [7]. Bidirectional NetFlow has the ability to capture packets and bytes in both directions, along with other functionalities.

2.2. Traffic Anomaly Detection

Machine learning has becoming extensively utilized for detecting traffic anomalies due to the ongoing advancements in artificial intelligence and cloud computing technology. In 1980, Anderson [8] introduced the notion of intrusion detection technology with the goal of rapidly detecting anomalous behaviors in the network and mitigating the resulting losses. Anomaly detection technology takes advantage of the continuous updating of new technologies. The purpose of these new methods is to perceive anomalies with precise prediction accuracy and improve real-time prediction efficiency by extracting different patterns from network traffic to distinguish abnormal traffic from regular traffic.

Researchers have dedicated significant effort to proposing diverse network intrusion detection systems with the aim of identifying and thwarting irregular attacks on network traffic. Currently, the predominant machine learning techniques used in intrusion detection are supervised learning approaches, including random forest (RF) [9], K-closest neighbor (KNN) [10], and support vector machine (SVM) [11]. Chowdhury et al. [12] suggested merging two machine learning techniques to categorize incursions that are based on signatures. Their study utilized the simulated annealing approach to produce three random feature sets and employed the SVM algorithm to detect unusual behaviors. Yang Min and colleagues [13] introduced an advanced semi-supervised framework (ESeT) for network intrusion detection. The framework comprises a multi-level feature extraction module and a semi-supervised learning module, which leverage a limited quantity of labelled data to enhance detection performance. Nevertheless, because of the inherent characteristics of identifying familiar dangers and the constraints of conventional machine learning techniques, a significant proportion of advanced cyber assaults can currently evade signature repositories. The aforementioned methods exhibit a high rate of false alarms and a low rate of detection when it comes to identifying traffic irregularities. The unresolved research problem pertains to the development of an efficient detection system.

Furthermore, deep learning exhibits strong flexibility, self-organization, and generalization skills. Consequently, it is capable of effectively addressing the issues that arise in conventional machine learning. In recent years, scholars have extensively researched the application of deep learning in order to enhance the detection system's efficiency. Tuor et al. [14] used deep neural network autoencoders for unsupervised network anomaly detection, using temporal aggregation statistics as features. Yan [15] constructed an intrusion detection system utilizing a convolutional neural network (CNN) and employed a generative adversarial network to produce synthetic attack trails. The empirical findings confirmed the efficacy of the approach.

2.3. *Transformer Architecture*

Although network communications are inherently sequential, current ML-based research often neglects sequential data and instead prioritizes the classification of individual network flow records in isolation. The introduction of the transformer architecture in the field of natural language processing marked a significant advancement in applying machine learning to sequential data. Vaswani [16] first built a transformer architecture based on the attention mechanism. Dosovitskiy [17] introduced BERT, a novel language representation model that utilizes transformers to pre-train on unlabeled text by simultaneously adjusting the left and right context. BERT achieved state-of-the-art performance on 11 natural language processing tasks at that time.

In addition, effectively identifying a significant fraction of attacks in network traffic necessitates taking into account the extended patterns and attributes of the network [18]. Transformer's ability to access remote information helps detect complex network traffic patterns that may indicate an attack. Therefore, studying transformer architecture has huge potential. Wu et al. [19] introduced a transformer-based intrusion detection system named RTIDS. This system utilizes position-embedding technology to establish connections between sequence information and features. Alkhatib et al. [20] showed that BERT can be effectively used to learn quorum identifier (ID) sequences in a controller area network (CAN) using a "masked language model" unsupervised training aim.

Secondly, although there are great improvements in combining the transformer architecture, applying transformer in the network field is not as simple as in the natural language field. Although the architecture for using transformers to process text data has been established, the same is not true for network traffic. In order to obtain network data and generate classifications from the transformer output, key decisions must be made independently of the transformer model itself [21]. To solve this problem, this paper proposes FSTDS, an anomaly traffic detection system based on feature fusion and sparse transformer. FSTDS leverages the distinct benefits of feature fusion and sparse transformer architecture to enhance both the accuracy of detecting aberrant network traffic and the speed at which the model is trained.

3. System Design

The overall framework of FSTDS is shown in Figure 1. In this section, we delve into each key step of FSTDS, including preprocessing technology, feature fusion network, sparse transformer, and classification head.

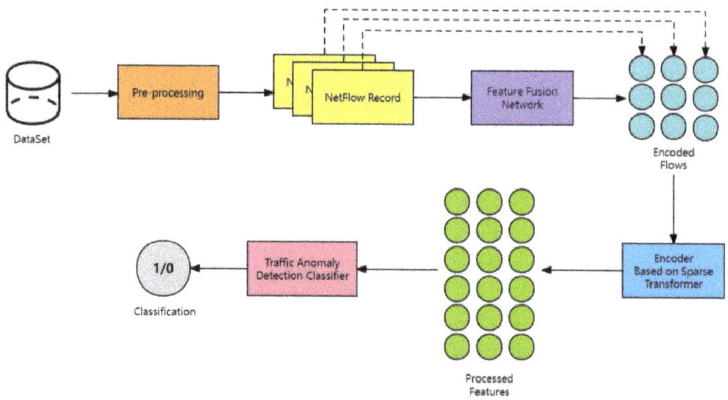

Figure 1. FSTDS Overall Framework Diagram.

3.1. Data Preprocessing

First, we collect the NetFlow streaming dataset of traffic through the NetFlow Analyzer tool and preprocess the dataset. The main steps of preprocessing are as follows:

1. One-hot encoding: The NetFlow streaming dataset contains categorical features that need to be translated into numerical values for optimal prediction results from our deep learning model. Thus, the columns were transformed into numerical values using the get_dummies function from the pandas package in Python for the preparation stage. We chose one-hot encoding instead of the label encoder because the label encoder will produce multiple numbers in the same column, and the model may misinterpret that the values are in a specific order, which will affect classification;
2. Normalization: Normalization refers to the process of rescaling data to a given range in order to minimize duplication and expedite model training. The study employs min–max normalization to rescale the data range to [0, 1]:

$$x_{[i]} = \frac{x_{[i]} - x_{min}}{x_{max} - x_{min}}; \tag{1}$$

3. S-fold stratified cross-validation: Stratification involves reorganizing the data to guarantee that each subset is a reliable representation of the entire dataset. The stratified S-fold cross-validation technique partitions the dataset into S subsets, and the model is trained on S-1 subsets while being validated on the S-th subset. This process continues until all folds have been utilized to validate the model. Stratification guarantees that every fold accurately represents the full dataset, facilitating parameter optimization and enhancing the model's ability to categorize attacks.

3.2. CNN-Based Feature Fusion

For the preprocessed stream records, the one-hot encoding of the classification field is connected with the numerical field and then put into the feature fusion network as input. The feature fusion network structure is shown in Figure 2. In this paper, we denote the stride by the lowercase letter "s" and the number of folds in S-fold cross-validation by the uppercase letter "S". This distinction ensures clarity in discussing these two concepts throughout the paper.

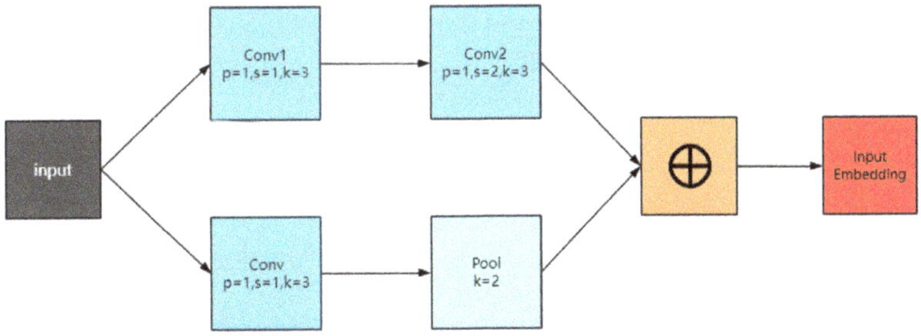

Figure 2. Feature fusion network structure.

The feature fusion network has two layers of parallel convolutional networks. The initial layer is composed of two stacked convolutional layers. The first convolutional layer has a stride of 1, while the second convolutional layer has a stride of 2 and a kernel size of 3. The second layer is composed of a convolutional layer and a pooling layer. The convolutional layer has a kernel size of 3 and a stride of 1, while the pooling layer has a stride of 2. The padding size utilized in the two-layer convolution process is 1 for both layers. To fully utilize the features obtained from the convolutional layer and pooling layer, the extracted features are combined to generate the encoded stream data.

In order to maintain the size of the input matrix during the convolution operation, it is necessary to execute a padding procedure:

$$X = \text{Padding}\,(X_0, 1) = \begin{bmatrix} 0 & \cdots & \cdots & \cdots & 0 \\ & x_{11} & \cdots & x_{1W} & \\ \vdots & \vdots & \cdots & \vdots & \vdots \\ & x_{H1} & \cdots & x_{HW} & \\ 0 & \cdots & \cdots & \cdots & 0 \end{bmatrix} \tag{2}$$

where X_0 represents the preprocessed stream record matrix data, and the variable W represents the width of the matrix, whereas the variable H represents the height.

The calculation process of the first layer in the feature fusion network is as follows:

X_1^1 represents the feature matrix obtained after the first convolution operation. Since the step size is 1, the output size remains unchanged.

$$X_1^1 = X \odot C = \begin{bmatrix} x_{11} & \cdots & x_{1k} \\ \vdots & \ddots & \vdots \\ x_{k1} & \cdots & x_{kk} \end{bmatrix} \odot \begin{bmatrix} c_{11} & \cdots & c_{1k} \\ \vdots & \ddots & \vdots \\ c_{k1} & \cdots & c_{kk} \end{bmatrix} \tag{3}$$

Among them, C represents the convolution kernel matrix, c_{ij} indicates the specific value within the convolution kernel matrix, and k denotes the size of the kernel.

$$X_1^2 = \text{padding}\left(X_1^1, 1\right) \tag{4}$$

X_1^3 represents the feature matrix that is derived from the second convolution operation. Since the step size is 2, the output size is halved.

$$X_1^3 = X_1^2 \odot C = \begin{bmatrix} x_{11}^2 & \cdots & x_{1k}^2 \\ \vdots & \ddots & \vdots \\ x_{k1}^2 & \cdots & x_{kk}^2 \end{bmatrix} \odot \begin{bmatrix} c_{11} & \cdots & c_{1k} \\ \vdots & \ddots & \vdots \\ c_{k1} & \cdots & c_{kk} \end{bmatrix} \tag{5}$$

The second layer calculation process of the feature fusion network is as follows:

X_2^1 represents the feature matrix extracted after the convolution operation. The step size is 1, so the output size does not change.

$$X_2^1 = X \odot C = \begin{bmatrix} x_{11} & \cdots & x_{1k} \\ \vdots & \ddots & \vdots \\ x_{k1} & \cdots & x_{kk} \end{bmatrix} \odot \begin{bmatrix} c_{11} & \cdots & c_{1k} \\ \vdots & \ddots & \vdots \\ c_{k1} & \cdots & c_{kk} \end{bmatrix} \tag{6}$$

The matrix X_2^2 indicates the result of applying the feature maximal pooling procedure, which reduces the size of the output feature matrix by half.

$$X_2^2 = \text{Maxpooling}\left(X_2^1\right) = \frac{max\left\{x_{ij}^1\right\}}{i,j \in [1,k]} \tag{7}$$

Then, the matrix results obtained by the two layers of parallel convolutional networks are feature-fused to obtain the encoded traffic feature X_f:

$$X_f = X_1^3 \oplus X_2^2 \tag{8}$$

3.3. Sparse Transformer Based on Memory Compression

Utilizing a transformer-based strategy offers numerous advantages to the system. Transformer's ability to support parallel execution sets it apart from other ways of processing sequential data, enabling efficient and scalable analysis of network data. Moreover, the transformer model adeptly captures intricate connections among various network flows, rendering it highly ideal for NetFlow processing.

The encoded stream data are input into a deep encoder based on sparse transformer and converted into a fixed-length feature vector sequence. The encoder is composed of several blocks, each comprising a multi-head sparse attention block and a multilayer perceptron (MLP) block. Normalization is applied before each block, and residual concatenation is applied after each block.

The method of calculating attention is to multiply the input vector sequence by the linear matrices W_q, W_k, and W_v to generate the query vector Q, key vector K, and value vector V for each position. The inner product of Q and K is performed and normalized to obtain the attention matrix of each position with respect to all positions and then multiplied by V to obtain the sequence representation of the input sequence after self-attention.

$$Attention(Q,K,V) = softmax\left(\frac{QK^T}{\sqrt{d_k}}\right)V \tag{9}$$

To design a sparse self-attention block method, we modify the transformer's multi-head self-attention to reduce memory usage by limiting the dot product between Q and K. Stride convolution is used to compress K and V on the sequence length, and the number of queries Q remains unchanged. First, a convolution sliding along the sequence length dimension is used to downsample the dimension to obtain a smaller matrix of key and value:

$$K_s^T = Conv\left(K^T\right) = \begin{bmatrix} k_{11} & \cdots & k_{N1} \\ \cdots & \cdots & \cdots \\ k_{D1} & \cdots & k_{DN} \end{bmatrix} \Longrightarrow \begin{bmatrix} k_{11} & \cdots & k_{L1} \\ \cdots & \cdots & \cdots \\ k_{D1} & \cdots & k_{DL} \end{bmatrix} \tag{10}$$

$$V_s^T = Conv\left(V^T\right) = \begin{bmatrix} v_{11} & \cdots & v_{N1} \\ \cdots & \cdots & \cdots \\ v_{D1} & \cdots & v_{DN} \end{bmatrix} \Longrightarrow \begin{bmatrix} v_{11} & \cdots & v_{L1} \\ \cdots & \cdots & \cdots \\ v_{D1} & \cdots & v_{DL} \end{bmatrix} \tag{11}$$

The memory compression principle of sparse transformer is shown in Figure 3. N is the initial length of the sequence, D represents the dimension, and L represents the length of the sequence after downsampling. It can be seen that the complexity of sparse self-attention matrix multiplication is $O(NL)$, while the complexity of standard Q and K calculations is $O(N^2)$. The size of L is often half or even less than N because strided convolution is based on this sparse method. It greatly decreases the amount of parameters that the transformer needs to train, better utilizes the information in the input sequence, and removes irrelevant information.

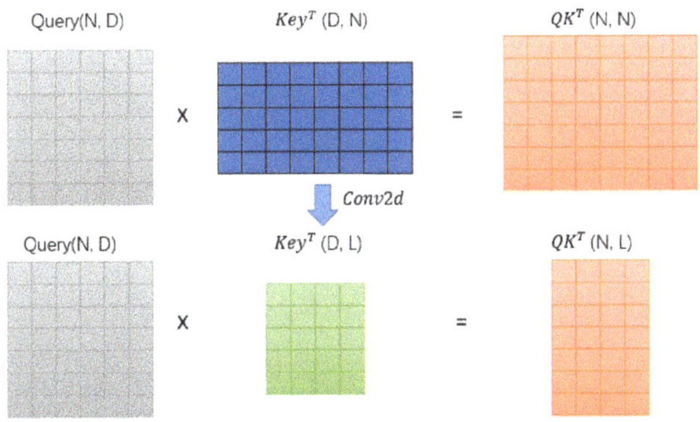

Figure 3. The difference in memory between standard self-attention and sparse self-attention.

Then, the multi-head attention value is obtained by splicing the head attention, and weighted fusion is performed through the learnable parameter W^o to obtain the final output label sequence.

$$Head_i = Attention\left(QW_i^Q, KW_i^K, VW_i^V\right) \tag{12}$$

$$Multihead(Q, K, V) = Concat(head_1, \ldots, head_b)W^o \tag{13}$$

3.4. MLP-Based Anomaly Classifier

The transformer is a type of model that operates on sequences where both the input and output are sequences. For the traffic anomaly detection system, we aim to have classification as output. The classification head retrieves the output token sequence from the transformer components and transforms it into predictions for one or several classes. The primary obstacle associated with the classification head is the issue of dimensionality. Transformers exhibit fast handling of sequences of any length. However, directly feeding the output into a dense neural network might lead to an exponential growth in the number of parameters. On the contrary, classification heads are usually created to choose particular components or condense the information obtained from the transformer. This way, they avoid experiencing the same rise in dimensionality as the sequence length increases.

For each feature in the contextual representation, we use densely connected multi-layer perceptron (MLP). This is a spatiotemporally distributed technique that enables the model to assign varying weights to different streams within the sequence. Typically, the classification task of traffic anomaly detection systems involves only the category of the last flow (e.g., benign or anomalous), and using only the embedding vector of the last context is sufficient. We use the last context embedding vector as the input of the multi-layer perceptron, which still includes information from previous streaming data due to the role of multi-head self-attention in the transformer.

Next, we compute the loss during the training process through the binary cross-entropy loss function:

$$Loss = -\frac{1}{N}\sum_{i=1}^{N} y_i \cdot log(p(y_i)) + (1 - y_i) \cdot log(1 - p(y_i)) \tag{14}$$

where $p(y_i)$ represents the probability output by the MLP for the y_i, and N represents the total number of samples contained within the training set.

The number of predefined MLP hidden layer neurons is 128, and the dropout rate is 10%. The gradient descent method is used for parameter training to obtain the final model for malicious network traffic detection, enabling anomaly traffic detection.

4. Experiment

4.1. Experimental Setup

4.1.1. Experimental Environment

This study performed experiments on FSTDS in the specific setting described in Table 1.

Table 1. Experimental environment.

CPU	Intel(R) Core(TM) i5-10400 CPU @ 2.90 GHz (Intel Corporation, Santa Clara, CA, USA)
RAM	16 GB DDR4 RAM (Kingston Technology, Fountain Valley, CA, USA)
GPU	NVIDIA GeForce RTX 2060 6G (NVIDIA Corporation, Santa Clara, CA, USA)
Compiler Environment	python 3.8 + tensorflow 2.0
Operating System	Windows 10 (Microsoft Corporation, Redmond, WA, USA)

4.1.2. Training Details

During the process of training the model, referring to FlowTransformer [4], we employed early stopping and epoch limitation. Early stopping was set to 10 epochs of patience, while the maximum number of epochs was restricted to 40. We chose 40 epochs because we observed in our initial experiments that by the 40th epoch, most models had converged to within 1% of their final performance. We used the Adam optimizer for training and specify a learning rate of 0.025.

4.1.3. Dataset

In this paper, we conduct a series of experiments using KDD-CUP99, UNSW-NB15, and Grid-Flow datasets.

1. KDD-CUP99 dataset: This dataset is utilized in conjunction with the Third International Knowledge Discovery and Data Mining Tools Competition, which took place simultaneously with the KDD-99 Fifth International Conference on Knowledge Discovery and Data Mining. The objective of the competition is to construct a network intrusion detector, which is a prognostic model with the ability to differentiate between "malicious" connections known as intrusions or attacks and "benign" normal connections. The dataset comprises a standardized collection of data that is subject to auditing, encompassing several incursions within a military network setting;
2. UNSW-NB15 dataset: The University of New South Wales released this dataset in 2015. Since its inception, the UNSW dataset has been extensively utilized. The UNSWNB15 dataset encompasses a wider range of attack families, a larger set of extracted features, and a distinct number of IP addresses employed for simulations and data collecting [10]. The dataset comprises a combination of genuine, up-to-date normal network traffic and current, extensive attack efforts;
3. Grid-Flow dataset: The Grid-Flow dataset consists of the grid flow collected from time to time by the Information and Communication Branch of State Grid Jiangsu Electric Power Co., Ltd. during October 2023 on the distributed resource aggregation platform during the information interaction between power grid enterprises, including but not limited to real-time flow data from various power sources, grid flow types, regional distribution, peak and valley periods, etc.

Table 2 shows a list of features available in Grid-Flow dataset. The feature distribution of KDD-CUP99 and UNSW-NB15 datasets refers to the work of J. Sinha et al. [22]. We utilized the findings presented in their research to support our analysis in this paper.

Table 2. Grid-Flow Dataset Attack Categories.

Category	Count
Normal	898,195
DoS	4268
Brute Force	167,412
Spoofing	25,112
DDoS	259,565
Recon	24,829
Web-based	35,738
Mirai	1364
Total	1,416,483

4.1.4. Evaluation Metrics

Several common metrics are used to evaluate the performance of binary classifiers:

- True positive (TP)—the number of attack flows correctly classified as attacks;
- False positive (FP)—the number of benign flows incorrectly classified as attacks;
- True negatives (TN)—the number of benign flows correctly classified as normal;
- False negatives (FN)—the number of attack flows incorrectly classified as normal.

Formula (15) provides the definition of accuracy (ACC), which is the percentage of all correct classifications. The definitions of precision, recall, and F1-score are shown in Formulas (16), (17) and (18), respectively. The first two metrics quantify the impact of misclassifications on the accuracy of accurate classifications, while the last metric provides a comprehensive evaluation of the balance between precision and recall.

$$Acc = \frac{TP + TN}{TP + TN + FP + FN} \tag{15}$$

$$Precision = \frac{TP}{TP + FP} \tag{16}$$

$$Recall = \frac{TP}{TP + FN} \tag{17}$$

$$F1 = \frac{2 * (Precision * Recall)}{Precision + Recall} \tag{18}$$

4.2. Overall Performance

We report the results of accuracy and F1-score evaluation of all methods in Table 3. The following observations are made:

1. Our proposed FSTDS model achieves the best performance. Compared to existing methods, it improved by 1.78% and 3.67% on the KDD-CUP99 and UNSW-NB15 datasets, respectively. Among all compared methods, FSTDS outperforms other baselines on both datasets. Specifically, it shows a relative ACC improvement of 1.76% and 0.88% over the strongest baseline respectively, demonstrating the effectiveness of FSTDS;
2. In conventional machine learning models, the support vector machine (SVM) and K-nearest neighbor (KNN) exhibit an accuracy of 81%. The KNN and SVM models, on the other hand, achieve accuracy rates of 92.96% and 93.17%, respectively. Isolation forest (IF) has the lowest accuracy among traditional ML models, at 55.05%. When comparing these models to deep learning models, a substantial enhancement in accuracy is seen. In particular, the convolutional neural network (CNN) and transformer

models significantly outperform all traditional ML models in the comparison. This conclusion demonstrates the effectiveness of our proposed FSTDS in the practical application, affirming its superiority over conventional ML and sophisticated deep learning methods in terms of model precision;

3. In Table 3, the performance of FSTDS and other baselines in the datasets is evaluated using ACC and F1. The superior performance of FSTDS on both datasets demonstrates that the feature fusion and sparse Transformer architecture model significantly improve the accuracy of security-related tasks.

Table 3. Performance of FSTDS on KDD-CUP99, UNSW-NB15, and Grid-Flow.

Dataset	Method	*Acc*	*F1*
KDD-CUP99	GAN [23]	70.80	87.00
	HELAD	90.10	89.10
	uPU [24]	84.14	81.55
	nnPU [24]	89.62	89.14
	VPU [25]	90.30	89.58
	NB	98.00	98.00
	SVM	99.00	99.00
	FastRNN [26]	99.60	99.71
	FSTDS	99.73	99.75
UNSW-NB15	SVM	99.13	92.96
	BERT Model	98.90	76.23
	CNN	99.23	93.51
	IF [27]	86.33	55.05
	NB [28]	99.25	93.68
	KNN	99.30	93.17
	NN [29]	99.25	93.68
	FSTDS	99.34	93.75
Grid-Flow	GAN [23]	82.26	81.69
	CNN	98.12	86.75
	IF [27]	84.97	79.23
	NN [29]	97.25	90.68
	FSTDS	98.47	91.77

4.3. Ablation Study

In this section, we discuss the changes in parameter quantities and the impact on experimental results after introducing sparse transformer.

As shown in Figure 4, the introduction of the sparse transformer significantly reduces the parameter count, but the detection performance remains largely unchanged. For example, in the UNSW-NB15 dataset, the number of parameters has decreased by 47.95% compared to the baseline, while the accuracy basically remained unchanged, that is, from 99.39% to 99.34%. This illustrates the effectiveness of our proposed sparse transformer for detecting network traffic anomalies.

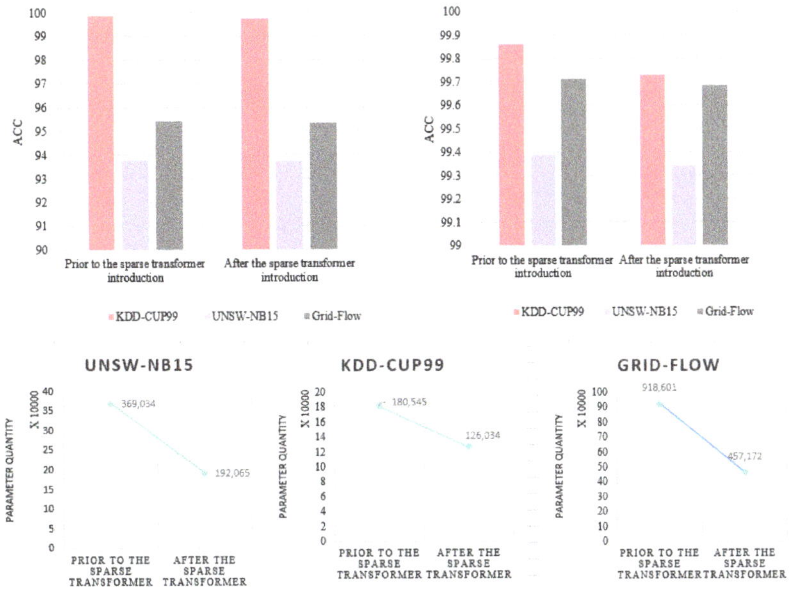

Figure 4. Comparison of ablation results before and after introducing sparse transformer.

4.4. *Visualization*

We randomly selected 2000 traffic data from the Grid-Flow dataset to visualize the embedding representation before and after the traffic enters FSTDS. The dimensions were first reduced to 20 dimensions by PCA [30] and then to 2 dimensions by UMAP [31]. The visualization results are shown in Figure 5.

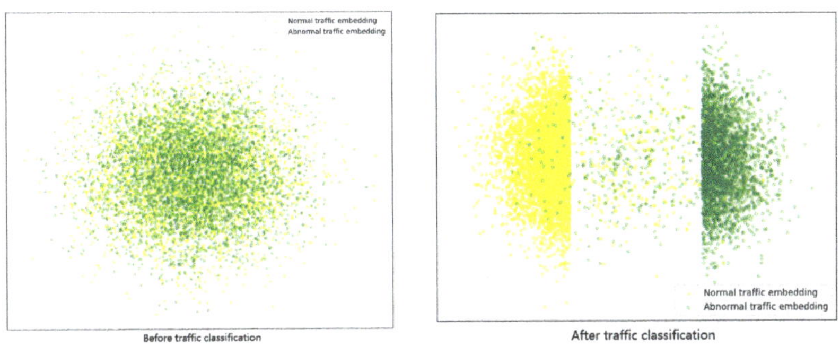

Figure 5. The embedding representation before and after the traffic enter FSTDS.

As we know from Figure 5, the characteristic representation of traffic data is chaotically distributed in the feature space before entering FSTDS. We cannot distinguish whether the traffic is abnormal through a single feature. After FSTDS classification, abnormal traffic and normal traffic are strictly distinguished in the feature space.

5. Conclusions

In this paper, we propose a powerful abnormal traffic detection system based on feature fusion and sparse transformer, called FSTDS, for accurate identification of abnormal traffic in the network. FSTDS provides an integrated abnormal traffic detection solution consisting of four modules: preprocessing technology, feature fusion network, sparse transformer, and a classification head. We designed a feature fusion network when encoding the input traffic data sequences, which uses two layers of parallel convolutional networks to extract shallow and deep feature extraction from the preprocessed flow data. These extract features to obtain the encoded flow data vectors. Subsequently, a deep encoder based on sparse transformer was utilized to capture the complex relationships between different network flows. Finally, a multi-layer perceptron was used to classify the traffic to detect abnormal traffic. The experimental results demonstrate that FSTDS outperforms mainstream classical and deep learning intrusion detection algorithms used in abnormal traffic detection systems.

The traffic detection system, in conjunction with the feature fusion and sparse transformer, performs exceptionally well in the area of anomalous traffic detection; however, the model's scalability is limited, and the accuracy of detecting novel forms of attack traffic that do not occur in the training set requires improvement in light of the evolving complexity of network environments and the emergence of novel attack types.

Our future work will focus on how to improve the speed of the sparse transformer for the abnormal traffic intrusion detection system to significantly reduce the damage caused by abnormal events. Furthermore, in the next work, we will consider adopting prompt learning methods to solve the fow-shot classification problem.

Author Contributions: Methodology, X.Z. and Y.J.; validation, X.Z., W.M. and G.Y.; formal analysis, X.Z., W.M. and S.Z.; investigation, X.Z., G.Y. and Y.J.; resources, Q.L.; writing—original draft, X.Z.; writing—review and editing, X.Z. and W.M.; visualization, X.Z.; supervision, Q.L.; project administration, W.M.; funding acquisition, X.Z. All authors have read and agreed to the published version of the manuscript.

Funding: This work was supported by the Science and Technology Project of State Grid Jiangsu Electric Power Company Ltd., under Grant J2023124.

Data Availability Statement: The data will be made available by the authors on request.

Conflicts of Interest: Authors Xinjian Zhao, Weiwei Miao, Guoquan Yuan and Song Zhang were employed by the company State Grid Jiangsu Electric Power Co., Ltd. The remaining authors declare that the research was conducted in the absence of any commercial or financial relationships that could be construed as a potential conflict of interest.

References

1. Wang, K.; Fu, Y.; Duan, X.; Liu, T.; Xu, J. Abnormal traffic detection system in SDN based on deep learning hybrid models. *Comput. Commun.* **2024**, *216*, 183–194. [CrossRef]
2. Xu, J. Research on abnormal traffic detection strategy for the Internet of Things based on machine learning. *Software* **2022**, *43*, 162–164.
3. Farnaaz, N.; Jabbar, M.A. Random forest modeling for network intrusion detection system. *Procedia Comput. Sci.* **2016**, *89*, 213–217. [CrossRef]
4. Manocchio, L.D.; Layeghy, S.; Lo, W.W.; Kulatilleke, G.K.; Sarhan, M.; Portmann, M. Flowtransformer: A transformer framework for flow-based network intrusion detection systems. *Expert Syst. Appl.* **2024**, *241*, 122564. [CrossRef]
5. Zhang, J.; Zulkernine, M.; Haque, A. Random-forests-based network intrusion detection systems. *IEEE Trans. Syst. Man Cybern. Part C Appl. Rev.* **2008**, *38*, 649–659. [CrossRef]
6. Li, Y.; Miao, R.; Kim, C.; Yu, M. {FlowRadar}: A better {NetFlow} for data centers. In Proceedings of the 13th USENIX SYMPOSIUM on Networked Systems Design and Implementation (NSDI 16), Santa Clara, CA, USA, 17–18 March 2016.
7. Mohanad, S.; Layeghy, S.; Moustafa, N.; Portmann, M. Netflow datasets for machine learning-based network intrusion detection systems. In *Big Data Technologies and Applications: 10th EAI International Conference, BDTA 2020, and 13th EAI International Con-ference on Wireless Internet, WiCON 2020, Virtual Event, 11 December 2020, Proceedings 10*; Springer International Publishing: Berlin/Heidelberg, Germany, 2021.
8. dos Santos, F.P.; Ribeiro, L.S.; Ponti, M.A. Generalization of feature embeddings transferred from different video anomaly detection domains. *J. Vis. Commun. Image Represent.* **2019**, *60*, 407–416. [CrossRef]
9. Kuang, F.; Xu, W.; Zhang, S. A novel hybrid KPCA and SVM with GA model for intrusion detection. *Appl. Soft Comput.* **2014**, *18*, 178–184. [CrossRef]
10. Salman, O.; Elhajj, I.H.; Chehab, A.; Kayssi, A. A machine learning based framework for IoT device identification and abnormal traffic detection. *Trans. Emerg. Telecommun. Technol.* **2022**, *33*, e3743. [CrossRef]

11. Reddy, R.R.; Ramadevi, Y.; Sunitha, K.V.N. Effective discriminant function for intrusion detection using SVM. In Proceedings of the 2016 International Conference on Advances in Computing, Communications and Informatics (ICACCI), Jaipur, India, 21–24 September 2016; IEEE: Piscataway, NJ, USA, 2016.
12. Nam, M.; Park, S.; Kim, D.S. Intrusion detection method using bidirectional GPT for in-vehicle controller area networks. *IEEE Access* **2021**, *9*, 124931–124944. [CrossRef]
13. Chowdhury; Nasimuzzaman, M.; Ferens, K.; Ferens, M. Network intrusion detection using machine learning. In Proceedings of the International Conference on Security and Management (SAM), Las Vegas, NV, USA, 25–28 July 2016; The Steering Committee of the World Congress in Computer Science, Computer Engineering and Applied Computing (WorldComp): Las Vegas, NV, USA, 2016.
14. Li, Y.; Yuan, X.; Li, W. An Extreme Semi-supervised Framework Based on Transformer for Network Intrusion Detection. In Proceedings of the 31st ACM International Conference on Information &Knowledge Management, Atlanta, GA, USA, 17–21 October 2022; pp. 4204–4208.
15. Alex, K.; Sutskever, I.; Hinton, G.E. Imagenet classification with deep convolutional neural networks. *Adv. Neural Inf. Process. Syst.* **2012**, *25*, 84–90.
16. Tuor, A.; Kaplan, S.; Hutchinson, B.; Nichols, N.; Robinson, S. Deep learning for unsupervised insider threat detection in structured cybersecurity data streams. In Proceedings of the Workshops at the Thirty-First AAAI Conference on Artificial Intelligence, San Francisco, CA, USA, 4–9 February 2017.
17. Yan, Q.; Wang, M.; Huang, W.; Luo, X.; Yu, F.R. Automatically synthesizing DoS attack traces using generative adversarial networks. *Int. J. Mach. Learn. Cybern.* **2019**, *10*, 3387–3396. [CrossRef]
18. Ashish, V.; Shazeer, N.; Parmar, N.; Uszkoreit, J.; Jones, L.; Gomez, A.N.; Kaiser, Ł. Attention is all you need. *arXiv* **2017**, arXiv:1706.03762.
19. Jiang, Y.; Liang, L.; Li, Q. Black-box Speech Adversarial Attack with Genetic Algorithm and Generic Attack Ideas. In *2023 IEEE International Conference on Dependable, Autonomic and Secure Computing, International Conference on Pervasive Intelligence and Computing, International Conference on Cloud and Big Data Computing, International Conference on Cyber Science and Technology Congress (DASC/PiCom/CBDCom/CyberSciTech)*; IEEE: Piscataway, NJ, USA, 2023.
20. Wu, Z.; Zhang, H.; Wang, P.; Sun, Z. RTIDS: A robust transformerbased approach for intrusion detection system. *IEEE Access* **2022**, *10*, 64375–64387. [CrossRef]
21. Shi, D.; Xia, Y.; Peng, T. Network abnormal traffic detection model based on semi-supervised deep reinforcement learning. *IEEE Trans. Netw. Serv. Manag.* **2021**, *18*, 4197–4212.
22. Jay, S.; Manollas, M. Efficient deep CNN-BiLSTM model for network intrusion detection. In Proceedings of the 2020 3rd International Conference on Artificial Intelligence and Pattern Recognition, Chengdu, China, 28–30 August 2020.
23. Yun, S.; Jeong, M.; Kim, R.; Kang, J.; Kim, H.J. Graph transformer networks. *arXiv* **2019**, arXiv:1911.06455.
24. Li, W.; Yi, P.; Wu, Y.; Pan, L.; Li, J. A new intrusion detection system based on KNN classification algorithm in wireless sensor network. *J. Electr. Comput. Eng.* **2014**, *2014*, 240217. [CrossRef]
25. Duan, X.; Fu, Y.; Wang, K. Network traffic anomaly detection method based on multi-scale residual classifier. *Comput. Commun.* **2023**, *198*, 206–216. [CrossRef]
26. Yin, C.; Zhu, Y.; Fei, J.; He, X. A deep learning approach for intrusion detection using recurrent neural networks. *IEEE Access* **2017**, *5*, 21954–21961. [CrossRef]
27. Mikolov, T.; Sutskever, I.; Chen, K.; Corrado, G.S.; Dean, J. Distributed representations of words and phrases and their compositionality. *arXiv* **2013**, arXiv:1310.4546.
28. Deng, H.; Li, X. Network traffic anomaly identification and detection based on deep learning. *Comput. Syst. Appl.* **2023**, *32*, 274–280.
29. Alkhatib, N.; Mushtaq, M.; Ghauch, H.; Danger, J.-L. Can-bert do it? controller area network intrusion detection system based on bert language model. In Proceedings of the 2022 IEEE/ACS 19th International Conference on Computer Systems and Applications (AICCSA), Abu Dhabi, United Arab Emirates, 5–8 December 2022; IEEE: Piscataway, NJ, USA, 2022; pp. 1–8.
30. Pearson, K. Liii. on lines and planes of closest fit to systems of points in space. *Lond. Edinb. Dublin Philos. Mag. J. Sci.* **1901**, *2*, 559–572. [CrossRef]
31. McInnes, L.; Healy, J.; Melville, J. Umap: Uniform manifold approximation and projection for dimension reduction. *arXiv* **2018**, arXiv:1802.03426.

mathematics

Review

Hallucination Mitigation for Retrieval-Augmented Large Language Models: A Review

Wan Zhang and Jing Zhang *

School of Cyber Science and Engineering, Southeast University, Nanjing 211189, China; zhangwan@seu.edu.cn
* Correspondence: jingz@seu.edu.cn

Abstract: Retrieval-augmented generation (RAG) leverages the strengths of information retrieval and generative models to enhance the handling of real-time and domain-specific knowledge. Despite its advantages, limitations within RAG components may cause hallucinations, or more precisely termed confabulations in generated outputs, driving extensive research to address these limitations and mitigate hallucinations. This review focuses on hallucination in retrieval-augmented large language models (LLMs). We first examine the causes of hallucinations from different sub-tasks in the retrieval and generation phases. Then, we provide a comprehensive overview of corresponding hallucination mitigation techniques, offering a targeted and complete framework for addressing hallucinations in retrieval-augmented LLMs. We also investigate methods to reduce the impact of hallucination through detection and correction. Finally, we discuss promising future research directions for mitigating hallucinations in retrieval-augmented LLMs.

Keywords: large language models; hallucination; retrieval-augmented generation; hallucination mitigation

MSC: 68T07

1. Introduction

In recent years, large language models (LLMs) such as GPT-4 [1], LLaMA [2], and Gemini [3] have rapidly advanced, achieving significant progress in the field of natural language processing (NLP). These models learn statistical representations of linguistic patterns and word distributions through complex deep learning architectures and pre-training on vast datasets and adapt to domain-specific tasks through supervised fine-tuning. They are widely used for various tasks, including semantic analysis [4], text generation [5], and reasoning [6]. However, due to their reliance on fixed parameters, LLMs often produce task-irrelevant outputs or generate factually inconsistent responses when faced with tasks beyond the scope of their training data. This limitation can be understood as the knowledge boundary of LLMs, which refers to the extent of their knowledge derived solely from the patterns and associations in the training data. This phenomenon, where the model generates responses that are inconsistent with facts or appear meaningless, is commonly referred to as hallucination or confabulation. Hallucinations undermine the reliability and trustworthiness of LLMs, and in scenarios requiring precise information, they can lead to severe consequences. To address the limitations of LLMs' knowledge boundaries and the high training costs, retrieval-augmented generation (RAG) [7] aims to alleviate knowledge deficiencies by retrieving external information and providing it to the LLM, improving the quality of domain-specific responses and reducing hallucinations. While RAG technology has shown great promise in

https://doi.org/10.3390/math13050856

mitigating hallucinations, the RAG paradigm itself also has limitations, with the insufficient capabilities of its components contributing to the generation of hallucinations.

Investigating the root causes of hallucinations in the RAG paradigm helps to understand the mechanisms of its components at different stages and how their limitations affect LLM-generated responses. It also provides guidance for developing hallucination mitigation strategies for retrieval-augmented LLMs. Based on the retrieval and generation phases of RAG, we categorize the sub-tasks in each phase and analyze the fundamental issues causing hallucinations in each sub-task. This classification spans the entire RAG process, allowing a comprehensive analysis of the root causes and mechanisms of hallucinations at each stage. Specifically, in the retrieval phase, we focus on data source, query, retriever, and retrieval strategy problems. In the generation phase, we address context noise, context conflict, and the middle curse in long contexts, alignment problems, and model capability boundary problems.

In addition, based on the causes of hallucinations, we surveyed and categorized corresponding hallucination mitigation methods. We found that prompt engineering plays a significant role in mitigating hallucinations, addressing tasks such as designing prompts to directly reduce hallucinations, using prompt techniques to automate the construction of resources like demonstrations and labeled datasets for hallucinations mitigation, and evaluating model performance on specific tasks to further guide the tuning of generative models. Given its simplicity, efficiency, universality, and interpretability compared to model optimization and supervised fine-tuning, most of the hallucination mitigation methods we reviewed extensively utilize prompt techniques. This review aims to encourage researchers to further explore the potential of prompt engineering in hallucination mitigation tasks while consciously adhering to the norms of using prompt engineering for various research tasks [8]. Considering that hallucinations are still unavoidable even after optimizing each subtask of RAG, it is also worth investigating methods to reduce the impact of hallucinations through detection and correction.

Finally, we also discuss the challenges faced by existing methods, provide some promising directions to mitigate hallucinations in retrieval-augmented LLMs, and offer suggestions for future research.

1.1. Comparison with Existing Reviews and Surveys

The hallucination or confabulation issue in generative artificial intelligence (GAI) has had a significant impact on the reliability and trustworthiness of many existing applications based on generative AI, making it a major challenge in the field. Numerous reviews and surveys have been conducted on this topic [9–14]. These surveys explore the hallucination problem from various perspectives and offer valuable insights. However, our review specifically focuses on hallucinations within the RAG paradigm. Liu et al. [9] provided an in-depth investigation of hallucinations in large visual language models (LVLMs), introducing innovative evaluation methods and benchmarks, analyzing the root causes of hallucinations, and discussing corresponding mitigation techniques. Sahoo et al. [10] established a precise definition and structured classification of hallucinations, offering a comprehensive overview of hallucination detection and mitigation techniques for multimodal foundation models. Alghamdi et al. [11] discussed knowledge graph-based enhancement techniques from three perspectives, knowledge-aware inference, training, and knowledge-aware validation, assessing their effectiveness in reducing hallucinations. Tonmoy et al. [12] classified hallucination mitigation techniques into prompt engineering and model design, providing a thorough review. Huang et al. [13] offered a hierarchical classification method for hallucinations and presented a detailed, coherent introduction to their causes and solutions across data, training, and inference stages. Zhang et al. [14] analyzed the causes of hallucinations in LLMs and provided a comprehensive review of mitigation methods across four stages: pre-training, supervised fine-tuning, reinforcement learning from human feedback (RLHF), and inference. However, our review specifically focuses on classifying and analyzing the root causes and mechanisms of hallucinations in the sub-tasks of the RAG paradigm and provides corresponding mitigation methods. These methods emphasize the potential of prompt engineering in reducing hallucinations.

1.2. *Organization of the Review*

This paper reviews recent research on hallucinations in retrieval-augmented LLMs. Figure 1 shows the internal organizational principles of this review, which include the causes of hallucinations and corresponding mitigation methods in retrieval-augmented LLMs. Specifically, the causes of hallucination mitigation in different subtasks of the generation deficiency and retrieval failure stages in Figure 1 are analyzed in detail in Section 3. Sections 4 and 5 review hallucination mitigation methods corresponding to the causes in the subtasks of the retrieval and generation stages, respectively. Additionally, Section 2 introduces the classical RAG pipeline, delineates the conceptual distinctions between hallucination and confabulation, summarizes existing taxonomies of hallucination phenomena, and overviews prompt techniques commonly employed in hallucination mitigation strategies. Section 6 covers techniques for mitigating hallucinations after detection. Finally, Section 7 discusses the challenges faced by current mitigation methods and provides suggestions for future research directions.

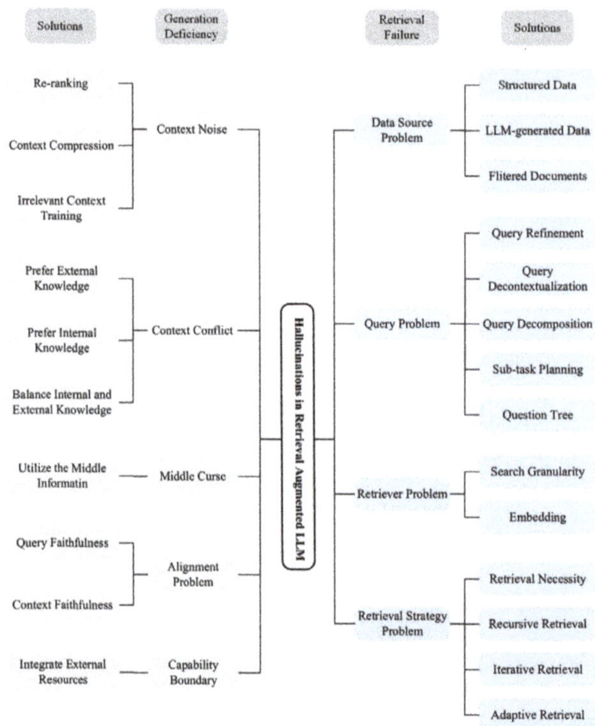

Figure 1. Causes of hallucinations and corresponding mitigation methods in retrieval-augmented LLMs. Hallucinations in RAG models arise from two primary stages: retrieval failure and generation deficiency. Retrieval failure includes four sub-problems: data sources, queries, retrievers, and retrieval strategy problems. Generation deficiency encompasses five sub-problems: context noise, context conflict, middle curse, alignment problems, and capability boundary. For each sub-problem, corresponding solutions for mitigating hallucinations are provided.

2. Concepts and Definitions

This section provides some important concepts and definitions related to retrieval-augmented LLMs.

2.1. Retrieval-Augmented Generation

A typical retrieval-augmented generation (RAG) process is shown in Figure 2. The user inputs a question about recent news, but due to the real-time nature of news, the LLM's internal parameters do not contain the necessary knowledge to answer the question. External knowledge needs to be retrieved and integrated to fill this information gap. In the retrieval phase, the input question is pre-processed and passed as a query to the retriever. RAG uses external retrieval engines such as BM25, TF-IDF, or more complex neural retrieval models to perform dense or sparse retrieval from web pages, pre-constructed document corpora, knowledge bases, or databases to find relevant documents or paragraphs. Dense retrieval involves encoding documents and queries using a pre-trained embedding model to generate dense vector representations. The retriever typically returns the top-k most relevant text segments based on the query-document relevance. In the generation phase, the retrieved documents or paragraphs are combined with the user's original question and passed to the generation model to generate a response for the user.

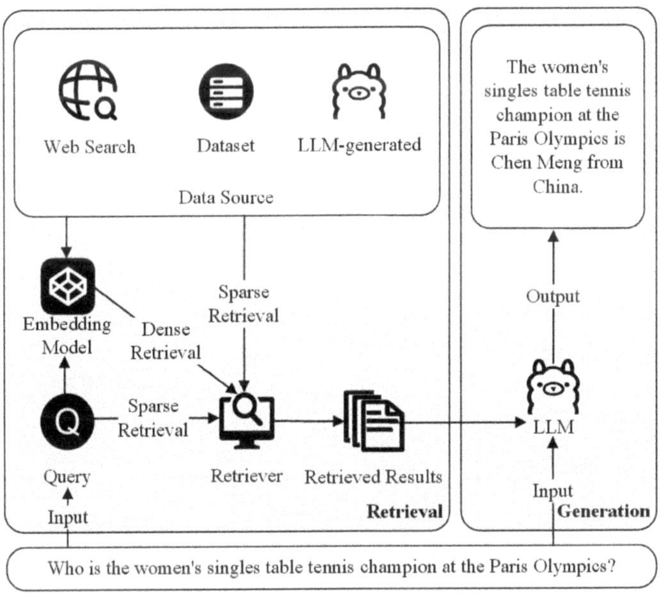

Figure 2. The basic workflow of retrieval-augmented generation.

2.2. Hallucinations or Confabulation in Large Language Models

The concept of hallucination originated in psychology, referring to perceptual experiences that occur without external stimuli or perceptions that deviate from reality [15]. In natural language processing, hallucinations typically refer to information generated by LLMs that is inconsistent with facts or nonsensical. However, Smith et al. [16] contend that the term hallucination inappropriately suggests that LLMs possess sensory perception, thereby constituting an imprecise metaphor. They propose the concept of confabulation, derived from psychiatry, as a more suitable alternative. Confabulation denotes the unconscious fabrication of false memories by individuals with impaired memory or cognitive deficits to fill gaps in their recollection [17]. Unlike perceptual experiences, confabulations represent erroneous reconstructions of information that are influenced by internal and external knowledge and the environment. This aligns more closely with the behavior of LLMs, which generate outputs that are erroneous yet plausible based on their training data and context. Although the term confabulation has gained traction in public discourse on artificial intelligence [18] and has garnered consensus among researchers, it has not yet been widely adopted in the academic literature. Consequently, we continue to employ the term hallucination to review and analyze the relevant methods.

Some researchers have categorized hallucinations based on different criteria. And we list examples of different types of hallucinations in Table 1. Ji et al. [19] categorized hallucinations in NLP into intrinsic and extrinsic based on whether they can be verified against the input source. Intrinsic hallucination occurs when the generated content contradicts the input, while extrinsic hallucination refers to content that cannot be verified from the input but may be correct in external knowledge. Huang et al. [13] refined this classification by introducing factuality hallucination and faithfulness hallucination based on the consistency with real-world knowledge and user-centered contexts. Factuality hallucination involves inconsistencies with real-world facts, such as factual contradiction (responses contradicting known facts) or factual fabrication (responses fabricated as facts). Faithfulness hallucination refers to inconsistencies with user instructions, context, or internal consistency, including instruction inconsistency (responses deviating from the original instructions), context inconsistency (responses inconsistent with provided context), and logical inconsistency (internal contradictions in responses). Rawte et al. [20] proposed several classification methods, including hallucinations caused by correct or incorrect prompts, the severity of hallucinations, and specific error types. They termed the responses that deviate from facts when LLMs process factually correct prompts as the factual mirage and the seemingly plausible but incorrect responses generated from factually incorrect prompts as the silver lining. They further categorized hallucinations into six specific types: acronym ambiguity, numeric nuisance, generated golem, virtual voice, geographic erratum, and time warp.

Table 1. Examples of different types of hallucinations.

Type	Question	Response	Explanation
Intrinsic Hallucination	Company A's financial report shows a net cash flow from operating activities of CNY 520 million. Analyze A's cash flow situation.	The net cash flow from investing activities is CNY 380 million.	The actual financial report shows a figure of CNY 520 million, which contradicts the facts.
Extrinsic Hallucination		The improvement in cash flow is attributed to the expansion in the Southeast Asian market.	The financial report does not disclose regional details, but it may be consistent with external knowledge.
Factuality Hallucination	Please introduce the history of the Great Wall of China.	The Great Wall of China was ordered to be built by Emperor Qin Shi Huang after he unified the six warring states.	After Emperor Qin Shi Huang unified the six warring states, he undertook large scale repairs and expansions of the Great Wall, but this was not the time when the Great Wall was originally built.

Table 1. *Cont.*

Type	Question	Response	Explanation
Faithfulness Hallucination	Translate: Who was the director of Avatar?	Avatar was directed by James Cameron.	The LLM's response is inconsistent with the instruction and failed to translate the sentence as required.
Factual Mirage	Conan Doyle is the author of the Sherlock Holmes series. Please introduce Conan Doyle.	Conan Doyle was awarded the title of "Royal Deective" for his exceptional reasoning skills.	Arthur Conan Doyle was never awarded the title of "Royal Detective". When LLM processes a factually correct prompt, the generated output may deviate from the truth.
Silver Lining	Why did Lin Daiyu uproot the weeping willow?	Lin Daiyu uprooted the weeping willow because she was sorrowful over her tragic fate, using it as a way to express her grief over the impermanence of life and the unfairness of destiny.	Lin Daiyu did not uproot the weeping willow. The LLM generated false content when handling prompts with factual errors.

In retrieval-augmented LLMs, hallucination caused by the inherent knowledge boundary of LLMs is mitigated by retrieving external information, but hallucinations may still occur [21]. When the retrieved information contains false, outdated content, or conflicts with the internal parameters of the model, factuality hallucination may occur. When the query does not accurately reflect the user's intention, the retrieved content does not accurately reflect the user's query, which will cause faithfulness hallucination. When LLMs cannot make good use of the context obtained from the query, both types of hallucinations may occur.

2.3. Common Prompt Techniques

Prompt engineering directs the model to generate higher-quality, more user-friendly responses through the careful design and construction of input prompts. Compared to other methods, such as model architecture modification or fine-tuning, prompt engineering offers significant advantages in terms of simplicity, efficiency, generality, and interpretability. It enables rapid adaptation to new tasks and efficient optimization by simply designing appropriate input prompts without the need to modify the model structure or retrain the model. Additionally, prompt techniques have minimal computational and data requirements, making them easy to implement and deploy. Prompt engineering also supports timely adjustment and optimization, maintaining its universality across different models. As a result, prompt engineering plays a crucial role in the study of hallucination mitigation in retrieval-augmented LLMs. On the one hand, well-constructed prompts can guide the model to generate outputs with higher semantic alignment to input queries by optimizing the conditional probability distribution over token sequences, leading to more accurate and consistent responses. On the other hand, prompt engineering can also automate the creation of labeled datasets, saving time and cost, and evaluate the model's performance, guiding further tuning. The following section introduces common prompt techniques used in the hallucination mitigation methods discussed later to help further understand the role of prompt engineering in these tasks. Table 2 shows examples of different prompt techniques.

- Clear and Precise Prompts

Constructing clear and specific prompts can effectively guide the model to generate the desired output. LLMs, pre-trained on vast datasets containing extensive knowledge, may struggle to interpret vague or broad prompts, often resulting in generalized responses. In contrast, clear and precise prompts can reduce ambiguity and polysemy in language, clearly point out the core content that users are concerned about, make it easier for the model to identify and match patterns related to these keywords, and provide more accurate and satisfactory responses.

- Role-Playing Prompts

Role-playing prompts [22] assign a specific role or identity to the LLMs, guiding them to generate responses that align with a particular style or area of expertise. This approach helps the model better emulate human conversational patterns, enhancing the accuracy and relevance of its output. For instance, in customer service applications, the model can assume the role of a customer service representative, thereby providing more professional and user-friendly interactions.

- Few-Shot Prompts

Few-shot prompts [23] involve providing a small number of carefully designed examples within the prompt to help the model quickly grasp the task requirements and the expected output format. This approach enhances the accuracy and consistency of the model's responses. The few-shot prompt is particularly beneficial in scenarios with limited data, as it reduces the reliance on large-scale annotated datasets while significantly improving the model's performance across various tasks.

- Chain-of-Thought (CoT) Prompts

CoT prompts [24] simulate the step-by-step reasoning process of humans when solving complex problems, guiding the model to generate intermediate reasoning steps and gradually work through each step to reach the final answer. This approach significantly enhances the model's performance in multi-step reasoning tasks, such as solving mathematical problems, common-sense reasoning, and symbolic reasoning. Zhang et al. [25] introduced Auto-CoT, which automatically prompts LLMs to generate reasoning chains by incorporating the phrase "Let's think step by step" into the prompt. These chain-of-thought promptings force the model to transform the implicit probability distribution calculation process into an explicit logical chain of text output. When the model answers complex problems step by step, it faces subtasks with lower entropy, making it easier to generate accurate responses and reducing the risk of error accumulation. As a result, it can better answer complex questions.

- Program-of-Thought (PoT) Prompts

PoT prompts [26] direct the language models to express their reasoning process using a programming language, delegating computational tasks to an external program interpreter through a clear task description, sample code, and specific questions. PoT decomposes complex reasoning processes into distinct coding steps, leveraging the iteration and loop structures of programming languages to efficiently manage tasks requiring multiple iterations. By utilizing a program interpreter for complex computations, PoT helps mitigate errors in the language model's calculations, thereby enhancing both the accuracy and efficiency of the model in numerical reasoning tasks.

- Opinion-Based Prompts

The opinion-based prompts [27] reformulate the context into a narrator's statement and transform the question into an inquiry about the narrator's opinion on that statement.

This approach alters the nature of the question, compelling the model to focus more on the specific statements in the context rather than its internally stored factual knowledge.

Table 2. Examples of different prompt techniques.

Type	Example Prompt	Explanation
Clear and Precise	I want to learn about healthy diets, especially low-sugar, high-fiber meal combinations suitable for diabetic patients to eat for breakfast.	The prompt "I want to learn about healthy diets" is too ambiguous, leading to generic suggestions. A clear prompt specifying the target audience, time, and needs helps the model provide more tailored advice.
Role-Playing	You are a professional customer service representative, responsible for providing customer support for an electronics company.	Assigning a role (such as a customer service representative) to the LLM in the prompt enables it to generate role-specific responses.
Few-Shot	Question: Classify the sentiment of the following sentences into "positive" or "negative". Examples: "I absolutely love this phone!" positive "The product is terrible. I hate it." negative Input: "The movie was amazing!" Output:	By showing it how to classify sentences as "positive" or "negative", the model can then apply this pattern to new inputs, like "The movie was amazing!"
CoT	Question: If the train leaves at 2:30 p.m. and the journey takes 3 h and 45 min, what time will it arrive? Step-by-step reasoning: 1. Start time: 2:30 p.m. 2. Add 3 h to 2:30 p.m. to get 5:35 p.m. 3. Add 5 min to 5:30 p.m. to get 5:30 p.m. Output:	Through step-by-step reasoning, the CoT prompt helps the model perform addition operations in chronological order to arrive at the correct arrival time.
Auto-CoT	What should be included when writing a proposal for regional environmental protection measures? Let's think step by step.	Using the Auto-CoT prompt with "Let's think step by step" gives model more time to process and reason.

PoT	Question: What is the sum of 1 to 100?
	# Python 3.8 code
	total_sum = 0
	for i in range(1, 101):
	    total_sum+=i
	print(total_sum)
		This PoT prompt uses a clear task description and example code to guide the model in reasoning through code. The program interpreter executes the task and computes the result efficiently.

Table 2. *Cont.*

Type	Example Prompt	Explanation
Opinion-Based	Li Hua said: "The new president of the United States is Donald Trump". According to Li Hua's opinion, who is the new president of the United States?	Opinion-based prompt makes the model focus on Li Hua's statement and reflect that individual's belief, not its internal knowledge.

3. Hallucination Causes in Retrieval-Augmented Generation Process

LLMs often suffer from hallucinations when generating text, which affects the reliability and accuracy of the model output. In order to mitigate hallucinations in LLMs and improve the factuality of their output, the RAG framework was proposed [28–31]. RAG combines the retrieval module and the generation module and uses the external knowledge base to provide the model with richer and more accurate contextual information, thereby improving the accuracy and credibility of the generated content. Although RAG has significant advantages in mitigating hallucinations, it still has the possibility of introducing hallucinations at different stages. Specifically, hallucinations in RAG models arise from two primary stages: retrieval failure and generation deficiency. In the retrieval stage, the retrieval module may not be able to provide accurate contextual information due to the unreliability of the data source, the ambiguity of the user query, or the limitations of the retriever and retrieval strategy. In the generation phase, the generation module may generate content inconsistent with the retrieved information or input requirements due to context noise, context conflict, middle curse or alignment problems, or inaccurate generation due to limited model capabilities. We will start from these two stages to reveal the specific mechanism of hallucination in the process of retrieval-enhanced generation and provide a theoretical basis for subsequent research.

3.1. Retrieval Failure

In the retrieval augmentation system, the retrieval process plays a core role and is responsible for obtaining contextual information related to user queries from external knowledge bases to enhance the generation ability of language models. However, the retrieval process may cause hallucinations due to various reasons. This section will analyze the causes of hallucinations from four perspectives: data source problems, query problems, retriever problems, and retrieval strategy problems.

- Data Source Problem

Retrieval-augmented LLMs are prone to generate hallucinations due to three key data source issues: low quality, obsolescence, and singleness of retrieval sources. Low-quality data sources may rely on unverified and unreliable materials, such as inaccurate or biased information, which can easily cause the model to generate unrealistic responses based on wrong data. In particular, with the development of generative artificial intelligence, more and more LLM-generated content is published on the Internet. Modern retrieval models increasingly favor LLM-generated content over human-created sources. This preference stems from two factors: (1) the high semantic similarity between generated contexts and user queries and (2) the inherent incompleteness of retrieved contexts. The tendency of LLMs to produce factual hallucinations will aggravate the reliability problem of retrieval sources. In addition, various data poisoning attacks against knowledge bases will also affect the correctness of data sources. Outdated data sources often contain data that have not been updated on time, causing LLMs to make inferences based on outdated research or data, thereby producing hallucinations that are inconsistent with current knowledge. The singleness problem is that the model relies on only a limited or single type of data source, ignoring relevant information in other fields, which will lead to incomplete or wrong inferences. In short, these problems affect the reliability and completeness of information, prompting LLMs to generate inaccurate or unrealistic content.

- Query Problem

User queries play a fundamental role in RAG, which directly determines the direction and accuracy of the information obtained by the retrieval system. However, ambiguous queries and complex queries often cause RAG systems to generate hallucinations, affecting the quality of generated content. Ambiguous queries refer to user queries that contain omissions, coreferences, and ambiguities. Due to the lack of clarity or the existence of multiple possible interpretations, such queries make it difficult for the retrieval system to accurately identify the user's true intentions, thereby increasing the difficulty of obtaining accurate and relevant information. Table 3 lists several examples of ambiguous queries. Complex queries usually require intensive reasoning capabilities or involve information retrieval from multiple aspects. Such queries may exceed the capabilities of current retrieval methods based on keywords or semantic matching, resulting in one-sided or wrong retrieval results. Complex queries require advanced processing and decomposition capabilities to accurately retrieve and integrate information from multiple sources to generate accurate responses. These two types of query problems not only affect the quality of retrieval results but also reduce the credibility of the responses generated by the model, ultimately affecting the user experience.

- Retriever Problem

The role of the retriever in RAG is crucial. It is responsible for finding information related to user input from the knowledge base or document library to provide contextual support for the subsequent generation process. However, the retriever may also become the source of large model hallucination, mainly in terms of retrieval granularity and embedding.

Table 3. Examples of ambiguous queries that can cause hallucinations.

Type	Example Dialog	Explanation
Ambiguity	Query: Apple is very popular, why?	The word "Apple" in this query is ambiguous, referring to either the fruit or the phone brand. The system erroneously retrieved and explained information about the phone brand.
	Retrieved Paragraph: Apple's popularity is driven by its innovative products, which blend style with functionality...	
	Answer: Apple's popularity can be attributed to its innovative approach in combining style and functionality... making it a preferred choice for many consumers.	
Omission	Query: Who is the 2024 Olympic 100 m champion?	The question omitted a specific 100 m race, so the system only searched for the men's 100 m race results and gave the champion of the men's 100 m race.
	Retrieved Paragraph: USA sprinter Noah Lyles won the men's 100 m title at the Paris 2024 Olympic Games by the smallest of margins in a dramatic photo finish.	
	Answer: The 2024 Olympic 100 m champion is Noah Lyles from the United States. He won the gold medal with a time of 9.784 s, narrowly defeating Jamaica's Kishane Thompson by just five-thousandths of a second.	

Table 3. *Cont.*

Type	Example Dialog	Explanation
Coreference	Query: Li Hua recommended a history book to Xiaoming. He thought it was very interesting and bought it. Who bought a history book?	The query gives two people, but "He" does not clearly indicate who they are, which causes the system to perform inappropriate retrieval and incorrect model generation.
	Retrieved Paragraph: Li Hua is a common protagonist in English exam essays, often set as a character who recommends books or shares experiences with others.	
	Answer: Li Hua is the one who recommended the book and found it interesting; it is likely that Li Hua is the one who bought the history book.	

First, the retrieval granularity determines the size and detail level of the retrieved information blocks. The retrieval structure matching different retrieval granularities will also affect the effectiveness of the retriever. If the retrieval granularity is too large, the retrieved information block may be too broad and contain a lot of irrelevant content, which will increase the burden of the language model to process information and may cause the generated answer to be inaccurate or even deviate from the core of the user's question. On the contrary, if the retrieval granularity is too small, although the information block is more targeted, it may not provide enough contextual information, making it difficult for the language model to integrate this fragmented knowledge, thus affecting the coherence and completeness of the answer. Secondly, many RAG frameworks rely on flat data representation, which cannot capture multi-hop relationship paths between encoded entities and limits the system's ability to capture complex relationships between entities. For example, when a user asks "How does artificial intelligence technology change the diagnosis and treatment methods in the medical industry?", the RAG system may retrieve separate documents on artificial intelligence, medical diagnosis, and treatment methods. However, due to the reliance on flat data representation, these systems may not be able to effectively integrate the complex relationships between these documents, resulting in fragmented generated answers. Finally, the quality of the embedding model directly affects the accuracy of retrieval. The embedding model converts text into a vector representation for calculating similarity scores. If the embedding model is suboptimal, it may reduce the matching degree between the retrieval results and the user query, which in turn affects the output of the language model and leads to hallucinations. Therefore, optimizing the retrieval granularity and embedding model of the retriever is crucial to improving the overall performance of RAG and reducing the generation of hallucinations.

- Retrieval Strategy Problem

Retrieval strategies involve the necessity, frequency, and timing of retrieval. Regarding the necessity of retrieval, not all queries require retrieval. When the internal knowledge of the model is sufficient to answer the question, blind retrieval may lead to conflicts between the retrieved information and the internal knowledge on the one hand and introduce noise into the context on the other hand, both of which will lead to misleading responses. Regarding the frequency and timing of retrieval, the earliest strategy of performing a single retrieval on the original input [32,33] achieved good performance in handling single-hop problems. However, a single retrieval often has difficulty handling complex queries, especially those that require multi-step reasoning or involve multiple sub-questions. In addition, a single retrieval requires extremely high precision and recall of the retrieval system. Otherwise, it is easy to affect the generation quality due to incomplete or inaccurate information retrieved. To better cope with complex information retrieval, it is necessary to propose a better strategy to overcome the defects of a single retrieval on the premise of determining the necessity of retrieval.

3.2. Generation Deficiency

After the retrieval process, the generation phase, as the final output core of RAG, is responsible for integrating the retrieved relevant information with the user input and generating accurate and context-related answers through LLMs. However, the generation process may lead to hallucinations due to various reasons. This section will specifically analyze the causes of hallucinations in relation to five aspects: context noise, context conflict, middle information utilization, alignment problems, and ability boundaries.

- Context Noise

Contextual noise is often caused by the failure of the retrieval process, which can result in the retrieved context containing information that is irrelevant or redundant to the user's question, fragmented information that lacks coherence and completeness, and wrong or outdated information. Cuconasu et al. [34] pointed out that a large number of interfering documents retrieved by the retriever may contain semantic information related to the query, but this information may not support the correct answer and may cause the LLM to generate incorrect answers based on misleading information. At the same time, they also found that adding irrelevant random documents to the context reduces the focus of attention, avoids entropy collapse, and can significantly improve the performance of LLMs. Zhao et al. [35] pointed out that since LLMs are trained on a large amount of historical text, there is an inherent risk that outdated information matches the model's internal knowledge base. This matching may prompt LLMs to tend to and perpetuate outdated information. In short, large language models are extremely sensitive to this noise information. After the noise information is passed to the generative model, the answers generated by the model may be logically incoherent or generate completely fictitious content, thus leading to hallucinations.

- Context Conflict

Context conflict mainly refers to the conflict between knowledge in the context and model internal parameter knowledge. RAG brings richer context to the model input, but it may also bring information that conflicts with the model's internal parameter knowledge. Xu et al. [36] believe that the conflict between context and model parameter knowledge is mainly caused by temporal misalignment and misinformation pollution. Temporal misalignment means that the temporal information based on pre-training data may be outdated, while the external contextual knowledge may contain the latest information. This temporal difference will cause the model to fail to accurately reflect the current reality when dealing with problems. Misinformation pollution refers to the possibility that the external context contains erroneous or misleading information, which may be mistakenly adopted by LLMs, resulting in the generation of wrong or hallucination content. Longpre et al. [37] replaced the entity mentioned in the standard document with another entity to create a conflicting context, revealing the model's tendency to over-rely on parameter knowledge. Chen et al. [38] used multiple paragraphs and found that when the model performed best, it mainly relied on contextual knowledge. They believe that the entity replacement method reduces the semantic coherence of the interfering paragraphs, and Longpre et al. [37]'s study is based on a single paragraph, which leads to the model's preference for parameter knowledge. Xie et al. [39] found that as long as the external knowledge is coherent and convincing, LLMs tend to obey external knowledge, even if this knowledge conflicts with internal parameter knowledge.

Many recent studies have also emphasized that the model tends to be consistent with the user's views—that is, the model exhibits "sycophancy" [40–43].

- Middle Curse

Despite retrieving factually correct and query-relevant information, LLMs may still exhibit degraded generation quality due to insufficient utilization of long contexts, especially the middle curse issue [44]. The self-attention mechanism in Transformer [45] models exhibits attention decay and insufficient resolution in positional encoding when processing long texts, compounded by limitations in memory and computational resources. These factors collectively lead to a significant degradation in the model's ability to capture information from the middle portion of the input text. When critical information is located in the middle of the context, LLMs often struggle to effectively localize and utilize such information, resulting in a notable decline in accuracy. This problem is particularly prominent in Multi-doc QA tasks. Recent studies have further demonstrated that the middle curse also exists in tasks such as abstraction [43], long-form QA [46], and paragraph ranking [47].

- Alignment Problem

The alignment problem is mainly reflected in two aspects: context-generation alignment and query-generation alignment in the retrieval-augmented large language model. Context-generation alignment emphasizes the consistency and relevance of the generated text with the input context in terms of content and logic. If the generative model fails to effectively integrate the retrieved contextual information, or the context is too complex, the generated text may deviate from the factual consistency of the input content, resulting in faithfulness hallucination. Query-generation alignment requires that the generated content maintains high semantic correspondence with the content and structural patterns of the user's query. In the RAG framework, there is a semantic, contextual, or structural mismatch between the query and the retrieved knowledge base. For example, there may be inconsistencies between the query raised by the user and the retrieved literature or data, resulting in the generated answer not aligning with the user's real needs. The root cause of this alignment problem is usually the complexity of the query, the diversity of external knowledge, and the limitations of the retrieval mechanism. If the retrieved knowledge does not fully meet the intent of the query, the generated answer may have information omissions or logical errors, thus causing hallucinations.

- Capability Boundary

The capability boundaries of LLMs are mainly reflected in the deficiencies in precise calculation, data retrieval, and complex logic processing. These deficiencies are mainly due to their design goals based on statistical learning and language patterns, rather than being built for mathematical reasoning or symbolic operations. LLMs lack built-in mathematical logic, and their training data mainly comes from unstructured natural language texts. The model does not specifically learn mathematical rules, resulting in reliance on language patterns rather than real mathematical operations when dealing with mathematical problems. In addition, LLMs have limited digital representation capabilities, and complex mathematical expressions will be split into multiple tokens, affecting the accuracy of calculations. The presentation of mathematical problems is also relatively limited, lacking strict mathematical formulas and reasoning, which makes the model lack a sufficient data foundation for precise calculations. In addition, the reasoning process of LLMs is based on language generation rather than logical reasoning, lacking an understanding of logical rules and causal relationships and having difficulty handling complex multi-step reasoning tasks. These capabilities make LLMs prone to hallucinations. Prompt methods such as chain-of-thought encourage LLMs to decompose the problem, but when solving the problem, even if the problem is correctly decomposed, LLMs often make mistakes in logic and arithmetic [48].

4. Solutions to Retrieval Failure

This section reviews several key solutions to the problem of retrieval failure. First, the accuracy and credibility of information can be significantly enhanced by ensuring the reliability of data sources. Second, effective query construction methods have been proposed to deal with ambiguous and complex queries. Third, the effectiveness of the retriever is enhanced from two aspects, retrieval granularity and the embedding method, which improves its ability to handle complex queries. Finally, well-designed retrieval strategies ensure the efficient execution of the retrieval process and the accuracy of the results. These solutions target different subproblems of retrieval failure, aiming to comprehensively improve the overall performance of the retrieval system and effectively reduce hallucinations in retrieval-augmented LLMs.

4.1. Data Source Reliability

Structured data, such as knowledge graphs (KGs), are usually built from verified data sources and are constantly updated. This verification process ensures their ability to deliver accurate, reliable knowledge. The modular retrieval-augmented LLM KnowledGPT [49] combines LLMs with knowledge bases (KBs). It generates Python 3.8 code through the program of thoughts (PoT) [26] to perform knowledge base operations, retrieves information from different knowledge bases, and enables multi-hop retrieval for complex questions. Additionally, KnowledGPT [49] introduces a personalized knowledge base (PKB). This allows users to store knowledge related to professional fields or personal interests according to their needs. It also supports multiple knowledge representation forms, including entity descriptions, relationship triples, and entity-aspect information, enabling a broader range of knowledge storage.

The context generated by LLMs is aligned with the pre-training target and, therefore, tends to contain more relevant information. GENREAD [50] replaces the retriever with an LLM generator, which first prompts the LLM to generate context documents based on a given question and then generates a final response based on the generated documents. Cheng et al. [51] found that the output of LLMs has a memory that is more similar to the data distribution during inference than the training data and thus proposed the selfmem framework to improve the generation quality by using the output of the model. Slefmem creates an unbounded memory pool by the retrieval-augmented generator and uses a memory selector to select output as the memory for subsequent generation rounds; it then iterates through the generation process to enhance the model generation performance.

In addition, filtering and evaluating the credibility of retrieval sources can also prevent retrieval failures. Inspired by common practices in pre-training data processing [52], Asai et al. [53] considered a quality filter to ensure the high quality of retrieval source data storage. Xie et al. [39] found that relying solely on internal knowledge to evaluate the credibility of information is unreliable. Pan et al. [54] proposed a credibility-aware (CAG) framework to assign credibility levels to document-level and sentence-level retrieval information based on the relevance, timeliness, and reliability of the source of the information. CoT [24] was used on an existing QA dataset to prompt the large language model to generate explanations based on questions, retrieved documents with credibility annotations, and golden answers. The LLM was fine-tuned through instructions to generate responses based on credibility, which mitigated the impact of introducing defective information in the retrieval process.

4.2. User Query Construction

4.2.1. Ambiguous Queries

Query refinement can supplement and improve background information and solve the problem of necessary background information that is short, ambiguous, and lacking in search queries. Query refinement can be achieved through query expansion or query rewriting.

Query expansion is used to achieve disambiguation and satisfy the user's rich intents. Wang et al. [55] proposed a query2doc query expansion method, which first generates pseudo-related documents that help query disambiguation and guide the retriever through a small number of samples to prompt LLMs, and then connects them with the original query to form a new query. KnowledGPT [49] uses the functions of the knowledge base to obtain candidate entities and related information and uses few-shot prompting to prompt LLMs to align the entities mentioned in the text with the entities in the knowledge base to achieve disambiguation, avoiding the introduction of irrelevant and erroneous knowledge due to ambiguous retrieval. Jagerman et al. [56] generate new query terms through LLMs and combine them with the original query terms repeated five times to form a new expanded query. Studies have shown that applying CoT prompts [24] to this query expansion effectively improves the search engine recall rate. Wang et al. [57] found that ambiguous, multi-faceted queries, such as "What is jazz?", often contain multiple sub-intents, and users want to obtain comprehensive answers covering multiple aspects. Based on this, Wang et al. [57] proposed the RichRAG framework, which explicitly models various sub-aspects of the query and retrieves external knowledge to build a diverse document candidate pool, thereby providing comprehensive long-form answers and satisfying the user's rich intent. Kim et al. [58] proposed the Tree of Clarification (ToC) framework to construct more effective queries by identifying all clarification questions for fuzzy queries. TOC recursively builds the clarification tree of AQ by leveraging external knowledge for few-shot hints and pruning when necessary. TOC solves the challenge of clarification from multiple dimensions through a recursive tree and satisfies the external knowledge required to identify clarification questions and their answers through the retriever.

Query rewriting is used to align queries with retrieval requirements. Ma et al. [59] proposed a re-writer trained by reinforcement learning. The re-writer uses the LLM performance as a reward, learning to adapt the retrieval query to improve the reader on downstream tasks. Mao et al. [60] used the feedback signal of a publicly available re-ranker to train the rewriting model, eliminating the dependence on labeled data.

Decontextualization is used to effectively solve dialog dependency problems presented by questions in conversational retrievals, such as omission, ambiguity, and coreference [61–63]. Choi et al. [64] first proposed the decontextualization task. This task aims to extract sentences from their rich contexts and rewrite them into independent sentences that can be understood without context while retaining their original meaning. Choi et al. [64] designed an annotation pipeline to provide a high-quality annotated dataset and evaluation scripts and trained an automatic decontextualization model. Yoon et al. [65] guided an advanced LLM to generate various potential rewrites through multiple prompting methods, collected the retrieval feedback on each rewrite, and constructed a large-scale dataset called RF_COLLECTION. The dataset contains retriever feedback on more than 410,000 query rewrites from 12,000 conversations optimized for retrieval. Then, Yoon et al. [65] optimized the rewriter based on this dataset to generate retriever-preferred query rewrites, achieving the goal of contextualization.

4.2.2. Complex Queries

Query decomposition is a common approach when faced with complex queries involving multiple aspects, as it breaks down complex queries into subqueries to retrieve information more accurately. Shao et al. [66] proposed a method named STROM, focusing on applying LLMs to write long texts in an organized and well-founded manner. This method decomposes topics into various perspectives by retrieving Wikipedia articles on similar topics and gives LLMs specific perspectives, simulating multiple rounds of dialogue between authors and experts to collect knowledge. Finally, a multi-level section heading outline is generated by combining the internal knowledge of LLMs and the collected information, and a long text is generated based on this.

Sub-task planning is often used to decompose and solve complex queries that require intensive reasoning step by step. Through sub-task planning, complex and intricate queries can be decomposed into manageable, sequential steps that can be addressed individually. When combined, these steps provide context for the original problem and answer it in full. To overcome the challenge of easy-to-hard generalization in the chain of thought, Zhou et al. [67] propose a novel prompting strategy, least-to-most prompting. The foundational premise of this approach is to systematically decompose a complex problem into a series of easily solvable sub-problems and then solve these sub-problems sequentially in order, with each sub-problem solved with the help of the answer of the previously solved sub-problem. Khot et al. [68] also proposed decomposed prompting (DECOMP) based on the idea of subproblem planning. Compared with least-to-most, DECOMP has the following advantages: First, DECOMP has a modular structure, and each sub-task is processed by a dedicated processor. The sub-task processor can be independently optimized, debugged, and upgraded. If necessary, the sub-tasks that are more difficult for LLMs can be further decomposed. The task can be recursively decomposed into the same task with smaller inputs. The symbolic information retrieval module can be easily integrated within the decomposition framework to improve the performance on long-text multi-hop question answering and open-domain multi-hop question answering tasks. Second, DECOMP can improve previous work by simply adding an error correction sub-task processor as a post-processing step. Finally, the sub-task processor can be shared between different tasks to improve the efficiency of task-solving.

Question tree structure enables complex reasoning in knowledge-intensive, multi-hop question answering by decomposing complex questions into hierarchical nodes, facilitating global reasoning, and avoiding negative retrieval through retrieving and aggregating answers from different knowledge sources at each node. Cao et al. [69] proposed probabilistic tree-of-thought reasoning (ProbTree). First, LLMs transform a complex question into a query tree, where each non-root node represents a sub-question of its parent node, and leaf nodes are atomic questions that cannot be further decomposed. Then, ProbTree performs probabilistic reasoning on the tree, from leaf nodes to root nodes, and solves the problem by post-order traversal while considering the confidence of question decomposition and answer. For leaf nodes, ProbTree selects more confident answers from closed-book question answering and open-book question answering, avoiding the problem of negative retrieval. For non-leaf nodes, the tree hierarchy is used to obtain information from child nodes for global reasoning, thereby recovering from local errors and alleviating the problem of error propagation. Chu et al. [70] proposed a reasoning framework called beam aggregation reasoning (BeamAggR). Compared with ProbTree, it first performs complementary multi-source reasoning on leaf nodes and then performs fine-grained answer aggregation, which can better perform knowledge collaboration. For non-leaf nodes, BeamAggR enumerates the combination of sub-questions that the node depends on. Then, it selects the most promising prediction through beam aggregation, optimizes the reasoning trajectory, and reduces cascading errors.

4.3. Retriever Validity

4.3.1. Search Granularity

Appropriate search granularity can better meet complex retrieval requirements. Chunk-structured data sources face the problem of balancing the length of the context and the completeness of the semantics. Gao et al. [71] proposed to narrow the semantic gap between questions and answers by adding metadata attachments to the blocks. This includes metadata filtering for retrieving the original document (e.g., page numbers, file names, authors, categories, and timestamps) as well as artificially constructed metadata, such as paragraph summaries and hypothetical questions.

Partitioning the complete database allows the retriever to focus more on key memories and reduce retrieval noise. Wang et al. [72] proposed to divide the external database into multiple partitions. Each partition serves as the basic unit for RAG execution, thereby achieving fine-grained retrieval and focusing on key memories. Through the multi-agent reinforcement learning framework, the two agents, Agent-S and Agent-R, are responsible for selecting appropriate partitions and refining the retrieved memories, respectively. This process further improves text generation performance.

Tree and graph structures are used to organize long document information. Their hierarchical nature allows them to represent complex relationships. This improves information retrieval efficiency and enhances the ability to process complex queries. It also addresses the limitations of fixed-size chunking, which struggles to capture the structure and dependencies of long documents.

In RAG systems, most existing methods only retrieve short, continuous text fragments from the retrieval corpus, which limits the effective utilization of document-level contextual information. This limitation is reflected in the model's inability to capture long-range dependencies and integrate cross-fragment semantics. Sarthi et al. [73] proposed recursive abstractive processing for tree-organized retrieval (RAPTOR), which recursively embeds, clusters, and summarizes text blocks to build a tree structure with different summary levels from the bottom up. RAPTOR retrieves information from this tree during reasoning and integrates information at different levels of abstraction in long documents.

Graph structure can represent complex dependencies between entities well [74]. It helps organize information from multiple sources into coherent and contextual information, significantly reducing the possibility of hallucinations. LightRAG [75] extracts entity nodes and relationship edges from text through LLMs to construct text key–value pairs. After deduplication, it obtains a knowledge graph and dynamically integrates new data through incremental updates. It not only enhances the ability to handle complex queries but also improves the efficiency of data updates and retrieval performance through optimized key–value data structures. LightRAG [75] adopts a two-level retrieval paradigm, where low-level retrieval focuses on retrieving specific entities and their detailed information, while high-level retrieval focuses on aggregating multiple entities and relations to provide insights into broad topics. In the retrieval process, the graph structure and vector representation are combined to extract local and global keywords in the query and match relevant entities and relations by using the few-shot hint LLMs of role assignment, thus achieving comprehensive and efficient retrieval. Experiments on four datasets from the UltraDomain benchmark [76] show that this method outperforms block-based retrieval methods [71,77,78] in handling large-scale token queries and complex queries. To capture the logical relationship between document content and structure, Knowledge Graph Prompting (KGP) [79] implements indexing between multiple documents by constructing a knowledge graph. It treats paragraphs (text content) and structures (e.g., pages and tables) as nodes. The semantic, lexical, or structural relationships between paragraphs are represented as edges. This approach effectively addresses knowledge retrieval across multiple documents. It answers questions by extracting subgraphs to retrieve relevant information.

In addition, Chen et al. [80] introduced propositions as a new retrieval granularity to strike a balance between reducing noise and providing complete content. A proposition is defined as an atomic expression in text that encapsulates a distinct fact, presented in concise and self-sufficient natural language.

4.3.2. Embedding

By fine-tuning the embedding model to adapt to the domain knowledge of different downstream tasks. Retrieve and plug (REPLUG) [31] prepends the retrieved documents to the input text, feeds it into the frozen black-box language model, and optimizes the retrieval model by using the output of the black-box language model as a supervisory signal. Muennighoff et al. [81] proposed a generative representational instruction tuning (GRIT) method, which distinguishes between generation and embedding tasks through instructions and trains large language models to handle both tasks simultaneously. GRIT reduces the number of forward passes during reasoning through caching operations, thereby improving efficiency. Zhang et al. [82] enhance the inaccessible black-box embedding model by introducing a trainable embedding model. Zhang et al. [82] concatenate the output of the black-box embedding model and the trainable white-box model to form a new embedding function. Different fine-tuning criteria are adopted based on the availability of relevance labels between queries and candidate passages.

4.4. Retrieval Strategies

To prevent unnecessary retrieval from introducing knowledge that conflicts with the internal parameters of the model, it is necessary to determine the necessity of retrieval. Asai et al. [83] evaluate the necessity of retrieval by introducing special retrieve tags. The model is trained to generate these tags by designing specific prompts and demonstrations. Wang et al. [84] proposed a self-knowledge-guided retrieval enhancement (SKR) method. It allows LLMs to refer to the problems they have encountered before and adaptively call external resources when dealing with new problems. SKR collects self-knowledge of training problems by comparing the performance with and without retrieval enhancement. It then proposes strategies such as direct prompting, in-context learning, training a classifier, and nearest neighbor search to detect the self-knowledge corresponding to a problem by referring to the collected training problems. Jiang et al. [85] decide whether external information needs to be retrieved based on the uncertainty in the generation process. If there are low-confidence words, the model will use the sentence as a retrieval query to retrieve relevant documents from the external knowledge base, and regenerate the sentence based on the retrieved information.

Retrieval frequency refers to the frequency of searching the external knowledge base during the generation process, which controls the degree of reliance on the search results and is usually more worthy of consideration than the necessity of the search. There are a variety of multiple search strategies, such as iterative retrieval [86,87], recursive retrieval [88,89], conditional retrieval, adaptive retrieval [90,91], etc.

In iterative retrieval, information is retrieved in multiple steps. Each step builds on the previous ones, making this approach suitable for tasks that require detailed exploration and improvement. Trivedi et al. [86] proposed an iterative retrieval method called IRCoT, in which retrieval and reasoning steps are performed alternately, allowing reasoning to guide retrieval and using retrieval results to improve reasoning. Shao et al. [87] proposed a method called ITER-RETGEN. This method also adopts an iterative strategy, using the generated output of the model as the context of retrieval, to more accurately obtain relevant knowledge and improve subsequent generation results. The iterative retrieval method solves the limitations of traditional single-shot retrieval methods in multi-step reasoning tasks. Combining dynamic retrieval and reasoning significantly improves the accuracy of retrieval and the performance of downstream question-answering tasks while reducing factual errors in the reasoning chain generated by the model.

Recursive retrieval creates a tree or graph structure of retrieval, which contains retrieval that can call itself and performs well in managing hierarchical information. Chen et al. [89] proposed the MemWalker method, which constructs a tree structure by splitting long text into small paragraphs and recursively generating summary nodes. After receiving the query, the model starts navigating from the root node of the tree, checks the summary content of the child nodes level by level, and decides which child node to enter to continue searching for relevant information through reasoning. When the current node information is insufficient to answer the question, it backtracks until it finds a node containing enough information and generates an answer. The hierarchical summarization and dynamic navigation of the tree structure break through the limitations of the context window of the language model, significantly improve the efficiency and accuracy of long text processing, enhance reasoning ability and interpretability, and support error recovery, making it perform well in long text question-answering tasks. Kang et al. [88] proposed the SURGE framework, which uses a recursive strategy in the knowledge graph to better capture dependencies between entities in context by extracting subgraphs related to the conversation context. The structured organization of the knowledge graph enables the systematic integration of multi-level information, improving the accuracy and contextual relevance of retrieved knowledge. This structured approach facilitates the generation of more coherent and contextually consistent conversational outputs.

Conditional retrieval ensures strict adherence to predefined criteria and is suitable for scenarios with clear rules and fixed requirements. Adaptive retrieval dynamically adjusts retrieval behavior according to current task requirements, contextual information, or model status, providing flexibility in dynamic environments. Jeong et al. [90] proposed Adaptive-RAG, which aims to dynamically adjust the retrieval strategy according to the complexity of the query. Adaptive-RAG uses a small LM as a classifier to predict the complexity label of the query and selects the most suitable method from a simple no-retrieval strategy to a complex multi-step retrieval strategy based on the prediction results. Islam et al. [91] proposed a hybrid adaptive retrieval method that dynamically decides whether to retrieve based on model confidence, balancing retrieval frequency and reasoning speed. Adaptive retrieval optimizes reasoning efficiency by dynamically adjusting the retrieval frequency, especially avoiding unnecessary retrieval overhead when processing simple queries and fully using retrieval information when processing complex queries.

5. Solutions to Generation Deficiency

This section reviews relevant solutions to several key issues in generation deficiency. First, we review improving the relevance of retrieved documents by reducing contextual noise. Second, we investigate methods to balance knowledge conflicts, aiming to coordinate the relationship between external knowledge and internal parameters of the model, to ensure the consistency and factual accuracy of generated content. Third, for the problem of middle curse, we outline ways to compress long texts and train models to extract key information, making full use of context. Finally, this section investigates how to ensure the alignment of generation with query and context, and how to break through the limitations of model capabilities by integrating external resources. These solutions help to comprehensively improve the performance of generation models and reduce deviations and errors in the generation process.

5.1. Reduce Context Noise

We begin with the strategy of reducing the impact of noise by re-ranking to retain more relevant context. RichRAG [57] builds a diverse pool of document candidates based on modeled latent sub-aspects to retrieve external knowledge, which often contains noise. To reduce the noise of retrieved documents, RichRAG re-ranks candidate documents and selects the top k documents as context. The multifaceted queries targeted by RichRAG require rich context, and the users of the information retrieval (IR) model are LLMs, which require the ranking of the ranker to be aligned with the preferences of the LLMs. Based on this, the optimization of the ranker is divided into two stages. The first stage is supervised fine-tuning (SFT), where a coverage utility function is used to create silver targets for training, enhancing the ranker's ability to cover query aspects. The second stage is reinforcement learning, which improves ranking quality and aligns it with LLM preferences using the direct preference optimization algorithm (DPO) [92] and a unilateral significance sampling strategy (US3) to build valuable training samples for stable optimization. Vu et al. [93] proposed a few-shot prompt method, FreshPrompt, which generates a list of evidence by extracting sources, dates, titles, highlighted words, etc., from the results retrieved from the search engine and sorts them from old to new in time, encouraging the model to focus on the latest evidence to reduce noise. Vu et al. [93] also proposed a new dynamic question-answering benchmark, FreshQA, which includes 600 natural questions, covering questions that require rapidly changing knowledge and require refutation of false premises, to measure the performance of LLMs in dealing with questions that require the latest world knowledge.

In addition, context compression is used to filter out irrelevant information. Jiang et al. [94] presented LLMLingua, a coarse-to-fine prompt compression method. It involves a budget controller to maintain semantic integrity under high compression ratios, a token-level iterative compression algorithm to better model the interdependence between compressed contents, and an instruction tuning-based method for distribution alignment between language models. However, the tokenizer differences between the small model and the large model may cause the prompt length to be underestimated. Li [95] proposed a method called Selective Context. It leverages self-information to evaluate the informativeness of vocabulary units (such as sentences, phrases, or tokens) in the context and selectively retains the highly informative content. This approach provides a more compact and efficient context representation without sacrificing the performance of the model on a variety of tasks. Wang et al. [96] proposed to identify useful contexts based on lexical and information-theoretic methods and train a context-filtering model that can filter the retrieved contexts to compress the contexts. Xu et al. [97] presented two compressors—the extractive compressor selects useful sentences from the retrieved documents, and the abstractive compressor generates summaries by synthesizing information from multiple documents. These compressors are trained to improve the performance of LLMs while keeping the prompts concise. Liu et al. [98] proposed summary compression and semantic compression. Summary compression achieves compression through summarization, while semantic compression deletes tags that have little impact on semantics.

However, filtering irrelevant paragraphs and information may also cause some relevant information to be discarded. A more effective solution is to train LLMs to ignore irrelevant context by adding irrelevant context to the training data. Chain-of-note (CoN) [99] uses GPT-4 to collect data from the Natural Questions (NQ) corpus [100] and trains the model in a standard supervised manner to generate continuous reading notes for each retrieved document. This process helps evaluate their relevance to a given question and identify the most critical and reliable information. If all documents are irrelevant, the model either relies on intrinsic knowledge to answer or answers "Unknown" when the answer cannot be accurately determined.

5.2. Balance Knowledge Conflicts

Context conflict mainly refers to the conflict between the model's internal parameters and the retrieved external knowledge, namely, context–memory conflict [36]. When external knowledge is relevant to the task and has high credibility, it should be aligned with the contextual knowledge [27]. When external knowledge is insufficient or unclear, the model should be encouraged to be skeptical of the context and support parameter knowledge [101,102]. A broader strategy is to treat context and knowledge separately, provide disentangled answers [103], or use context and parameter knowledge to improve the factuality of the answer [104].

Specifically, Zhou et al. [27] reconstructed the question by asking the narrator's point of view through opinion-based prompts and used counterfactual demonstrations to show examples of conflicts with memorized knowledge, jointly improving the model's attention to context. Pan et al. [101] built a misleading information dataset by prompting LLMs, trained a misleading information detection model, and guided LLMs to be more cautious by adding additional warnings or guidance in the prompts. Xu et al. [102] constructed a "Fact to Misinform" (Farm) dataset containing a series of factual questions and their corresponding misleading information, and based on this, tracked the changes in LLMs' beliefs when facing misleading information through multiple rounds of dialogue, revealing the vulnerability of LLMs when facing misleading information. Xu et al. [102] used system prompts to remind LLMs to be vigilant about potential misinformation and list all the supporting evidence before responding. Both of the above methods improve the ability to adhere to factual and parameter information of the model when facing potential misinformation through vigilant prompts. Wang et al. [103] aims to consider LLM's ability to detect conflicts, locate conflicts, and generate different answers based on conflicting information. Wang et al. [103] prompted LLMs to generate entity lists in different subject areas and create conflicts through in-domain named entity substitution and in-domain entity shuffling. The chain-of-thought prompts that generate knowledge decompose context, classify conflicts sentence by sentence, and finally improve the ability to detect conflicts of LLMs. By clearly distinguishing the two knowledge sources and repeating the questions, the model's ability to generate different answers based on the knowledge source is improved. Zhang et al. [104] considered pairing the retrieved paragraphs with LLM-generated paragraphs obtained via specially designed prompts to form compatible pairs to generate the final answer. Zhang et al. [104] first evaluated whether the retrieved paragraphs contained correct evidence and then evaluated whether LLM-generated paragraphs were consistent with the retrieved paragraphs. By screening and matching factual and consistent paragraph pairs, the negative impact of knowledge conflicts on the model is reduced.

5.3. Utilize Middle Information

To address the middle curse issue in LLMs, recent studies have focused on effectively utilizing the middle information within long contexts. These approaches aim to enhance the model's ability to capture and leverage critical information located in the middle portions of the input text, thereby improving overall generation quality. Wang et al. [105] proposed a method called SoftPromptComp, which compresses long text into a concise but semantically rich representation through natural language summarization technology and then integrates it into the input of an LLM through soft prompts. This approach not only reduces the computational overhead by decreasing the volume of text processed but also enhances the model's performance in processing and generating compressed text through the dynamic adaptability of soft prompts. He et al. [44] proposed a method called Position-Agnostic Multi-step QA (PAM QA), which trains the model to accurately identify and extract key information from long texts through position-independent multi-step reasoning. Specifically, PAM QA reinforces the model's attention to the question through question repetition, assists in filtering relevant information via index prediction, and produces the final output through answer summarization, thereby improving the model's retrieval and summarization performance on long texts. Ravaut et al. [106] analyzed the contextual utilization of LLMs in long text summarization, revealed its bias in processing long inputs, and explored three alternative reasoning methods: hierarchical summarization, incremental summarization, and focus prompt. Hierarchical summarization aggregates information through block summarization and secondary summarization, incremental summarization updates the summary content block by block, and focus prompt guides LLMs to focus on the middle part of the input through prompts. Ravaut et al. [106] also sampled from a long-input summarization dataset to ensure that the key information is in the middle part of the context window, constructing a new evaluation benchmark MiddleSum.

5.4. Alignment Resolution

The alignment problem here mainly focuses on the alignment between context and generation, namely, context faithfulness, and the alignment between query and generation, namely, query faithfulness.

5.4.1. Context Faithfulness

Contextual faithfulness refers to the consistency and relevance of the generated text to the input context in terms of content and logic. Better contextual faithfulness is usually achieved by attributing the generated response to the context. Gao et al. [107] proposed the ALCE framework, which aims to enable LLMs to generate text with citations, thereby improving the accuracy and verifiability of their output. The ALCE framework first retrieves text fragments related to the question from the corpus and then guides LLMs to generate answers and cite supporting fragments through different prompting strategies (such as VANILLA, SUMM, SNIPPET, INLINESEARCH, etc.). Fierro et al. [108] proposed a plan-based text generation method that aims to improve the credibility and attribution quality of generated text by generating citations. The method decomposes the text generation task into a series of questions, which serve as the blueprint for the generated content. The model then generates a summary based on the blueprint and generates citations simultaneously during the generation process to ensure that the generated content is supported by reliable external evidence. These methods address the shortcomings of existing generative models in attribution, such as credibility issues caused by inaccurate or lacking citations. However, prompt-based methods can only provide sentence-level attribution and rely on the internal knowledge of LLMs, which have high computational overhead. Incomplete compliance with instructions by LLMs can also lead to problems such as incorrect citation format, citing non-existent sources, or failing to accurately reflect contextual usage.

Given the inherent defects of prompt-based methods, Ye et al. [109] proposed the AGREE method, which aims to improve the accuracy and credibility of answers by fine-tuning LLMs to cite retrieved document fragments as support when generating answers automatically. AGREE first uses unlabeled queries and natural language inference (NLI) models to automatically generate training data with citations. Then, LLMs are fine-tuned through supervised learning to enable them to generate accurate answers based on retrieved fragments and clearly annotate the citation sources. Finally, in the test phase, AGREE uses an iterative reasoning strategy in the retest phase to allow LLMs to actively retrieve additional information based on self-evaluation results to further optimize the answer. Qi et al. [110] proposed the MIRAGE method, which aims to enhance the credibility of answer attribution in RAG systems by leveraging model internals. MIRAGE first identifies the words affected by the context in the generated sentences by comparing the changes in the model's predicted distribution with and without context. Then, it uses feature attribution techniques such as gradients to attribute the generation of these sensitive words to specific context words and converts the results into a standard reference format. MIRAGE directly uses the calculation process inside the model to reflect the importance of the input in the generation process, thereby avoiding the inaccuracy and computational overhead that may be caused by external validators.

5.4.2. Query Faithfulness

Query faithfulness refers to how well the generated content aligns with the user's query and its semantic intent. Zhang et al. [111] proposed the MixAlign framework, which aims to address the knowledge alignment problem that occurs when LLMs interact with external knowledge bases—i.e., there is a semantic, contextual, structural, or logical mismatch between the user's question and the retrieved knowledge. MixAlign automatically detects these mismatches through interaction with users and knowledge bases. It generates clarifying questions to obtain further guidance from users, enhancing the model's knowledge utilization performance. Peng et al. [112] proposed a plug-and-play LLM-Augmenter framework for revising prompts through feedback on the responses of LLMs. The framework first integrates the retrieved external knowledge, constructs an evidence chain by linking related entities and pruning irrelevant information, and generates a response based on the evidence chain. It then evaluates the alignment between the response and specific business requirements using rule-based or model-based utility functions, generates feedback information to revise the prompt, and queries the LLM again. This process repeats until the generated response is verified.

5.5. Integrate External Resources

By combining the reasoning capabilities of LLMs with external tools, external resources (computing power, data retrieval capabilities, complex logic processing, etc.) can be effectively utilized to allow the model to adapt to new tasks with only a small number of examples or feedback, and to solve various challenges in complex tasks. Yao et al. [113] proposed ReAct, which aims to combine the reasoning and acting capabilities of LLMs to solve complex language and decision-making tasks. ReAct enables the model to dynamically adjust action plans during the reasoning process by alternately generating reasoning traces and task-related actions and obtaining necessary information to support reasoning through interaction with the external environment. Paranjape et al. [114] proposed the ART method, which solves the reasoning limitations and insufficient tool use of LLMs in dealing with complex tasks through automated multi-step reasoning and tool calls. ART retrieves relevant task examples from the task library as prompts, uses LLMs to generate programs containing intermediate reasoning steps and tool calls, pauses the generation to call the tool and integrate the output, and finally, continues to generate the final answer. In addition, ART also supports human feedback, and users can optimize performance by editing programs or adding tools. To compensate for the deficiencies of LLMs in computation and reasoning, Gao et al. [48] propose program-aided language models (PALs). These employ LLMs to decompose natural language problems and generate programs as intermediate reasoning steps through least-to-most prompting. PALs offload the solution step to a runtime such as a Python interpreter, separating problem decomposition from solution execution.

6. Mitigation After Hallucination Detection

Although the components of RAG have been optimized based on the causes of hallucination to mitigate its occurrence, hallucinations remain inevitable. However, their impact can be reduced through detection and correction.

Active hallucination detection and mitigation techniques detect and correct hallucinations in real-time during the generation process to prevent the accumulation and propagation of hallucinations. Varshney et al. [115] proposed an active hallucination detection and mitigation method. In the detection stage, it identifies the key concepts in the generated sentences and creates verification questions for these concepts. It retrieves relevant knowledge and answers verification questions through web searches and model parameter queries to verify the response knowledge in the generated sentences to detect hallucinations. In the mitigation stage, the retrieved knowledge is used as evidence to repair sentences that may have hallucinations, and the corrected sentences are appended to the generation context. The real-time verification and rectification (EVER) framework proposed by Kang et al. [116] also realizes hallucination detection and mitigation through three stages: generation, verification, and correction. In the verification stage, EVER divides hallucinations into internal hallucinations and external hallucinations, corrects internal hallucinations, and rewrites external hallucinations. The corrected sentences will be verified again. If the external illusion still exists, the system will choose to mark the user to warn or give up the answer according to the task requirements, thereby enhancing the credibility of the output content. EVER also uses the data it generates to build preference data pairs, and further improves the factuality of the model through preference adjustment.

Detecting and editing the output of LLMs is universal in hallucination detection and mitigation for different tasks. Gao et al. [117] proposed the retrofit attribution using the research and revision (RARR) method. RARR is divided into research and revision stages. In the research stage, query generation and evidence retrieval are performed for the responses of LLMs to achieve attribution. In the revision stage, the consistency model detects disagreements, and the editing model corrects the text based on the disagreements and retains the structural and stylistic properties of the original text. RARR also proposed a new metric for the attribution editing task, emphasizing the balance between attribution and preservation. Rawte et al. [20] considered replacing high-entropy words in the generation to mitigate hallucinations. Due to the inaccessibility of many LLMs, Rawte et al. [20] used open-source LLMs to identify high-entropy words and defined the hallucination vulnerability index (HVI) of LLMs. High-entropy words were replaced with LLMs based on lower HVI to mitigate hallucinations in generation. They also reported effective models for detecting and replacing high-entropy words, respectively.

7. Conclusions

In this review, we conducted a comprehensive investigation into the hallucination phenomenon caused by the RAG paradigm, including the causes of hallucinations in each subtask at different stages of the RAG framework and the corresponding hallucination mitigation methods. Additionally, we explored techniques for reducing hallucinations through detection and subsequent mitigation. We also provided a summary of the metrics, datasets, and challenges of representative hallucination mitigation methods in subtasks at different stages in Table 4.

Among the methods we reviewed, even though prompt techniques are widely used, they still have the following limitations that we should be concerned about: (1) Prompt techniques have weak generalization ability, and multiple iterations are required to fine-tune the prompts in practical applications, which may be very time-consuming. (2) Some mitigation methods have restrictions on the length of the prompt [94]. (3) The good performance of prompt engineering also depends on the powerful capabilities of the embedding model [82] and the generative model [99].

Despite extensive research and significant achievements in hallucination mitigation, hallucinations in retrieval-augmented LLMs remain a highly concerning issue and continue to face multifaceted challenges. For example, current multimodal retrieval-augmented LLMs extend the knowledge sources beyond text to include data from multiple modalities, such as images, audio, video, and code. This expansion enriches the context and supplements textual information, enabling the model to generate more satisfactory responses [118,119]. However, the diversity of data sources also introduces additional factors that can lead to hallucinations. Large language models may struggle to accurately interpret the relationships between entities in images, which further leads to the generation of hallucinations. Therefore, further research into hallucination mitigation strategies for multimodal retrieval-augmented LLMs is necessary. Moreover, malicious external attacks, such as carefully crafted jailbreaking prompts [120] and adversarial prompts [121], can induce the model to generate specific hallucinations. Research into attack and defense strategies for inducing hallucinations represents a promising direction for future work. Finally, we hope that this review provides valuable research materials for the development of more reliable and trustworthy LLMs.

Table 4. Summary of metrics, datasets, and challenges of representative hallucination mitigation methods in different stages of subtasks.

Category	Method	Metric	Dataset	Challenges
Data Source	CAG [54]	EM; Noise Ratio; Document Credibility	HotpotQA [122]; 2WikiMQA [123]; MuSiQue [124]; ASQA [125]; RGB [126]; EvolvTempQA [54]; NewsPolluQA [54]	Reliance on additional training data and annotations; limited scope for external resource integration
Query	RETPO [65]	MRR; NDCG; Recall@k; Clarity; Conciseness; Informativeness	QReCC [62]; TopiOCQA [63]	Limited testing scope; limited prompting methods
	Beam AggR [70]	F1	Bamboogle [127]; MuSiQue [124]; HotpotQA [122]; 2WikiMQA [123]	Multi-source reasoning and probabilistic aggregation raise computational costs; external knowledge is unstructured

Table 4. *Cont.*

Category	Method	Metric	Dataset	Challenges
Retriever	KGP [79]	Acc; EM; F1; PDFTriage; Struct-EM	MuSiQue [124]; HotpotQA [122]; 2WikiMQA [123]; IIRC [128]; PDFTriage [129]	Details not provided
	GRIT [81]	Acc; MAP; AP; V-Measure; nDCG; SC; EM; pass@1; Win Ratio	E5 [130];Tülu2 [131]; MMLU [4]; TyDi QA [132] GSM8K [133]; MTEB [134]; HumanEvalSyn [135]; AlpacaEval [136];	Lack of autonomous retrieval capability; insufficient pre-training data; lengthy GRITLM format
Retrieval Strategy	Adaptive RAG [90]	F1; EM; Acc	SQuAD [137]; NQ [100]; TabularQA [138]; MuSiQue [124]; HotpotQA [122]; 2WikiMQA [123]	Lack of datasets for training query complexity classifier; not good performance of classifier
Context Noise	CoN [99]	EM; F1; Reject Ratio; Acc	NQ [100]; TriviaQA [139]; WebQuestions [140]; RealTimeQA [141]	The sequential generation of reading notes extends response times
Knowledge Conflicts	COMBO [104]	EM; F1	NQ [100]; TriviaQA [139]; HotpotQA [122]; WebQ [140]	Lack of adaptability to multi-hop question answering tasks
Utilize Context	SPC [105]	Processing Time; Acc; Cost; Compression Rate	CNN/Daily Mail [142]; SST-2 [143]; AG News [144]; SQuAD v2.0 [137]	Need to balance efficiency and thoroughness to avoid losing important information through excessive compression
Alignment	Plan-based Text Generation [108]	Correctness; Attribution; ROUGE-L; Answerability; AutoAIS; ANLI	AQuAMuSe [145]; NQ [100];	Explore decoder-only models, passage indexing; use questions as additional training signals for retrieval
	Mix-Align [111]	Gold Answer Coverage; Accepted; Hallucination	FuzzyQA [111]	Clarification steps add computational load and time cost; no causal path links question, evidence, and answer

Table 4. *Cont.*

Category	Method	Metric	Dataset	Challenges
External Resource	PAL [48]	Acc	GSM8K [133]; SVAMP [146]; ASDIV [147]; MAWPS [148]; BIG-BenchHard [149];	Details not provided
Mitigation after Detection	Active Detection [115]	Precision; Hallucination Ratio; Recall; Mitigation Success Ratio	HotpotQA [122]; Manual	Details not provided
	Entropy Word [20]	HVI; Hallucination Ratio; Mitigation Success Rate	HILT [20];	Details not provided

Author Contributions: Conceptualization, W.Z. and J.Z.; methodology, W.Z.; investigation, W.Z.; resources, J.Z.; writing—original draft preparation, W.Z.; writing—review and editing, W.Z. and J.Z.; visualization, W.Z.; supervision, J.Z.; funding acquisition, J.Z. All authors have read and agreed to the published version of the manuscript.

Funding: This research was funded Fundamental Research Funds for the Central Universities, No. RF1028623059.

Data Availability Statement: The original contributions presented in this study are included in the article; further inquiries can be directed to the corresponding author.

Acknowledgments: The authors thank the MDPI *Mathematics* editorial team for inviting us to publish this review in this Special Issue.

Conflicts of Interest: The authors declare no conflicts of interest.

References

1. Achiam, J.; Adler, S.; Agarwal, S.; Ahmad, L.; Akkaya, I.; Aleman, F.L.; Almeida, D.; Altenschmidt, J.; Altman, S.; Anadkat, S.; et al. Gpt-4 technical report. *arXiv* **2023**, arXiv:2303.08774.
2. Touvron, H.; Lavril, T.; Izacard, G.; Martinet, X.; Lachaux, M.A.; Lacroix, T.; Rozière, B.; Goyal, N.; Hambro, E.; Azhar, F.; et al. Llama: Open and efficient foundation language models. *arXiv* **2023**, arXiv:2302.13971.
3. Team, G.; Anil, R.; Borgeaud, S.; Alayrac, J.B.; Yu, J.; Soricut, R.; Schalkwyk, J.; Dai, A.M.; Hauth, A.; Millican, K.; et al. Gemini: A family of highly capable multimodal models. *arXiv* **2023**, arXiv:2312.11805.
4. Hendrycks, D.; Burns, C.; Basart, S.; Zou, A.; Mazeika, M.; Song, D.; Steinhardt, J. Measuring massive multitask language understanding. *arXiv* **2020**, arXiv:2009.03300.
5. Zhang, T.; Ladhak, F.; Durmus, E.; Liang, P.; McKeown, K.; Hashimoto, T.B. Benchmarking large language models for news summarization. *Trans. Assoc. Comput. Linguist.* **2024**, *12*, 39–57. [CrossRef]
6. Yu, F.; Zhang, H.; Tiwari, P.; Wang, B. Natural language reasoning, a survey. *ACM Comput. Surv.* **2024**, *56*, 1–39. [CrossRef]
7. Kim, H.J.; Cho, H.; Kim, J.; Kim, T.; Yoo, K.M.; Lee, S.g. Self-generated in-context learning: Leveraging auto-regressive language models as a demonstration generator. *arXiv* **2022**, arXiv:2206.08082.
8. Morris, M.R. Prompting Considered Harmful. *Commun. ACM* **2024**, *67*, 28–30. [CrossRef]
9. Liu, H.; Xue, W.; Chen, Y.; Chen, D.; Zhao, X.; Wang, K.; Hou, L.; Li, R.; Peng, W. A survey on hallucination in large vision-language models. *arXiv* **2024**, arXiv:2402.00253.
10. Sahoo, P.; Meharia, P.; Ghosh, A.; Saha, S.; Jain, V.; Chadha, A. A comprehensive survey of hallucination in large language, image, video and audio foundation models. In *Findings of the Association for Computational Linguistics: EMNLP 2024*; Association for Computational Linguistics: Miami, FL, USA, 2024; pp. 11709–11724.
11. Alghamdi, G.A.T.K.Z.; Liu, H. Can Knowledge Graphs Reduce Hallucinations in LLMs?: A Survey. *arXiv* **2023**, arXiv:2311.07914.

12. Tonmoy, S.; Zaman, S.; Jain, V.; Rani, A.; Rawte, V.; Chadha, A.; Das, A. A comprehensive survey of hallucination mitigation techniques in large language models. *arXiv* **2024**, arXiv:2401.01313.
13. Huang, L.; Yu, W.; Ma, W.; Zhong, W.; Feng, Z.; Wang, H.; Chen, Q.; Peng, W.; Feng, X.; Qin, B.; et al. A survey on hallucination in large language models: Principles, taxonomy, challenges, and open questions. *ACM Trans. Inf. Syst.* **2023**, *43*, 1–55. [CrossRef]
14. Zhang, Y.; Li, Y.; Cui, L.; Cai, D.; Liu, L.; Fu, T.; Huang, X.; Zhao, E.; Zhang, Y.; Chen, Y.; et al. Siren's song in the AI ocean: A survey on hallucination in large language models. *arXiv* **2023**, arXiv:2309.01219.
15. Macpherson, F.; Platchias, D. *Hallucination: Philosophy and Psychology*; EBL-Schweitzer, MIT Press: Cambridge, MA, USA, 2013.
16. Smith, A.L.; Greaves, F.; Panch, T. Hallucination or confabulation? Neuroanatomy as metaphor in large language models. *PLoS Digit. Health* **2023**, *2*, e0000388. [CrossRef]
17. Weinstein, E.A. Linguistic aspects of amnesia and confabulation. In *Principles, Practices, and Positions in Neuropsychiatric Research*; Elsevier: Amsterdam, The Netherlands, 1972; pp. 439–444.
18. Sui, P.; Duede, E.; Wu, S.; So, R.J. Confabulation: The Surprising Value of Large Language Model Hallucinations. *arXiv* **2024**, arXiv:2406.04175.
19. Ji, Z.; Lee, N.; Frieske, R.; Yu, T.; Su, D.; Xu, Y.; Ishii, E.; Bang, Y.J.; Madotto, A.; Fung, P. Survey of hallucination in natural language generation. *ACM Comput. Surv.* **2023**, *55*, 1–38. [CrossRef]
20. Rawte, V.; Chakraborty, S.; Pathak, A.; Sarkar, A.; Tonmoy, S.; Chadha, A.; Sheth, A.P.; Das, A. The troubling emergence of hallucination in large language models–an extensive definition, quantification, and prescriptive remediations. *arXiv* **2023**, arXiv:2310.04988.
21. Barnett, S.; Kurniawan, S.; Thudumu, S.; Brannelly, Z.; Abdelrazek, M. Seven failure points when engineering a retrieval augmented generation system. In Proceedings of the IEEE/ACM 3rd International Conference on AI Engineering-Software Engineering for AI, Lisbon, Portugal, 14–15 April 2024; pp. 194–199.
22. Shanahan, M.; McDonell, K.; Reynolds, L. Role play with large language models. *Nature* **2023**, *623*, 493–498. [CrossRef]
23. Logan IV, R.L.; Balažević, I.; Wallace, E.; Petroni, F.; Singh, S.; Riedel, S. Cutting down on prompts and parameters: Simple few-shot learning with language models. *arXiv* **2021**, arXiv:2106.13353.
24. Wei, J.; Wang, X.; Schuurmans, D.; Bosma, M.; Xia, F.; Chi, E.; Le, Q.V.; Zhou, D. Chain-of-thought prompting elicits reasoning in large language models. *Adv. Neural Inf. Process. Syst.* **2022**, *35*, 24824–24837.
25. Zhang, Z.; Zhang, A.; Li, M.; Smola, A. Automatic chain of thought prompting in large language models. *arXiv* **2022**, arXiv:2210.03493.
26. Chen, W.; Ma, X.; Wang, X.; Cohen, W.W. Program of thoughts prompting: Disentangling computation from reasoning for numerical reasoning tasks. *arXiv* **2022**, arXiv:2211.12588.
27. Zhou, W.; Zhang, S.; Poon, H.; Chen, M. Context-faithful prompting for large language models. *arXiv* **2023**, arXiv:2303.11315.
28. Izacard, G.; Lewis, P.; Lomeli, M.; Hosseini, L.; Petroni, F.; Schick, T.; Dwivedi-Yu, J.; Joulin, A.; Riedel, S.; Grave, E. Atlas: Few-shot learning with retrieval augmented language models. *J. Mach. Learn. Res.* **2023**, *24*, 1–43.
29. Lewis, P.; Perez, E.; Piktus, A.; Petroni, F.; Karpukhin, V.; Goyal, N.; Küttler, H.; Lewis, M.; Yih, W.t.; Rocktäschel, T.; et al. Retrieval-augmented generation for knowledge-intensive nlp tasks. *Adv. Neural Inf. Process. Syst.* **2020**, *33*, 9459–9474.
30. Ram, O.; Levine, Y.; Dalmedigos, I.; Muhlgay, D.; Shashua, A.; Leyton-Brown, K.; Shoham, Y. In-context retrieval-augmented language models. *Trans. Assoc. Comput. Linguist.* **2023**, *11*, 1316–1331. [CrossRef]
31. Shi, W.; Min, S.; Yasunaga, M.; Seo, M.; James, R.; Lewis, M.; Zettlemoyer, L.; Yih, W.T. Replug: Retrieval-augmented black-box language models. *arXiv* **2023**, arXiv:2301.12652.
32. Lazaridou, A.; Gribovskaya, E.; Stokowiec, W.; Grigorev, N. Internet-augmented language models through few-shot prompting for open-domain question answering. *arXiv* **2022**, arXiv:2203.05115.
33. Borgeaud, S.; Mensch, A.; Hoffmann, J.; Cai, T.; Rutherford, E.; Millican, K.; Van Den Driessche, G.B.; Lespiau, J.B.; Damoc, B.; Clark, A.; et al. Improving language models by retrieving from trillions of tokens. In Proceedings of the International Conference on Machine Learning, PMLR, Baltimore, MD, USA, 17–23 July 2022; pp. 2206–2240.
34. Cuconasu, F.; Trappolini, G.; Siciliano, F.; Filice, S.; Campagnano, C.; Maarek, Y.; Tonellotto, N.; Silvestri, F. The power of noise: Redefining retrieval for rag systems. In Proceedings of the 47th International ACM SIGIR Conference on Research and Development in Information Retrieval, Washington, DC, USA, 14–18 July 2024; pp. 719–729.
35. Zhao, B.; Brumbaugh, Z.; Wang, Y.; Hajishirzi, H.; Smith, N.A. Set the clock: Temporal alignment of pretrained language models. *arXiv* **2024**, arXiv:2402.16797.
36. Xu, R.; Qi, Z.; Guo, Z.; Wang, C.; Wang, H.; Zhang, Y.; Xu, W. Knowledge conflicts for llms: A survey. *arXiv* **2024**, arXiv:2403.08319.
37. Longpre, S.; Perisetla, K.; Chen, A.; Ramesh, N.; DuBois, C.; Singh, S. Entity-based knowledge conflicts in question answering. *arXiv* **2021**, arXiv:2109.05052.
38. Chen, H.T.; Zhang, M.J.; Choi, E. Rich knowledge sources bring complex knowledge conflicts: Recalibrating models to reflect conflicting evidence. *arXiv* **2022**, arXiv:2210.13701.

39. Xie, J.; Zhang, K.; Chen, J.; Lou, R.; Su, Y. Adaptive chameleon or stubborn sloth: Revealing the behavior of large language models in knowledge conflicts. *arXiv* **2023**, arXiv:2305.13300.
40. Perez, E.; Ringer, S.; Lukošiūtė, K.; Nguyen, K.; Chen, E.; Heiner, S.; Pettit, C.; Olsson, C.; Kundu, S.; Kadavath, S.; et al. Discovering language model behaviors with model-written evaluations. *arXiv* **2022**, arXiv:2212.09251.
41. Turpin, M.; Michael, J.; Perez, E.; Bowman, S. Language models don't always say what they think: Unfaithful explanations in chain-of-thought prompting. *Adv. Neural Inf. Process. Syst.* **2024**, *36*, 74952–74965.
42. Wei, J.; Huang, D.; Lu, Y.; Zhou, D.; Le, Q.V. Simple synthetic data reduces sycophancy in large language models. *arXiv* **2023**, arXiv:2308.03958.
43. Sharma, M.; Tong, M.; Korbak, T.; Duvenaud, D.; Askell, A.; Bowman, S.R.; Cheng, N.; Durmus, E.; Hatfield-Dodds, Z.; Johnston, S.R.; et al. Towards understanding sycophancy in language models. *arXiv* **2023**, arXiv:2310.13548.
44. He, J.; Pan, K.; Dong, X.; Song, Z.; Liu, Y.; Liang, Y.; Wang, H.; Sun, Q.; Zhang, S.; Xie, Z. Never lost in the middle: Improving large language models via attention strengthening question answering. *arXiv* **2023**, arXiv:2311.09198.
45. Waswani, A.; Shazeer, N.; Parmar, N.; Uszkoreit, J.; Jones, L.; Gomez, A.; Kaiser, L.; Polosukhin, I. Attention is all you need. In Proceedings of the NIPS 2017, Beach, CA, USA, 7 December 2017.
46. Chen, H.T.; Xu, F.; Arora, S.; Choi, E. Understanding retrieval augmentation for long-form question answering. *arXiv* **2023**, arXiv:2310.12150.
47. Tang, R.; Zhang, X.; Ma, X.; Lin, J.; Ture, F. Found in the middle: Permutation self-consistency improves listwise ranking in large language models. *arXiv* **2023**, arXiv:2310.07712.
48. Gao, L.; Madaan, A.; Zhou, S.; Alon, U.; Liu, P.; Yang, Y.; Callan, J.; Neubig, G. Pal: Program-aided language models. In Proceedings of the International Conference on Machine Learning, PMLR 2023, Honolulu, HI, USA, 23–29 July 2023; pp. 10764–10799.
49. Wang, X.; Yang, Q.; Qiu, Y.; Liang, J.; He, Q.; Gu, Z.; Xiao, Y.; Wang, W. Knowledgpt: Enhancing large language models with retrieval and storage access on knowledge bases. *arXiv* **2023**, arXiv:2308.11761.
50. Yu, W.; Iter, D.; Wang, S.; Xu, Y.; Ju, M.; Sanyal, S.; Zhu, C.; Zeng, M.; Jiang, M. Generate rather than retrieve: Large language models are strong context generators. *arXiv* **2022**, arXiv:2209.10063.
51. Cheng, X.; Luo, D.; Chen, X.; Liu, L.; Zhao, D.; Yan, R. Lift yourself up: Retrieval-augmented text generation with self-memory. *Adv. Neural Inf. Process. Syst.* **2024**, *36*, 43780–43799.
52. Black, S.; Biderman, S.; Hallahan, E.; Anthony, Q.; Gao, L.; Golding, L.; He, H.; Leahy, C.; McDonell, K.; Phang, J.; et al. Gpt-neox-20b: An open-source autoregressive language model. *arXiv* **2022**, arXiv:2204.06745.
53. Asai, A.; Zhong, Z.; Chen, D.; Koh, P.W.; Zettlemoyer, L.; Hajishirzi, H.; Yih, W.T. Reliable, adaptable, and attributable language models with retrieval. *arXiv* **2024**, arXiv:2403.03187.
54. Pan, R.; Cao, B.; Lin, H.; Han, X.; Zheng, J.; Wang, S.; Cai, X.; Sun, L. Not All Contexts Are Equal: Teaching LLMs Credibility-aware Generation. *arXiv* **2024**, arXiv:2404.06809.
55. Wang, L.; Yang, N.; Wei, F. Query2doc: Query expansion with large language models. *arXiv* **2023**, arXiv:2303.07678.
56. Jagerman, R.; Zhuang, H.; Qin, Z.; Wang, X.; Bendersky, M. Query expansion by prompting large language models. *arXiv* **2023**, arXiv:2305.03653.
57. Wang, S.; Yu, X.; Wang, M.; Chen, W.; Zhu, Y.; Dou, Z. Richrag: Crafting rich responses for multi-faceted queries in retrieval-augmented generation. *arXiv* **2024**, arXiv:2406.12566.
58. Kim, G.; Kim, S.; Jeon, B.; Park, J.; Kang, J. Tree of clarifications: Answering ambiguous questions with retrieval-augmented large language models. *arXiv* **2023**, arXiv:2310.14696.
59. Ma, X.; Gong, Y.; He, P.; Zhao, H.; Duan, N. Query rewriting for retrieval-augmented large language models. *arXiv* **2023**, arXiv:2305.14283.
60. Mao, S.; Jiang, Y.; Chen, B.; Li, X.; Wang, P.; Wang, X.; Xie, P.; Huang, F.; Chen, H.; Zhang, N. RaFe: Ranking Feedback Improves Query Rewriting for RAG. *arXiv* **2024**, arXiv:2405.14431.
61. Qu, C.; Yang, L.; Chen, C.; Qiu, M.; Croft, W.B.; Iyyer, M. Open-retrieval conversational question answering. In Proceedings of the 43rd International ACM SIGIR Conference on Research and Development in Information Retrieval, Xi'an, China, 25–30 July 2020; pp. 539–548.
62. Anantha, R.; Vakulenko, S.; Tu, Z.; Longpre, S.; Pulman, S.; Chappidi, S. Open-domain question answering goes conversational via question rewriting. *arXiv* **2020**, arXiv:2010.04898.
63. Adlakha, V.; Dhuliawala, S.; Suleman, K.; de Vries, H.; Reddy, S. Topiocqa: Open-domain conversational question answering with topic switching. *Trans. Assoc. Comput. Linguist.* **2022**, *10*, 468–483. [CrossRef]
64. Choi, E.; Palomaki, J.; Lamm, M.; Kwiatkowski, T.; Das, D.; Collins, M. Decontextualization: Making sentences stand-alone. *Trans. Assoc. Comput. Linguist.* **2021**, *9*, 447–461. [CrossRef]
65. Yoon, C.; Kim, G.; Jeon, B.; Kim, S.; Jo, Y.; Kang, J. Ask Optimal Questions: Aligning Large Language Models with Retriever's Preference in Conversational Search. *arXiv* **2024**, arXiv:2402.11827.

66. Shao, Y.; Jiang, Y.; Kanell, T.A.; Xu, P.; Khattab, O.; Lam, M.S. Assisting in writing wikipedia-like articles from scratch with large language models. *arXiv* **2024**, arXiv:2402.14207.
67. Zhou, D.; Schärli, N.; Hou, L.; Wei, J.; Scales, N.; Wang, X.; Schuurmans, D.; Cui, C.; Bousquet, O.; Le, Q.; et al. Least-to-most prompting enables complex reasoning in large language models. *arXiv* **2022**, arXiv:2205.10625.
68. Khot, T.; Trivedi, H.; Finlayson, M.; Fu, Y.; Richardson, K.; Clark, P.; Sabharwal, A. Decomposed prompting: A modular approach for solving complex tasks. *arXiv* **2022**, arXiv:2210.02406.
69. Cao, S.; Zhang, J.; Shi, J.; Lv, X.; Yao, Z.; Tian, Q.; Li, J.; Hou, L. Probabilistic Tree-of-thought Reasoning for Answering Knowledge-intensive Complex Questions. *arXiv* **2023**, arXiv:2311.13982.
70. Chu, Z.; Chen, J.; Chen, Q.; Wang, H.; Zhu, K.; Du, X.; Yu, W.; Liu, M.; Qin, B. BeamAggR: Beam Aggregation Reasoning over Multi-source Knowledge for Multi-hop Question Answering. *arXiv* **2024**, arXiv:2406.19820.
71. Gao, Y.; Xiong, Y.; Gao, X.; Jia, K.; Pan, J.; Bi, Y.; Dai, Y.; Sun, J.; Wang, H. Retrieval-augmented generation for large language models: A survey. *arXiv* **2023**, arXiv:2312.10997.
72. Wang, Z.; Teo, S.X.; Ouyang, J.; Xu, Y.; Shi, W. M-RAG: Reinforcing Large Language Model Performance through Retrieval-Augmented Generation with Multiple Partitions. *arXiv* **2024**, arXiv:2405.16420.
73. Sarthi, P.; Abdullah, S.; Tuli, A.; Khanna, S.; Goldie, A.; Manning, C.D. Raptor: Recursive abstractive processing for tree-organized retrieval. *arXiv* **2024**, arXiv:2401.18059.
74. Rampášek, L.; Galkin, M.; Dwivedi, V.P.; Luu, A.T.; Wolf, G.; Beaini, D. Recipe for a general, powerful, scalable graph transformer. *Adv. Neural Inf. Process. Syst.* **2022**, *35*, 14501–14515.
75. Guo, Z.; Xia, L.; Yu, Y.; Ao, T.; Huang, C. Lightrag: Simple and fast retrieval-augmented generation. *arXiv* **2024**, arXiv:2410.05779.
76. Qian, H.; Zhang, P.; Liu, Z.; Mao, K.; Dou, Z. Memorag: Moving towards next-gen rag via memory-inspired knowledge discovery. *arXiv* **2024**, arXiv:2409.05591.
77. Gao, L.; Ma, X.; Lin, J.; Callan, J. Precise zero-shot dense retrieval without relevance labels. *arXiv* **2022**, arXiv:2212.10496.
78. Chan, C.M.; Xu, C.; Yuan, R.; Luo, H.; Xue, W.; Guo, Y.; Fu, J. Rq-rag: Learning to refine queries for retrieval augmented generation. *arXiv* **2024**, arXiv:2404.00610.
79. Wang, Y.; Lipka, N.; Rossi, R.A.; Siu, A.; Zhang, R.; Derr, T. Knowledge graph prompting for multi-document question answering. In Proceedings of the AAAI Conference on Artificial Intelligence, Vancouver, BC, Canada, 26 February 2024; Volume 38, pp. 19206–19214.
80. Chen, T.; Wang, H.; Chen, S.; Yu, W.; Ma, K.; Zhao, X.; Zhang, H.; Yu, D. Dense x retrieval: What retrieval granularity should we use? *arXiv* **2023**, arXiv:2312.06648.
81. Muennighoff, N.; Su, H.; Wang, L.; Yang, N.; Wei, F.; Yu, T.; Singh, A.; Kiela, D. Generative representational instruction tuning. *arXiv* **2024**, arXiv:2402.09906.
82. Zhang, M.; Lan, S.; Hayes, P.; Barber, D. Mafin: Enhancing Black-Box Embeddings with Model Augmented Fine-tuning. *arXiv* **2024**, arXiv:2402.12177.
83. Asai, A.; Wu, Z.; Wang, Y.; Sil, A.; Hajishirzi, H. Self-rag: Learning to retrieve, generate, and critique through self-reflection. *arXiv* **2023**, arXiv:2310.11511.
84. Wang, Y.; Li, P.; Sun, M.; Liu, Y. Self-knowledge guided retrieval augmentation for large language models. *arXiv* **2023**, arXiv:2310.05002.
85. Jiang, Z.; Xu, F.F.; Gao, L.; Sun, Z.; Liu, Q.; Dwivedi-Yu, J.; Yang, Y.; Callan, J.; Neubig, G. Active retrieval augmented generation. *arXiv* **2023**, arXiv:2305.06983.
86. Trivedi, H.; Balasubramanian, N.; Khot, T.; Sabharwal, A. Interleaving retrieval with chain-of-thought reasoning for knowledge-intensive multi-step questions. *arXiv* **2022**, arXiv:2212.10509.
87. Shao, Z.; Gong, Y.; Shen, Y.; Huang, M.; Duan, N.; Chen, W. Enhancing retrieval-augmented large language models with iterative retrieval-generation synergy. *arXiv* **2023**, arXiv:2305.15294.
88. Kang, M.; Kwak, J.M.; Baek, J.; Hwang, S.J. Knowledge graph-augmented language models for knowledge-grounded dialogue generation. *arXiv* **2023**, arXiv:2305.18846.
89. Chen, H.; Pasunuru, R.; Weston, J.; Celikyilmaz, A. Walking down the memory maze: Beyond context limit through interactive reading. *arXiv* **2023**, arXiv:2310.05029.
90. Jeong, S.; Baek, J.; Cho, S.; Hwang, S.J.; Park, J.C. Adaptive-rag: Learning to adapt retrieval-augmented large language models through question complexity. *arXiv* **2024**, arXiv:2403.14403.
91. Islam, S.B.; Rahman, M.A.; Hossain, K.; Hoque, E.; Joty, S.; Parvez, M.R. OPEN-RAG: Enhanced Retrieval-Augmented Reasoning with Open-Source Large Language Models. *arXiv* **2024**, arXiv:2410.01782.

92. Rafailov, R.; Sharma, A.; Mitchell, E.; Manning, C.D.; Ermon, S.; Finn, C. Direct preference optimization: Your language model is secretly a reward model. *Adv. Neural Inf. Process. Syst.* **2024**, *36*, 53728–53741.
93. Vu, T.; Iyyer, M.; Wang, X.; Constant, N.; Wei, J.; Wei, J.; Tar, C.; Sung, Y.H.; Zhou, D.; Le, Q.; et al. Freshllms: Refreshing large language models with search engine augmentation. *arXiv* **2023**, arXiv:2310.03214.
94. Jiang, H.; Wu, Q.; Lin, C.Y.; Yang, Y.; Qiu, L. Llmlingua: Compressing prompts for accelerated inference of large language models. *arXiv* **2023**, arXiv:2310.05736.
95. Li, Y. Unlocking context constraints of llms: Enhancing context efficiency of llms with self-information-based content filtering. *arXiv* **2023**, arXiv:2304.12102.
96. Wang, Z.; Araki, J.; Jiang, Z.; Parvez, M.R.; Neubig, G. Learning to filter context for retrieval-augmented generation. *arXiv* **2023**, arXiv:2311.08377.
97. Xu, F.; Shi, W.; Choi, E. Recomp: Improving retrieval-augmented lms with compression and selective augmentation. *arXiv* **2023**, arXiv:2310.04408.
98. Liu, J.; Li, L.; Xiang, T.; Wang, B.; Qian, Y. Tcra-llm: Token compression retrieval augmented large language model for inference cost reduction. *arXiv* **2023**, arXiv:2310.15556.
99. Yu, W.; Zhang, H.; Pan, X.; Ma, K.; Wang, H.; Yu, D. Chain-of-note: Enhancing robustness in retrieval-augmented language models. *arXiv* **2023**, arXiv:2311.09210.
100. Kwiatkowski, T.; Palomaki, J.; Redfield, O.; Collins, M.; Parikh, A.; Alberti, C.; Epstein, D.; Polosukhin, I.; Devlin, J.; Lee, K.; et al. Natural questions: A benchmark for question answering research. *Trans. Assoc. Comput. Linguist.* **2019**, *7*, 453–466. [CrossRef]
101. Pan, Y.; Pan, L.; Chen, W.; Nakov, P.; Kan, M.Y.; Wang, W.Y. On the risk of misinformation pollution with large language models. *arXiv* **2023**, arXiv:2305.13661.
102. Xu, R.; Lin, B.S.; Yang, S.; Zhang, T.; Shi, W.; Zhang, T.; Fang, Z.; Xu, W.; Qiu, H. The Earth is Flat because...: Investigating LLMs' Belief towards Misinformation via Persuasive Conversation. *arXiv* **2023**, arXiv:2312.09085.
103. Wang, Y.; Feng, S.; Wang, H.; Shi, W.; Balachandran, V.; He, T.; Tsvetkov, Y. Resolving knowledge conflicts in large language models. *arXiv* **2023**, arXiv:2310.00935.
104. Zhang, Y.; Khalifa, M.; Logeswaran, L.; Lee, M.; Lee, H.; Wang, L. Merging generated and retrieved knowledge for open-domain QA. *arXiv* **2023**, arXiv:2310.14393.
105. Wang, C.; Yang, Y.; Li, R.; Sun, D.; Cai, R.; Zhang, Y.; Fu, C. Adapting llms for efficient context processing through soft prompt compression. In Proceedings of the International Conference on Modeling, Natural Language Processing and Machine Learning, Xi'an, China, 17–19 May 2024; pp. 91–97.
106. Ravaut, M.; Joty, S.; Sun, A.; Chen, N.F. On position bias in summarization with large language models. *arXiv* **2023**, arXiv:2310.10570.
107. Gao, T.; Yen, H.; Yu, J.; Chen, D. Enabling large language models to generate text with citations. *arXiv* **2023**, arXiv:2305.14627.
108. Fierro, C.; Amplayo, R.K.; Huot, F.; De Cao, N.; Maynez, J.; Narayan, S.; Lapata, M. Learning to Plan and Generate Text with Citations. *arXiv* **2024**, arXiv:2404.03381.
109. Ye, X.; Sun, R.; Arik, S.Ö.; Pfister, T. Effective large language model adaptation for improved grounding. *arXiv* **2023**, arXiv:2311.09533.
110. Qi, J.; Sarti, G.; Fernández, R.; Bisazza, A. Model Internals-based Answer Attribution for Trustworthy Retrieval-Augmented Generation. *arXiv* **2024**, arXiv:2406.13663.
111. Zhang, S.; Pan, L.; Zhao, J.; Wang, W.Y. The knowledge alignment problem: Bridging human and external knowledge for large language models. *arXiv* **2023**, arXiv:2305.13669.
112. Peng, B.; Galley, M.; He, P.; Cheng, H.; Xie, Y.; Hu, Y.; Huang, Q.; Liden, L.; Yu, Z.; Chen, W.; et al. Check your facts and try again: Improving large language models with external knowledge and automated feedback. *arXiv* **2023**, arXiv:2302.12813.
113. Yao, S.; Zhao, J.; Yu, D.; Du, N.; Shafran, I.; Narasimhan, K.; Cao, Y. React: Synergizing reasoning and acting in language models. *arXiv* **2022**, arXiv:2210.03629.
114. Paranjape, B.; Lundberg, S.; Singh, S.; Hajishirzi, H.; Zettlemoyer, L.; Ribeiro, M.T. Art: Automatic multi-step reasoning and tool-use for large language models. *arXiv* **2023**, arXiv:2303.09014.
115. Varshney, N.; Yao, W.; Zhang, H.; Chen, J.; Yu, D. A stitch in time saves nine: Detecting and mitigating hallucinations of llms by validating low-confidence generation. *arXiv* **2023**, arXiv:2307.03987.
116. Kang, H.; Ni, J.; Yao, H. Ever: Mitigating hallucination in large language models through real-time verification and rectification. *arXiv* **2023**, arXiv:2311.09114.
117. Gao, L.; Dai, Z.; Pasupat, P.; Chen, A.; Chaganty, A.T.; Fan, Y.; Zhao, V.Y.; Lao, N.; Lee, H.; Juan, D.C.; et al. Rarr: Researching and revising what language models say, using language models. *arXiv* **2022**, arXiv:2210.08726.
118. Hu, Z.; Iscen, A.; Sun, C.; Wang, Z.; Chang, K.W.; Sun, Y.; Schmid, C.; Ross, D.A.; Fathi, A. Reveal: Retrieval-augmented visual-language pre-training with multi-source multimodal knowledge memory. In Proceedings of the IEEE/CVF Conference on Computer Vision and Pattern Recognition, Vancouver, BC, Canada, 17–24 June 2023; pp. 23369–23379.

119. Zhu, Y.; Ren, C.; Xie, S.; Liu, S.; Ji, H.; Wang, Z.; Sun, T.; He, L.; Li, Z.; Zhu, X.; et al. REALM: RAG-Driven Enhancement of Multimodal Electronic Health Records Analysis via Large Language Models. *arXiv* **2024**, arXiv:2402.07016.
120. Wei, A.; Haghtalab, N.; Steinhardt, J. Jailbroken: How does llm safety training fail? *Adv. Neural Inf. Process. Syst.* **2024**, *36*, 80079–80110.
121. Paulus, A.; Zharmagambetov, A.; Guo, C.; Amos, B.; Tian, Y. Advprompter: Fast adaptive adversarial prompting for llms. *arXiv* **2024**, arXiv:2404.16873.
122. Yang, Z.; Qi, P.; Zhang, S.; Bengio, Y.; Cohen, W.W.; Salakhutdinov, R.; Manning, C.D. HotpotQA: A dataset for diverse, explainable multi-hop question answering. *arXiv* **2018**, arXiv:1809.09600.
123. Ho, X.; Nguyen, A.K.D.; Sugawara, S.; Aizawa, A. Constructing a multi-hop qa dataset for comprehensive evaluation of reasoning steps. *arXiv* **2020**, arXiv:2011.01060.
124. Trivedi, H.; Balasubramanian, N.; Khot, T.; Sabharwal, A. MuSiQue: Multihop Questions via Single-hop Question Composition. *Trans. Assoc. Comput. Linguist.* **2022**, *10*, 539–554. [CrossRef]
125. Stelmakh, I.; Luan, Y.; Dhingra, B.; Chang, M.W. ASQA: Factoid questions meet long-form answers. *arXiv* **2022**, arXiv:2204.06092.
126. Chen, J.; Lin, H.; Han, X.; Sun, L. Benchmarking large language models in retrieval-augmented generation. In Proceedings of the AAAI Conference on Artificial Intelligence, Vancouver, BC, Canada, 26–27 February 2024; Volume 38, pp. 17754–17762.
127. Press, O.; Zhang, M.; Min, S.; Schmidt, L.; Smith, N.A.; Lewis, M. Measuring and narrowing the compositionality gap in language models. *arXiv* **2022**, arXiv:2210.03350.
128. Ferguson, J.; Gardner, M.; Hajishirzi, H.; Khot, T.; Dasigi, P. IIRC: A dataset of incomplete information reading comprehension questions. *arXiv* **2020**, arXiv:2011.07127.
129. Saad-Falcon, J.; Barrow, J.; Siu, A.; Nenkova, A.; Yoon, D.S.; Rossi, R.A.; Dernoncourt, F. Pdftriage: Question answering over long, structured documents. *arXiv* **2023**, arXiv:2309.08872.
130. Wang, L.; Yang, N.; Huang, X.; Yang, L.; Majumder, R.; Wei, F. Improving text embeddings with large language models. *arXiv* **2023**, arXiv:2401.00368.
131. Ivison, H.; Wang, Y.; Pyatkin, V.; Lambert, N.; Peters, M.; Dasigi, P.; Jang, J.; Wadden, D.; Smith, N.A.; Beltagy, I.; et al. Camels in a changing climate: Enhancing lm adaptation with tulu 2. *arXiv* **2023**, arXiv:2311.10702.
132. Clark, J.H.; Choi, E.; Collins, M.; Garrette, D.; Kwiatkowski, T.; Nikolaev, V.; Palomaki, J. Tydi qa: A benchmark for information-seeking question answering in ty pologically di verse languages. *Trans. Assoc. Comput. Linguist.* **2020**, *8*, 454–470. [CrossRef]
133. Cobbe, K.; Kosaraju, V.; Bavarian, M.; Chen, M.; Jun, H.; Kaiser, L.; Plappert, M.; Tworek, J.; Hilton, J.; Nakano, R.; et al. Training verifiers to solve math word problems. *arXiv* **2021**, arXiv:2110.14168.
134. Muennighoff, N.; Tazi, N.; Magne, L.; Reimers, N. MTEB: Massive text embedding benchmark. *arXiv* **2022**, arXiv:2210.07316.
135. Muennighoff, N.; Liu, Q.; Zebaze, A.; Zheng, Q.; Hui, B.; Zhuo, T.Y.; Singh, S.; Tang, X.; Von Werra, L.; Longpre, S. Octopack: Instruction tuning code large language models. In Proceedings of the NeurIPS 2023 Workshop on Instruction Tuning and Instruction Following, Montréal, QC, Canada, 8–10 August 2023.
136. Li, X.; Zhang, T.; Dubois, Y.; Taori, R.; Gulrajani, I.; Guestrin, C.; Liang, P.; Hashimoto, T.B. *Alpacaeval: An Automatic Evaluator of Instruction-Following Models*; GitHub: San Francisco, CA, USA, 2023.
137. Rajpurkar, P.; Zhang, J.; Lopyrev, K.; Liang, P. Squad: 100,000+ questions for machine comprehension of text. *arXiv* **2016**, arXiv:1606.05250.
138. Gupta, V.; Mehta, M.; Nokhiz, P.; Srikumar, V. INFOTABS: Inference on tables as semi-structured data. *arXiv* **2020**, arXiv:2005.06117.
139. Joshi, M.; Choi, E.; Weld, D.S.; Zettlemoyer, L. Triviaqa: A large scale distantly supervised challenge dataset for reading comprehension. *arXiv* **2017**, arXiv:1705.03551.
140. Berant, J.; Chou, A.; Frostig, R.; Liang, P. Semantic parsing on freebase from question-answer pairs. In Proceedings of the 2013 Conference on Empirical Methods in Natural Language Processing, Seattle, WD, USA, 18–21 October 2013; pp. 1533–1544.
141. Kasai, J.; Sakaguchi, K.; Le Bras, R.; Asai, A.; Yu, X.; Radev, D.; Smith, N.A.; Choi, Y.; Inui, K. Realtime qa: What's the answer right now? *Adv. Neural Inf. Process. Syst.* **2023**, *36*, 49025–49043.
142. Nallapati, R.; Zhou, B.; Gulcehre, C.; Xiang, B. Abstractive text summarization using sequence-to-sequence rnns and beyond. *arXiv* **2016**, arXiv:1602.06023.
143. Socher, R.; Perelygin, A.; Wu, J.; Chuang, J.; Manning, C.D.; Ng, A.Y.; Potts, C. Recursive deep models for semantic compositionality over a sentiment treebank. In Proceedings of the 2013 Conference on Empirical Methods in Natural Language Processing, Seattle, WA, USA, 18–21 October 2013; pp. 1631–1642.
144. Zhang, X.; Zhao, J.; LeCun, Y. Character-level convolutional networks for text classification. *Adv. Neural Inf. Process. Syst.* **2015**, *28*.
145. Kulkarni, S.; Chammas, S.; Zhu, W.; Sha, F.; Ie, E. Aquamuse: Automatically generating datasets for query-based multi-document summarization. *arXiv* **2020**, arXiv:2010.12694.
146. Patel, A.; Bhattamishra, S.; Goyal, N. Are NLP models really able to solve simple math word problems? *arXiv* **2021**, arXiv:2103.07191.
147. Miao, S.Y.; Liang, C.C.; Su, K.Y. A diverse corpus for evaluating and developing English math word problem solvers. *arXiv* **2021**, arXiv:2106.15772.

148. Koncel-Kedziorski, R.; Roy, S.; Amini, A.; Kushman, N.; Hajishirzi, H. MAWPS: A math word problem repository. In Proceedings of the 2016 Conference of the North American Chapter of the Association for Computational Linguistics: Human Language Technologies, San Diego, CA, USA, 12–17 June 2016; pp. 1152–1157.
149. Suzgun, M.; Scales, N.; Schärli, N.; Gehrmann, S.; Tay, Y.; Chung, H.W.; Chowdhery, A.; Le, Q.V.; Chi, E.H.; Zhou, D.; et al. Challenging big-bench tasks and whether chain-of-thought can solve them. *arXiv* **2022**, arXiv:2210.09261.

MDPI AG
Grosspeteranlage 5
4052 Basel
Switzerland
Tel.: +41 61 683 77 34

Mathematics Editorial Office
E-mail: mathematics@mdpi.com
www.mdpi.com/journal/mathematics

www.ingramcontent.com/pod-product-compliance
Lightning Source LLC
Chambersburg PA
CBHW061843210926
51850CB00006B/962
9783725866441